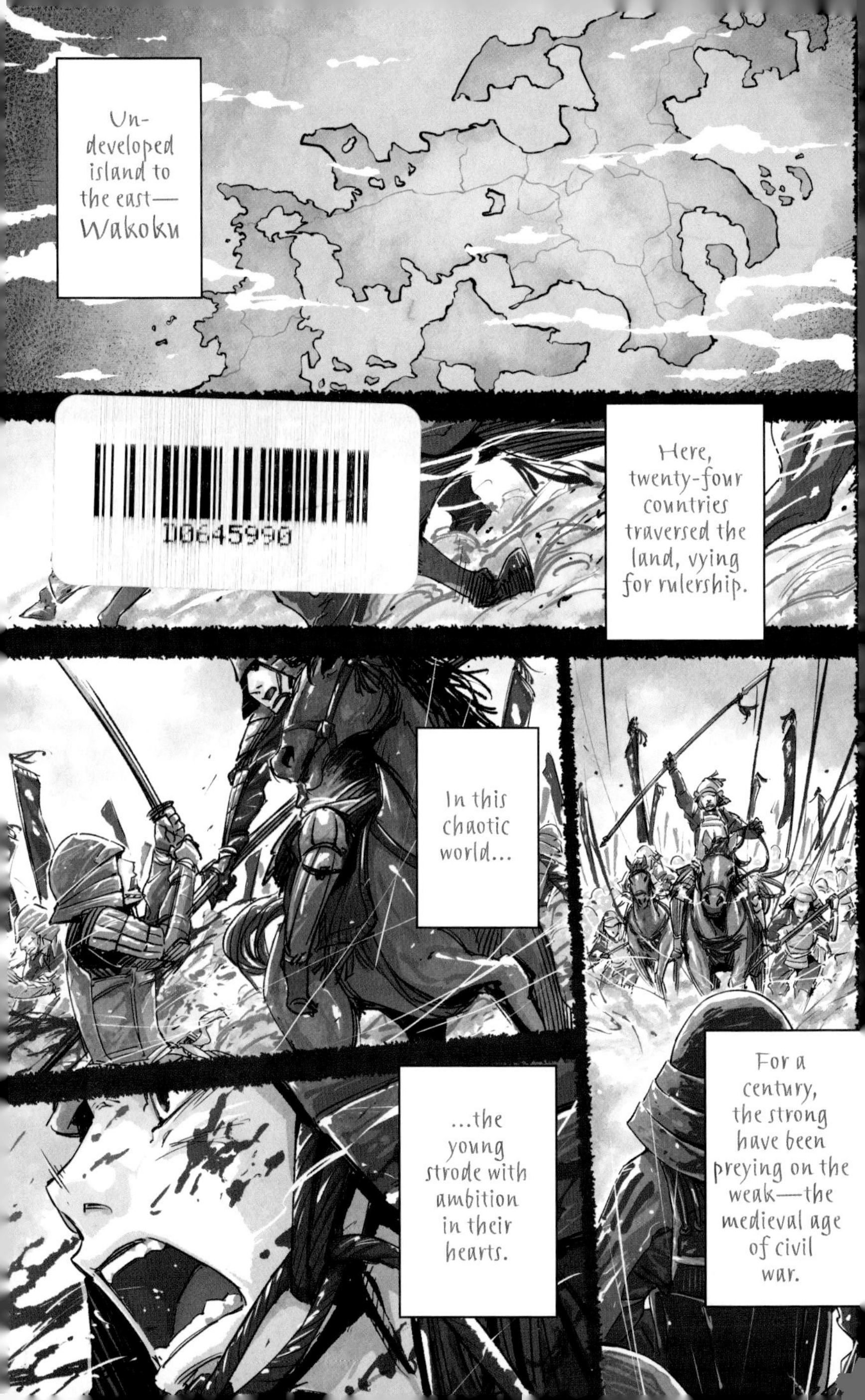
Un-developed island to the east—Wakoku
Here, twenty-four countries traversed the land, vying for rulership.
For a century, the strong have been preying on the weak—the medieval age of civil war.
In this chaotic world...
...the young strode with ambition in their hearts.

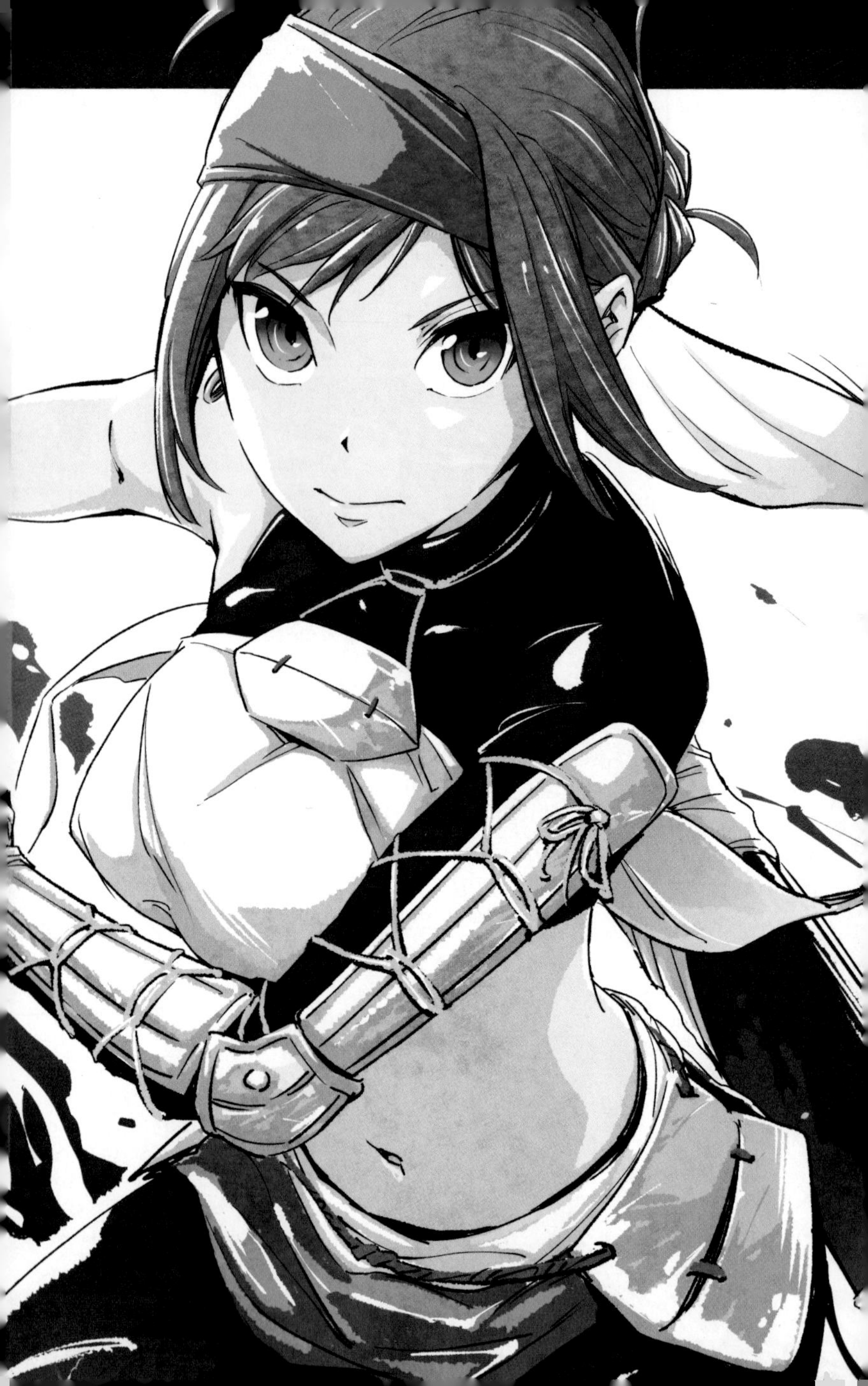

# Hinowa ga CRUSH!

1

Story: TAKAHIRO

Art: strelka

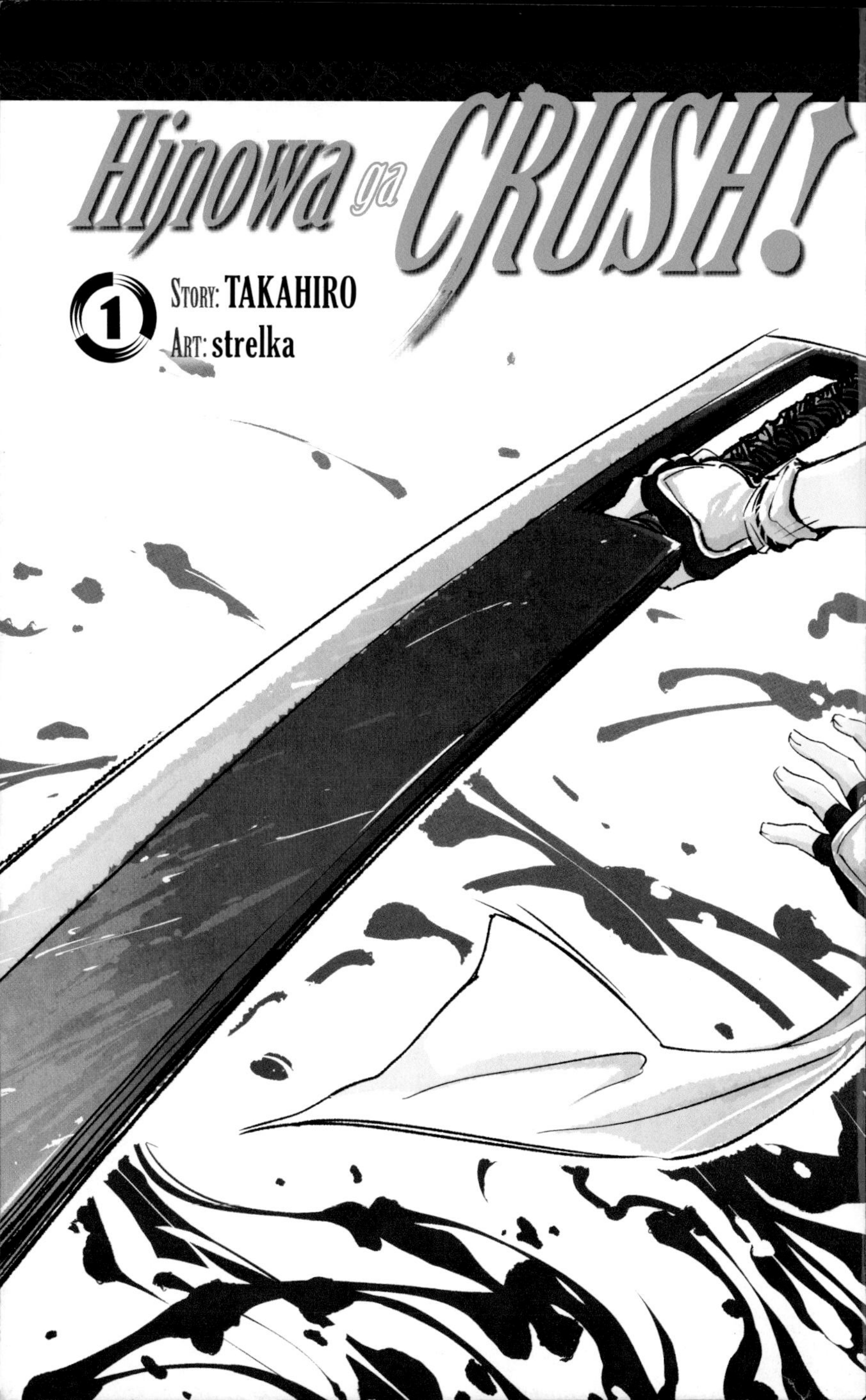

# Contents

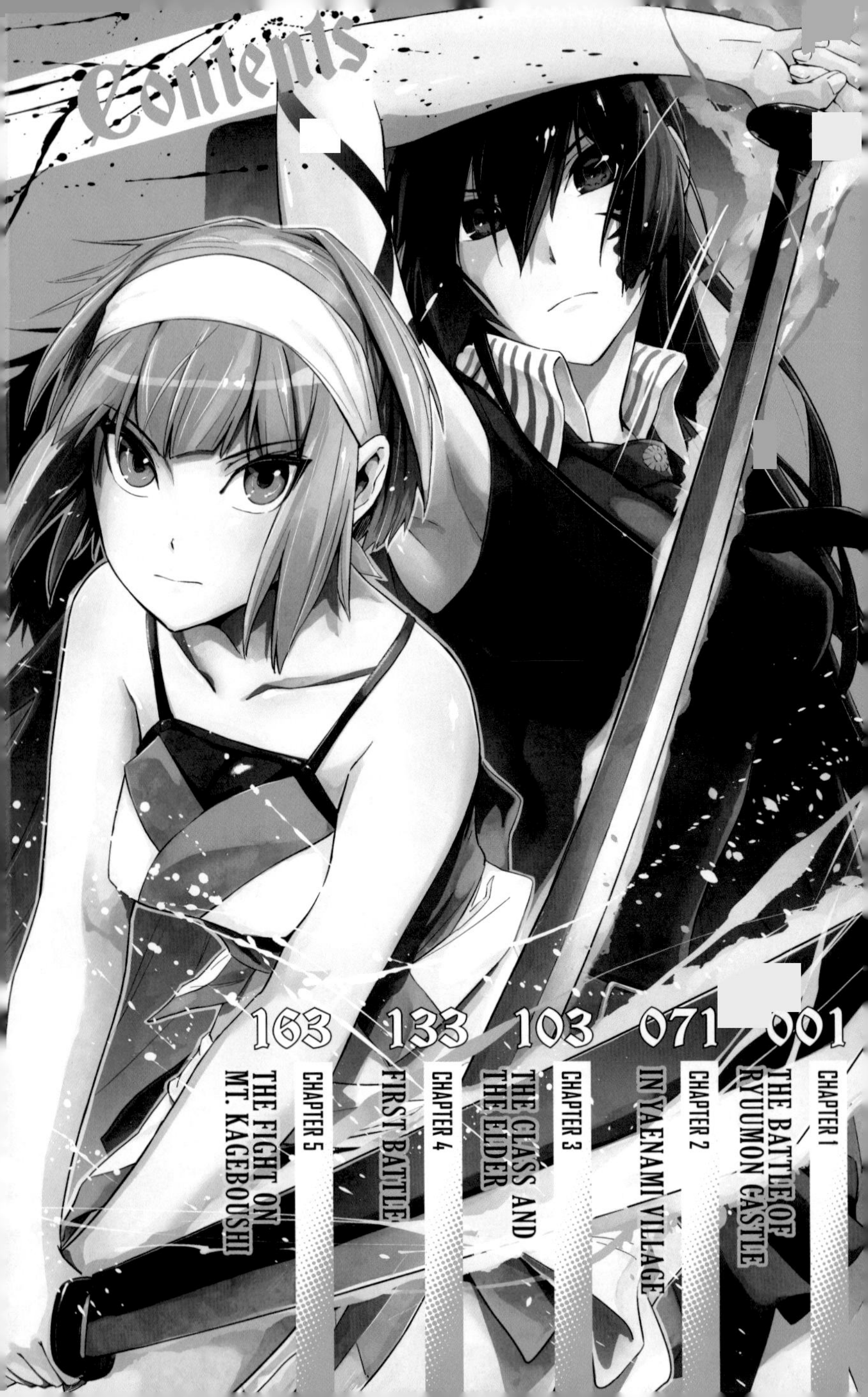

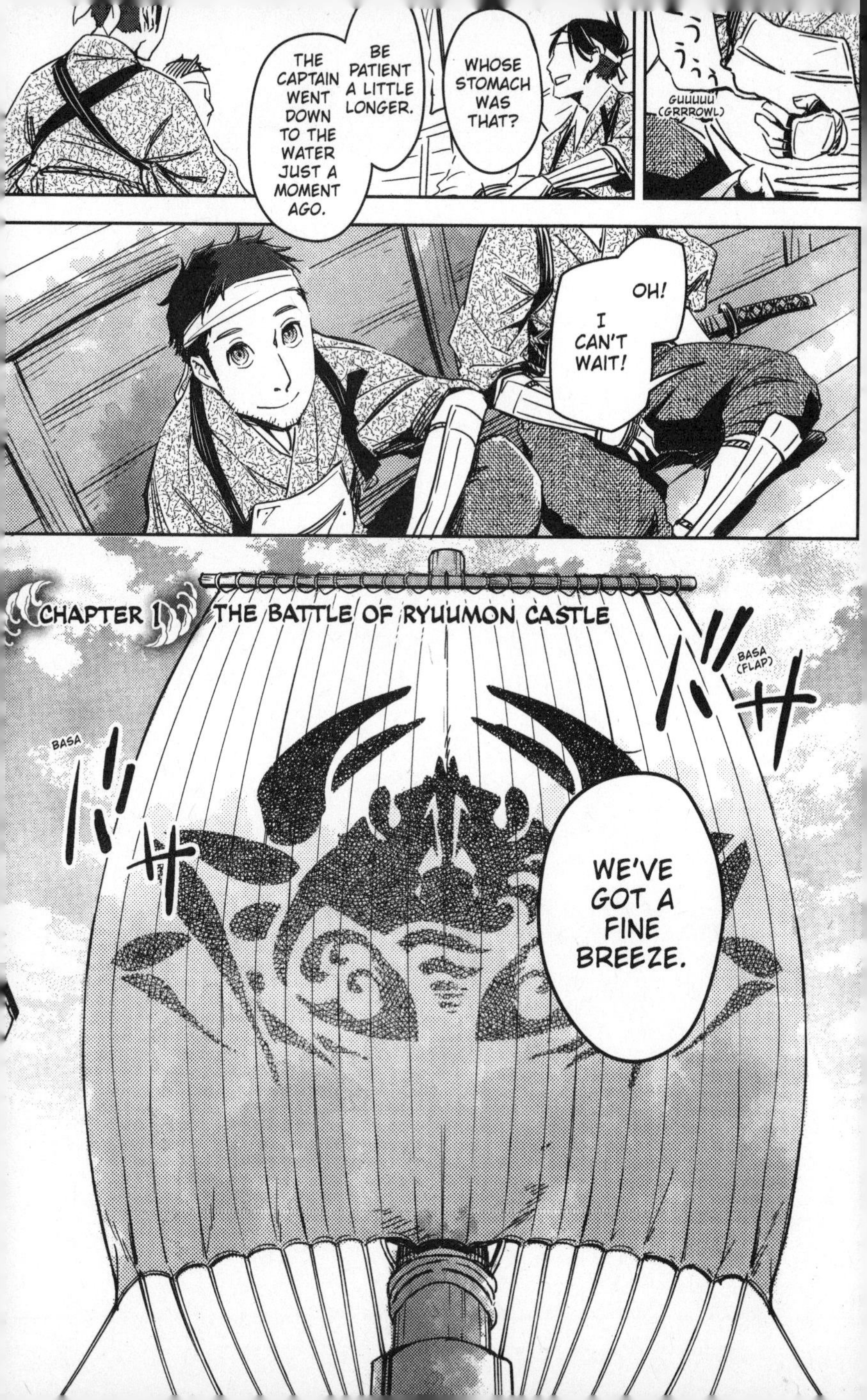
GUUUUU (GRRROWL)
WHOSE STOMACH WAS THAT?
BE PATIENT A LITTLE LONGER.
THE CAPTAIN WENT DOWN TO THE WATER JUST A MOMENT AGO.
OH! I CAN'T WAIT!
CHAPTER 1 THE BATTLE OF RYUUMON CASTLE
BASA (FLAP)
BASA
WE'VE GOT A FINE BREEZE.

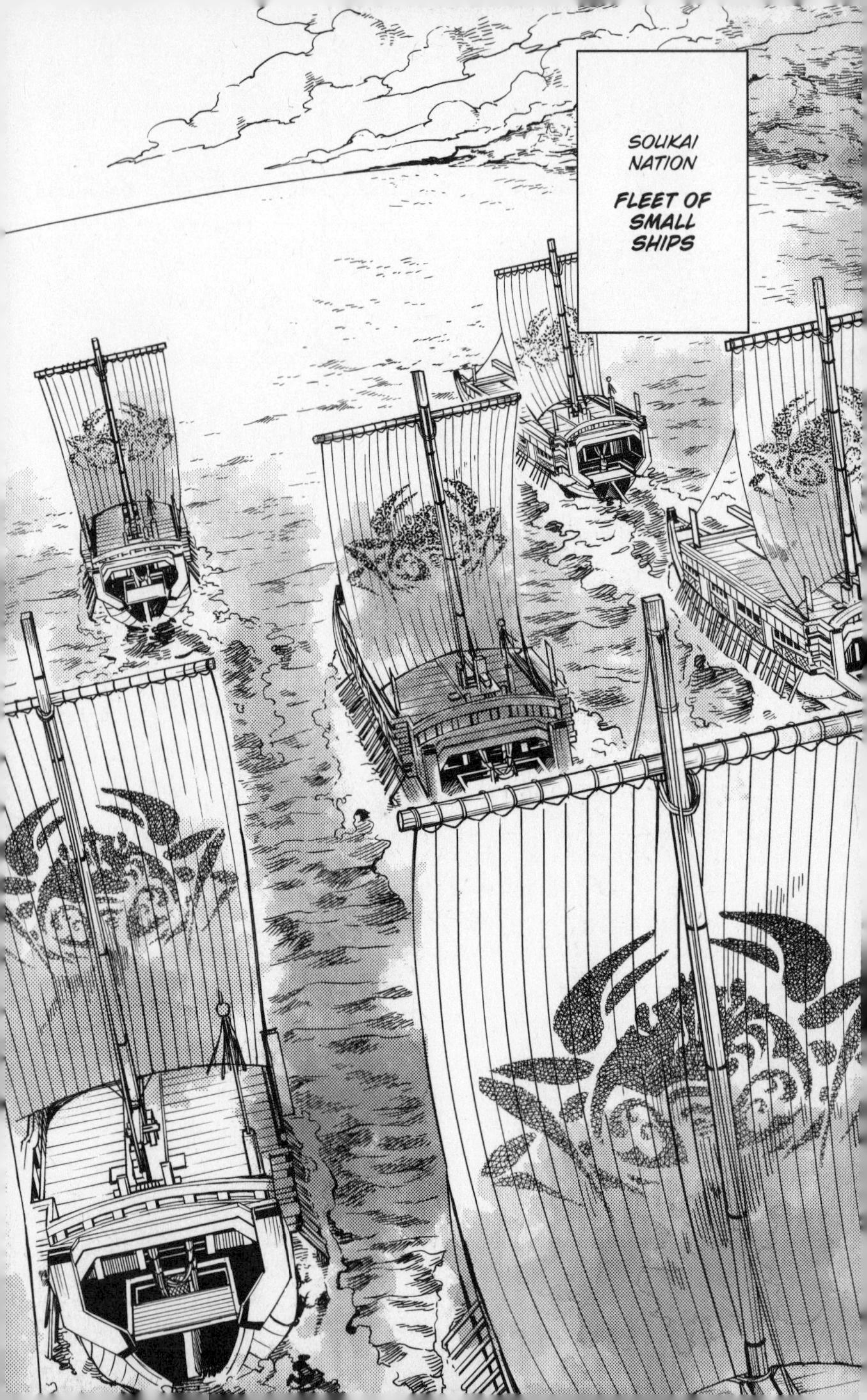
SOUKAI NATION
FLEET OF SMALL SHIPS

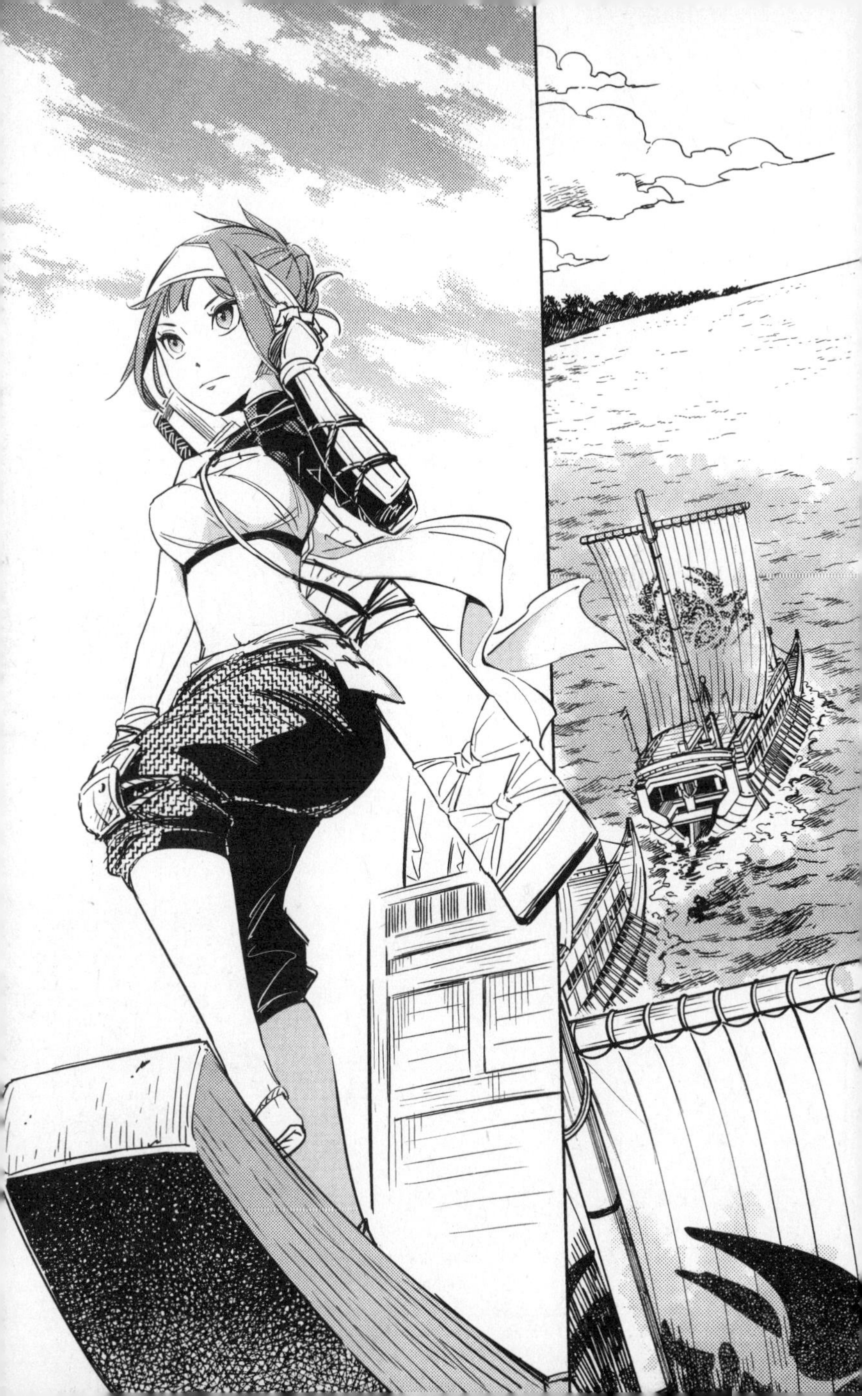

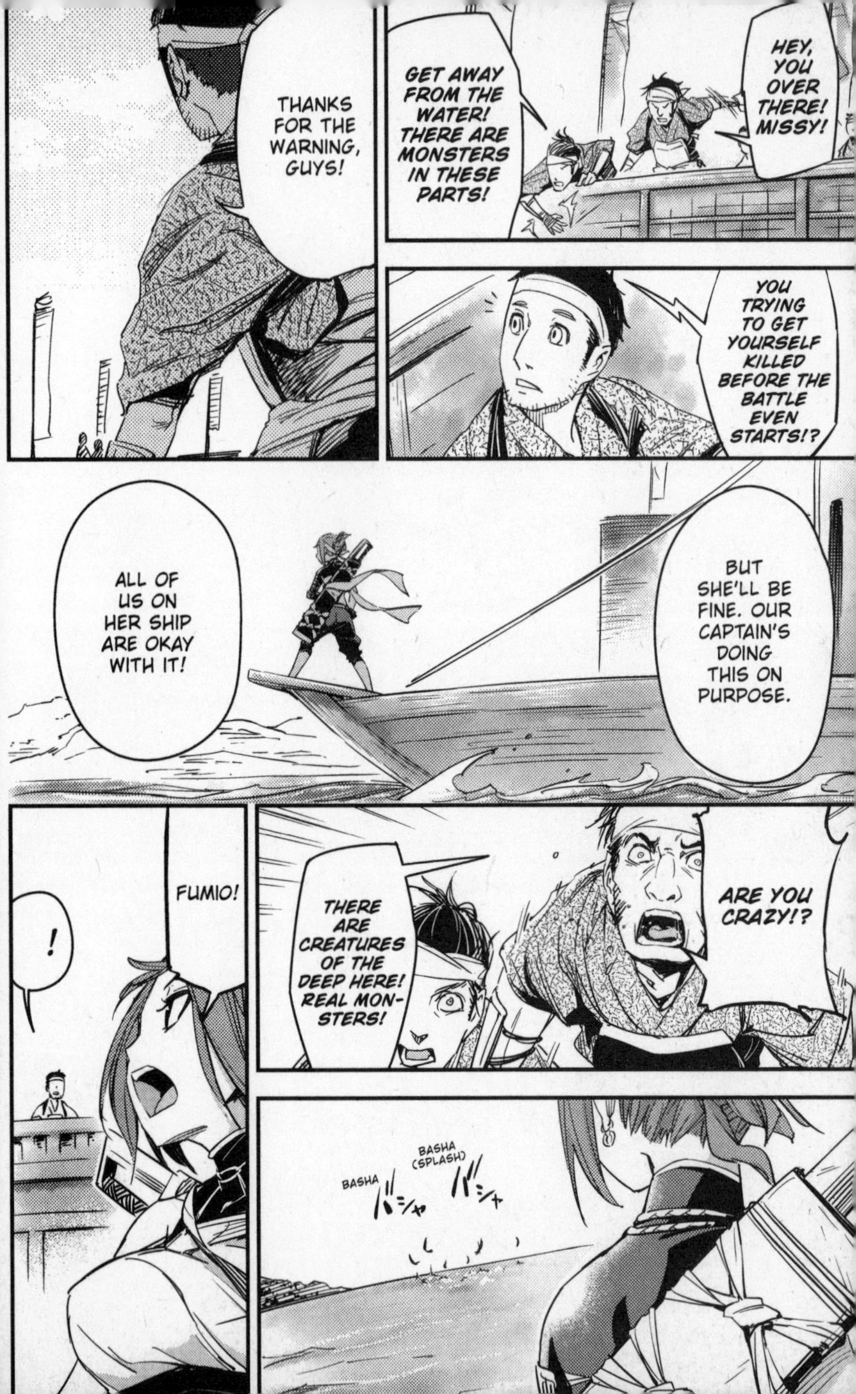
HEY, YOU OVER THERE! MISSY!
GET AWAY FROM THE WATER! THERE ARE MONSTERS IN THESE PARTS!
YOU TRYING TO GET YOURSELF KILLED BEFORE THE BATTLE EVEN STARTS!?
THANKS FOR THE WARNING, GUYS!
BUT SHE'LL BE FINE. OUR CAPTAIN'S DOING THIS ON PURPOSE.
ALL OF US ON HER SHIP ARE OKAY WITH IT!
ARE YOU CRAZY!?
THERE ARE CREATURES OF THE DEEP HERE! REAL MON-STERS!
BASHA (SPLASH)
BASHA
FUMIO!
!

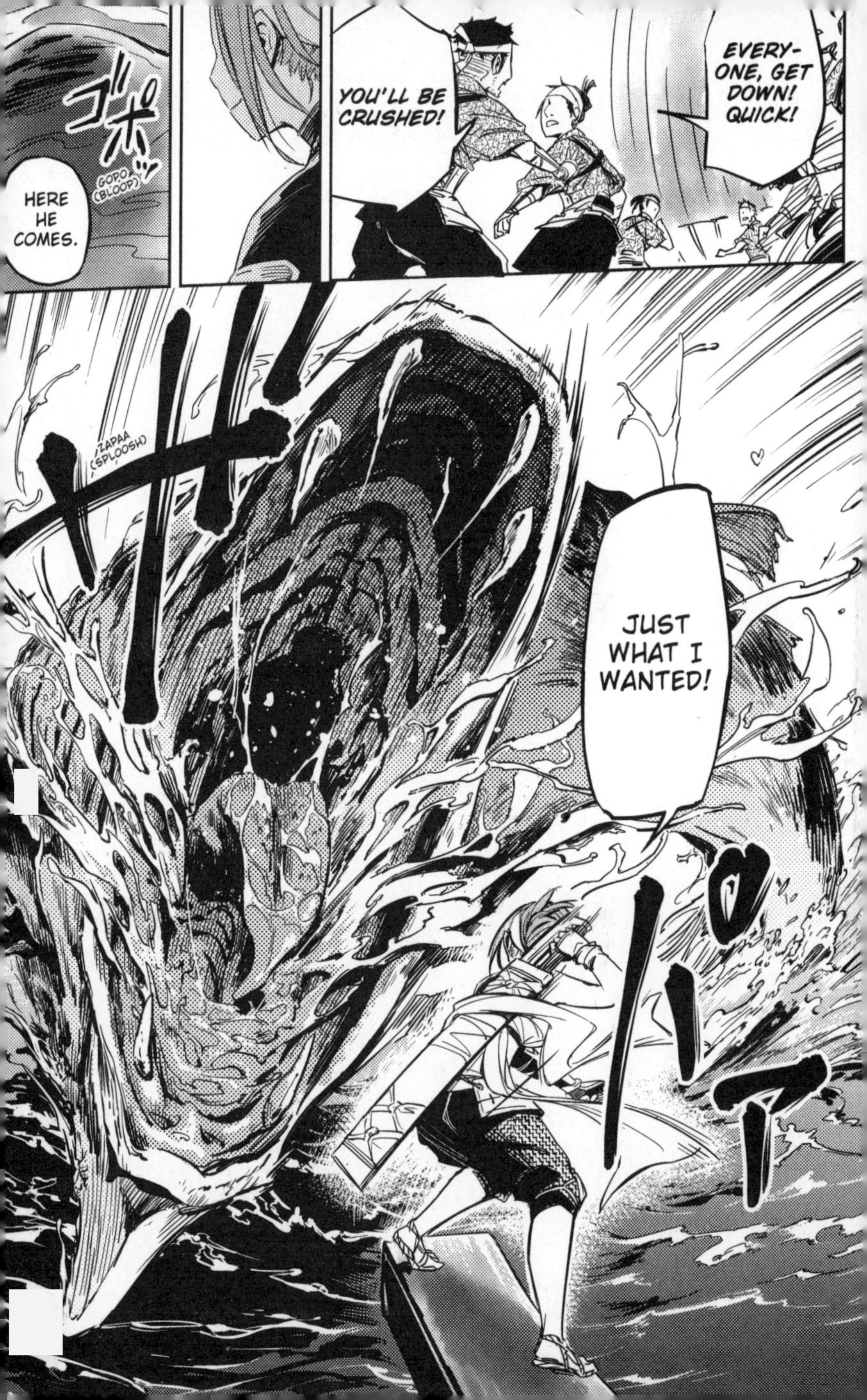
EVERY-ONE, GET DOWN! QUICK!
YOU'LL BE CRUSHED!
GOPO (BLOOP)
HERE HE COMES.
JUST WHAT I WANTED!
ZAPAA (SPLOOSH)

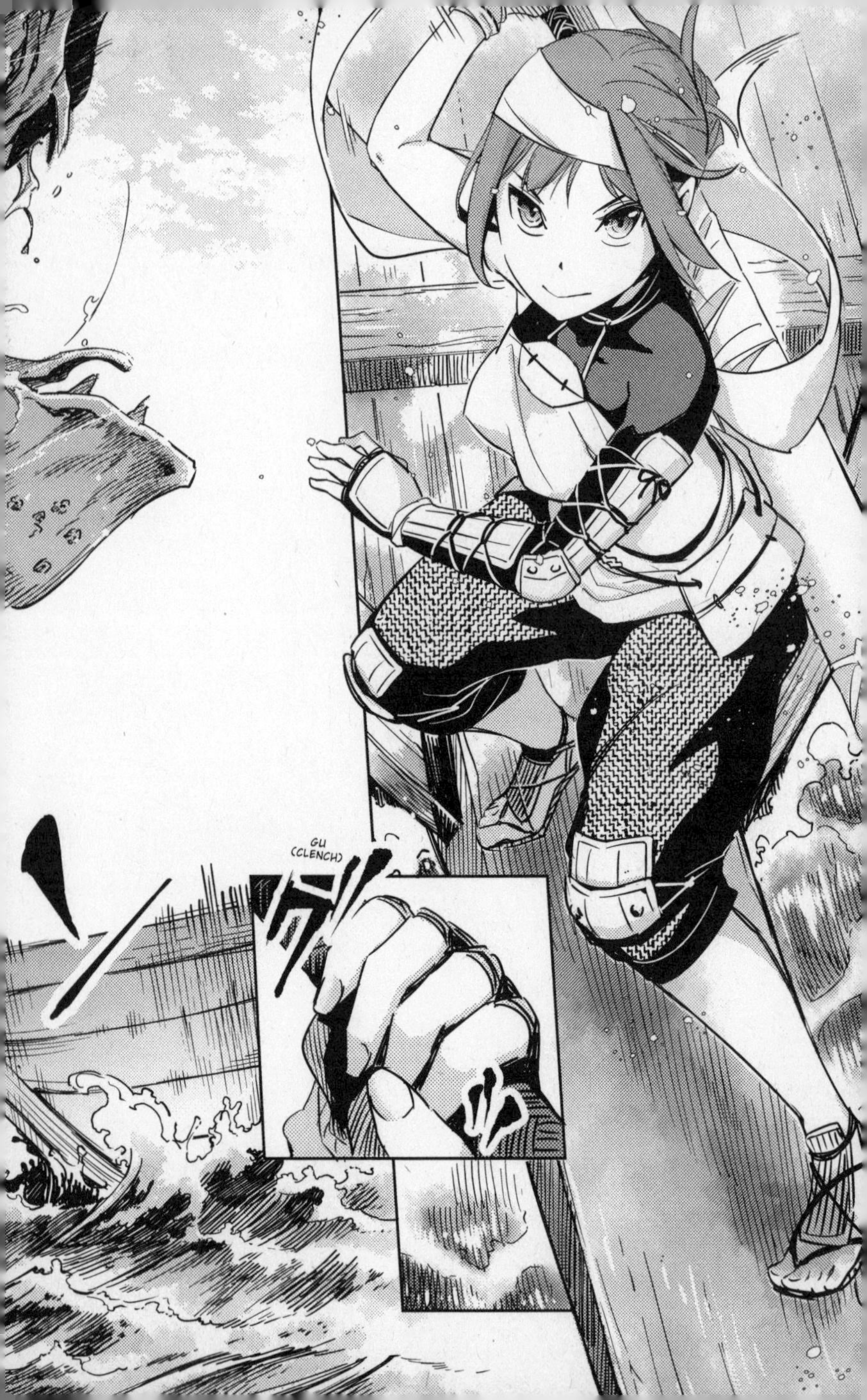
GU
(CLENCH)

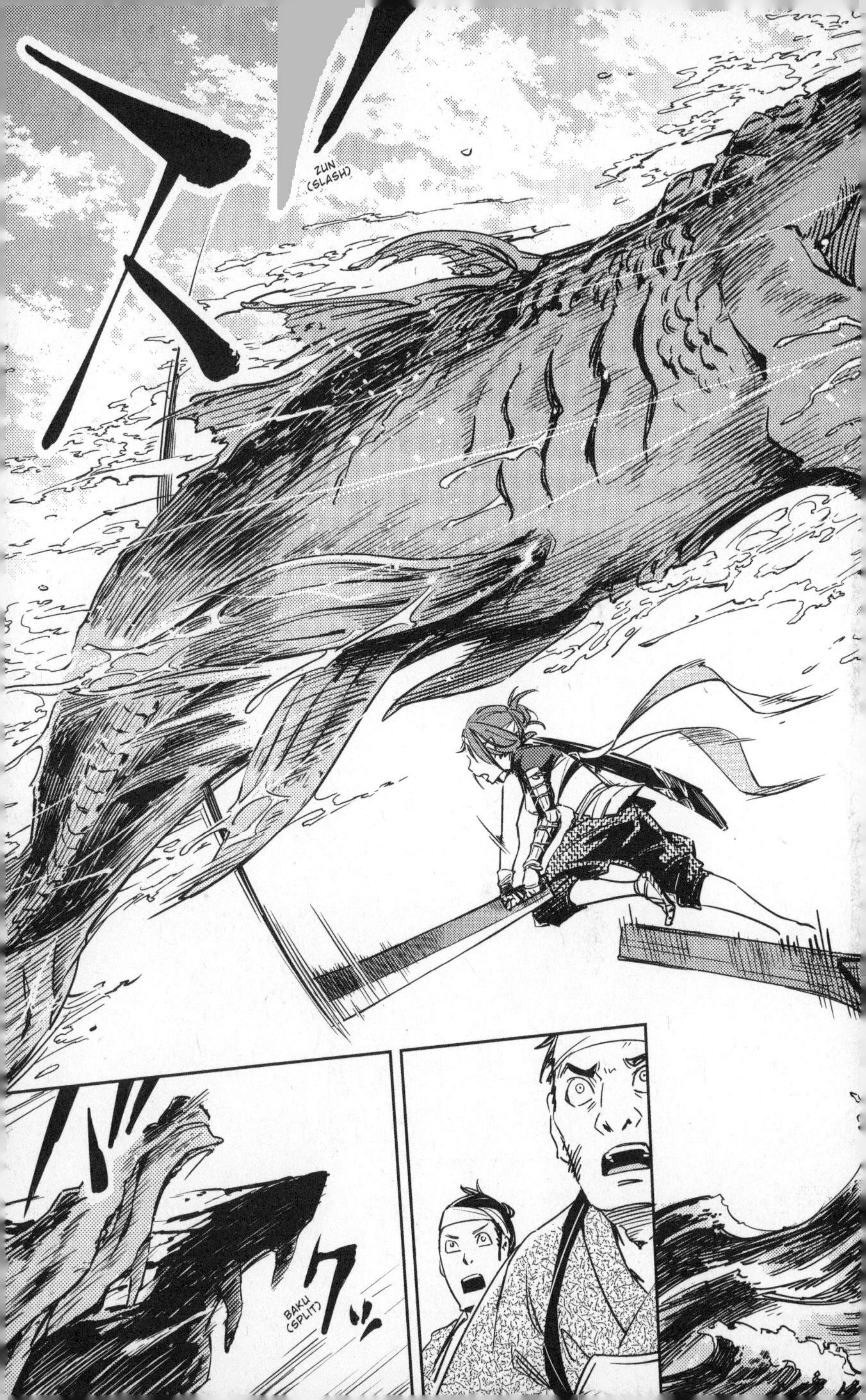
ZUN (SLASH)
BAKU (SPLIT)

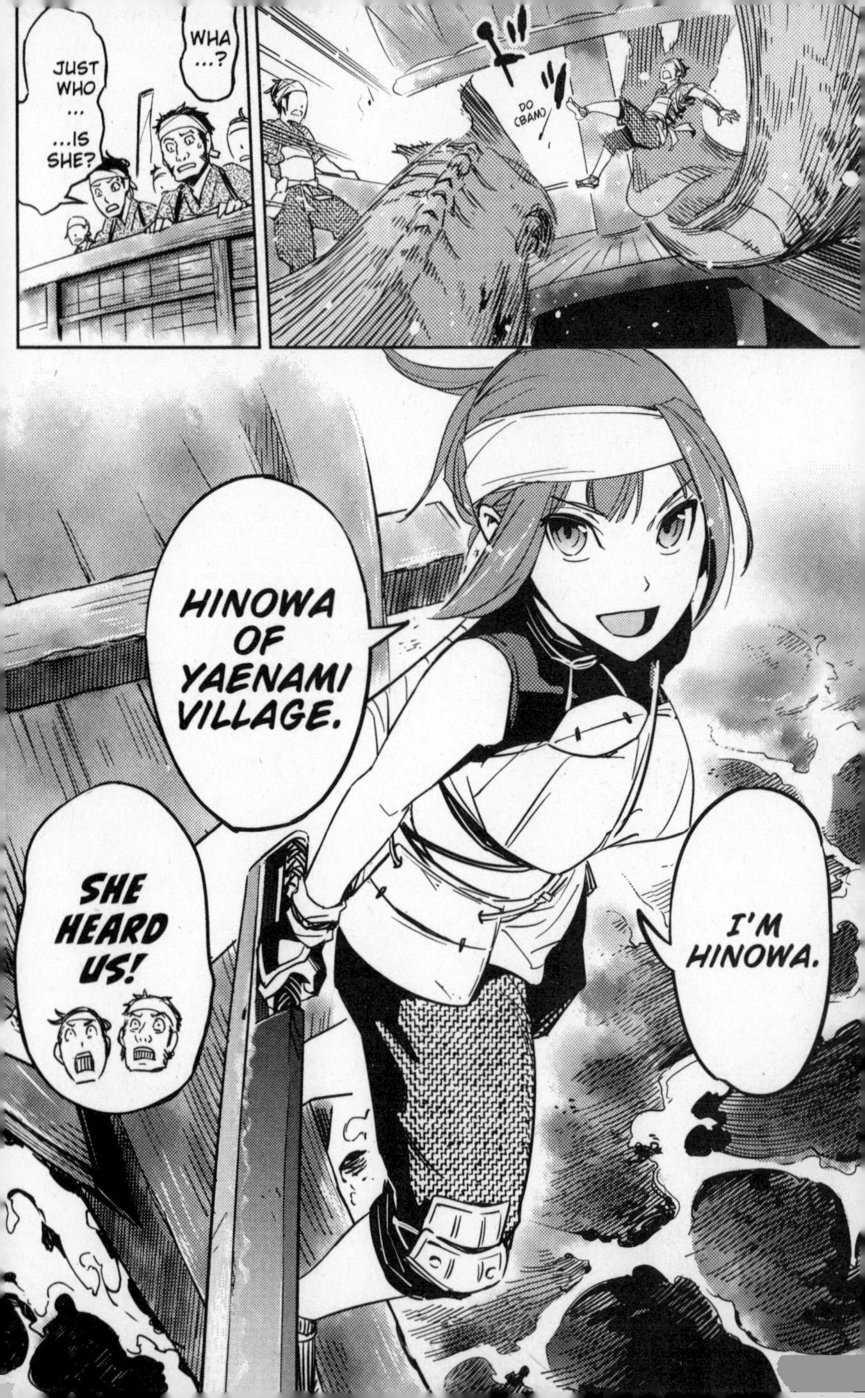
DO (BAM)
WHA ...?
JUST WHO ... ...IS SHE?
I'M HINOWA.
HINOWA OF YAENAMI VILLAGE.
SHE HEARD US!

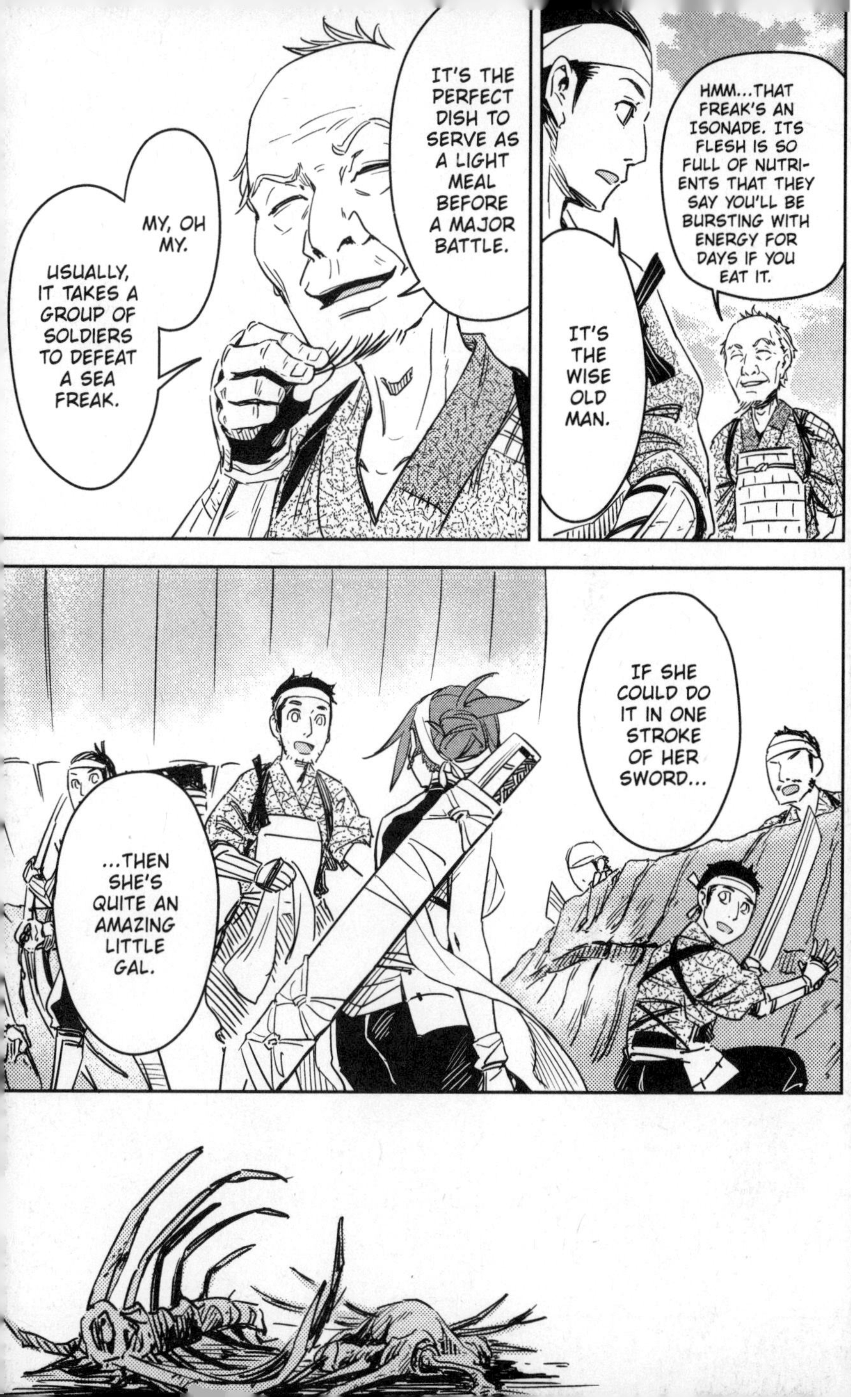
HMM...THAT FREAK'S AN ISONADE. ITS FLESH IS SO FULL OF NUTRI-ENTS THAT THEY SAY YOU'LL BE BURSTING WITH ENERGY FOR DAYS IF YOU EAT IT.
IT'S THE WISE OLD MAN.
IT'S THE PERFECT DISH TO SERVE AS A LIGHT MEAL BEFORE A MAJOR BATTLE.
MY, OH MY.
USUALLY, IT TAKES A GROUP OF SOLDIERS TO DEFEAT A SEA FREAK.
IF SHE COULD DO IT IN ONE STROKE OF HER SWORD...
...THEN SHE'S QUITE AN AMAZING LITTLE GAL.

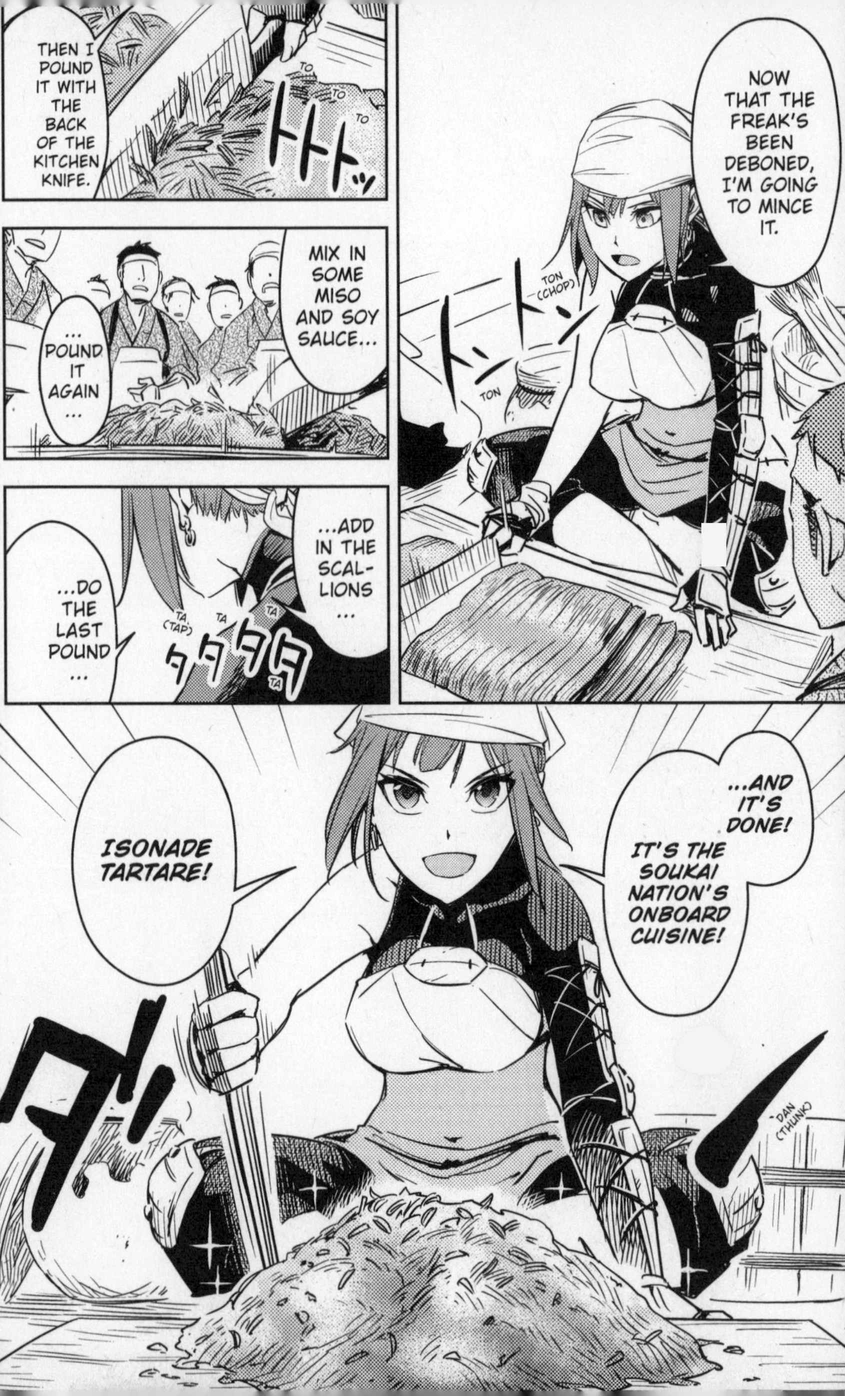
NOW THAT THE FREAK'S BEEN DEBONED, I'M GOING TO MINCE IT.
TON (CHOP)
TON
THEN I POUND IT WITH THE BACK OF THE KITCHEN KNIFE.
TO
TO
TO
MIX IN SOME MISO AND SOY SAUCE...
...POUND IT AGAIN...
...ADD IN THE SCALLIONS...
...DO THE LAST POUND...
TA (TAP)
TA
TA
TA
...AND IT'S DONE!
IT'S THE SOUKAI NATION'S ONBOARD CUISINE!
ISONADE TARTARE!
DAN (THUNK)

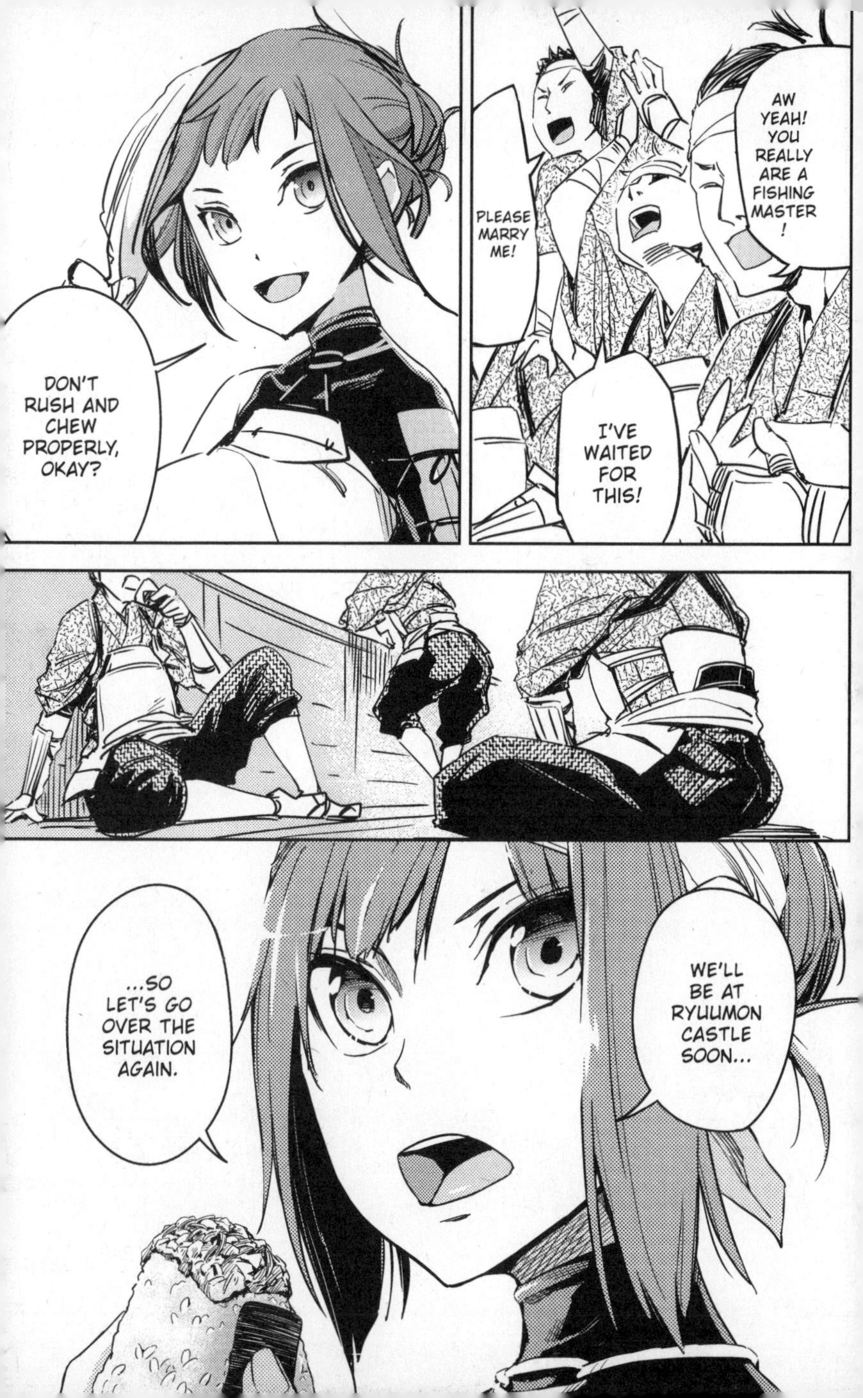
AW YEAH! YOU REALLY ARE A FISHING MASTER!
PLEASE MARRY ME!
I'VE WAITED FOR THIS!
DON'T RUSH AND CHEW PROPERLY, OKAY?
WE'LL BE AT RYUUMON CASTLE SOON...
...SO LET'S GO OVER THE SITUATION AGAIN.

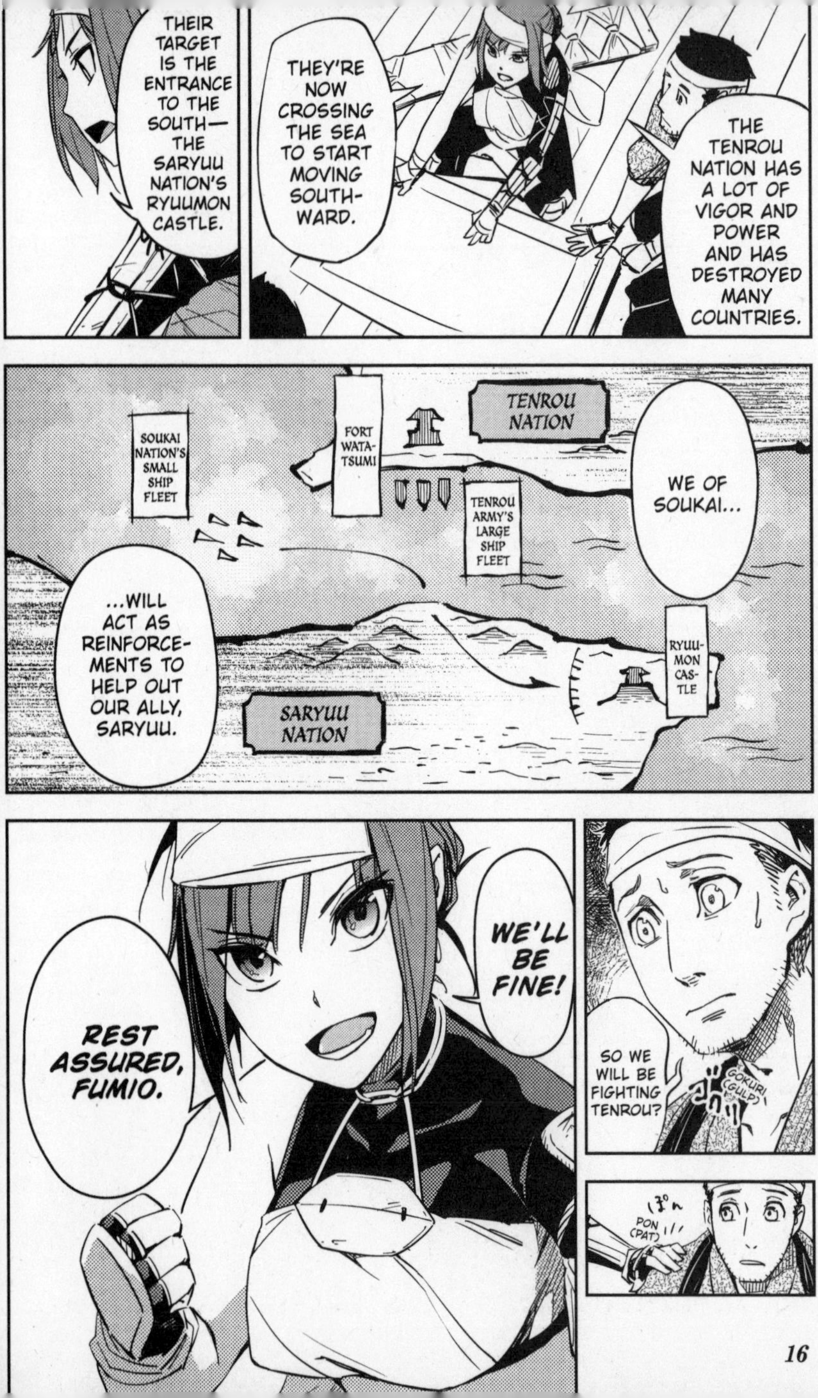
THE TENROU NATION HAS A LOT OF VIGOR AND POWER AND HAS DESTROYED MANY COUNTRIES.
THEY'RE NOW CROSSING THE SEA TO START MOVING SOUTHWARD.
THEIR TARGET IS THE ENTRANCE TO THE SOUTH—THE SARYUU NATION'S RYUUMON CASTLE.
WE OF SOUKAI...
TENROU NATION
FORT WATATSUMI
SOUKAI NATION'S SMALL SHIP FLEET
TENROU ARMY'S LARGE SHIP FLEET
RYUUMON CASTLE
SARYUU NATION
...WILL ACT AS REINFORCEMENTS TO HELP OUT OUR ALLY, SARYUU.
SO WE WILL BE FIGHTING TENROU?
GOKURI (GULP)
PON (PAT)
WE'LL BE FINE!
REST ASSURED, FUMIO.

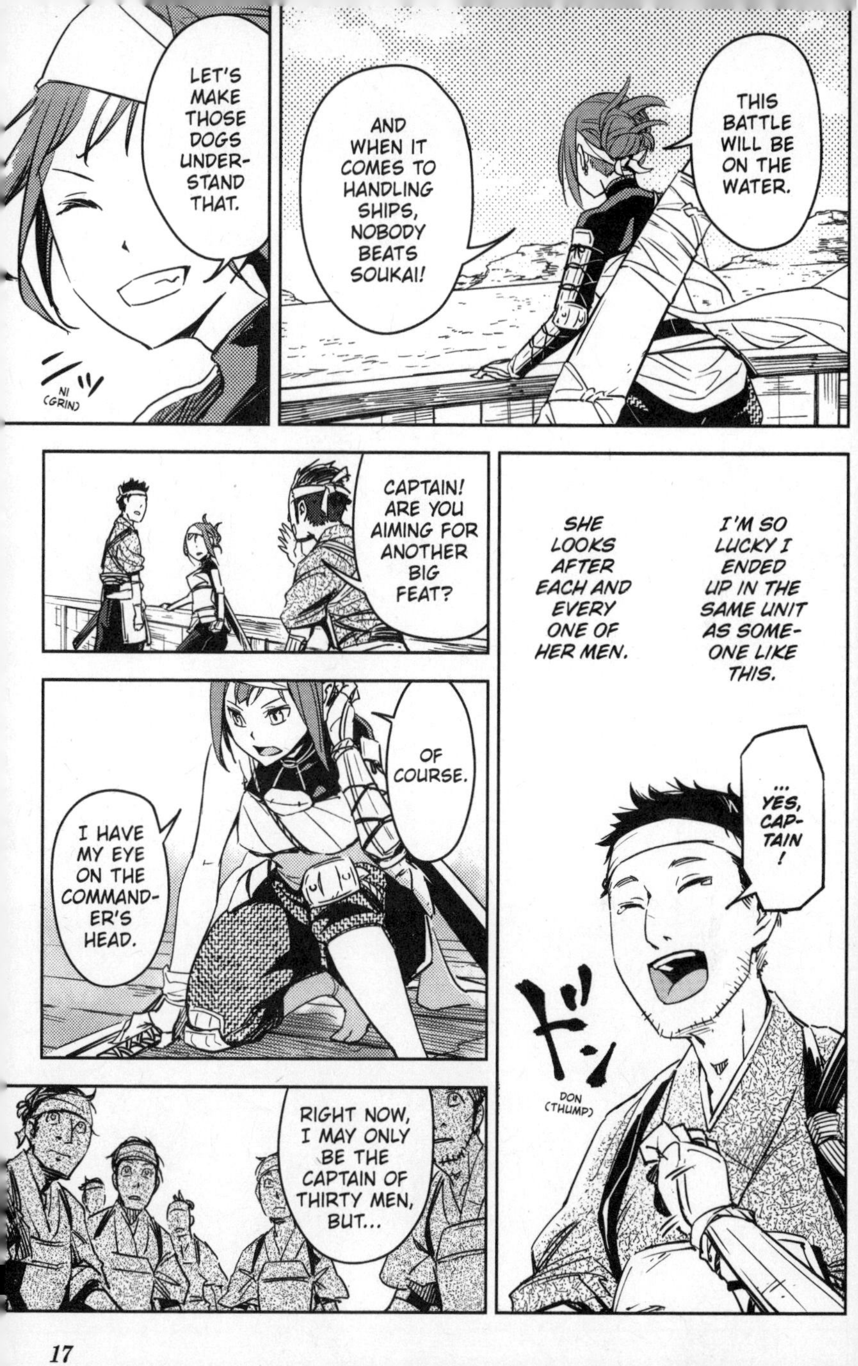
THIS BATTLE WILL BE ON THE WATER.
AND WHEN IT COMES TO HANDLING SHIPS, NOBODY BEATS SOUKAI!
LET'S MAKE THOSE DOGS UNDER-STAND THAT.
NI (GRIN)
I'M SO LUCKY I ENDED UP IN THE SAME UNIT AS SOME-ONE LIKE THIS.
SHE LOOKS AFTER EACH AND EVERY ONE OF HER MEN.
...YES, CAP-TAIN!
DON (THUMP)
CAPTAIN! ARE YOU AIMING FOR ANOTHER BIG FEAT?
OF COURSE.
I HAVE MY EYE ON THE COMMAND-ER'S HEAD.
RIGHT NOW, I MAY ONLY BE THE CAPTAIN OF THIRTY MEN, BUT...

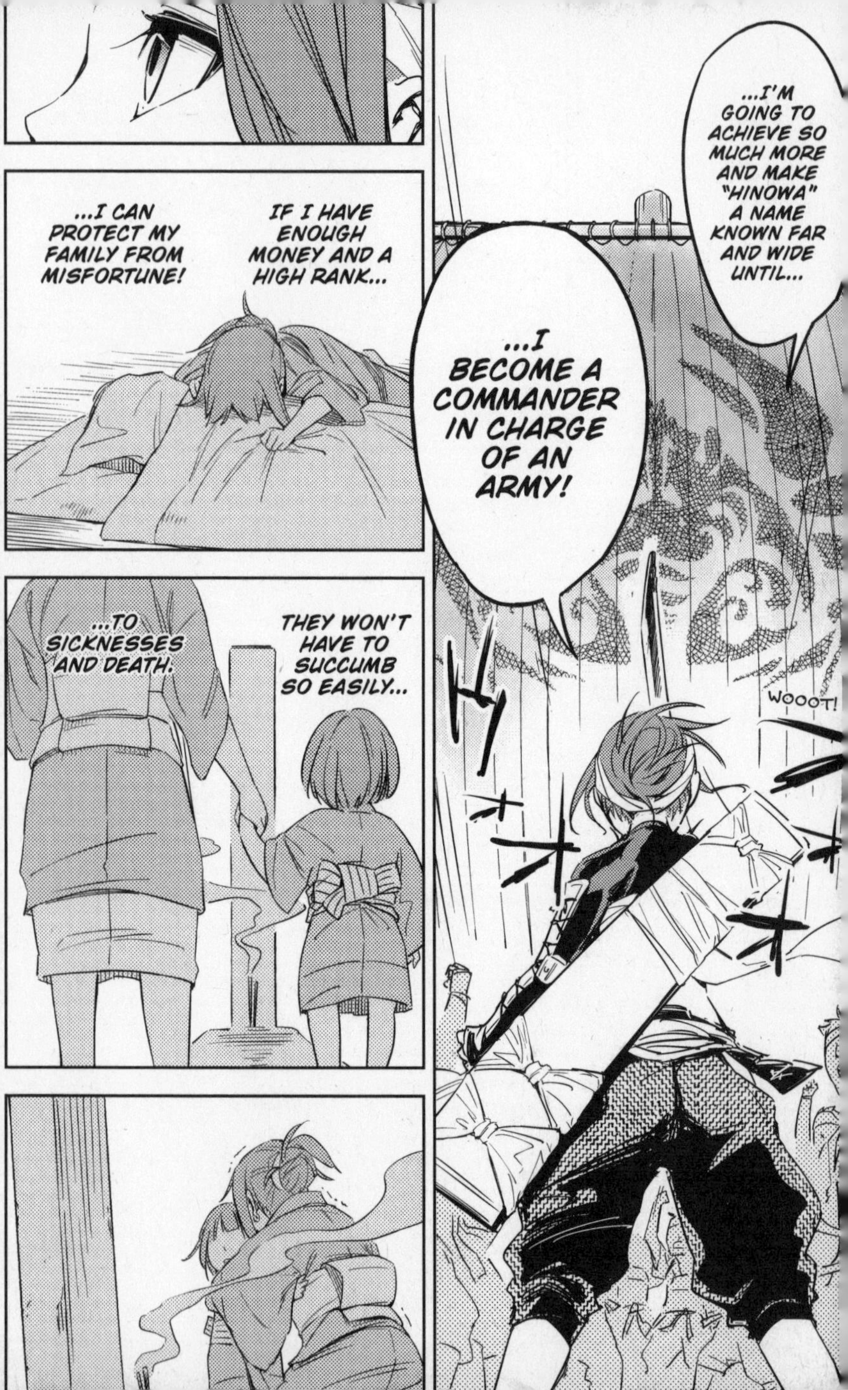
...I'M GOING TO ACHIEVE SO MUCH MORE AND MAKE "HINOWA" A NAME KNOWN FAR AND WIDE UNTIL...
...I BECOME A COMMANDER IN CHARGE OF AN ARMY!
WOOOT!
IF I HAVE ENOUGH MONEY AND A HIGH RANK...
...I CAN PROTECT MY FAMILY FROM MISFORTUNE!
THEY WON'T HAVE TO SUCCUMB SO EASILY...
...TO SICKNESSES AND DEATH.

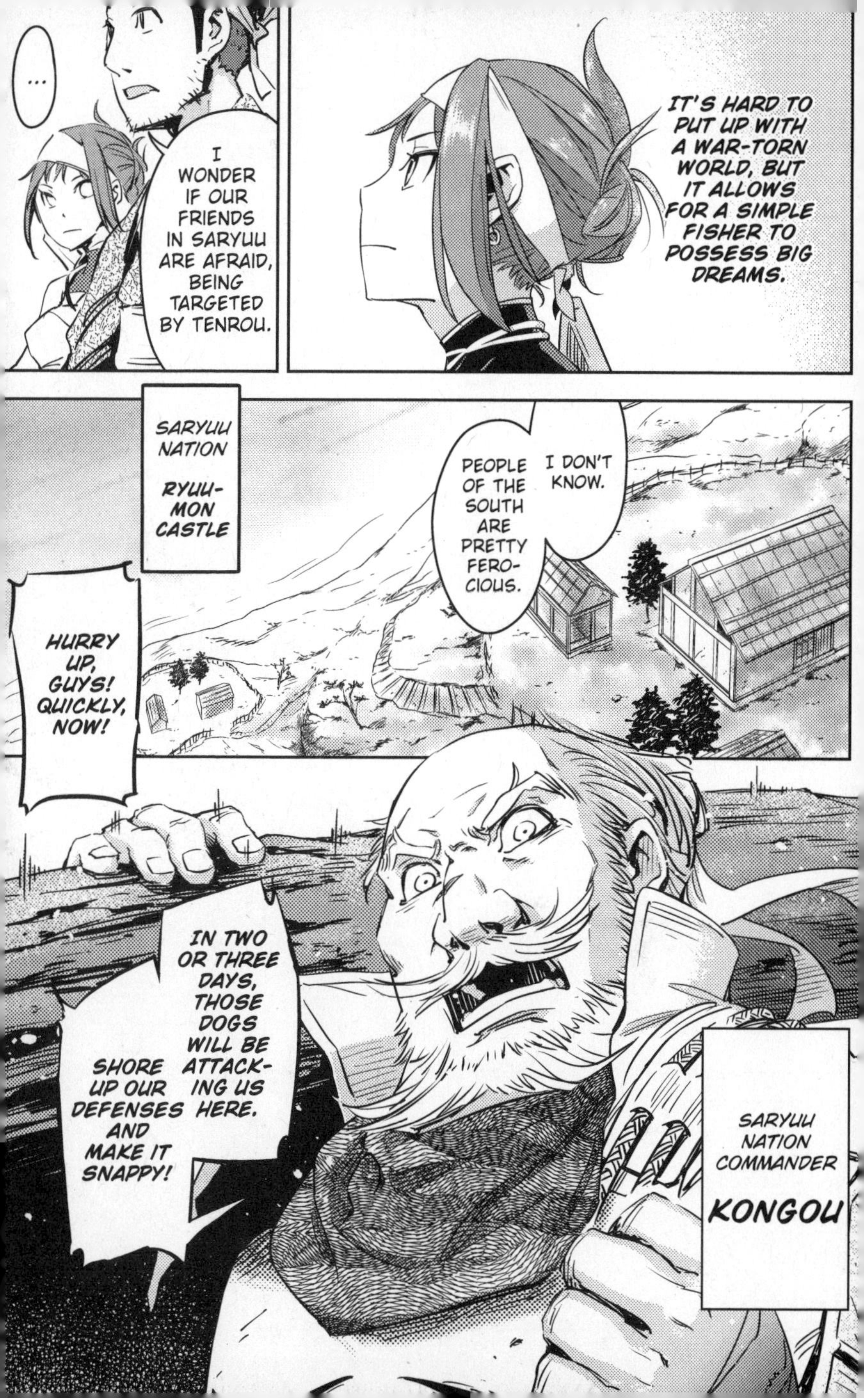
IT'S HARD TO PUT UP WITH A WAR-TORN WORLD, BUT IT ALLOWS FOR A SIMPLE FISHER TO POSSESS BIG DREAMS.
...
I WONDER IF OUR FRIENDS IN SARYUU ARE AFRAID, BEING TARGETED BY TENROU.
I DON'T KNOW.
PEOPLE OF THE SOUTH ARE PRETTY FERO-CIOUS.
SARYUU NATION
RYUU-MON CASTLE
SARYUU NATION COMMANDER
KONGOU
HURRY UP, GUYS! QUICKLY, NOW!
IN TWO OR THREE DAYS, THOSE DOGS WILL BE ATTACK-ING US HERE.
SHORE UP OUR DEFENSES AND MAKE IT SNAPPY!

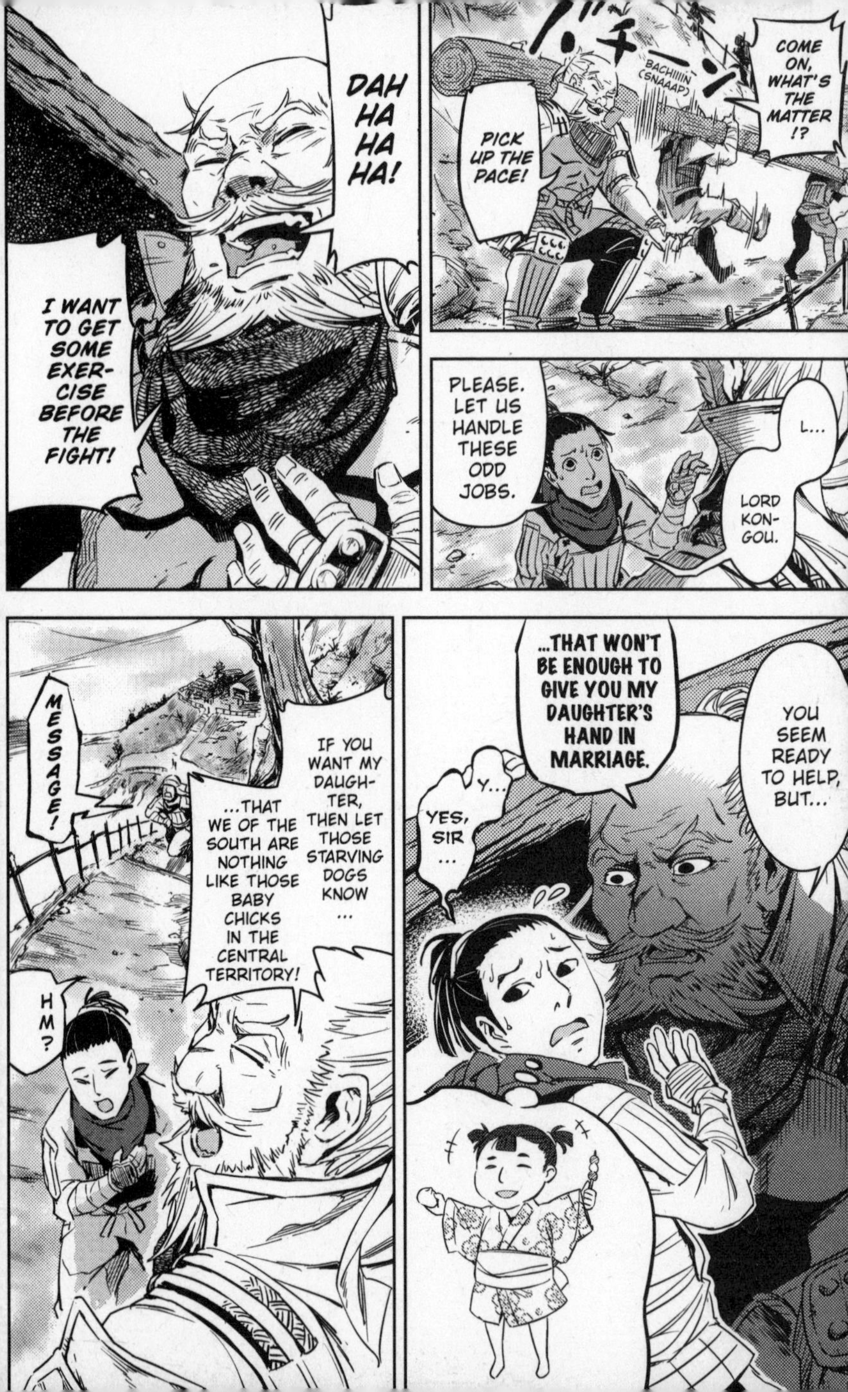

COME ON, WHAT'S THE MATTER !?
BACHIIIIN (SNAAAP)
PICK UP THE PACE!
L... LORD KON-GOU.
PLEASE. LET US HANDLE THESE ODD JOBS.
DAH HA HA HA!
I WANT TO GET SOME EXER-CISE BEFORE THE FIGHT!
YOU SEEM READY TO HELP, BUT...
...THAT WON'T BE ENOUGH TO GIVE YOU MY DAUGHTER'S HAND IN MARRIAGE.
Y...
YES, SIR ...
MESSAGE!
IF YOU WANT MY DAUGH-TER, THEN LET THOSE STARVING DOGS KNOW ...
...THAT WE OF THE SOUTH ARE NOTHING LIKE THOSE BABY CHICKS IN THE CENTRAL TERRITORY!
HM?

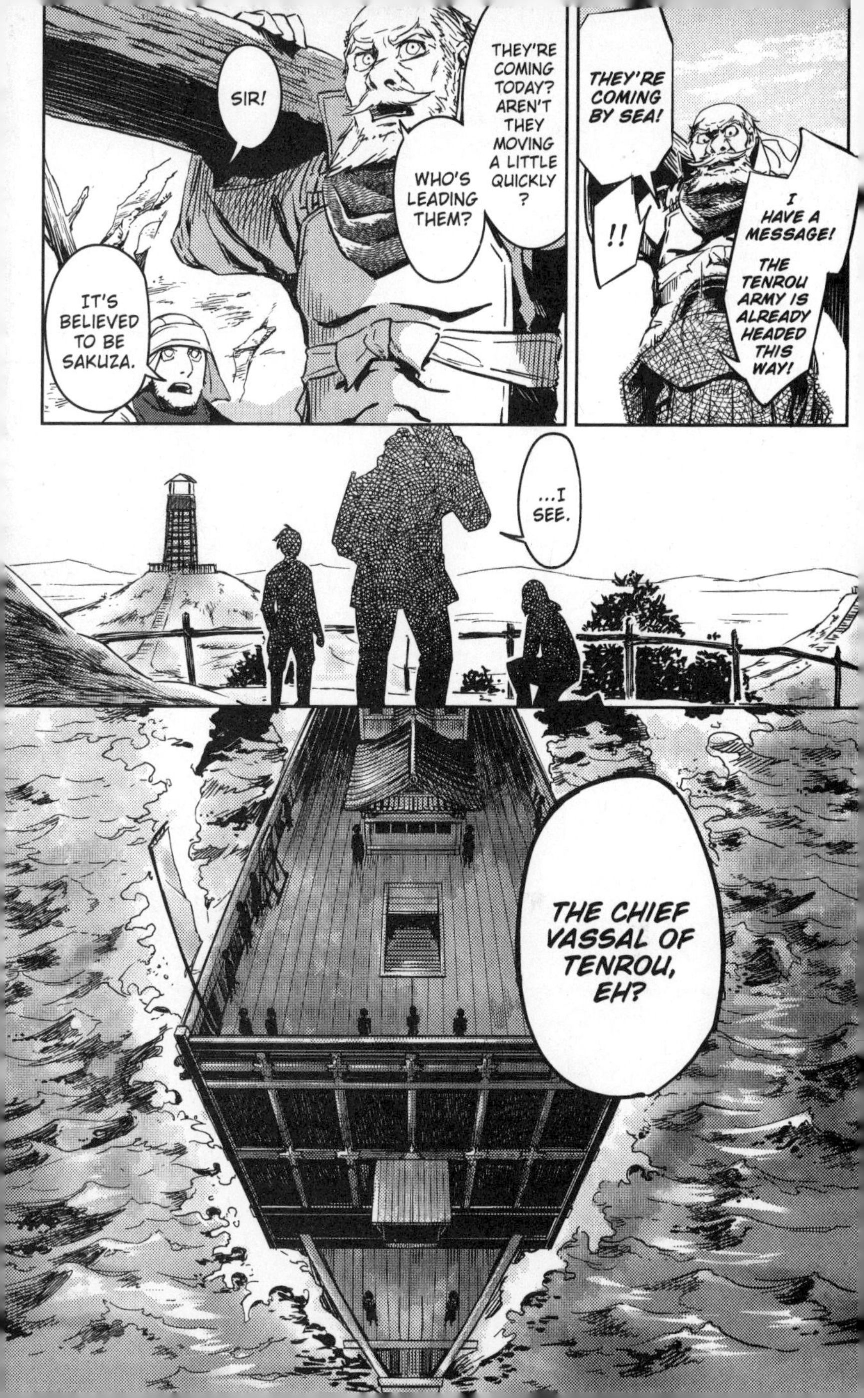
I HAVE A MESSAGE!
THE TENROU ARMY IS ALREADY HEADED THIS WAY!
!!
THEY'RE COMING BY SEA!
SIR!
THEY'RE COMING TODAY? AREN'T THEY MOVING A LITTLE QUICKLY?
WHO'S LEADING THEM?
IT'S BELIEVED TO BE SAKUZA.
...I SEE.
THE CHIEF VASSAL OF TENROU, EH?

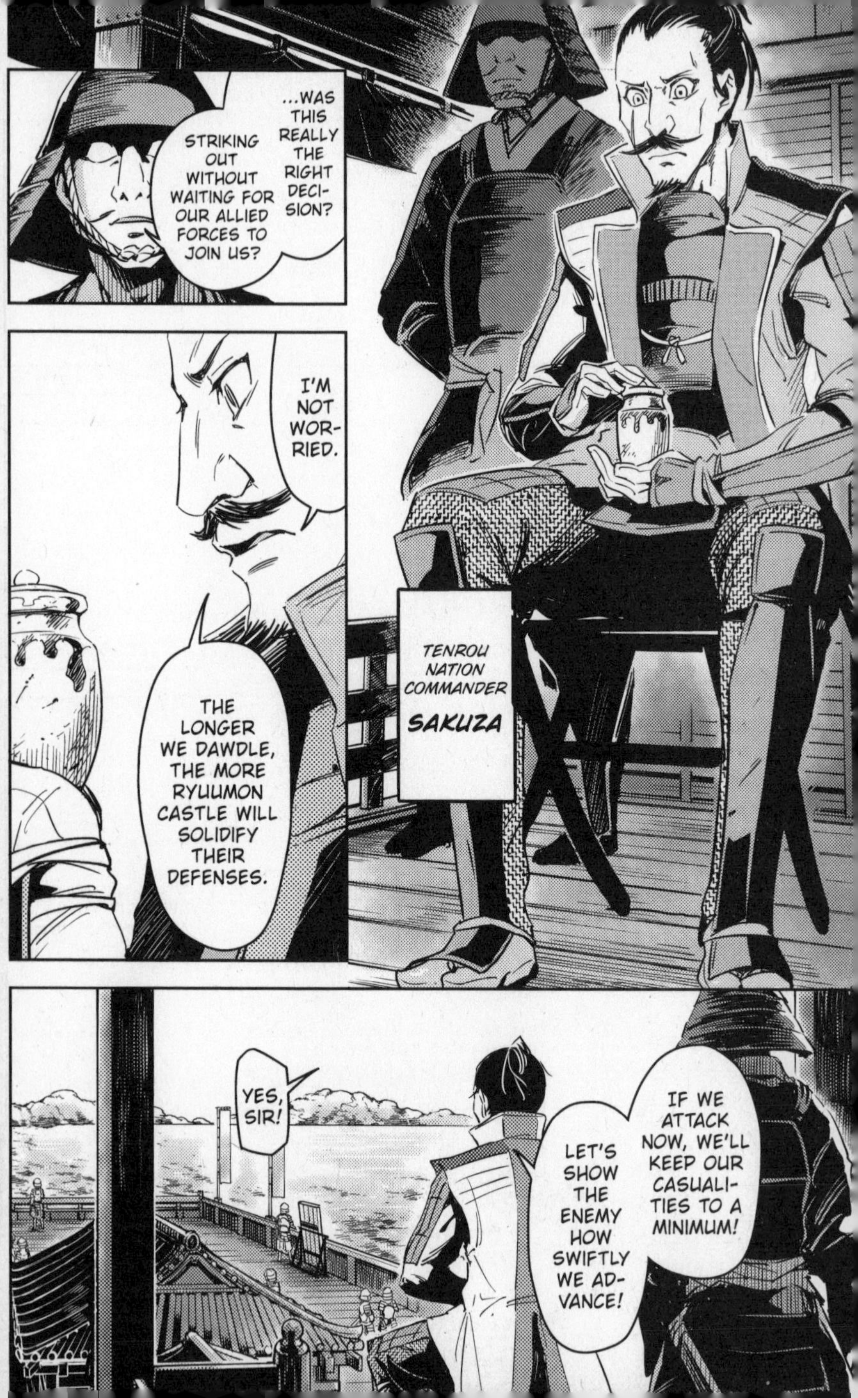
TENROU NATION COMMANDER
SAKUZA
STRIKING OUT WITHOUT WAITING FOR OUR ALLIED FORCES TO JOIN US?
...WAS THIS REALLY THE RIGHT DECI-SION?
I'M NOT WOR-RIED.
THE LONGER WE DAWDLE, THE MORE RYUUMON CASTLE WILL SOLIDIFY THEIR DEFENSES.
IF WE ATTACK NOW, WE'LL KEEP OUR CASUALI-TIES TO A MINIMUM!
LET'S SHOW THE ENEMY HOW SWIFTLY WE AD-VANCE!
YES, SIR!

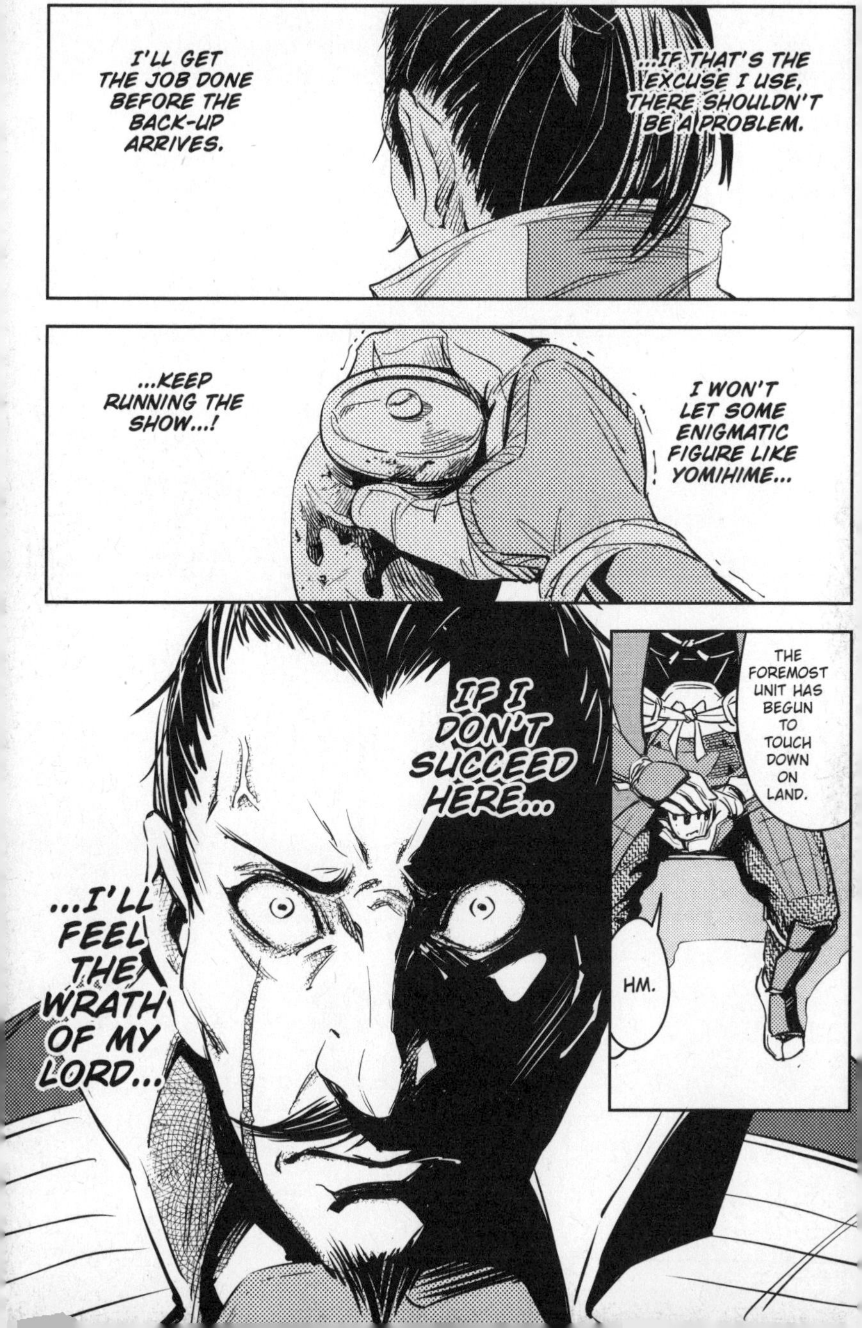

...IF THAT'S THE EXCUSE I USE, THERE SHOULDN'T BE A PROBLEM.
I'LL GET THE JOB DONE BEFORE THE BACK-UP ARRIVES.
I WON'T LET SOME ENIGMATIC FIGURE LIKE YOMIHIME...
...KEEP RUNNING THE SHOW...!
THE FOREMOST UNIT HAS BEGUN TO TOUCH DOWN ON LAND.
HM.
IF I DON'T SUCCEED HERE...
...I'LL FEEL THE WRATH OF MY LORD...

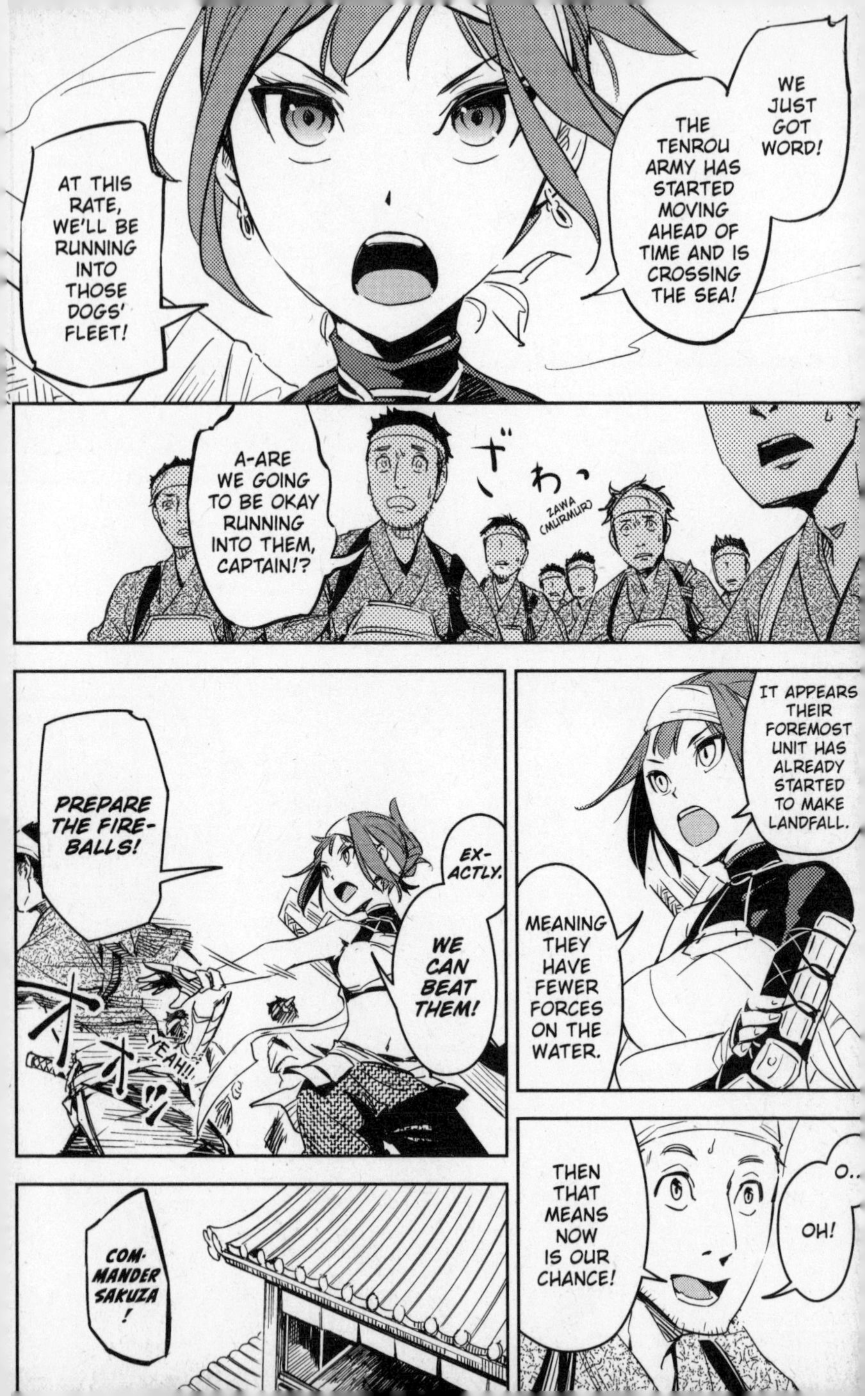
WE JUST GOT WORD!
THE TENROU ARMY HAS STARTED MOVING AHEAD OF TIME AND IS CROSSING THE SEA!
AT THIS RATE, WE'LL BE RUNNING INTO THOSE DOGS' FLEET!
ざわっ
ZAWA (MURMUR)
A-ARE WE GOING TO BE OKAY RUNNING INTO THEM, CAPTAIN!?
IT APPEARS THEIR FOREMOST UNIT HAS ALREADY STARTED TO MAKE LANDFALL.
MEANING THEY HAVE FEWER FORCES ON THE WATER.
O...
OH!
THEN THAT MEANS NOW IS OUR CHANCE!
EX-ACTLY.
WE CAN BEAT THEM!
PREPARE THE FIRE-BALLS!
YEAH!!
COM-MANDER SAKUZA!

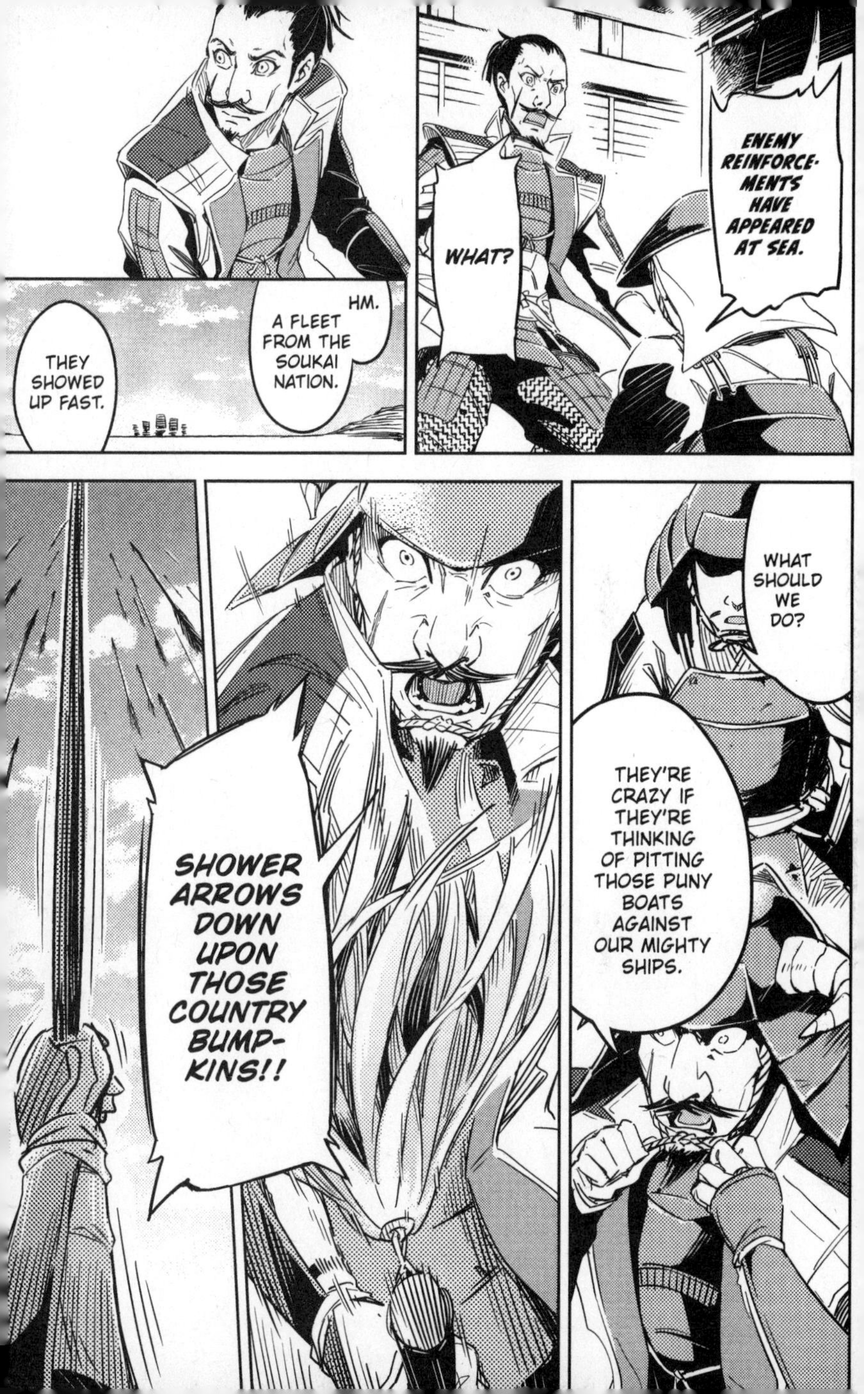
ENEMY REINFORCEMENTS HAVE APPEARED AT SEA.
WHAT?
HM. A FLEET FROM THE SOUKAI NATION.
THEY SHOWED UP FAST.
WHAT SHOULD WE DO?
THEY'RE CRAZY IF THEY'RE THINKING OF PITTING THOSE PUNY BOATS AGAINST OUR MIGHTY SHIPS.
SHOWER ARROWS DOWN UPON THOSE COUNTRY BUMPKINS!!

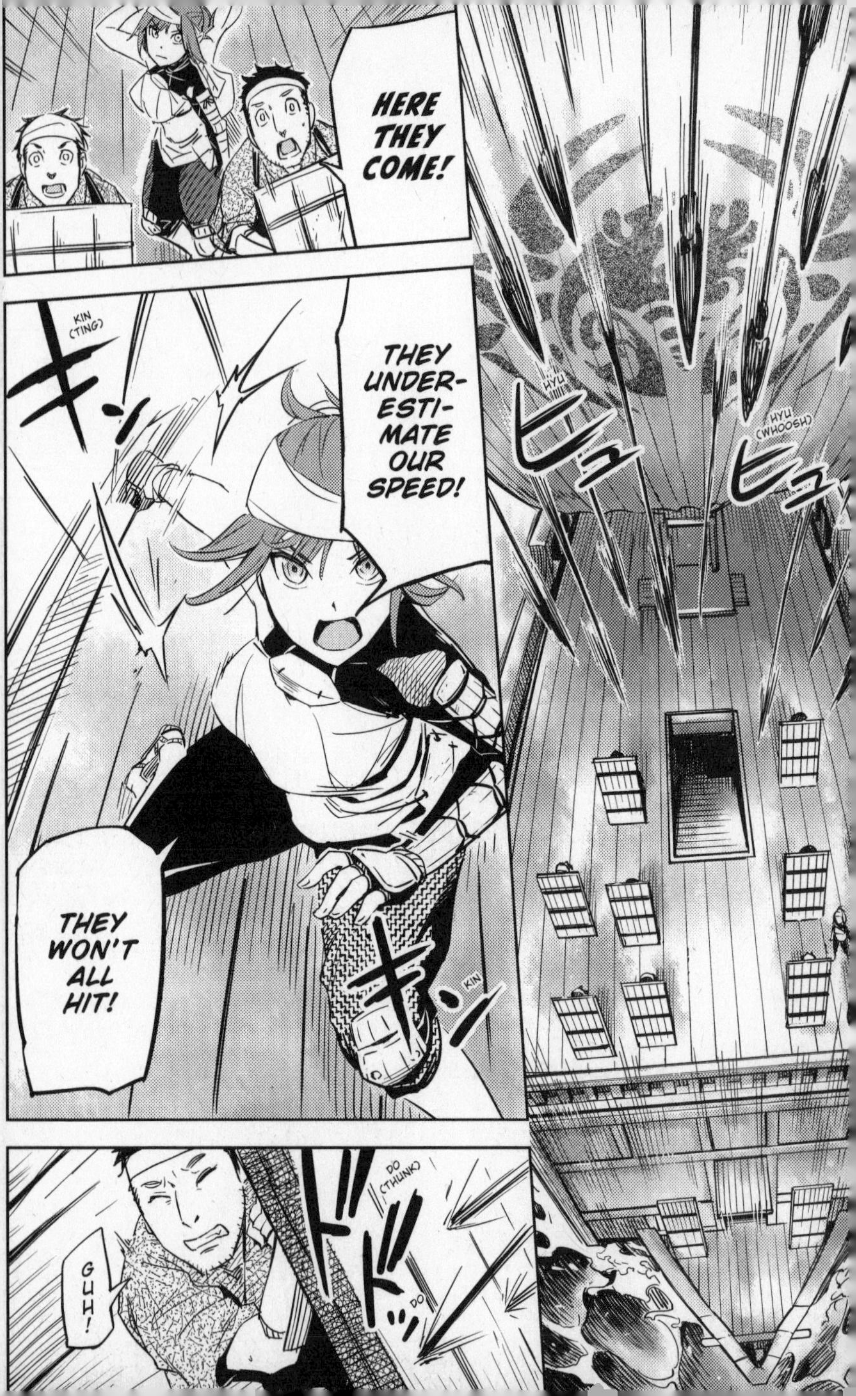

HYU
HYU (WHOOSH)
HERE THEY COME!
THEY UNDER-ESTIMATE OUR SPEED!
KIN (TING)
KIN
THEY WON'T ALL HIT!
DO (THUNK)
DO
GUH!

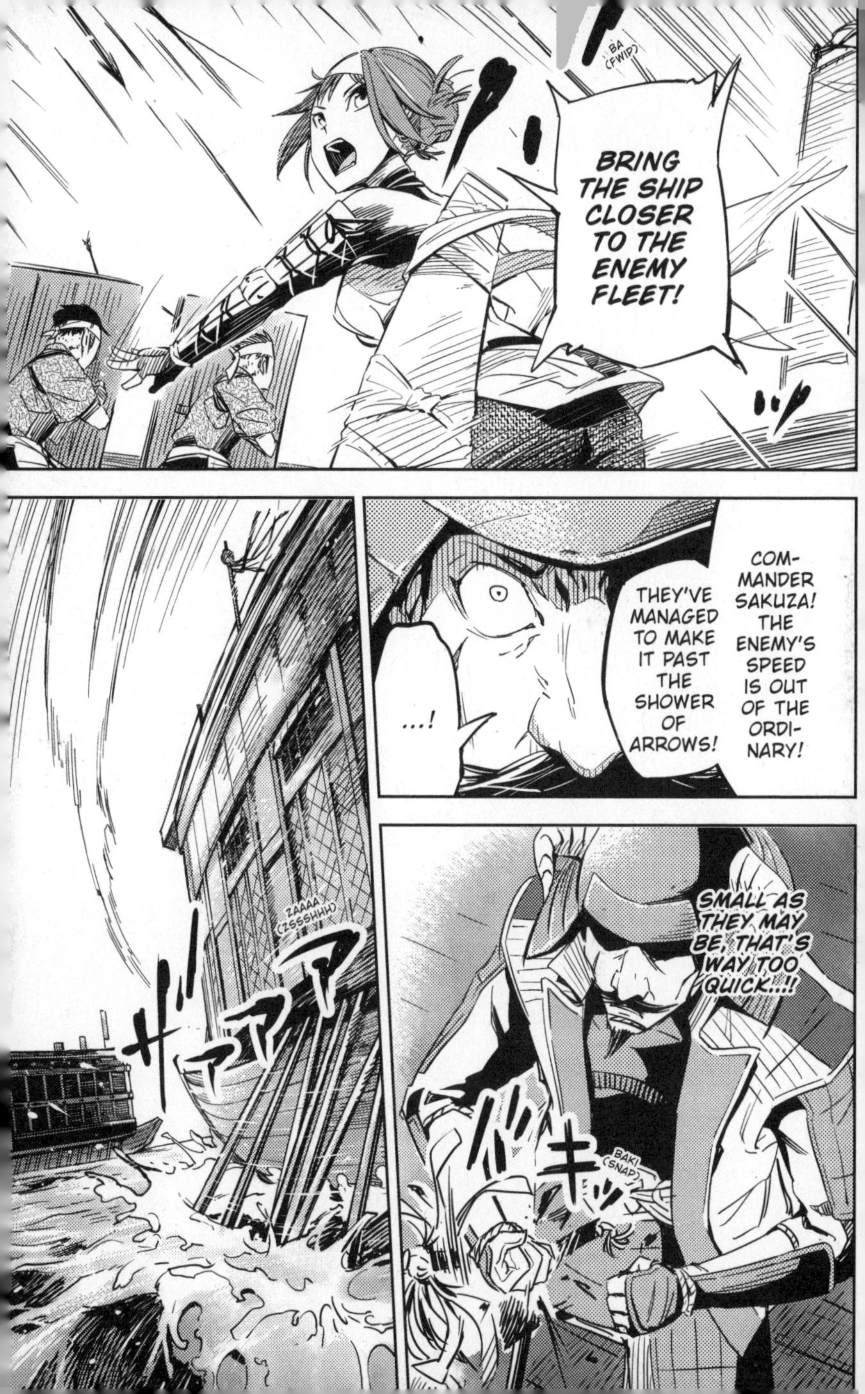
BA (FWIP)
BRING THE SHIP CLOSER TO THE ENEMY FLEET!
COMMANDER SAKUZA! THE ENEMY'S SPEED IS OUT OF THE ORDINARY!
THEY'VE MANAGED TO MAKE IT PAST THE SHOWER OF ARROWS!
...!
SMALL AS THEY MAY BE, THAT'S WAY TOO QUICK...!!
BAKI (SNAP)
ZAAAA (ZSSSHHH)

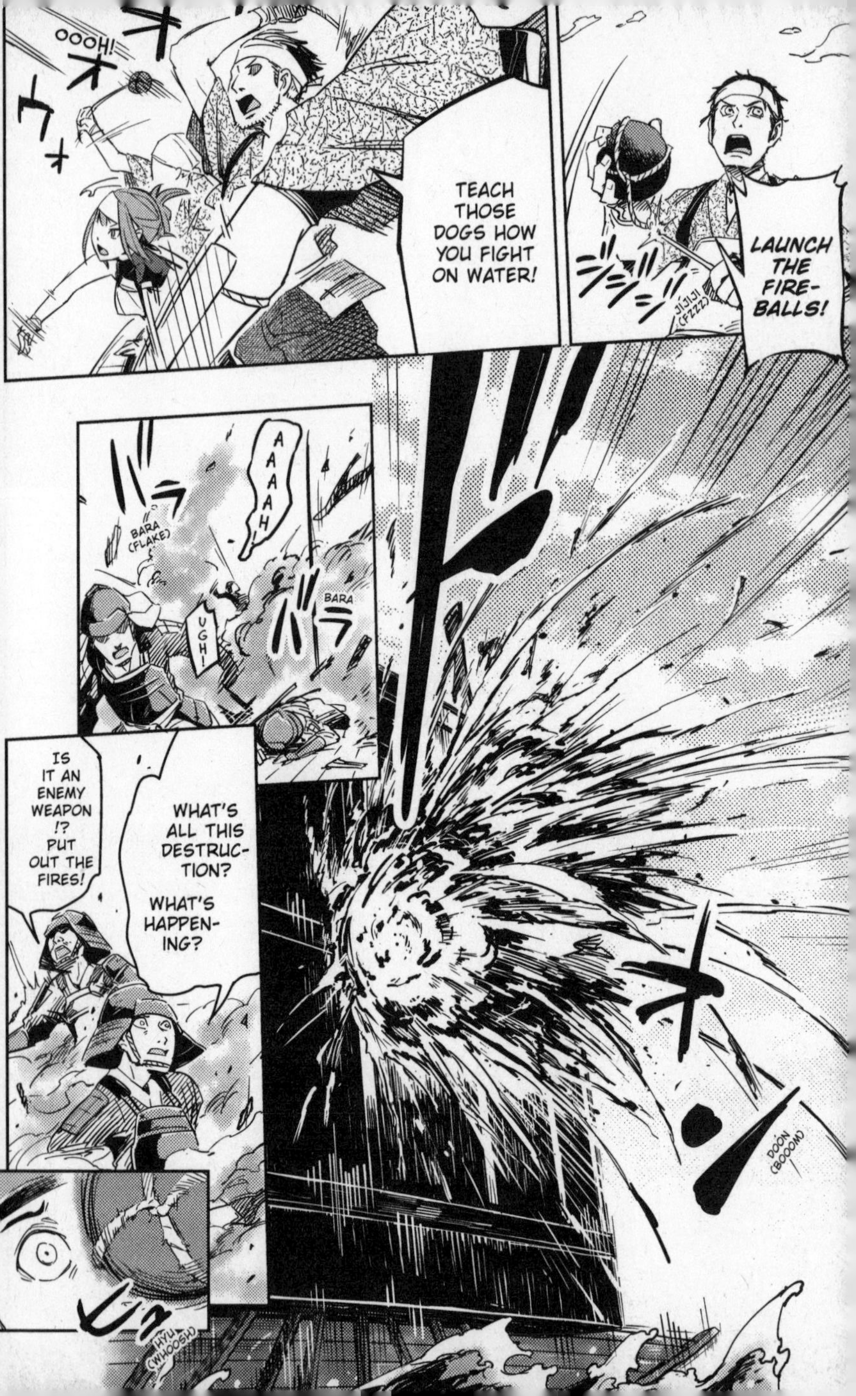

LAUNCH THE FIRE-BALLS!
JIJIJI (FZZZ)
TEACH THOSE DOGS HOW YOU FIGHT ON WATER!
OOOH!
DOON (BOOOM)
AAAAH
BARA (FLAKE)
BARA
UGH!
WHAT'S ALL THIS DESTRUCTION?
WHAT'S HAPPENING?
IS IT AN ENEMY WEAPON!? PUT OUT THE FIRES!
HYU (WHOOSH)

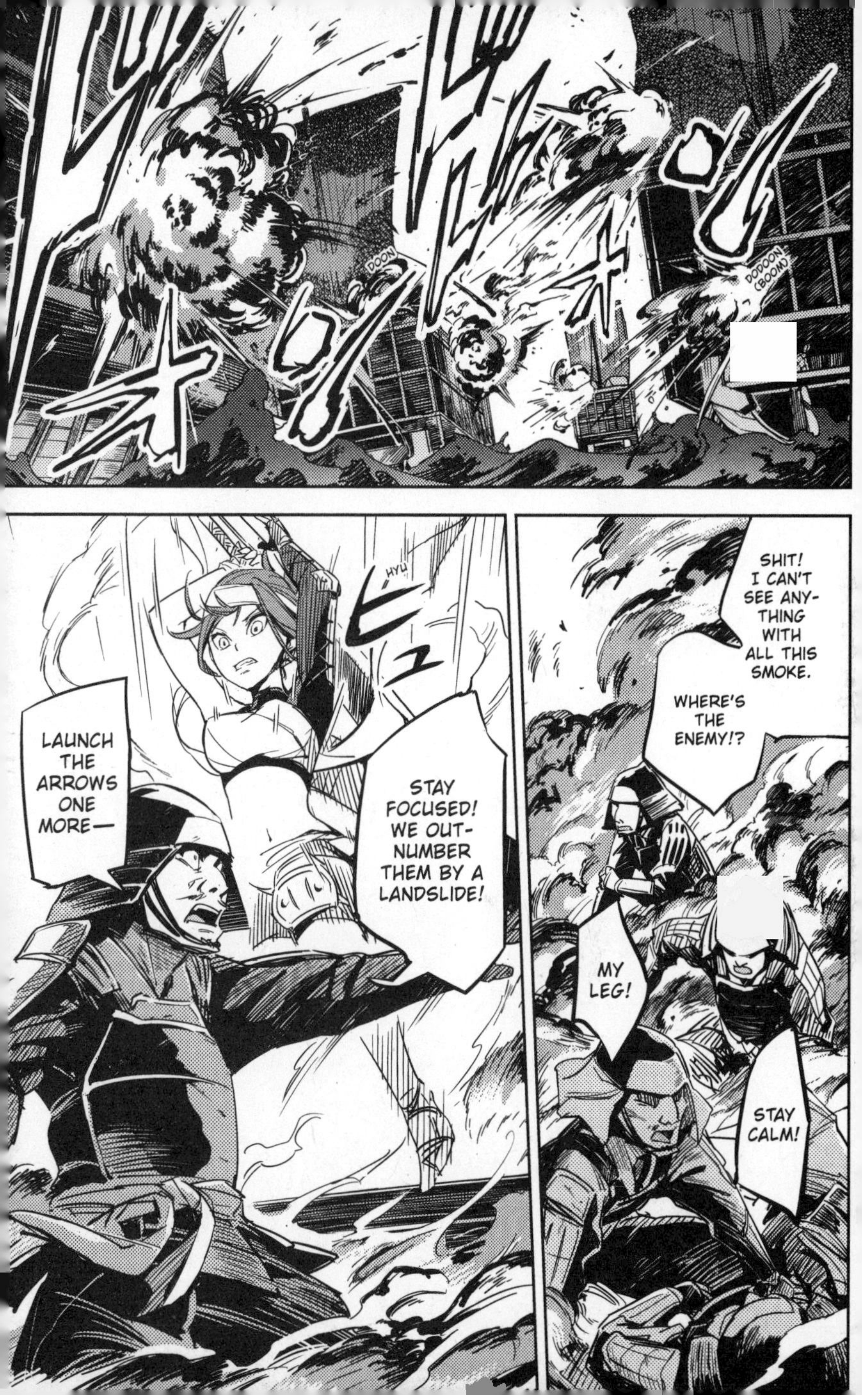
DODOON (BOOM)
DOON
SHIT! I CAN'T SEE ANY-THING WITH ALL THIS SMOKE.
WHERE'S THE ENEMY!?
MY LEG!
STAY CALM!
HYU
STAY FOCUSED! WE OUT-NUMBER THEM BY A LANDSLIDE!
LAUNCH THE ARROWS ONE MORE—

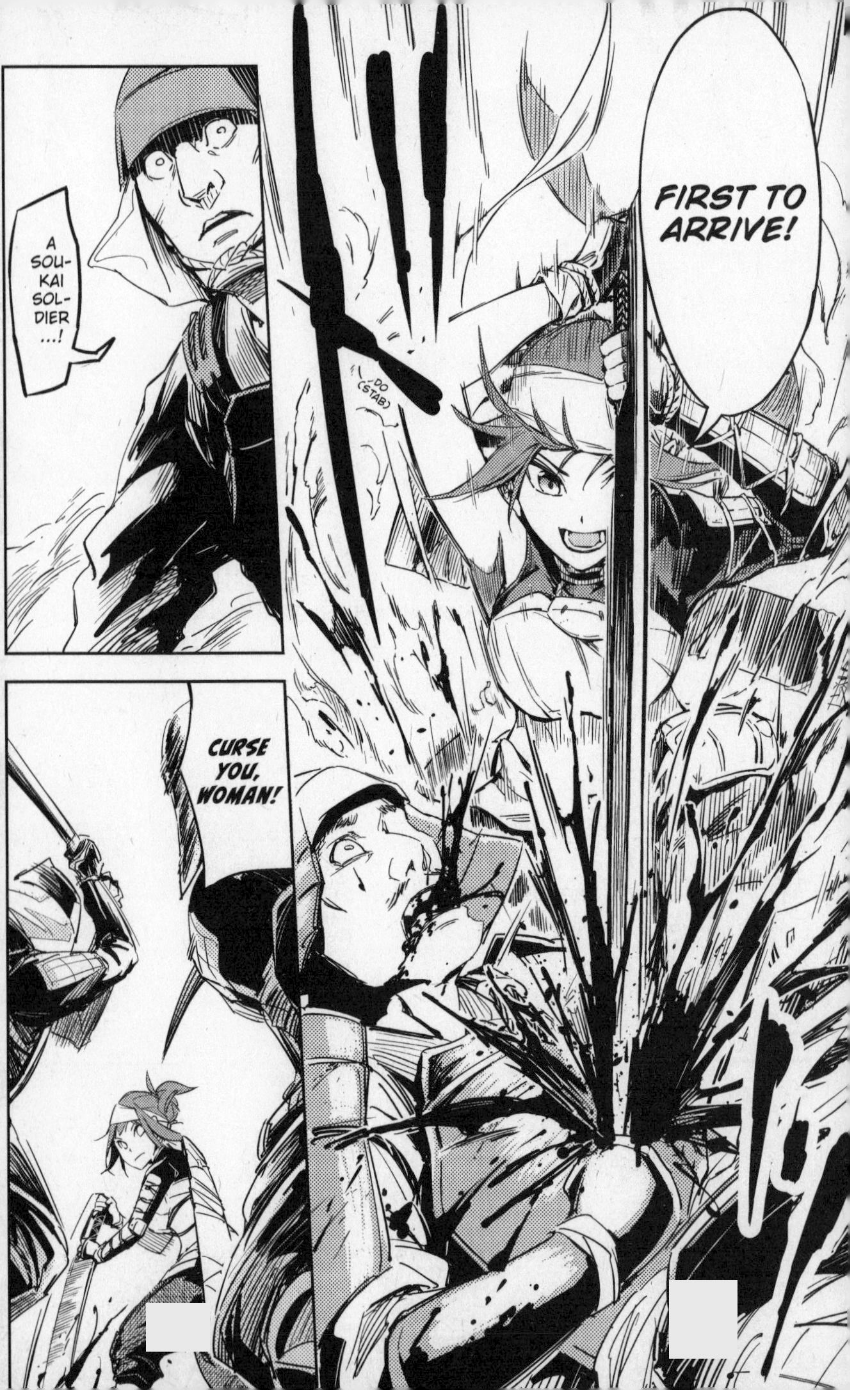
FIRST TO ARRIVE!
DO (STAB)
A SOU-KAI SOL-DIER ...!
CURSE YOU, WOMAN!

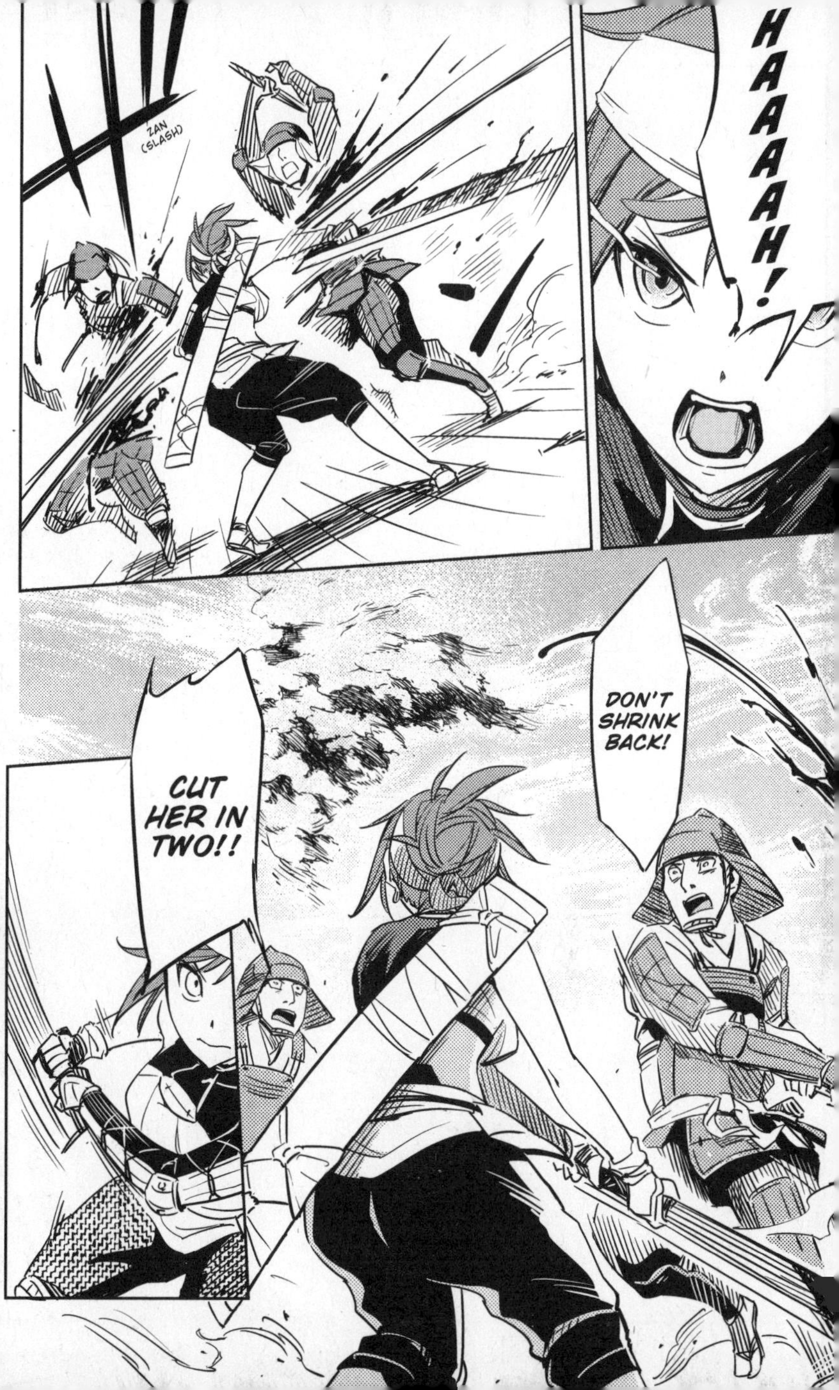
HAAAAAH!
ZAN (SLASH)
DON'T SHRINK BACK!
CUT HER IN TWO!!

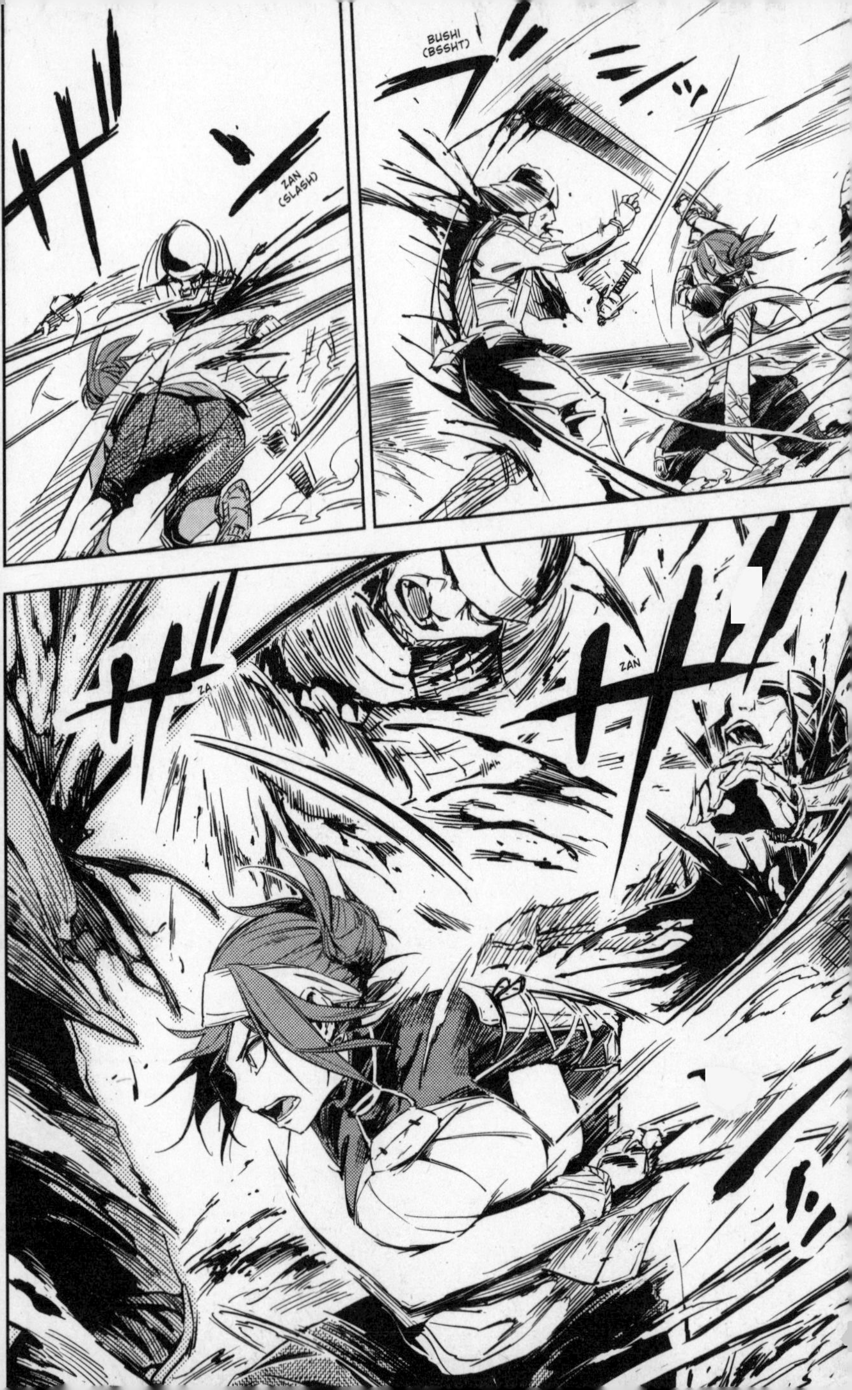
BUSHI
(BSSHT)
ZAN
(SLASH)
ZAN
ZA...

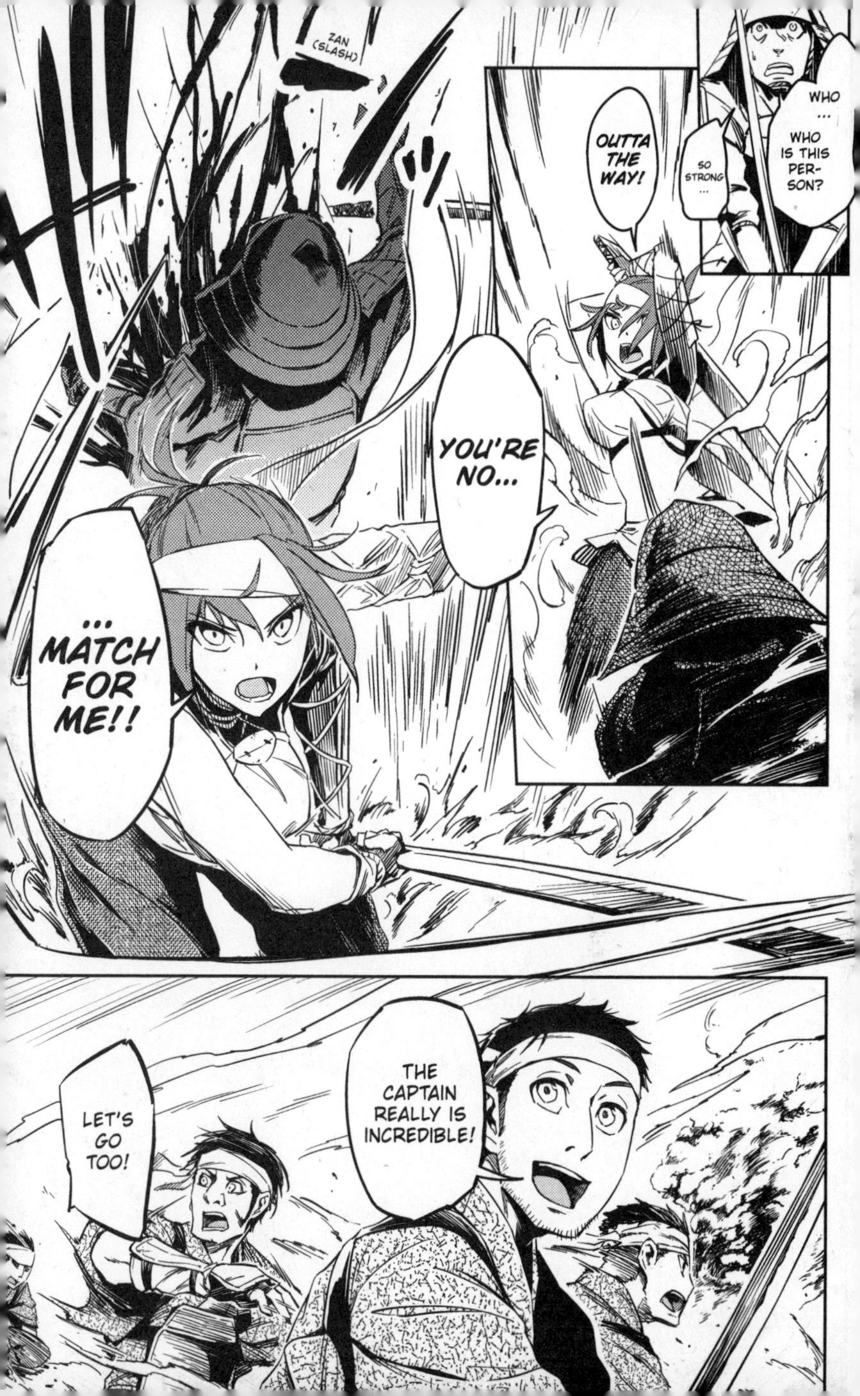
WHO... WHO IS THIS PER-SON?
SO STRONG...
OUTTA THE WAY!
ZAN (SLASH)
YOU'RE NO...
... MATCH FOR ME!!
THE CAPTAIN REALLY IS INCREDIBLE!
LET'S GO TOO!

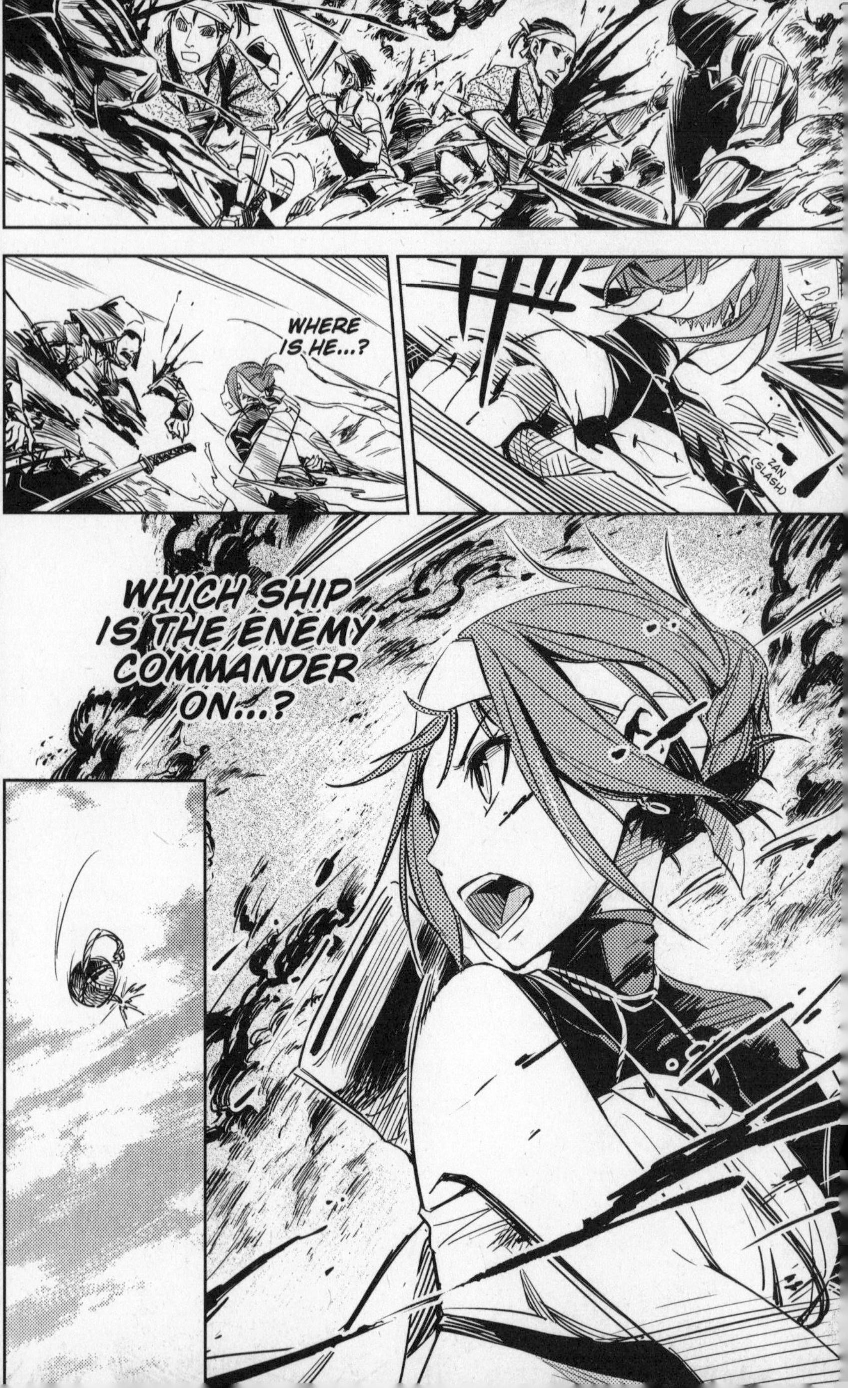
ZAN (SLASH)
WHERE IS HE...?
WHICH SHIP IS THE ENEMY COMMANDER ON...?

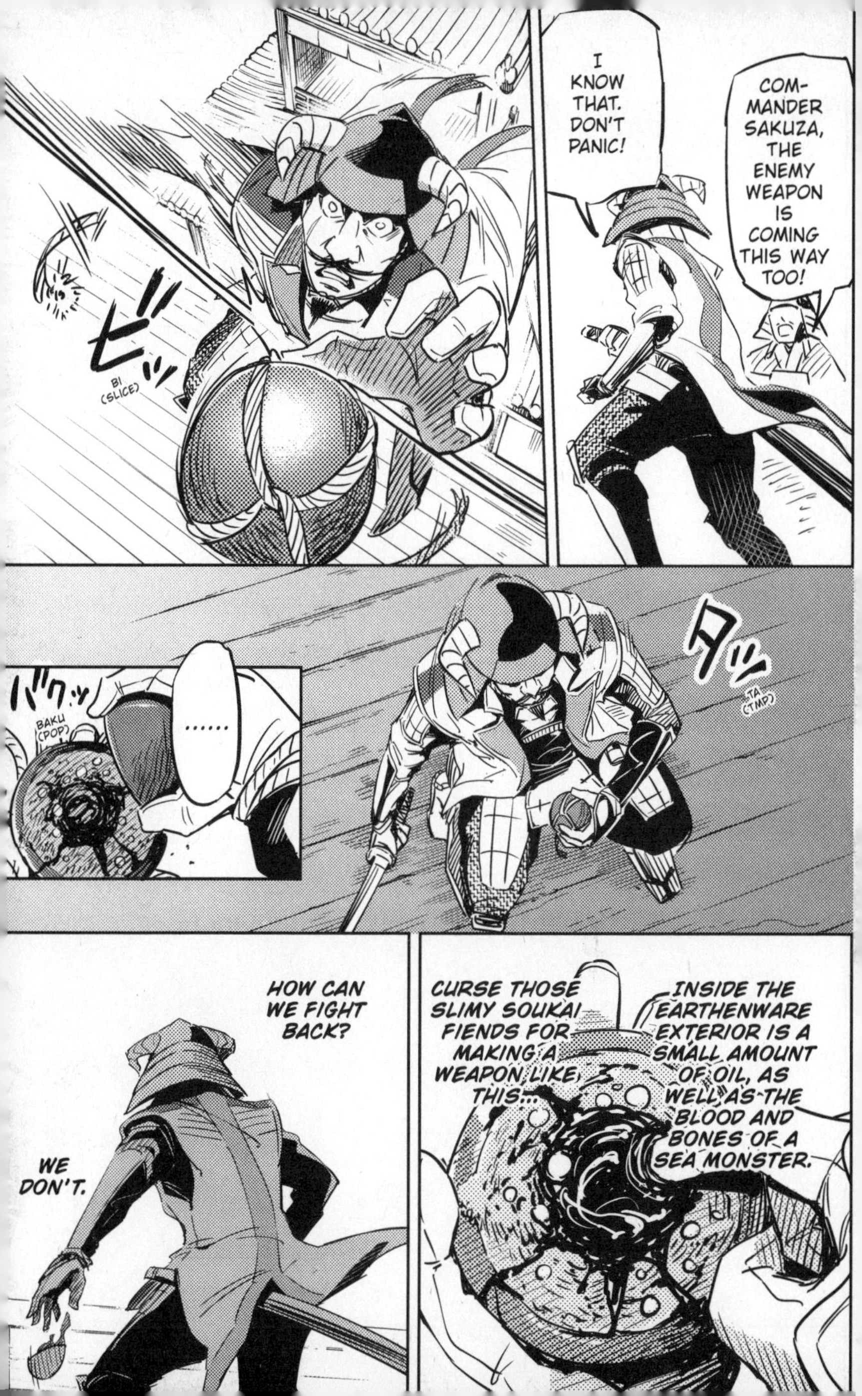

COM-MANDER SAKUZA, THE ENEMY WEAPON IS COMING THIS WAY TOO!
I KNOW THAT. DON'T PANIC!
ビッ
BI (SLICE)
タッ
TA (TMP)
......
バクッ
BAKU (POP)
INSIDE THE EARTHENWARE EXTERIOR IS A SMALL AMOUNT OF OIL, AS WELL AS THE BLOOD AND BONES OF A SEA MONSTER.
CURSE THOSE SLIMY SOUKAI FIENDS FOR MAKING A WEAPON LIKE THIS...
HOW CAN WE FIGHT BACK?
WE DON'T.

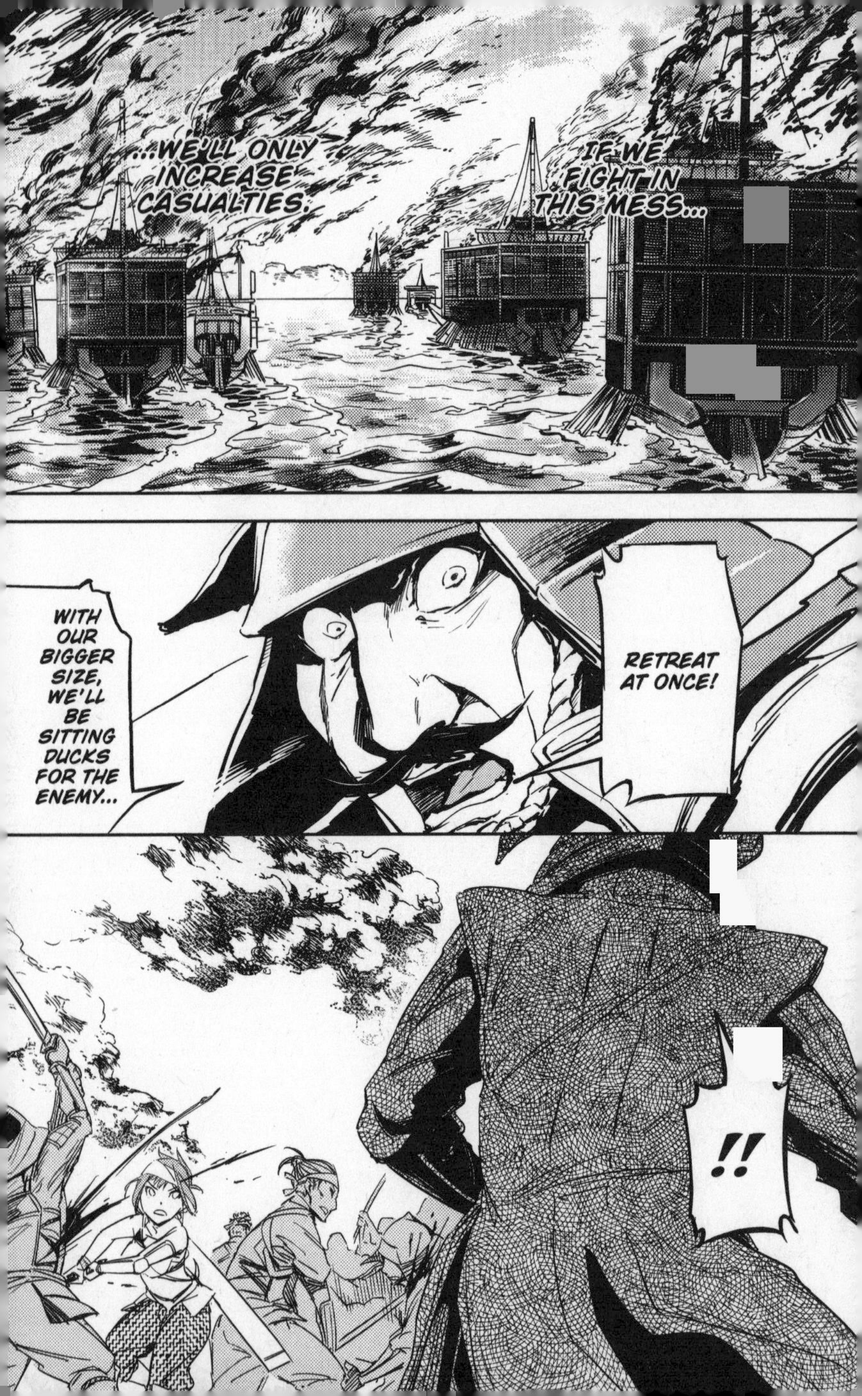
IF WE FIGHT IN THIS MESS...
...WE'LL ONLY INCREASE CASUALTIES.
RETREAT AT ONCE!
WITH OUR BIGGER SIZE, WE'LL BE SITTING DUCKS FOR THE ENEMY...
!!

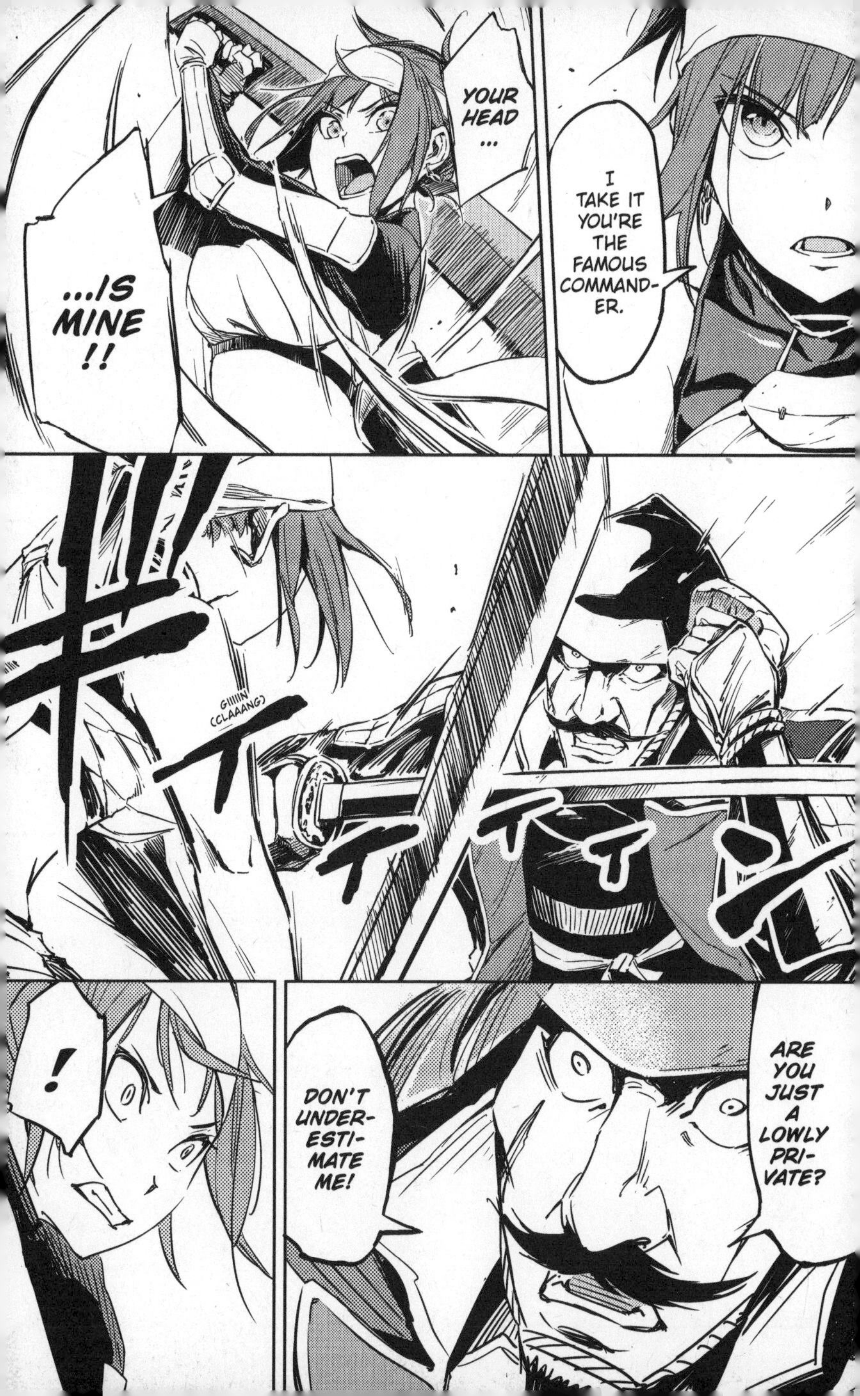
I TAKE IT YOU'RE THE FAMOUS COMMANDER.
YOUR HEAD ...
...IS MINE !!
GIIIIN (CLAAANG)
ARE YOU JUST A LOWLY PRIVATE?
DON'T UNDERESTIMATE ME!
!

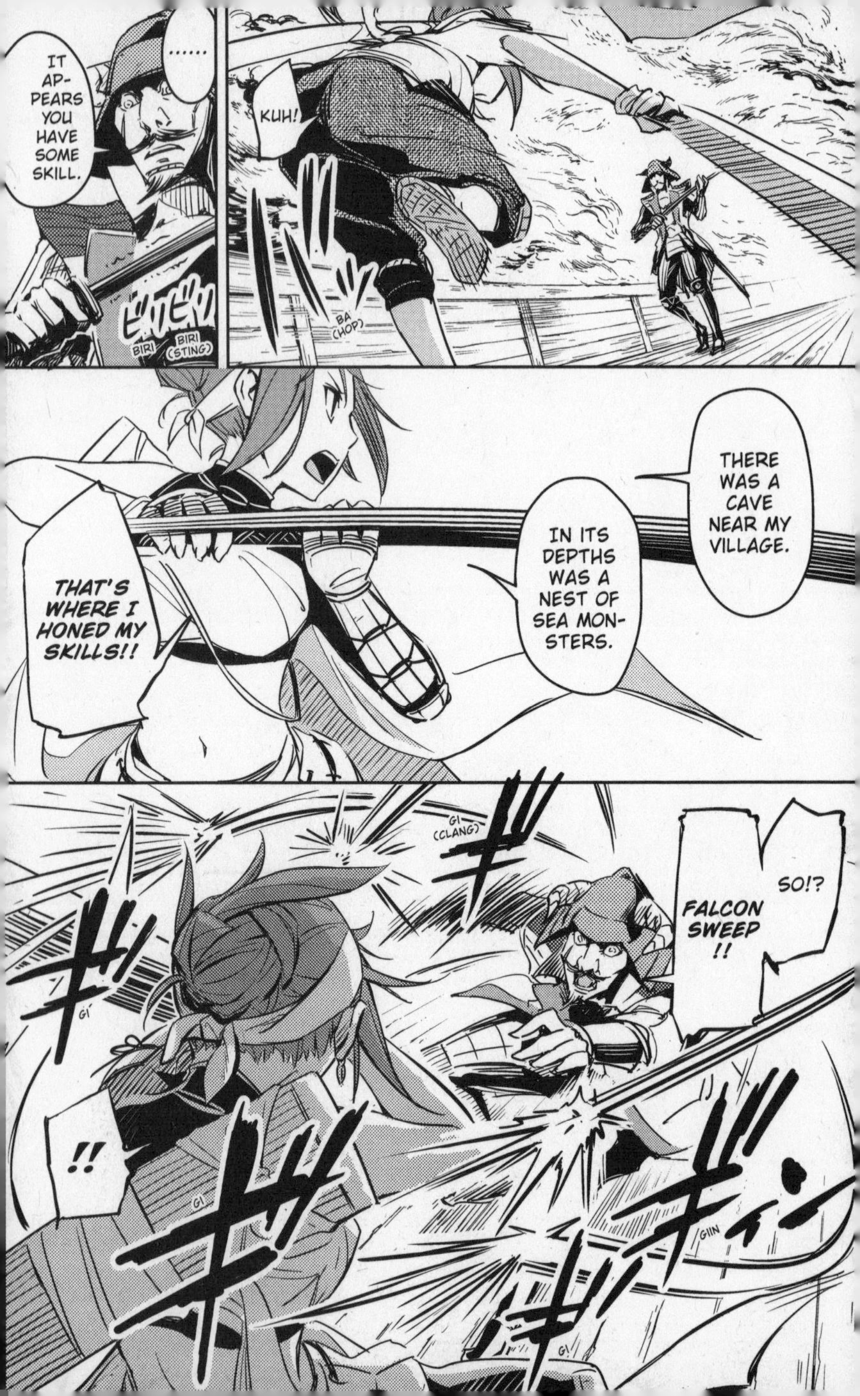
.......
KUH!
BA (HOP)
IT APPEARS YOU HAVE SOME SKILL.
BIRI BIRI (STING)
THERE WAS A CAVE NEAR MY VILLAGE.
IN ITS DEPTHS WAS A NEST OF SEA MONSTERS.
THAT'S WHERE I HONED MY SKILLS!!
SO!?
FALCON SWEEP!!
GI (CLANG)
GI
!!
GIIN
GI
GI!

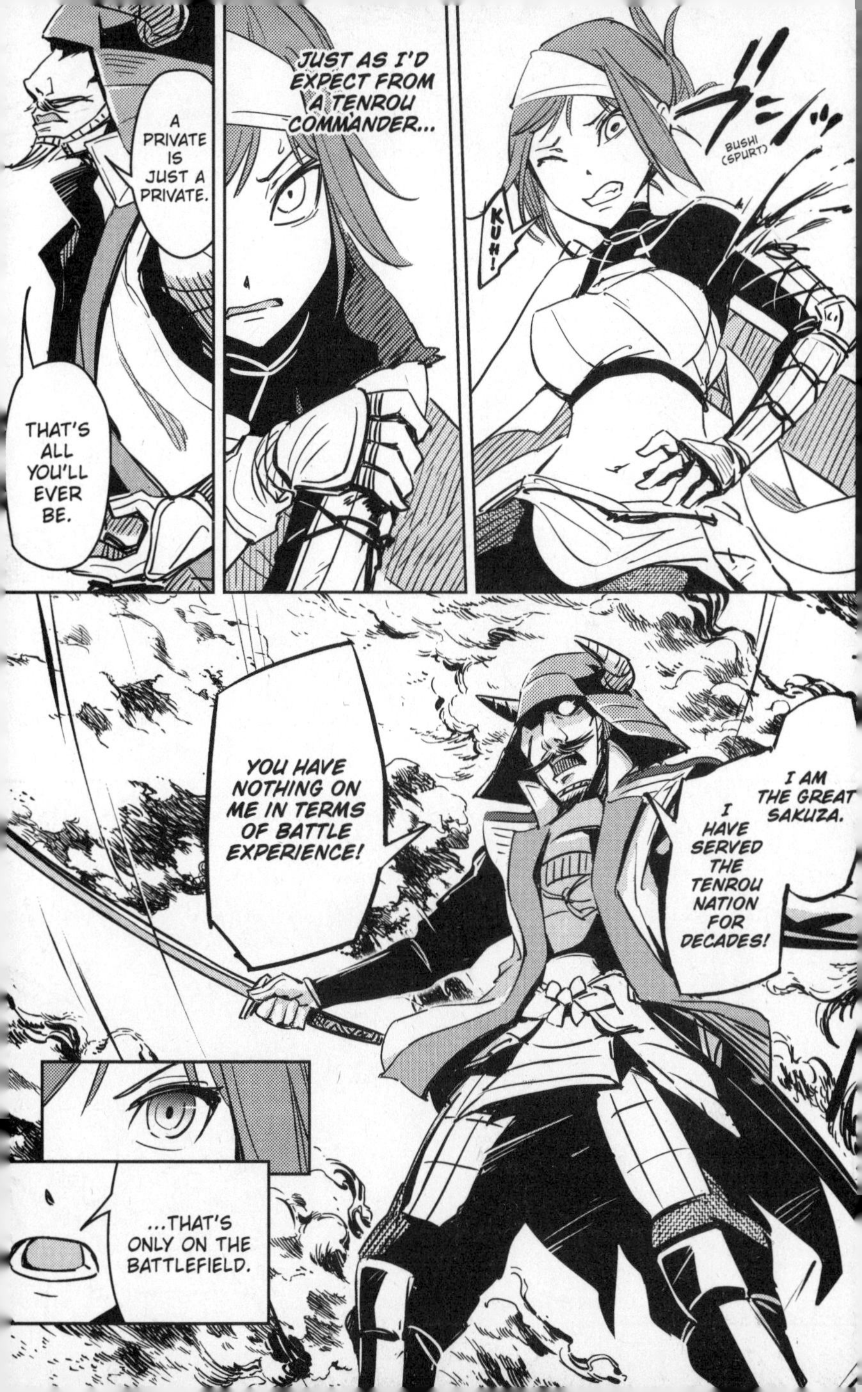
BUSHI (SPURT)
KUH!
JUST AS I'D EXPECT FROM A TENROU COMMANDER...
A PRIVATE IS JUST A PRIVATE.
THAT'S ALL YOU'LL EVER BE.
I AM THE GREAT SAKUZA.
I HAVE SERVED THE TENROU NATION FOR DECADES!
YOU HAVE NOTHING ON ME IN TERMS OF BATTLE EXPERIENCE!
...THAT'S ONLY ON THE BATTLEFIELD.

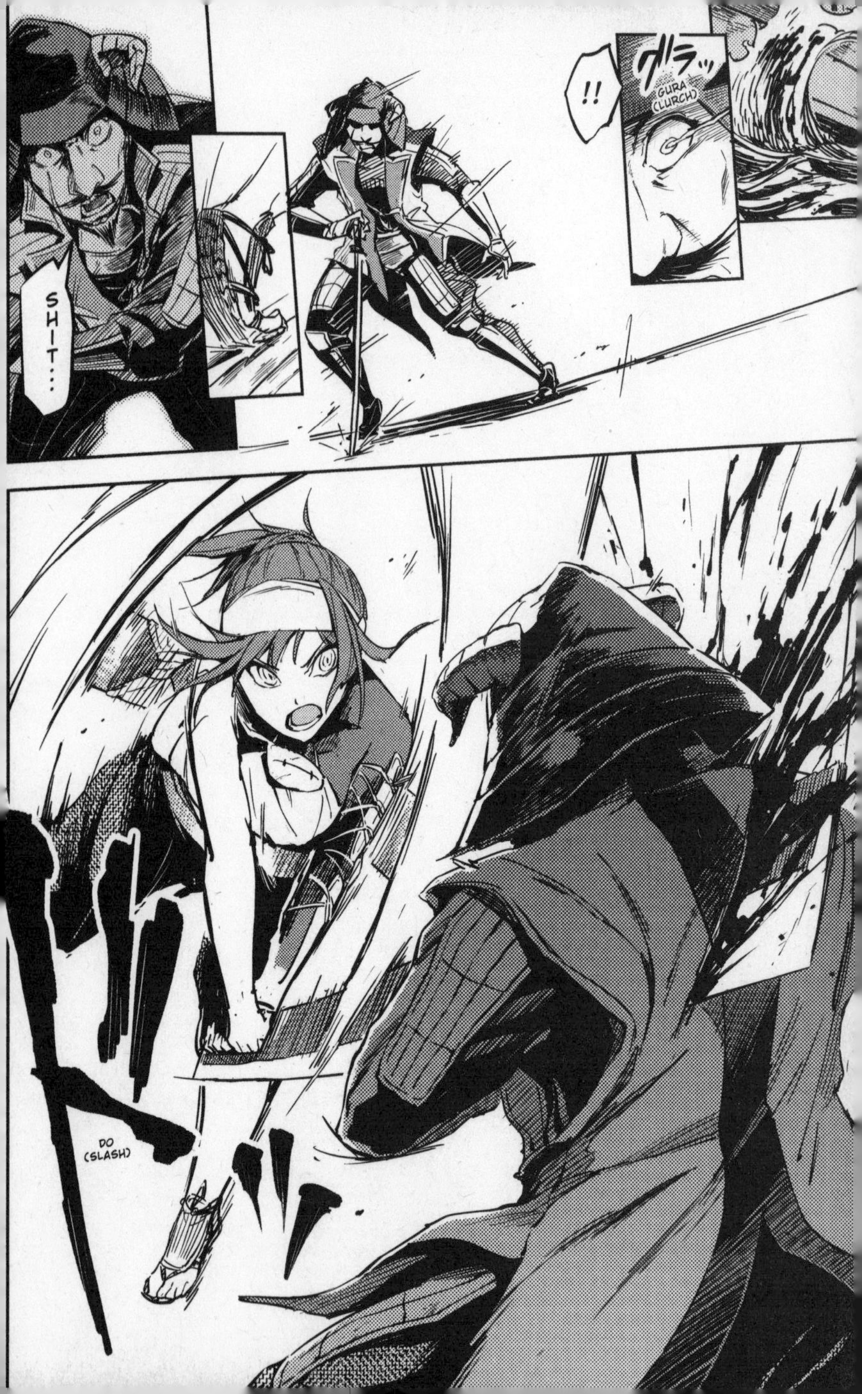
グラッ
GURA (LURCH)
!!
SHIT...
DO (SLASH)

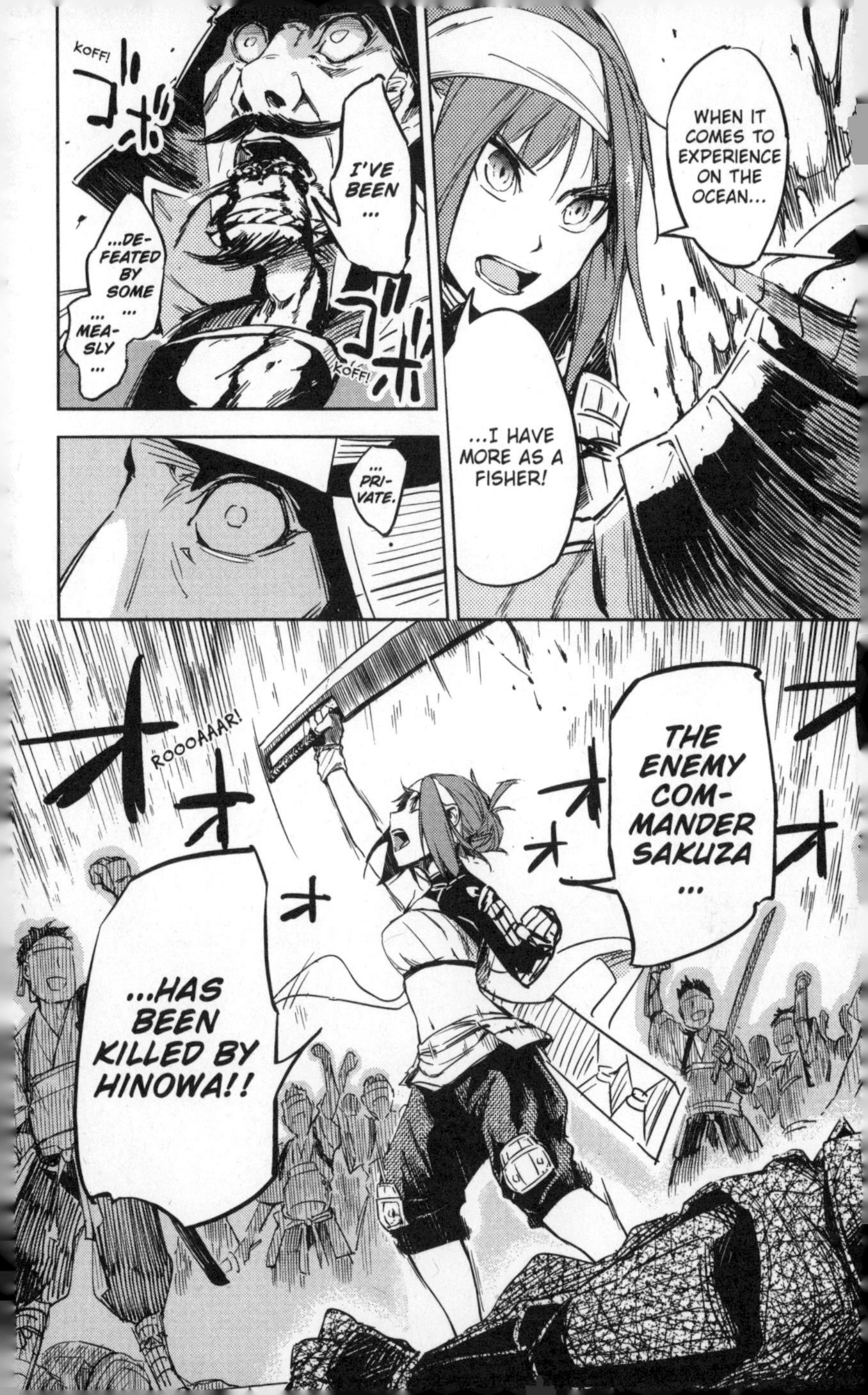
WHEN IT COMES TO EXPERIENCE ON THE OCEAN...
...I HAVE MORE AS A FISHER!
KOFF!
ゴボ
I'VE BEEN ...
...DEFEATED BY SOME ... MEASLY ...
ゴボ
KOFF!
... PRIVATE.
THE ENEMY COMMANDER SAKUZA ...
ROOOAAAR!
...HAS BEEN KILLED BY HINOWA!!

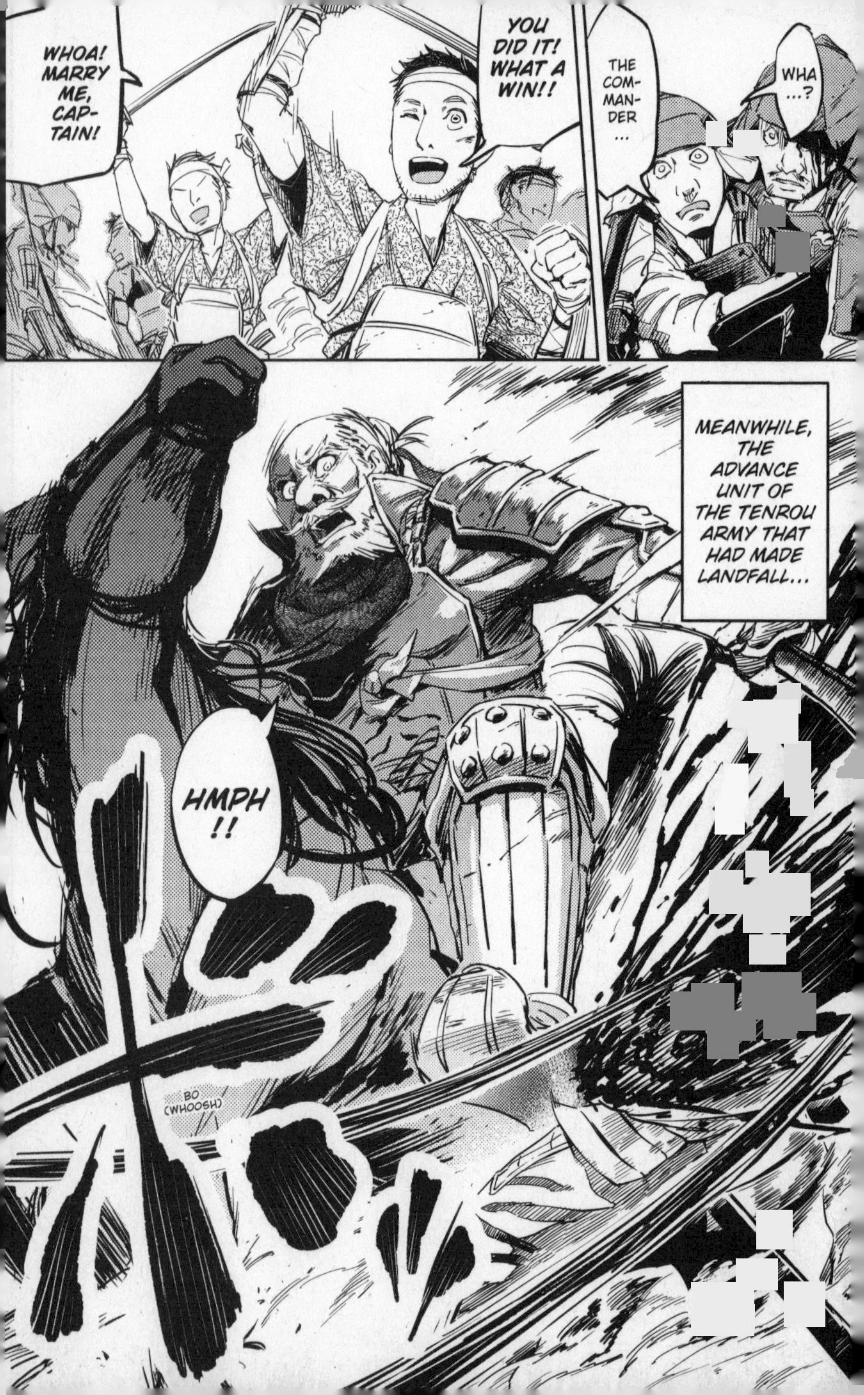
WHA...?
THE COM-MAN-DER...
YOU DID IT! WHAT A WIN!!
WHOA! MARRY ME, CAP-TAIN!
MEANWHILE, THE ADVANCE UNIT OF THE TENROU ARMY THAT HAD MADE LANDFALL...
HMPH!!
BO (WHOOSH)

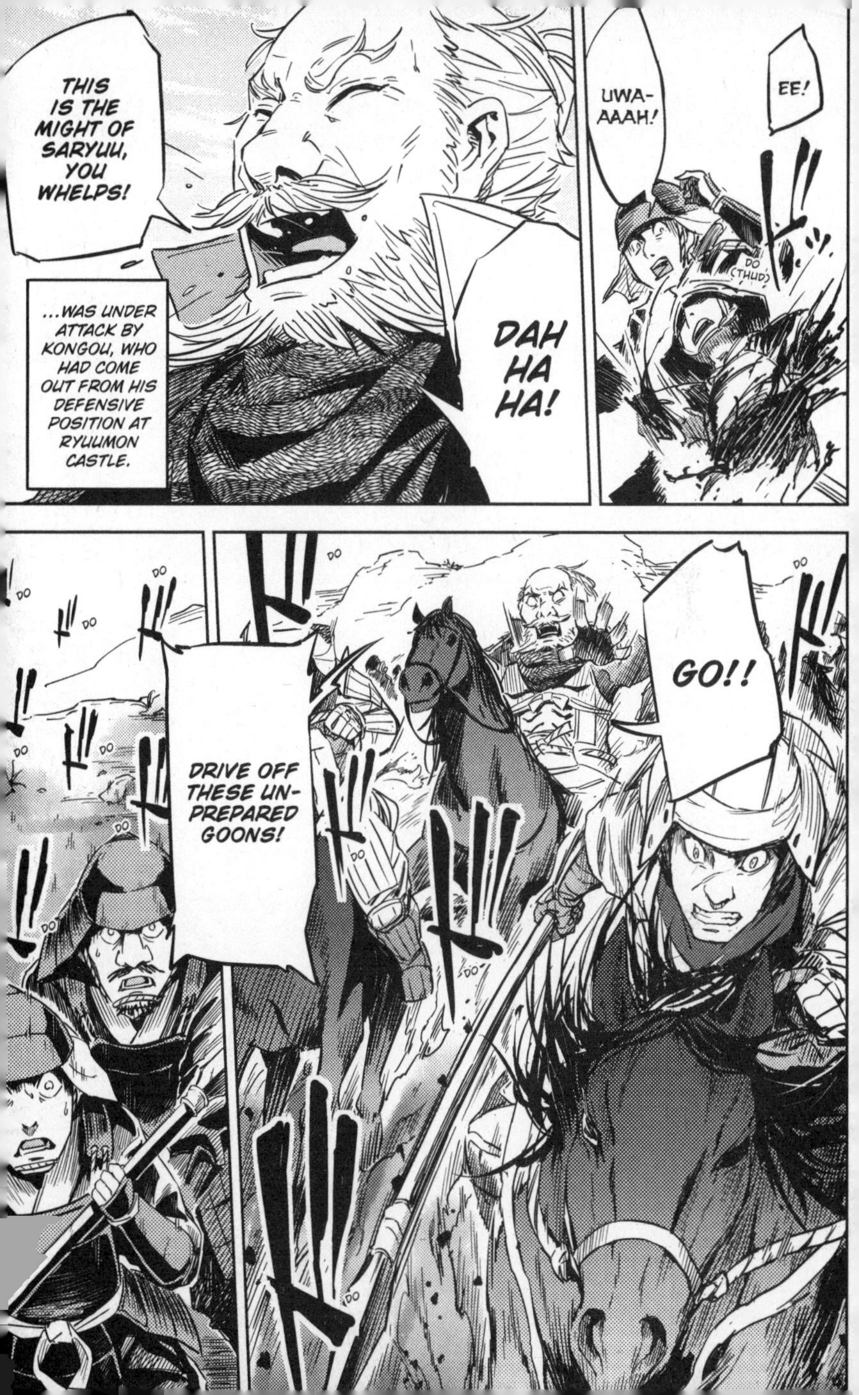
EE!
UWA-AAAH!
DO (THUD)
THIS IS THE MIGHT OF SARYUU, YOU WHELPS!
DAH HA HA!
...WAS UNDER ATTACK BY KONGOU, WHO HAD COME OUT FROM HIS DEFENSIVE POSITION AT RYUUMON CASTLE.
DO
GO!!
DO
DRIVE OFF THESE UN-PREPARED GOONS!
DO
DO
DO
DO
DO
DO
DO
DO
DO

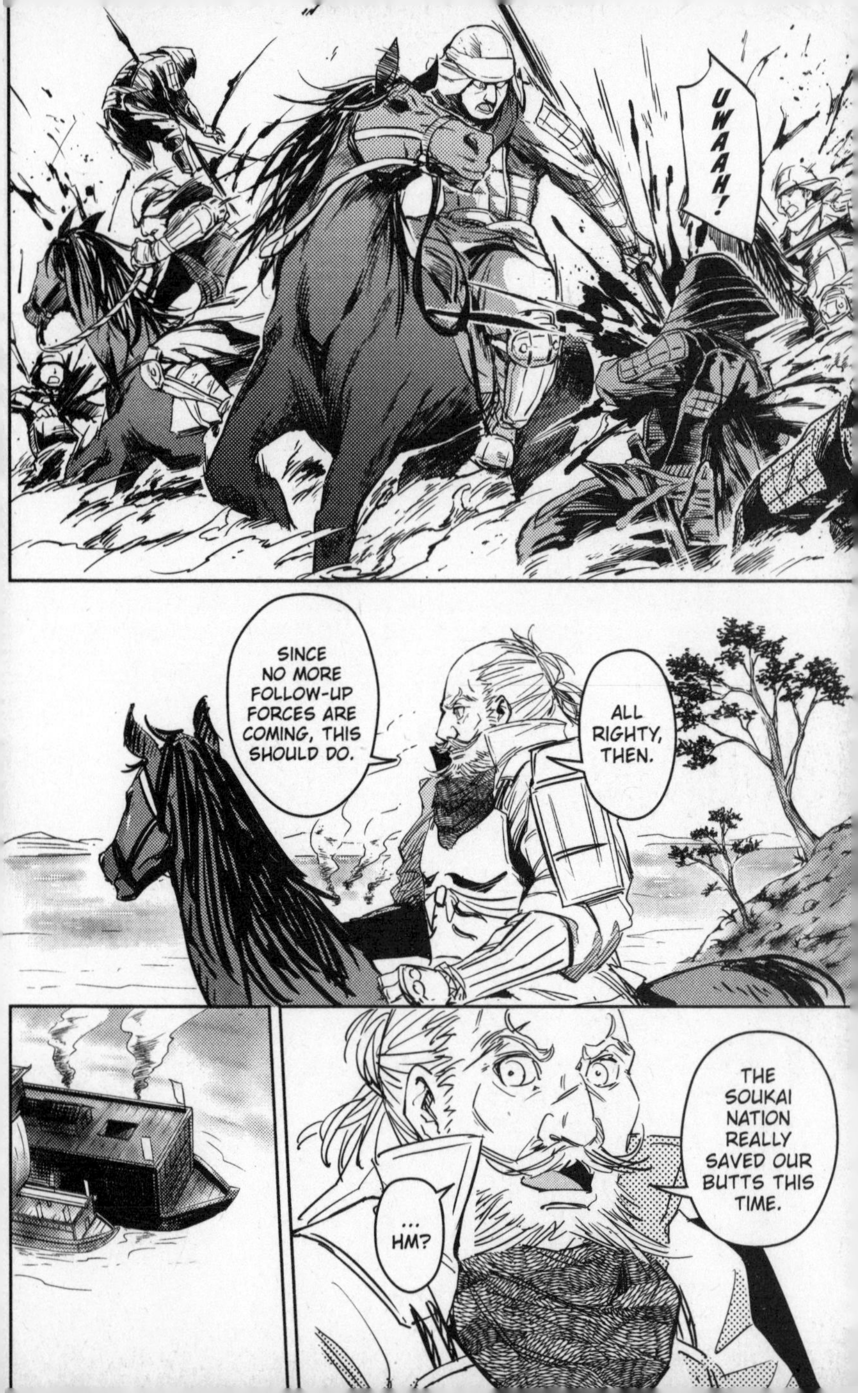
UWAAH!
ALL RIGHTY, THEN.
SINCE NO MORE FOLLOW-UP FORCES ARE COMING, THIS SHOULD DO.
THE SOUKAI NATION REALLY SAVED OUR BUTTS THIS TIME.
... HM?

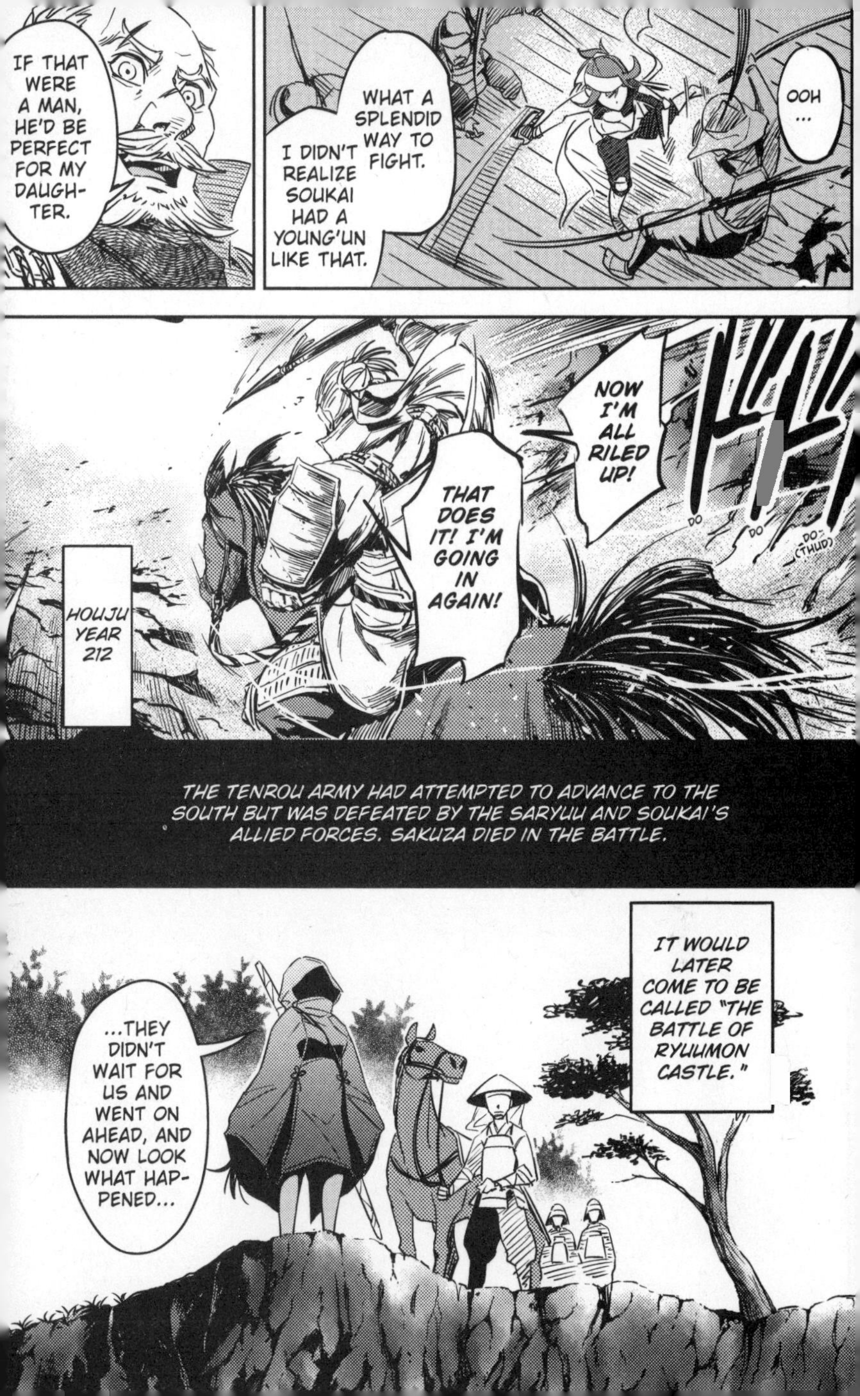
OOH...
WHAT A SPLENDID WAY TO FIGHT.
I DIDN'T REALIZE SOUKAI HAD A YOUNG'UN LIKE THAT.
IF THAT WERE A MAN, HE'D BE PERFECT FOR MY DAUGH-TER.
DO DO DO (THUD)
NOW I'M ALL RILED UP!
THAT DOES IT! I'M GOING IN AGAIN!
HOUJU YEAR 212
THE TENROU ARMY HAD ATTEMPTED TO ADVANCE TO THE SOUTH BUT WAS DEFEATED BY THE SARYUU AND SOUKAI'S ALLIED FORCES. SAKUZA DIED IN THE BATTLE.
IT WOULD LATER COME TO BE CALLED "THE BATTLE OF RYUUMON CASTLE."
...THEY DIDN'T WAIT FOR US AND WENT ON AHEAD, AND NOW LOOK WHAT HAP-PENED...

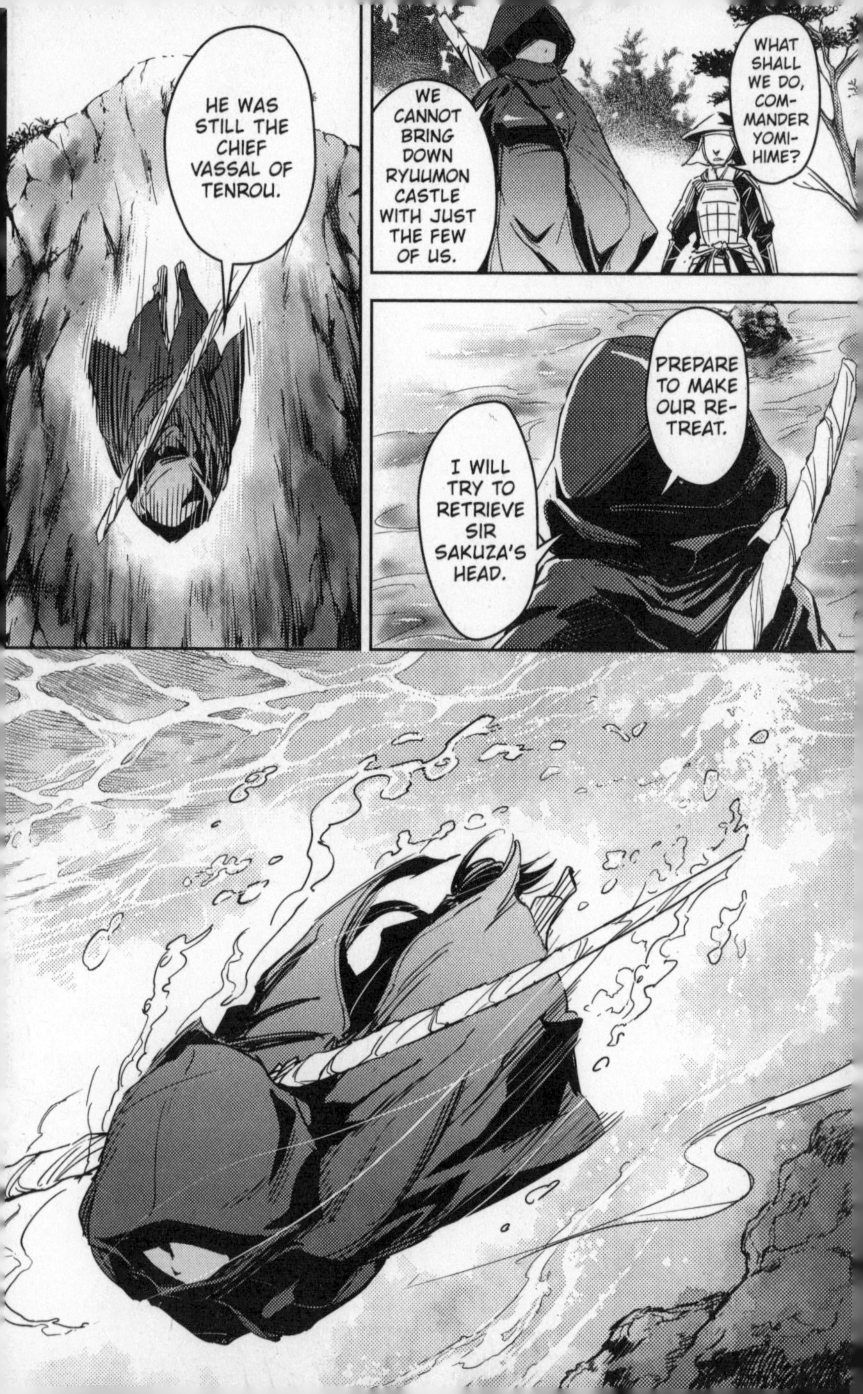
WHAT SHALL WE DO, COM-MANDER YOMI-HIME?
WE CANNOT BRING DOWN RYUUMON CASTLE WITH JUST THE FEW OF US.
PREPARE TO MAKE OUR RE-TREAT.
I WILL TRY TO RETRIEVE SIR SAKUZA'S HEAD.
HE WAS STILL THE CHIEF VASSAL OF TENROU.

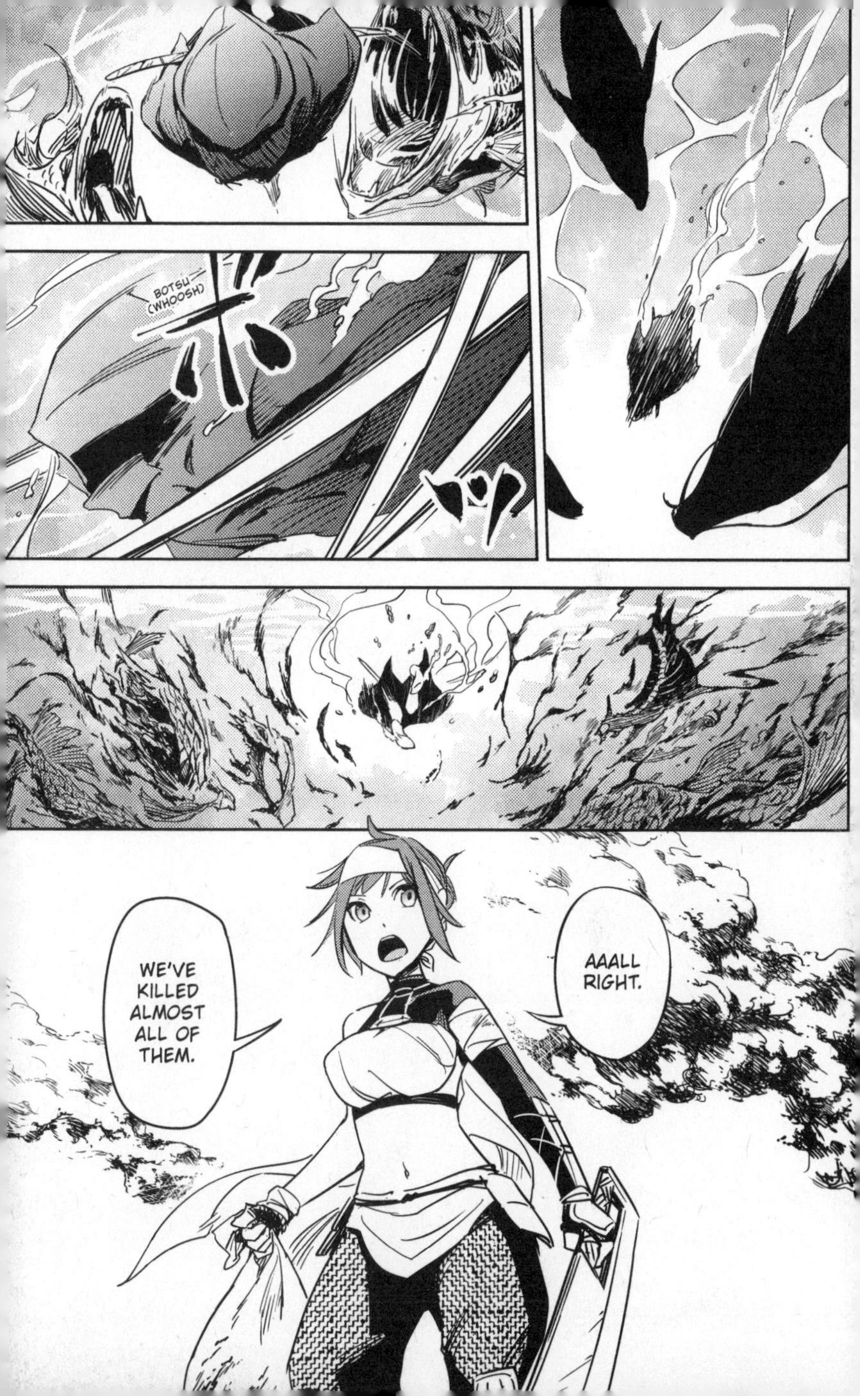
BOTSU (WHOOSH)
AAALL RIGHT.
WE'VE KILLED ALMOST ALL OF THEM.

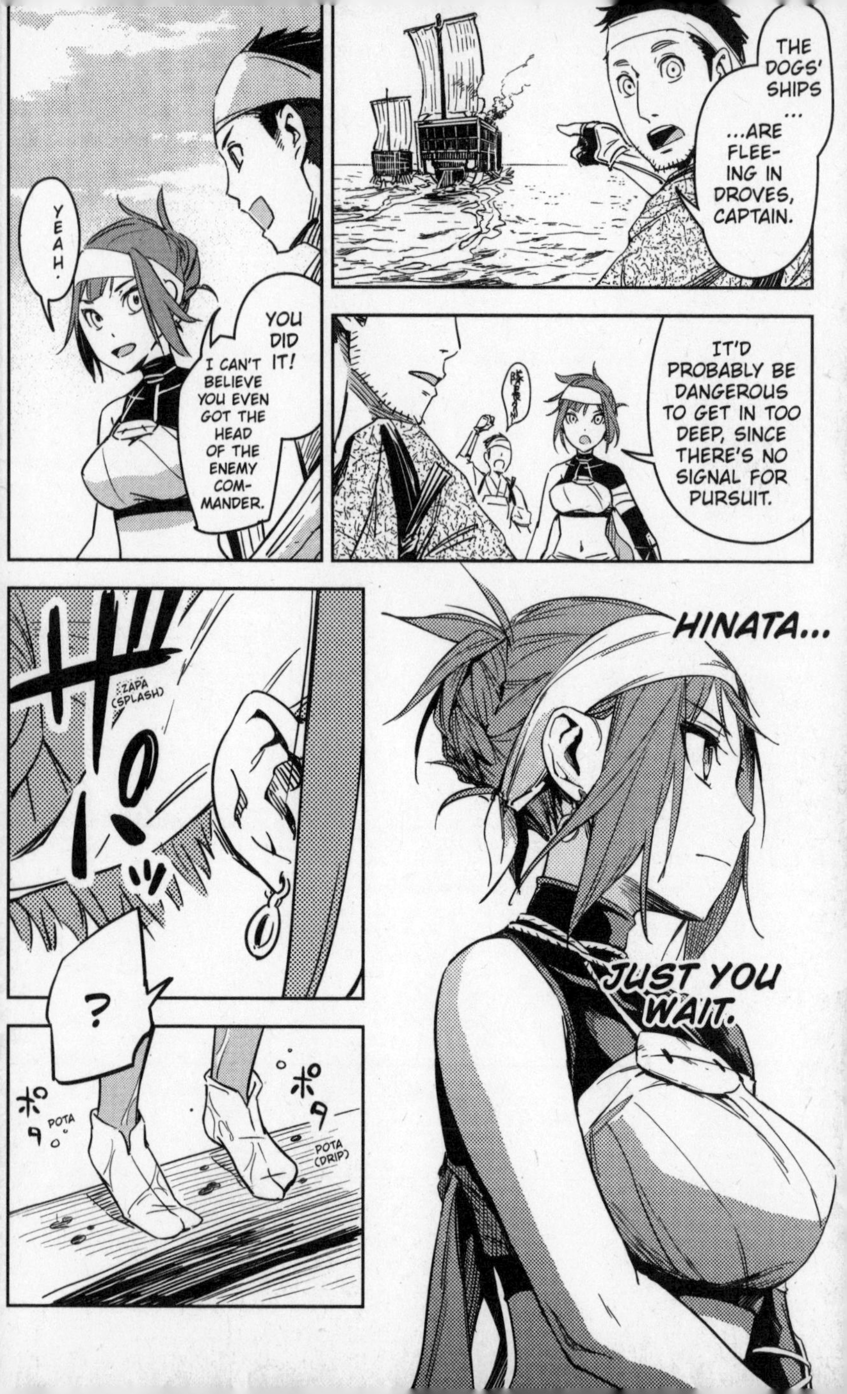
THE DOGS' SHIPS ...
...ARE FLEEING IN DROVES, CAPTAIN.
IT'D PROBABLY BE DANGEROUS TO GET IN TOO DEEP, SINCE THERE'S NO SIGNAL FOR PURSUIT.
YOU DID IT! I CAN'T BELIEVE YOU EVEN GOT THE HEAD OF THE ENEMY COMMANDER.
YEAH.
HINATA...
JUST YOU WAIT.
ZAPA (SPLASH)
?
ポタ
POTA (DRIP)
ポタ
POTA

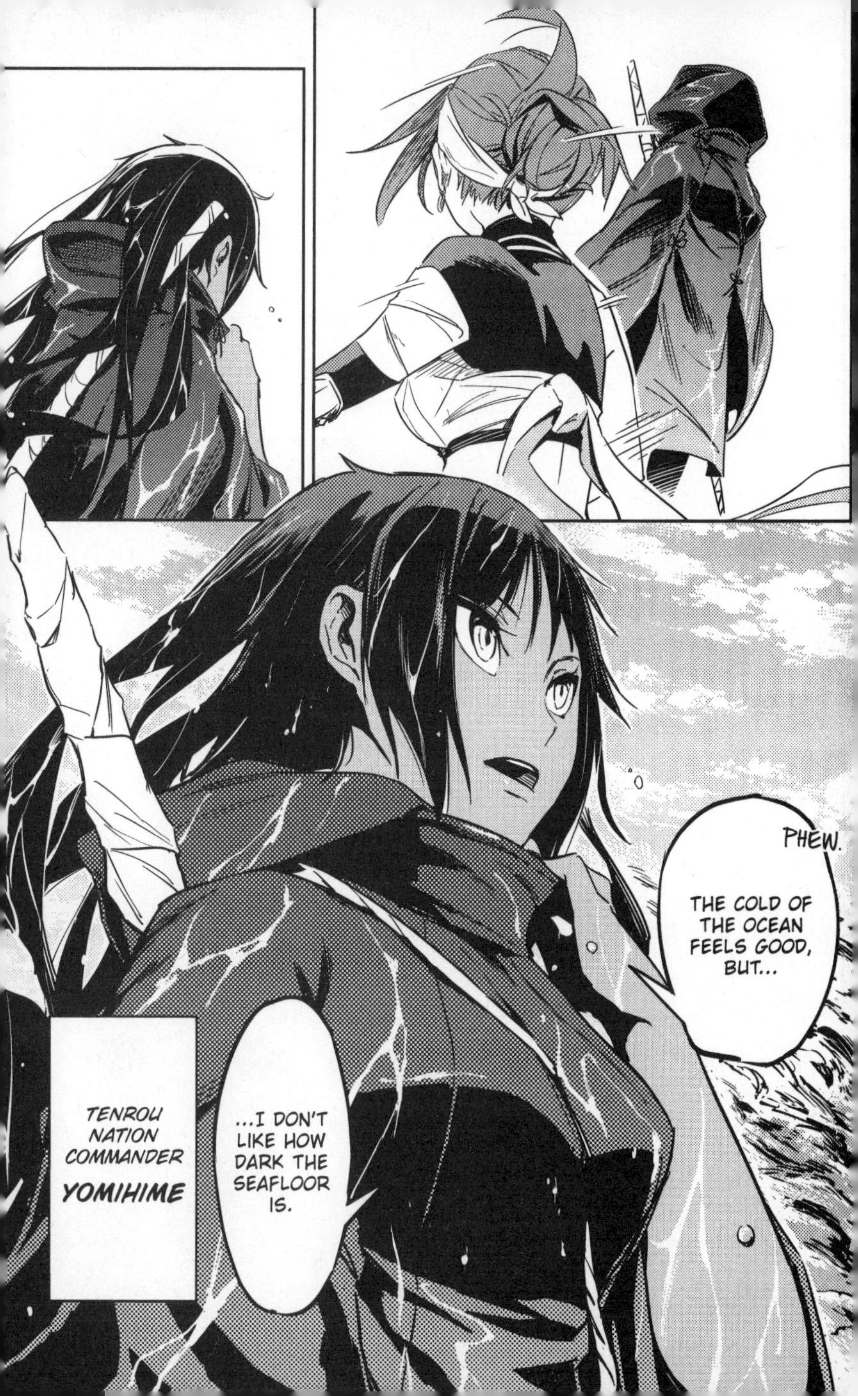
PHEW.
THE COLD OF THE OCEAN FEELS GOOD, BUT...
...I DON'T LIKE HOW DARK THE SEAFLOOR IS.
TENROU NATION COMMANDER YOMIHIME

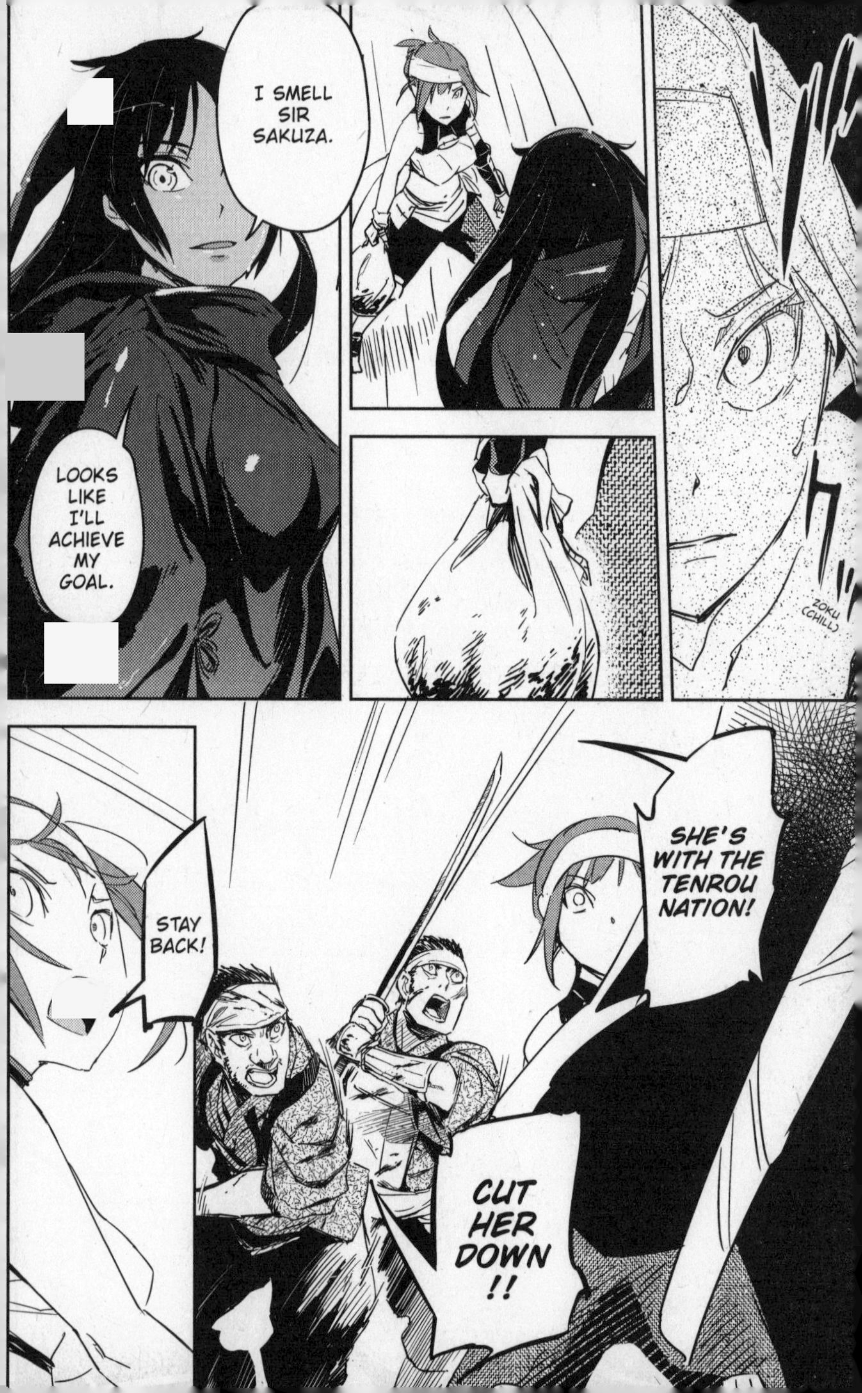
ZOKU (CHILL)
I SMELL SIR SAKUZA.
LOOKS LIKE I'LL ACHIEVE MY GOAL.
SHE'S WITH THE TENROU NATION!
CUT HER DOWN!!
STAY BACK!

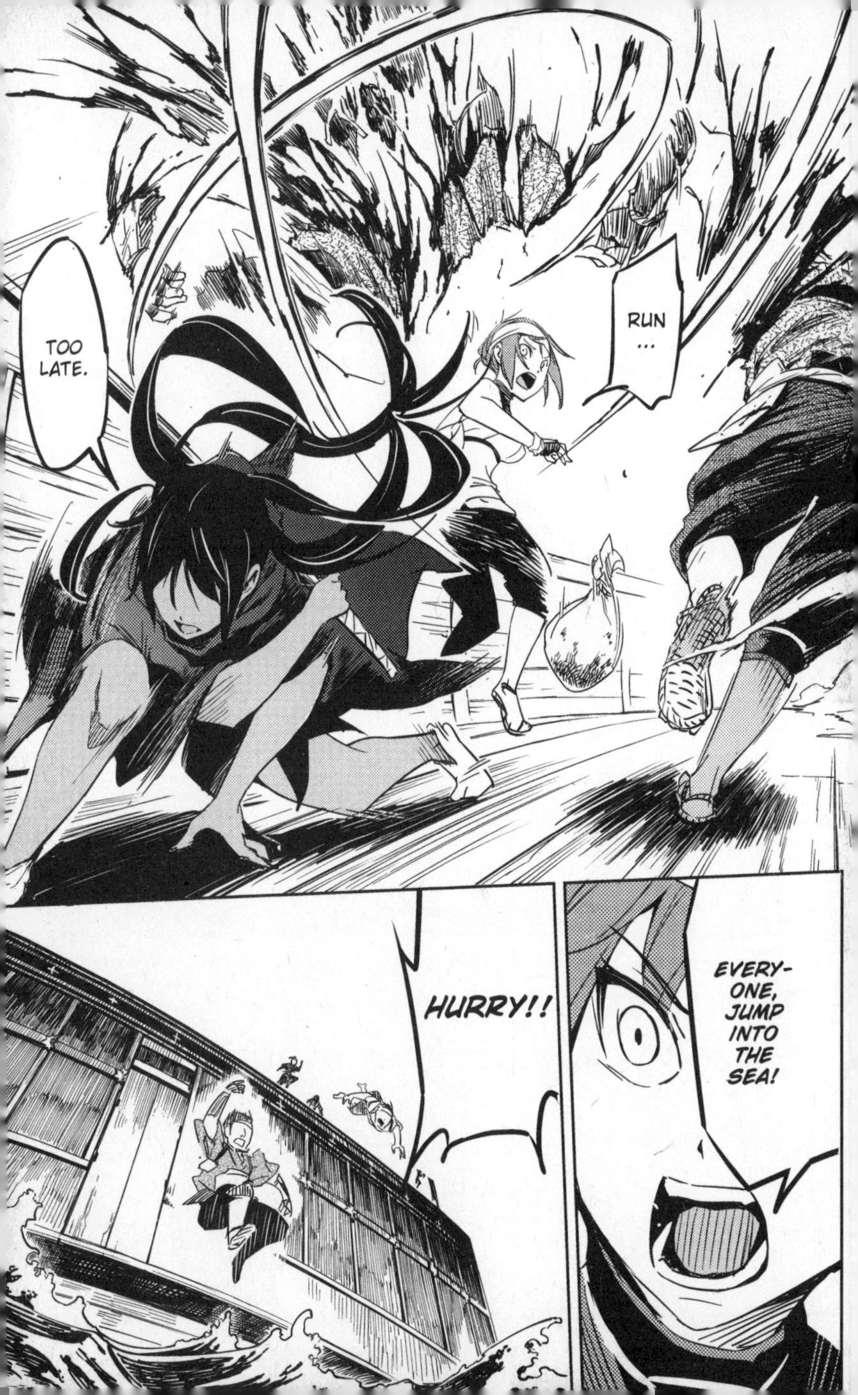
RUN ...
TOO LATE.
EVERY-ONE, JUMP INTO THE SEA!
HURRY!!

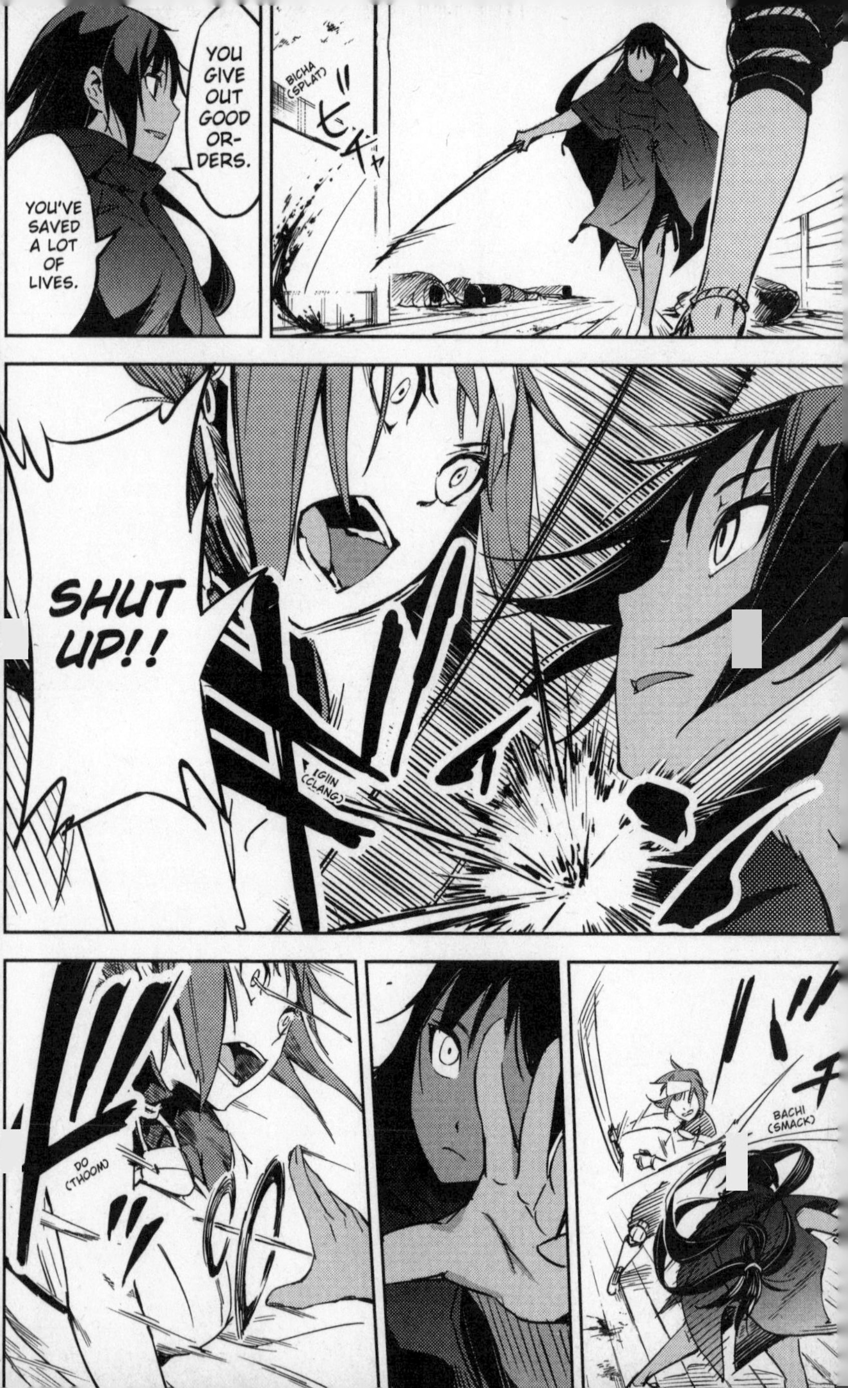
BICHA (SPLAT)
YOU GIVE OUT GOOD OR-DERS.
YOU'VE SAVED A LOT OF LIVES.
SHUT UP!!
GIIN (CLANG)
BACHI (SMACK)
DO (THOOM)

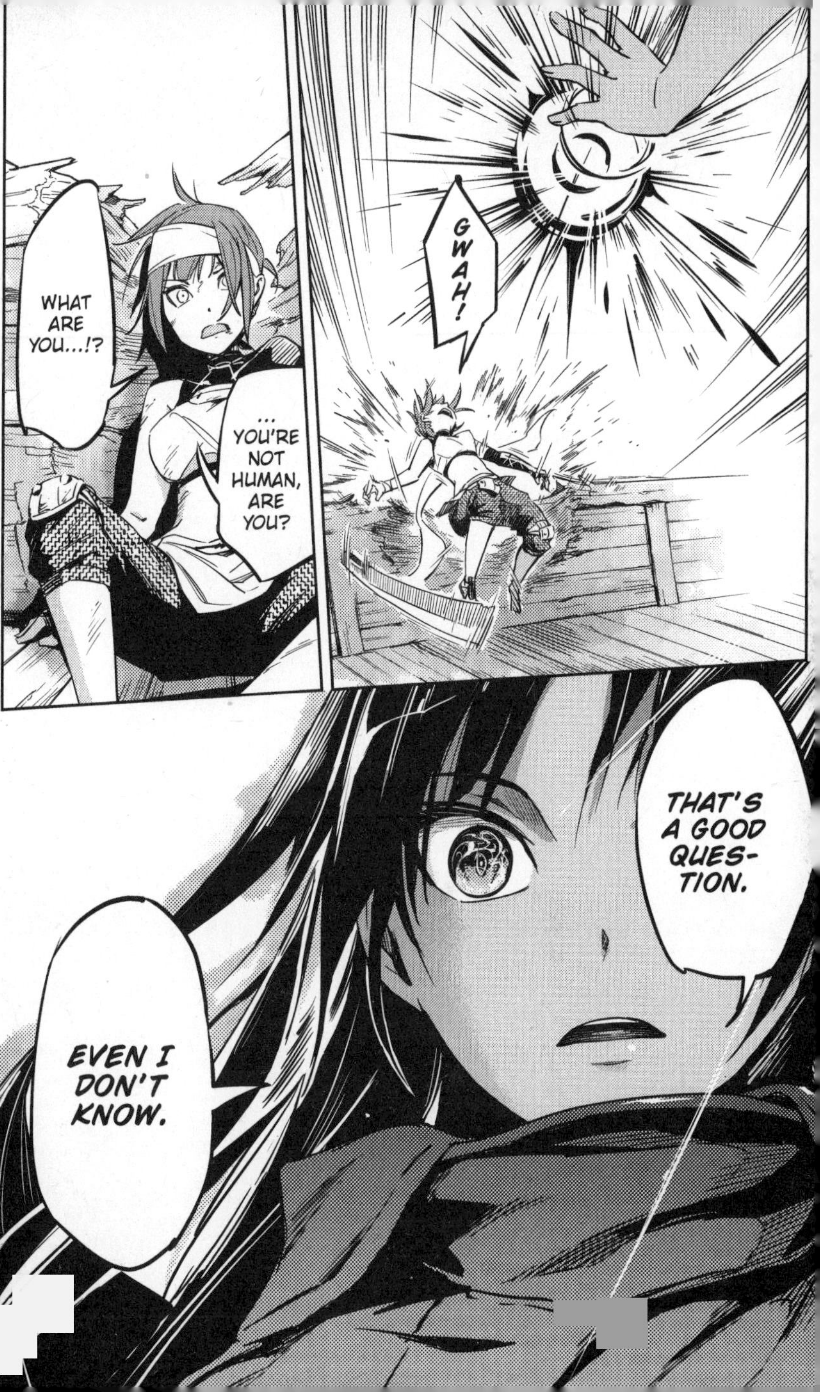
GWAH!
WHAT ARE YOU...!?
... YOU'RE NOT HUMAN, ARE YOU?
THAT'S A GOOD QUES-TION.
EVEN I DON'T KNOW.

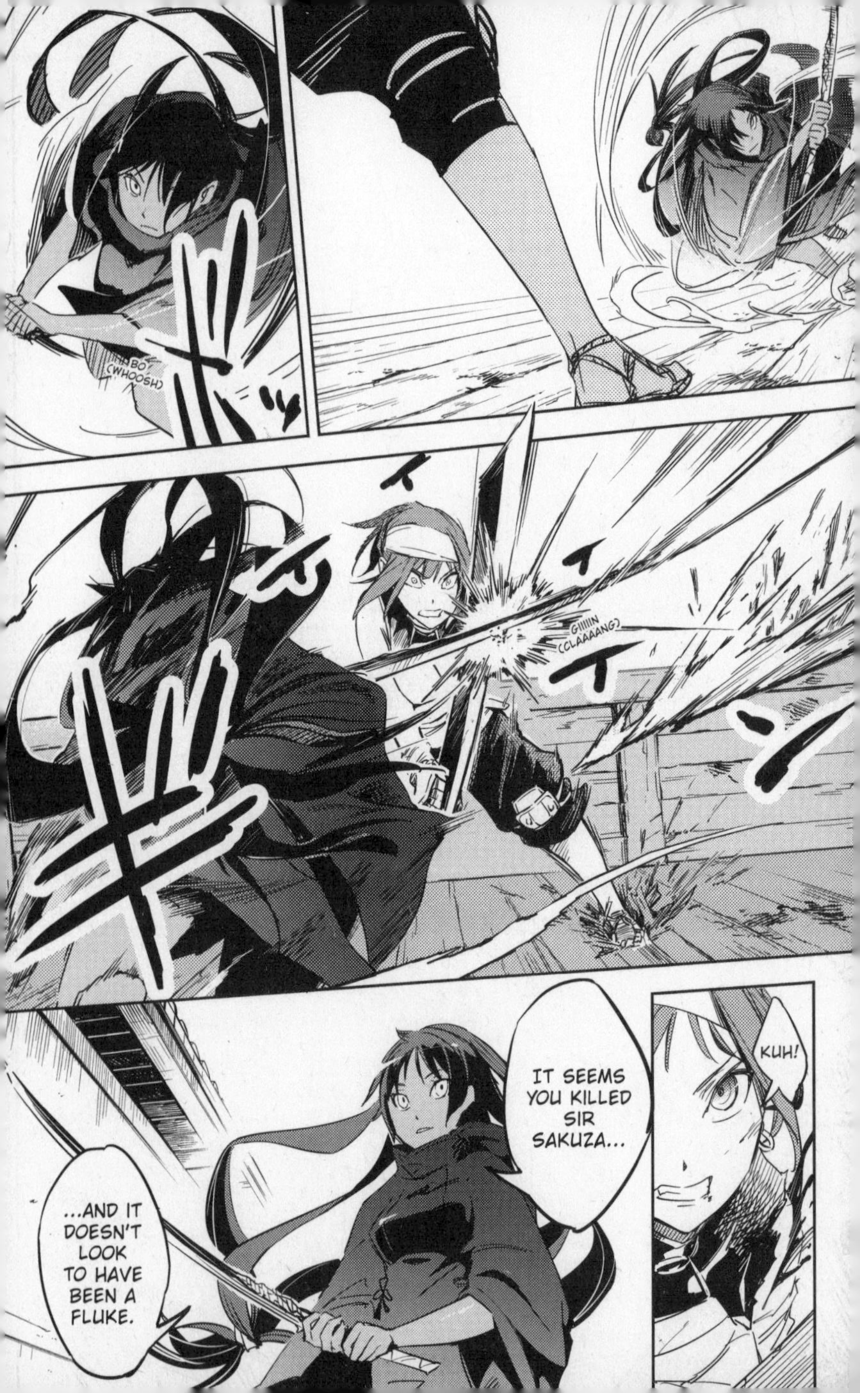
BO (WHOOSH)
GIIIIIN (CLAAAANG)
KUH!
IT SEEMS YOU KILLED SIR SAKUZA...
...AND IT DOESN'T LOOK TO HAVE BEEN A FLUKE.

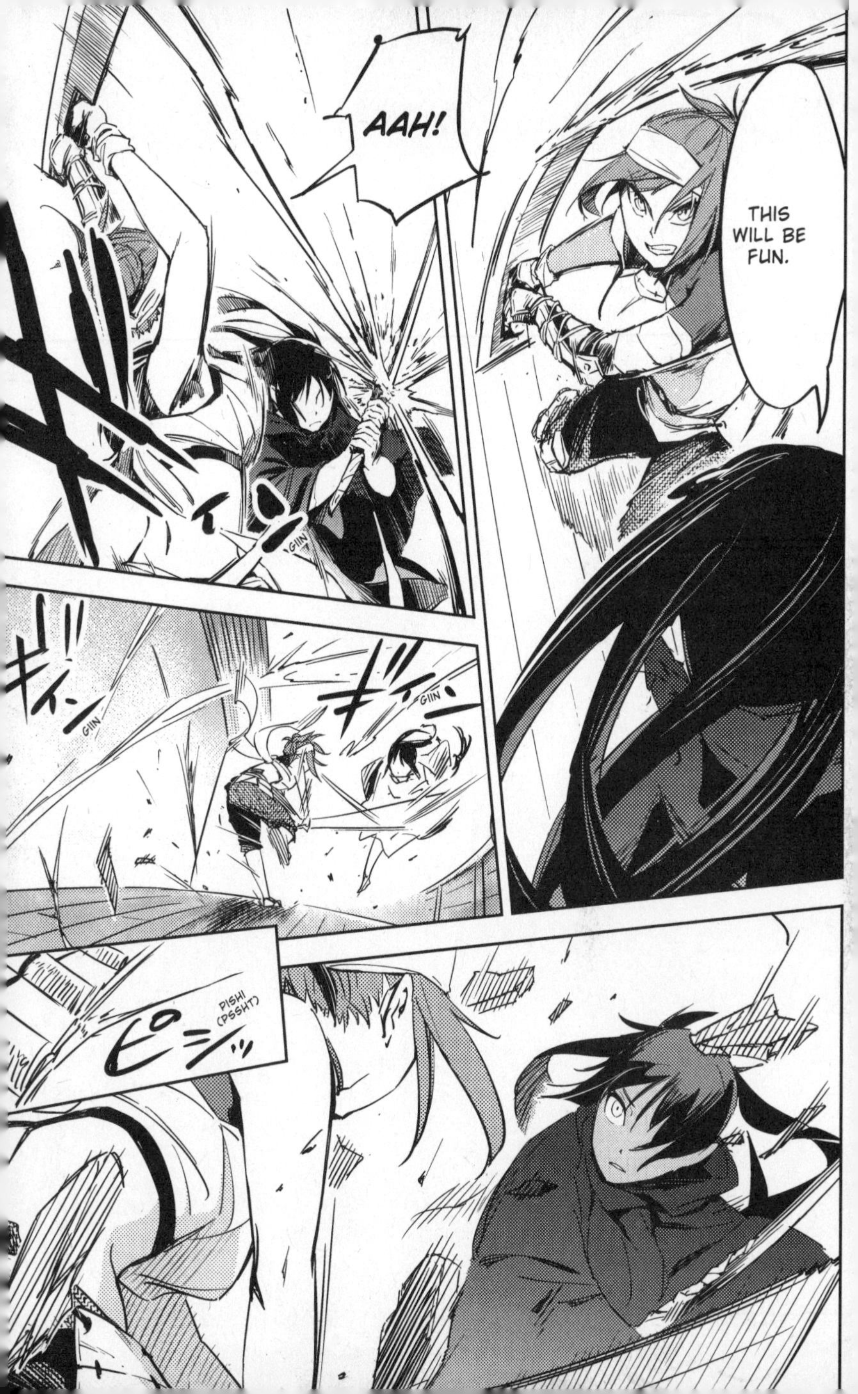
THIS WILL BE FUN.
AAH!
GIIN
GIIN
GIIN
PISHI (PSSHT)

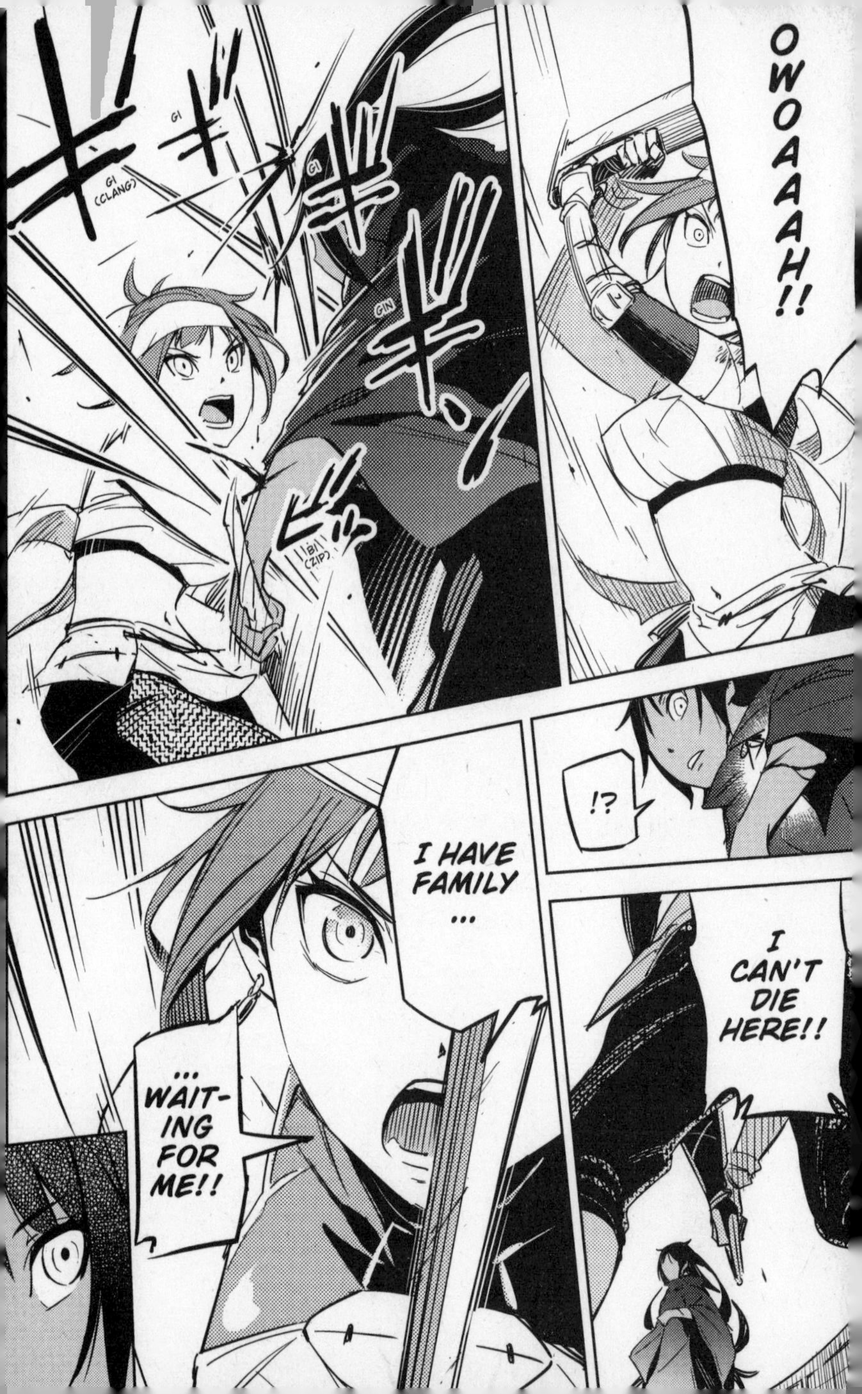
OWOAAAAH!!
GI
GI
GI (CLANG)
GIN
BI (ZIP)
!?
I CAN'T DIE HERE!!
I HAVE FAMILY ...
... WAITING FOR ME!!

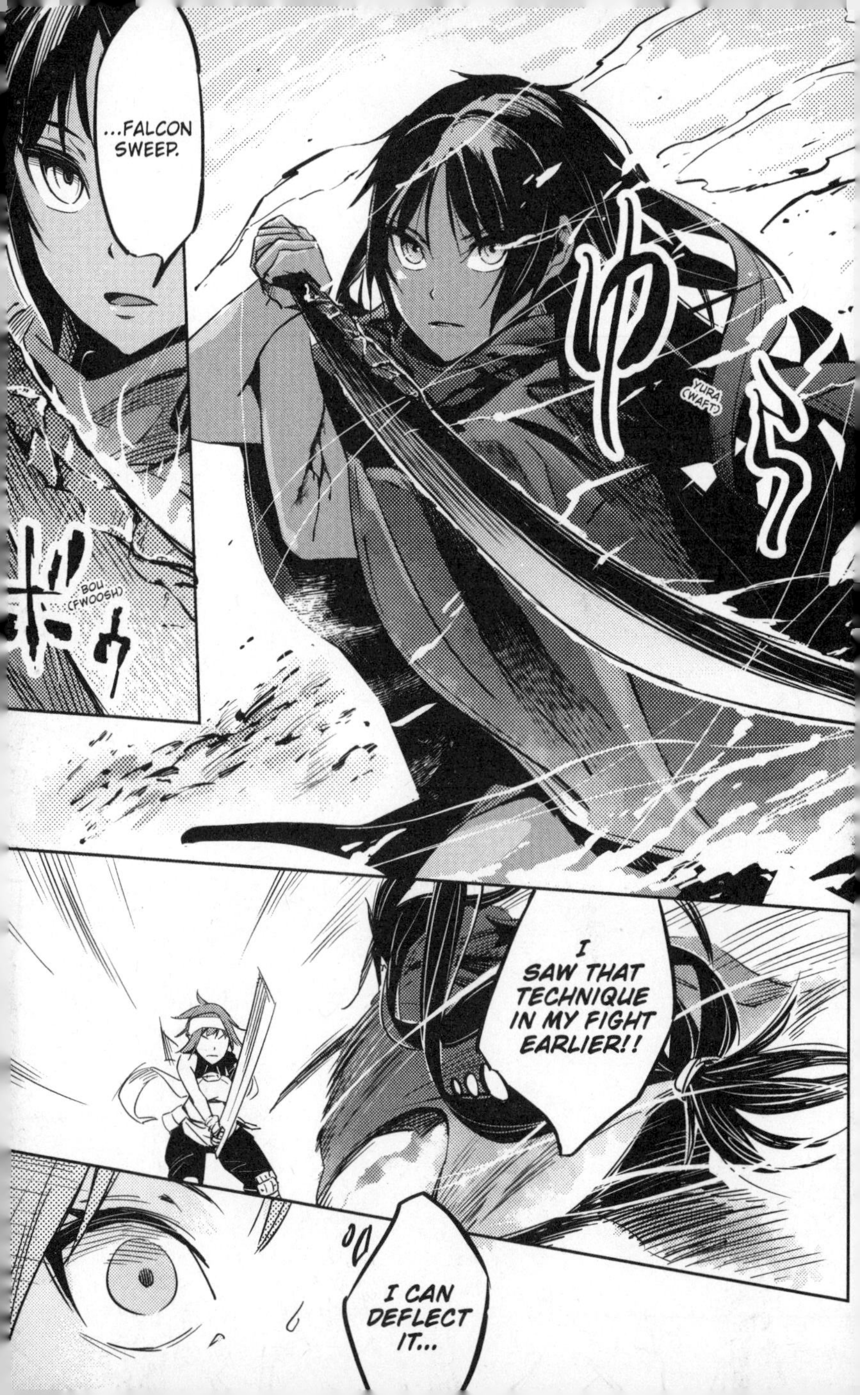
YURA (WAFT)
...FALCON SWEEP.
BOU (FWOOSH)
I SAW THAT TECHNIQUE IN MY FIGHT EARLIER!!
I CAN DEFLECT IT...

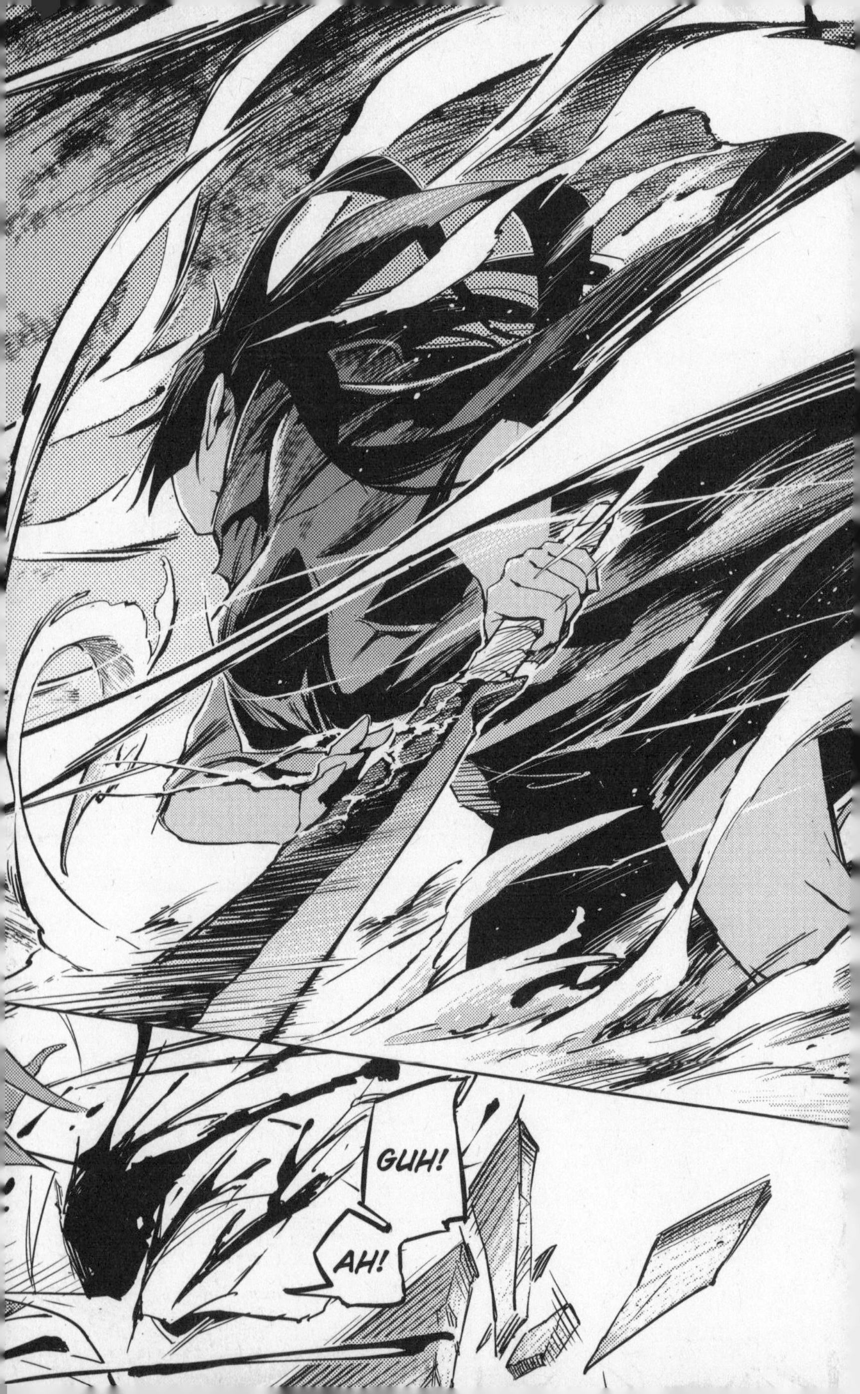
GUH!
AH!

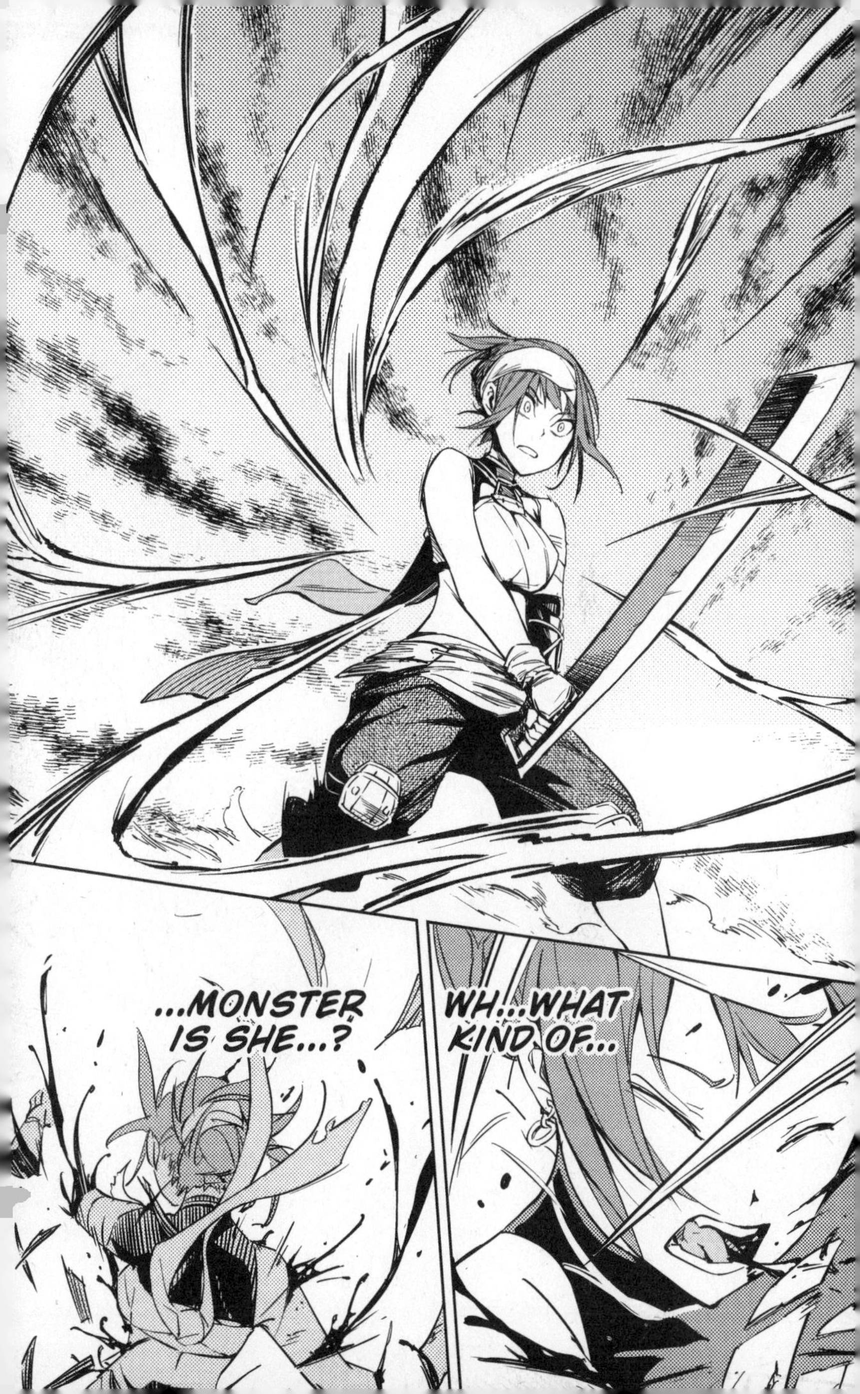
WH...WHAT KIND OF...
...MONSTER IS SHE...?

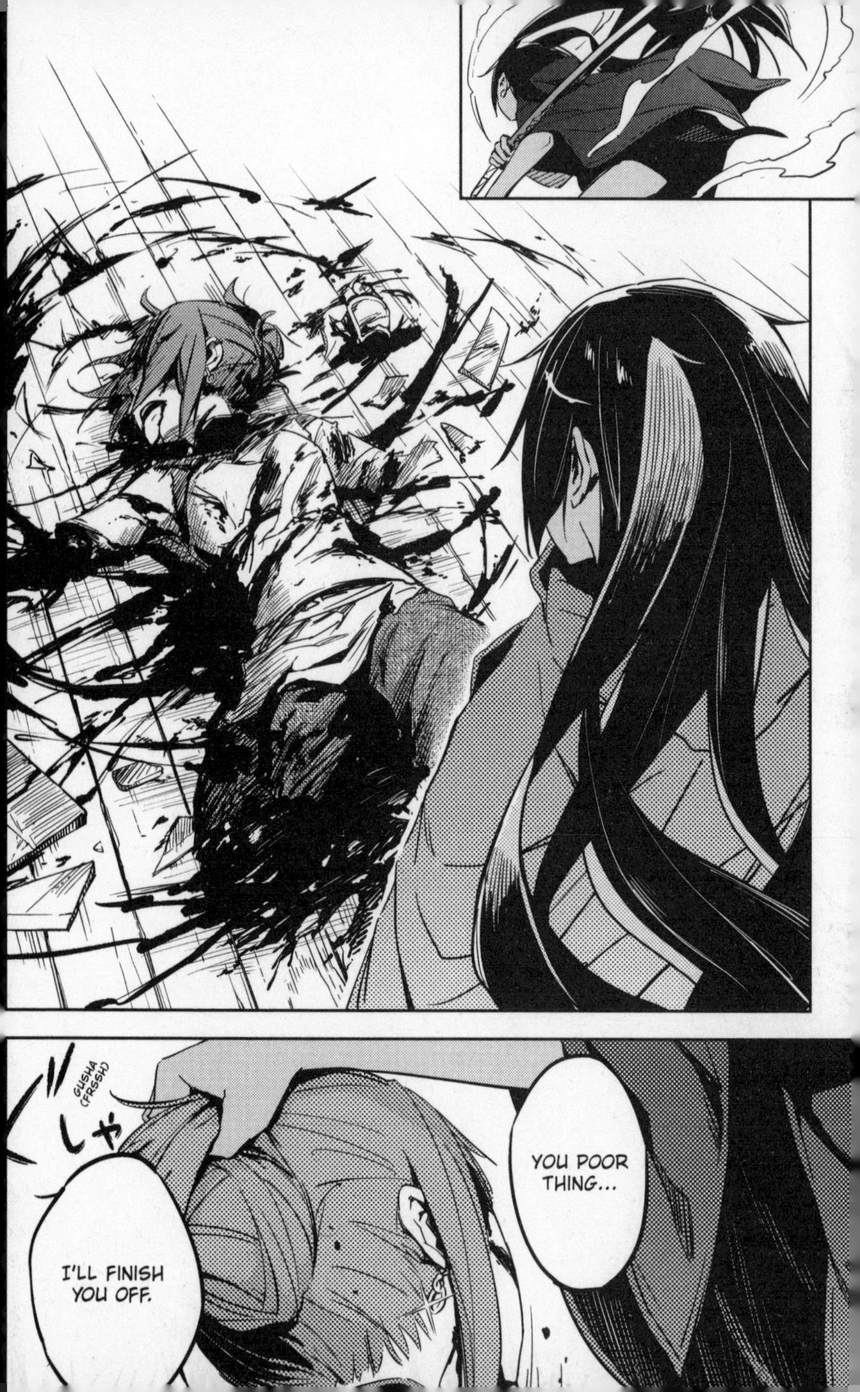
YOU POOR THING...
GUSHA (FRSSH)
I'LL FINISH YOU OFF.

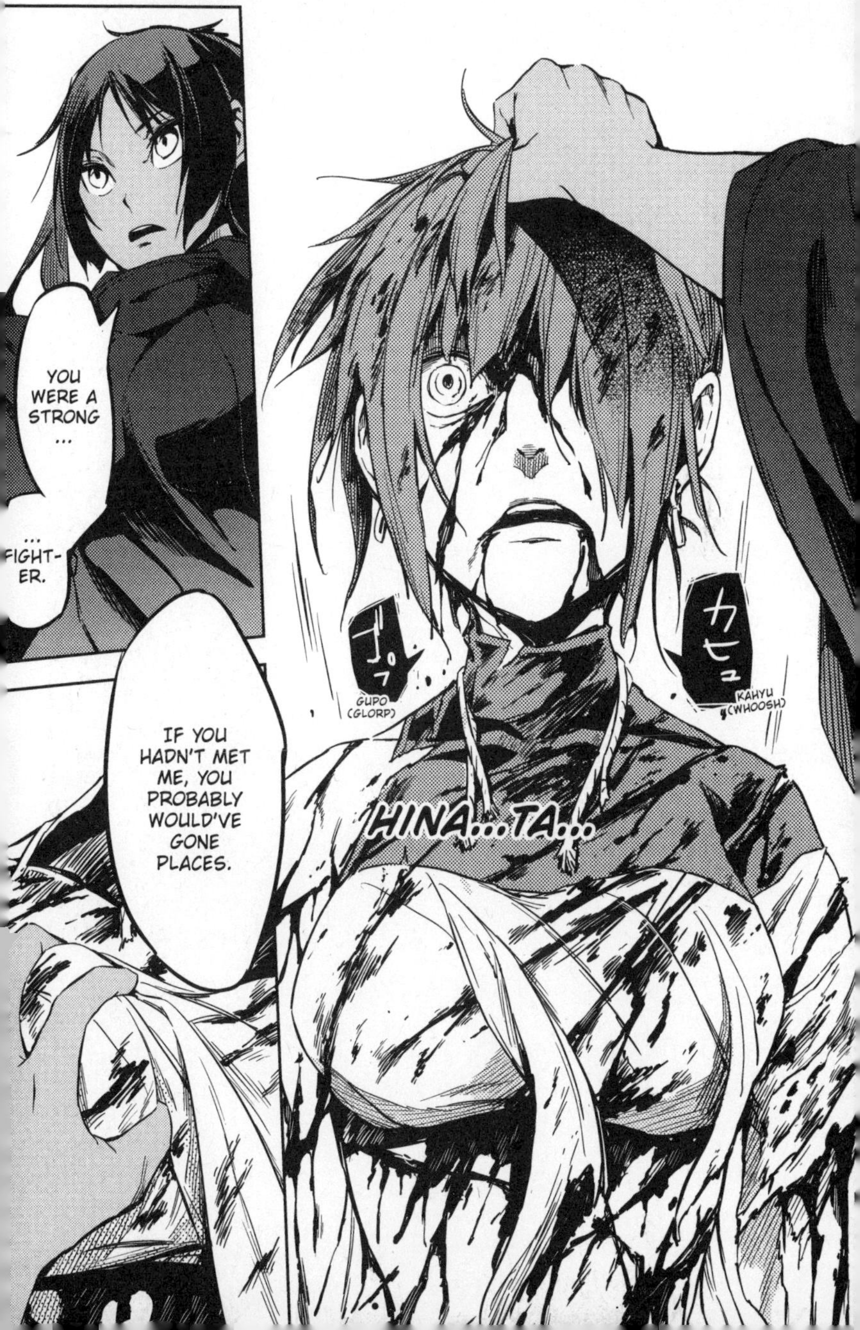
カヒュ
KAHYU (WHOOSH)
ゴプ
GUPO (GLORP)
HINA...TA...
YOU WERE A STRONG ...
... FIGHT-ER.
IF YOU HADN'T MET ME, YOU PROBABLY WOULD'VE GONE PLACES.

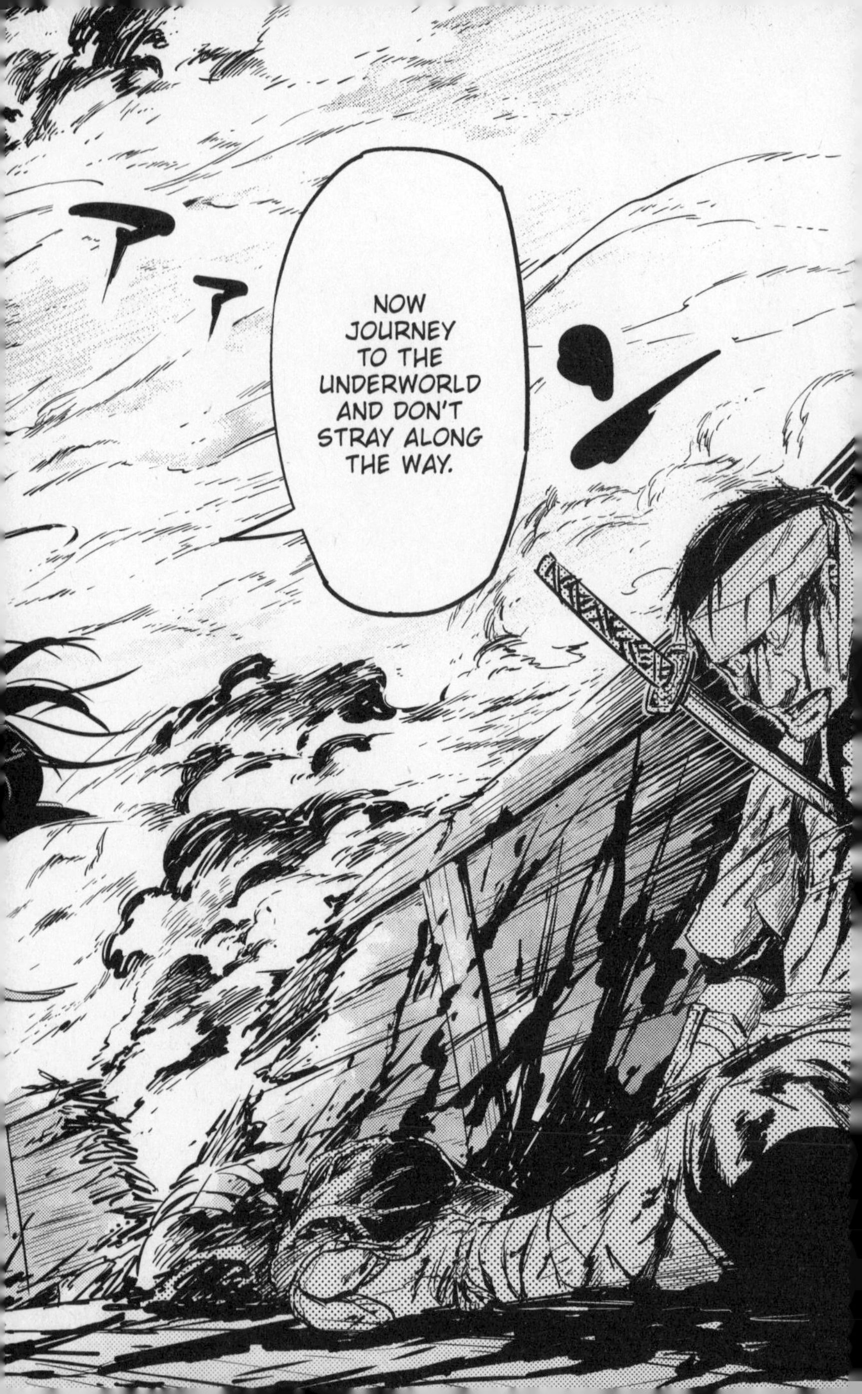
NOW JOURNEY TO THE UNDERWORLD AND DON'T STRAY ALONG THE WAY.

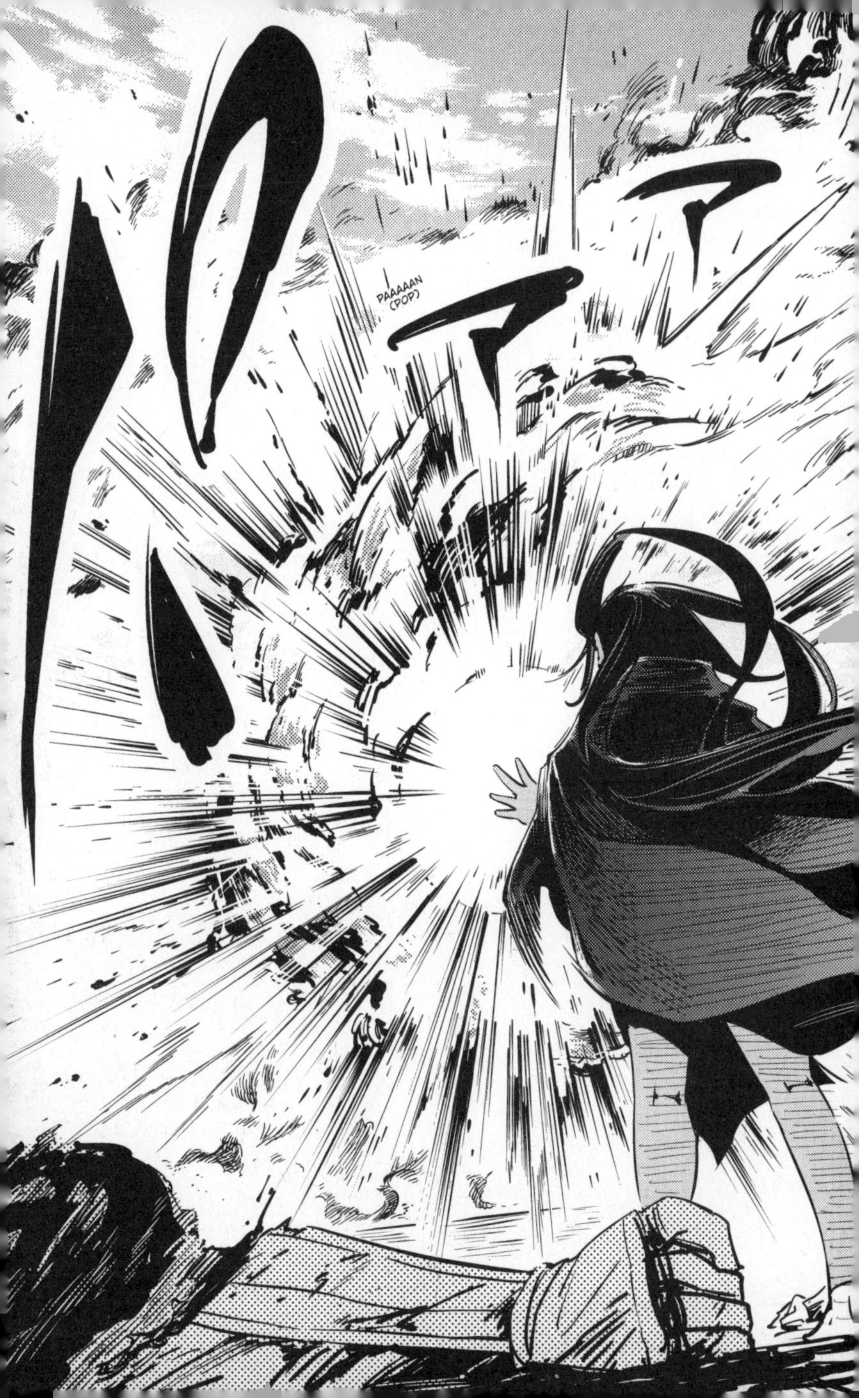
PAAAAAN
(POP)

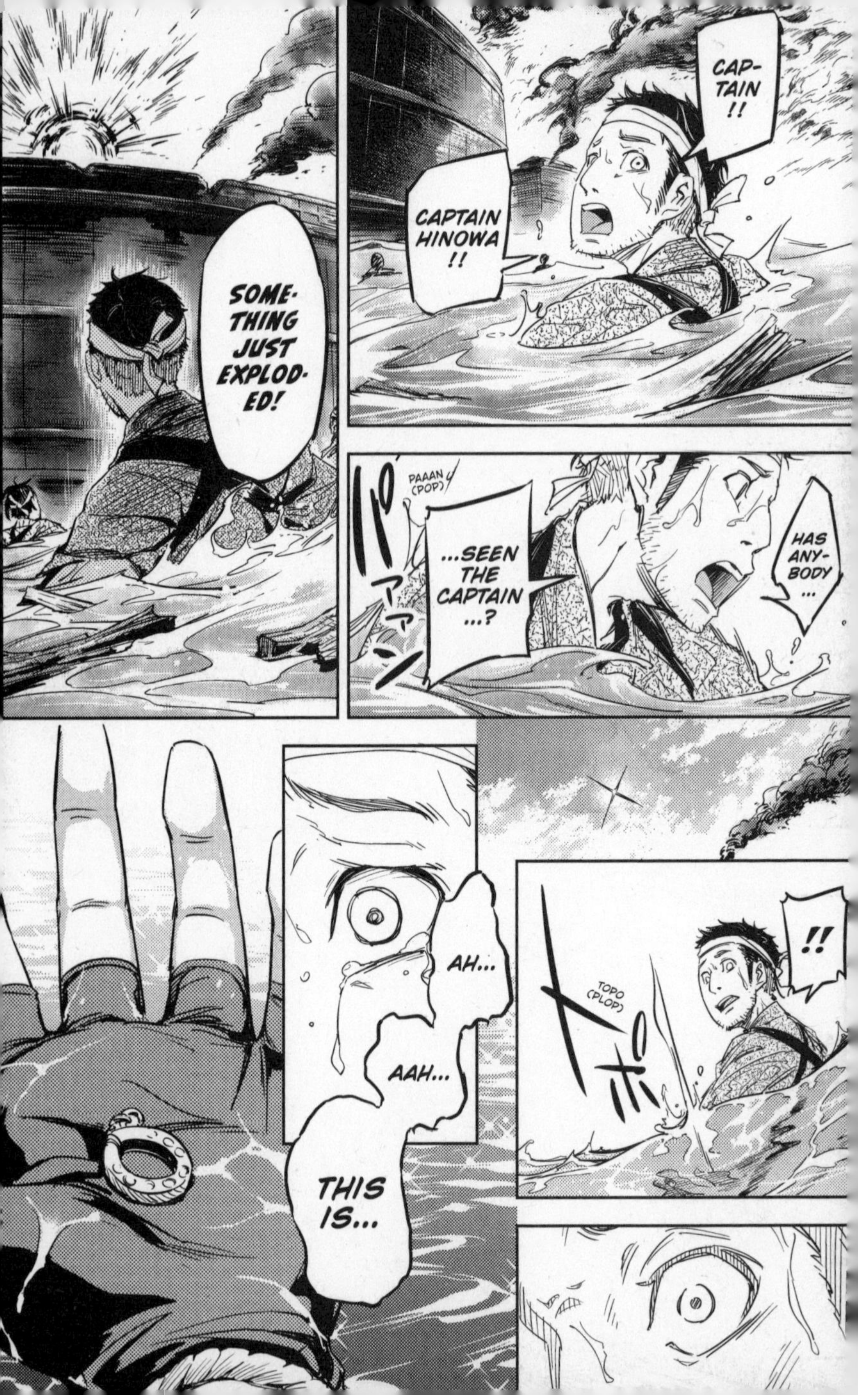
CAP-TAIN !!
CAPTAIN HINOWA !!
HAS ANY-BODY ...
PAAAN (POP)
...SEEN THE CAPTAIN ...?
SOME-THING JUST EXPLOD-ED!
!!
TOPO (PLOP)
AH...
AAH...
THIS IS...

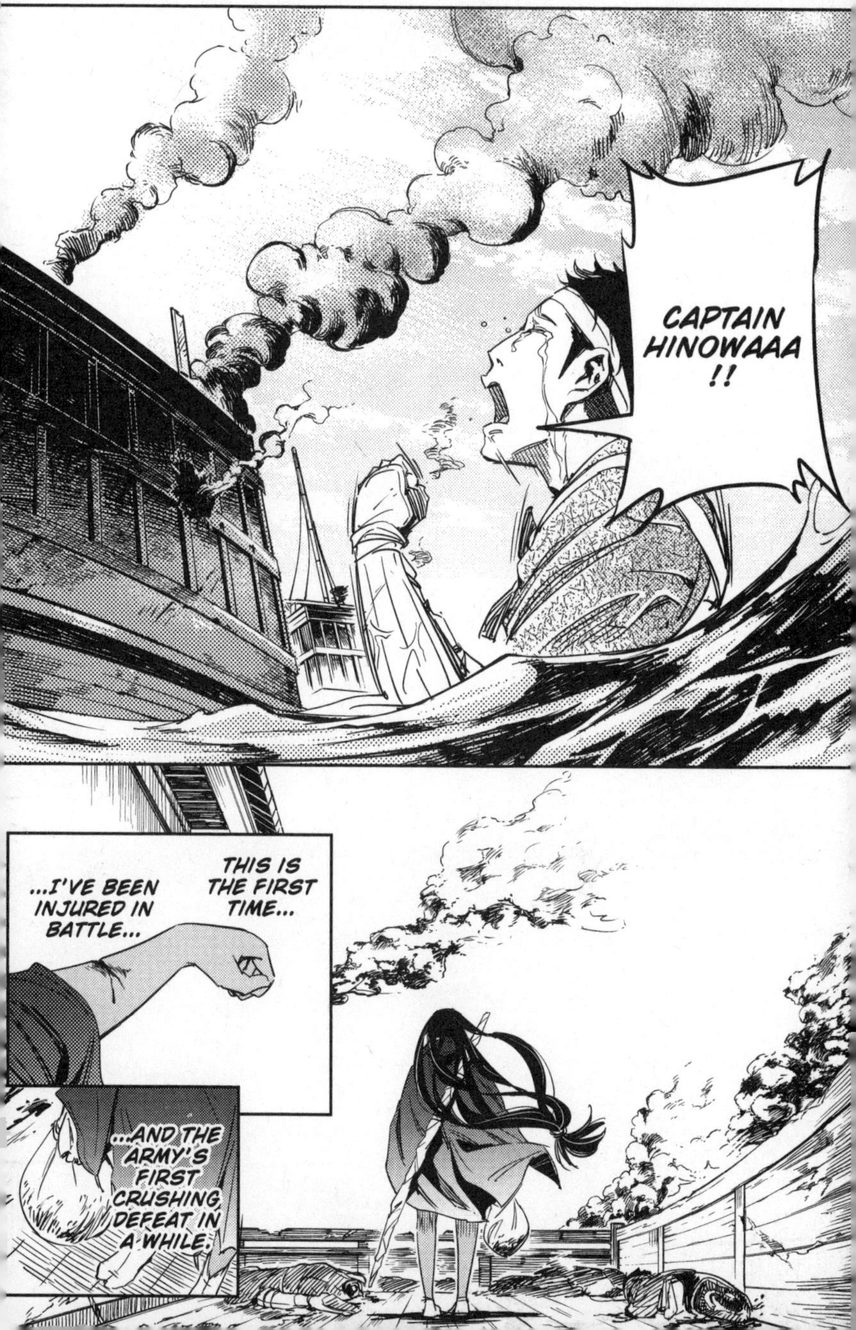
CAPTAIN HINOWAAA!!
THIS IS THE FIRST TIME...
...I'VE BEEN INJURED IN BATTLE...
...AND THE ARMY'S FIRST CRUSHING DEFEAT IN A WHILE.

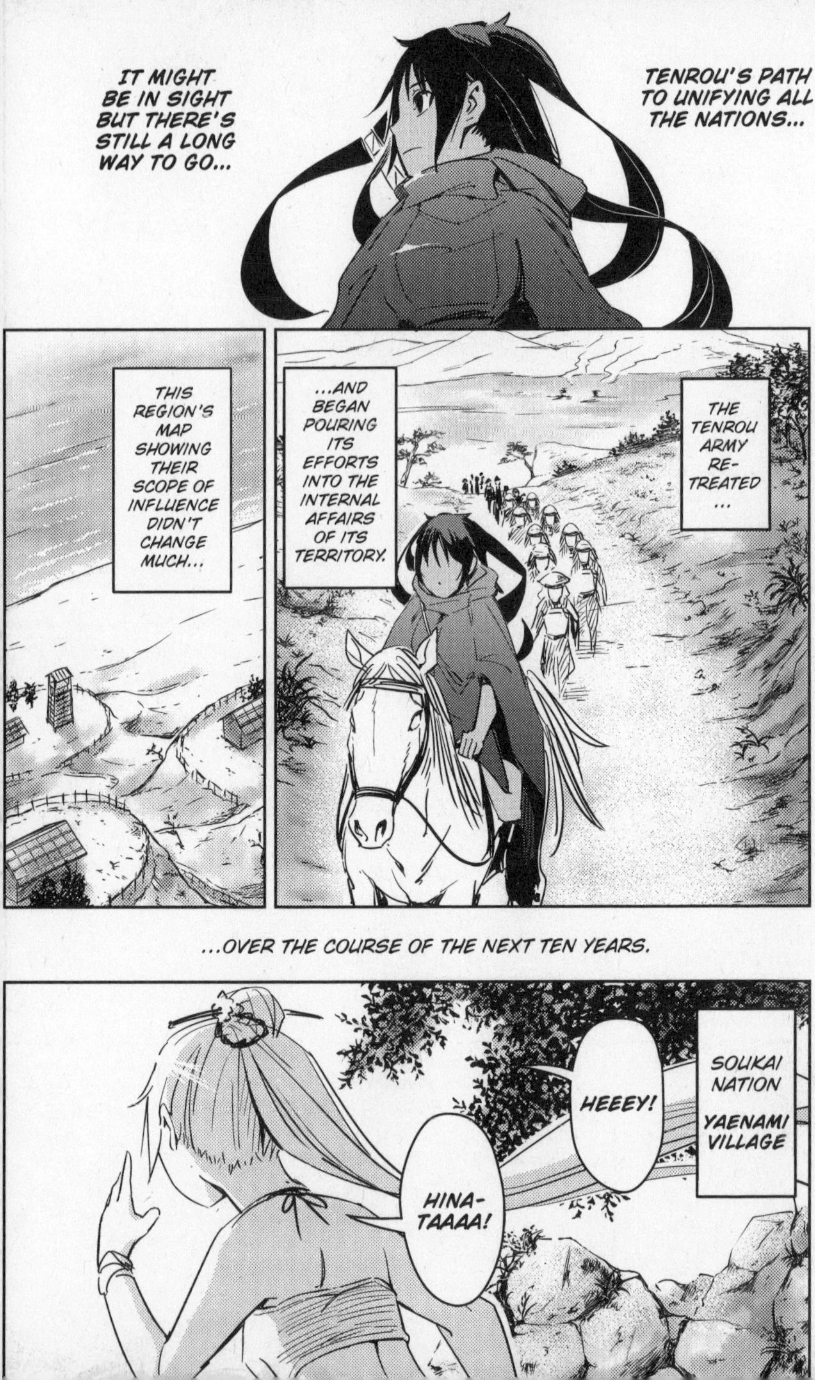
TENROU'S PATH TO UNIFYING ALL THE NATIONS...
IT MIGHT BE IN SIGHT BUT THERE'S STILL A LONG WAY TO GO...
THE TENROU ARMY RE-TREATED...
...AND BEGAN POURING ITS EFFORTS INTO THE INTERNAL AFFAIRS OF ITS TERRITORY.
THIS REGION'S MAP SHOWING THEIR SCOPE OF INFLUENCE DIDN'T CHANGE MUCH...
...OVER THE COURSE OF THE NEXT TEN YEARS.
SOUKAI NATION
YAENAMI VILLAGE
HEEEY!
HINA-TAAAA!

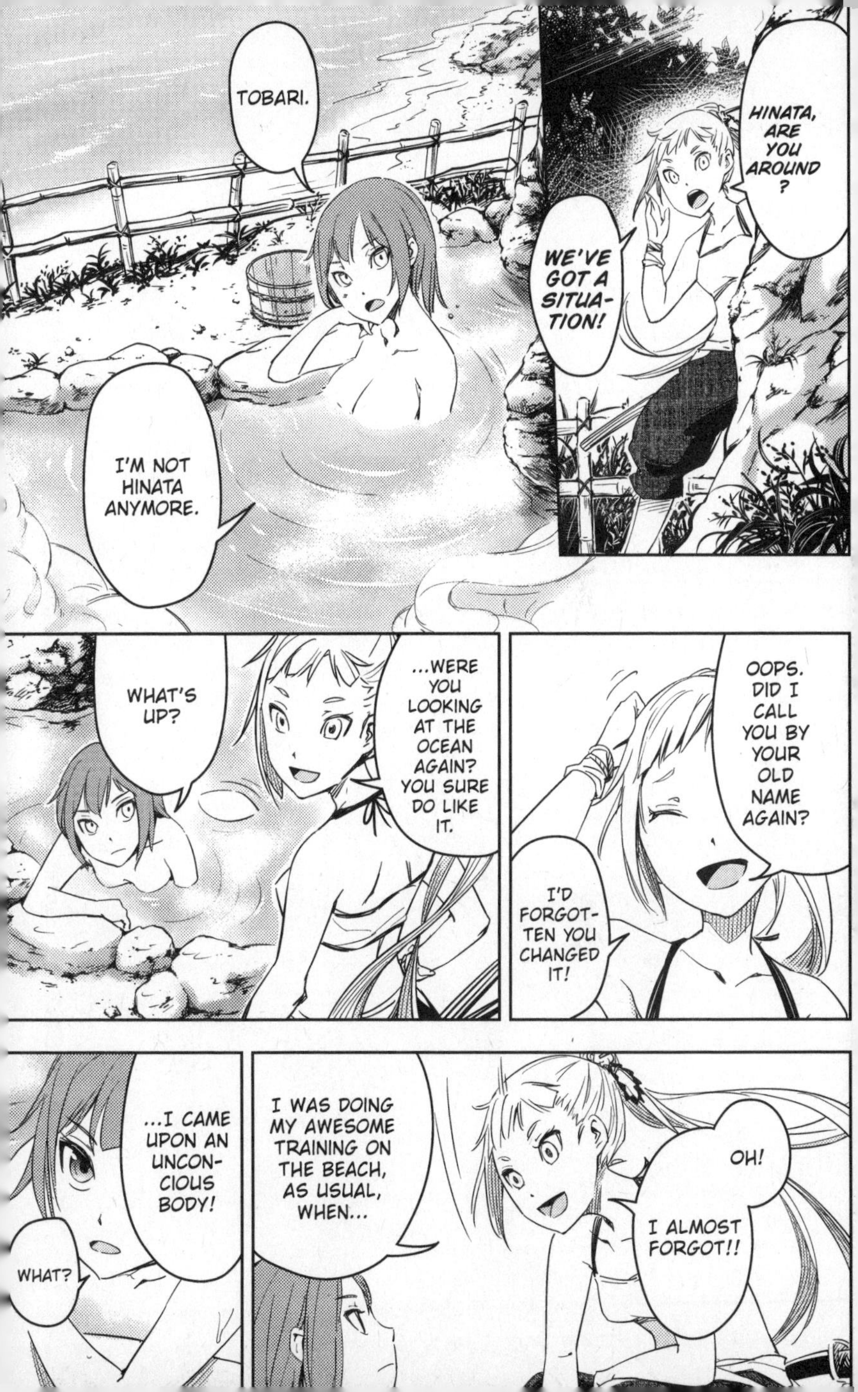

HINATA, ARE YOU AROUND?
WE'VE GOT A SITUATION!
TOBARI.
I'M NOT HINATA ANYMORE.
OOPS. DID I CALL YOU BY YOUR OLD NAME AGAIN?
I'D FORGOTTEN YOU CHANGED IT!
...WERE YOU LOOKING AT THE OCEAN AGAIN? YOU SURE DO LIKE IT.
WHAT'S UP?
OH!
I ALMOST FORGOT!!
I WAS DOING MY AWESOME TRAINING ON THE BEACH, AS USUAL, WHEN...
...I CAME UPON AN UNCONCIOUS BODY!
WHAT?

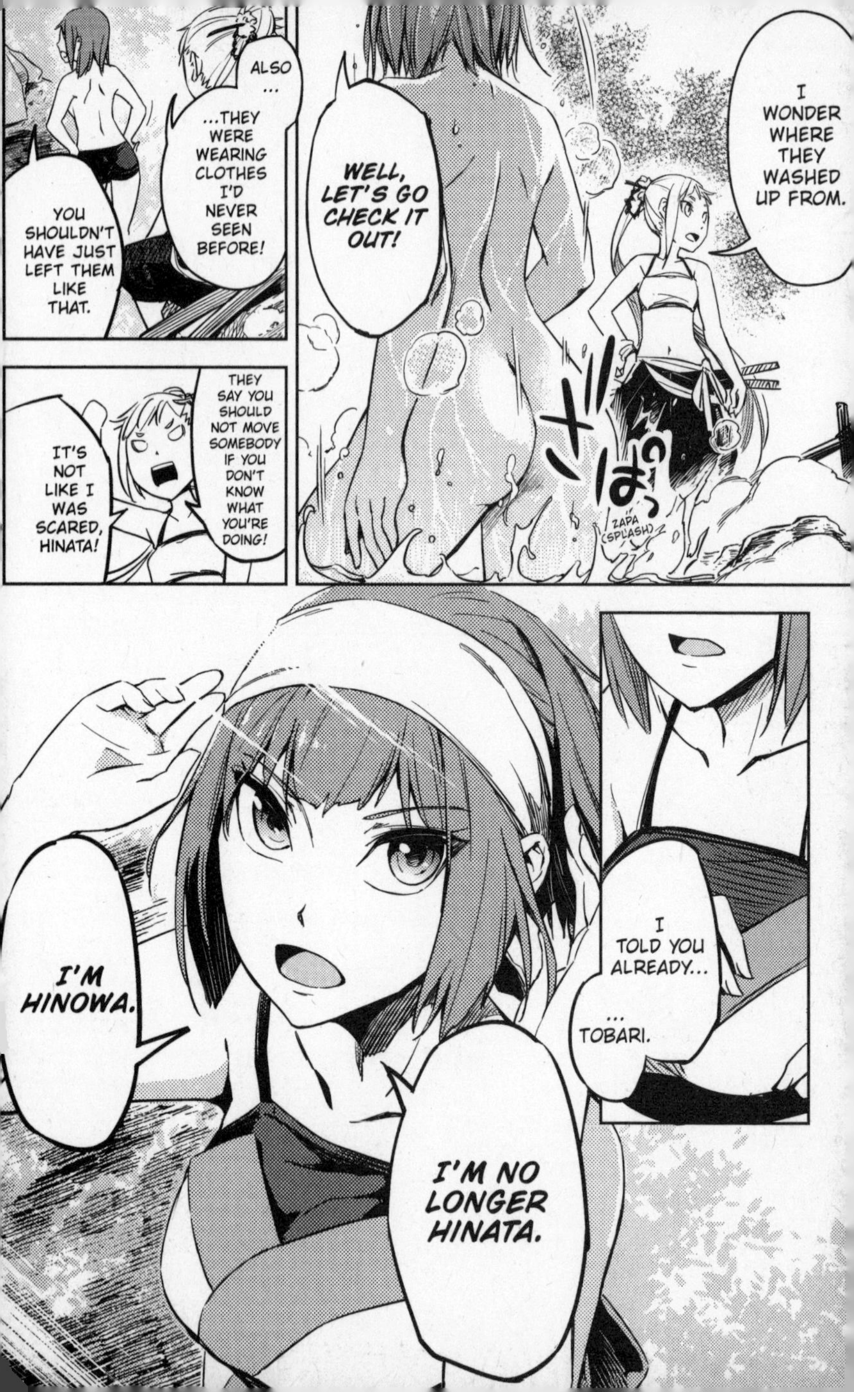
I WONDER WHERE THEY WASHED UP FROM.
WELL, LET'S GO CHECK IT OUT!
ZAPA (SPLASH)
ALSO ...
...THEY WERE WEARING CLOTHES I'D NEVER SEEN BEFORE!
YOU SHOULDN'T HAVE JUST LEFT THEM LIKE THAT.
THEY SAY YOU SHOULD NOT MOVE SOMEBODY IF YOU DON'T KNOW WHAT YOU'RE DOING!
IT'S NOT LIKE I WAS SCARED, HINATA!
I TOLD YOU ALREADY...
... TOBARI.
I'M NO LONGER HINATA.
I'M HINOWA.

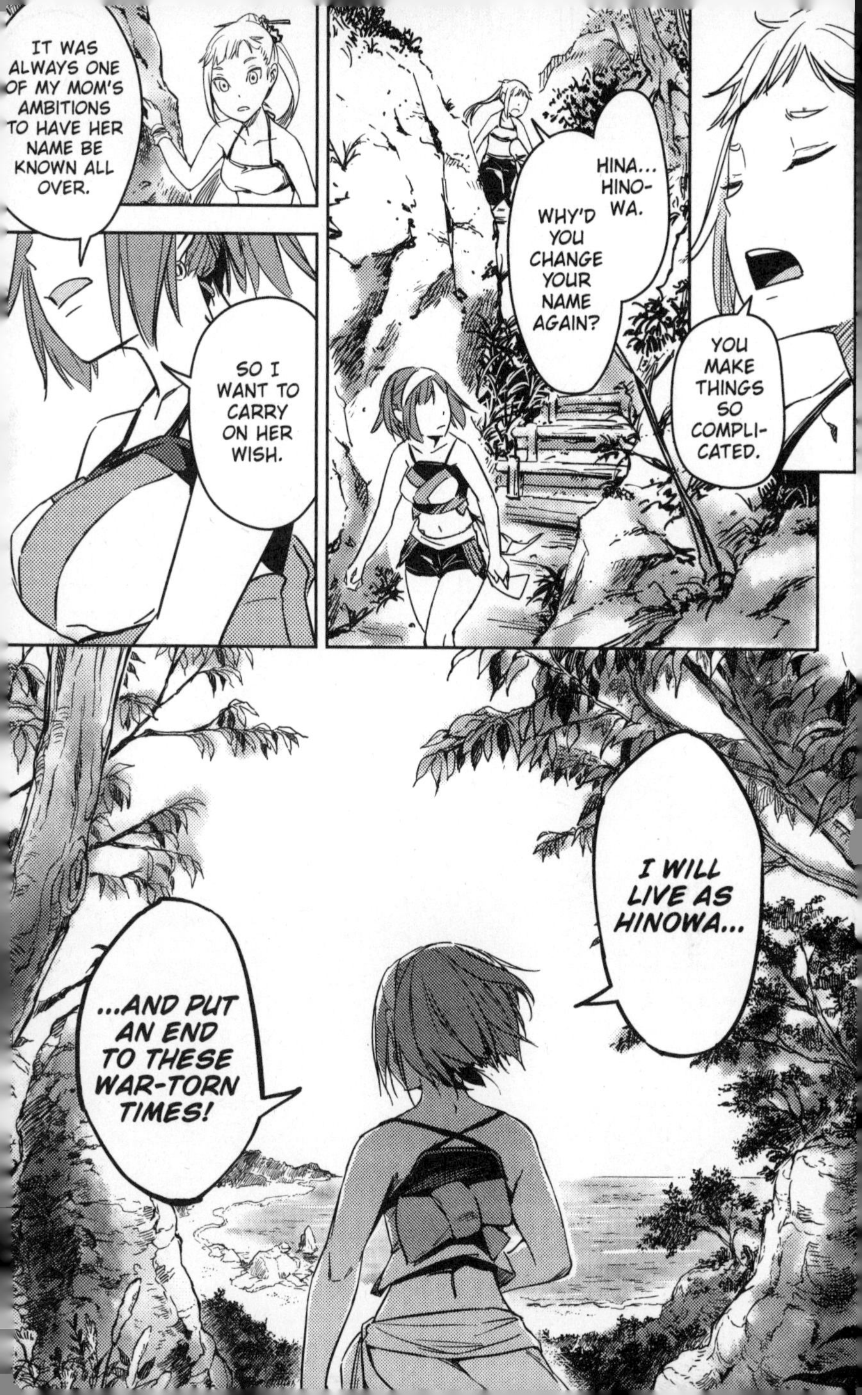
HINA... HINOWA.
WHY'D YOU CHANGE YOUR NAME AGAIN?
YOU MAKE THINGS SO COMPLICATED.
IT WAS ALWAYS ONE OF MY MOM'S AMBITIONS TO HAVE HER NAME BE KNOWN ALL OVER.
SO I WANT TO CARRY ON HER WISH.
I WILL LIVE AS HINOWA...
...AND PUT AN END TO THESE WAR-TORN TIMES!

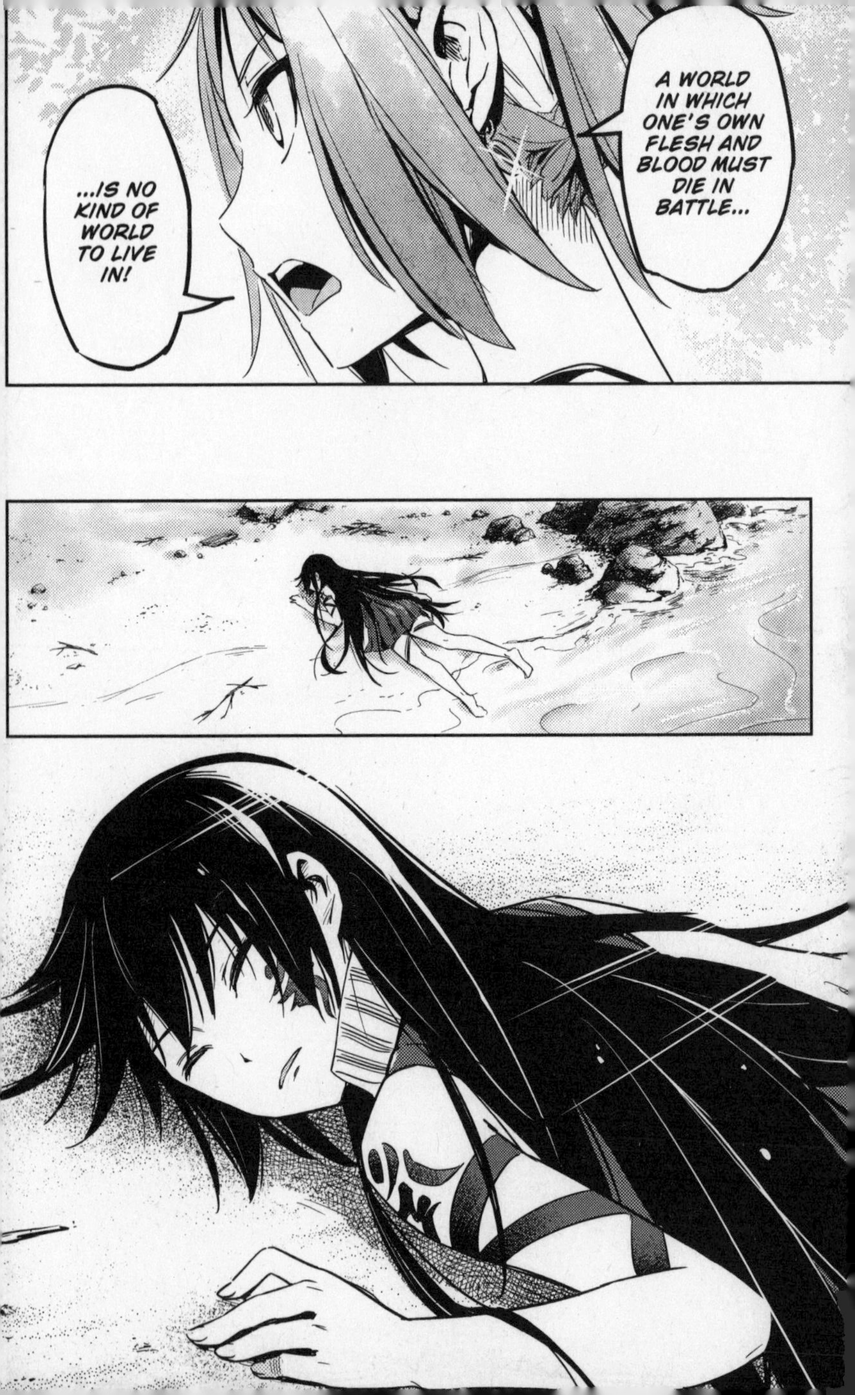
A WORLD IN WHICH ONE'S OWN FLESH AND BLOOD MUST DIE IN BATTLE...
...IS NO KIND OF WORLD TO LIVE IN!

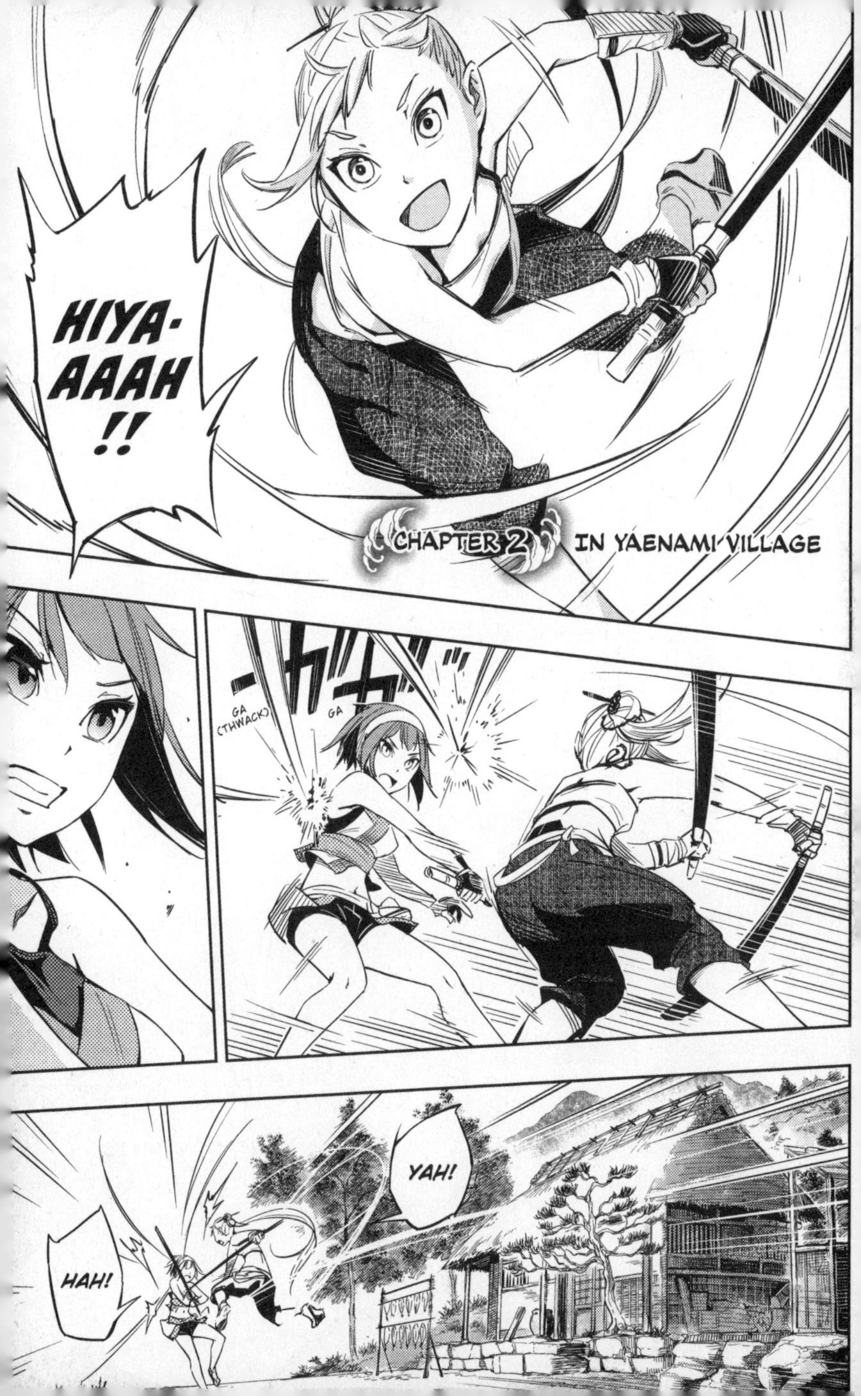
HIYA-AAAH!!
CHAPTER 2 IN YAENAMI VILLAGE
GA
GA (THWACK)
YAH!
HAH!

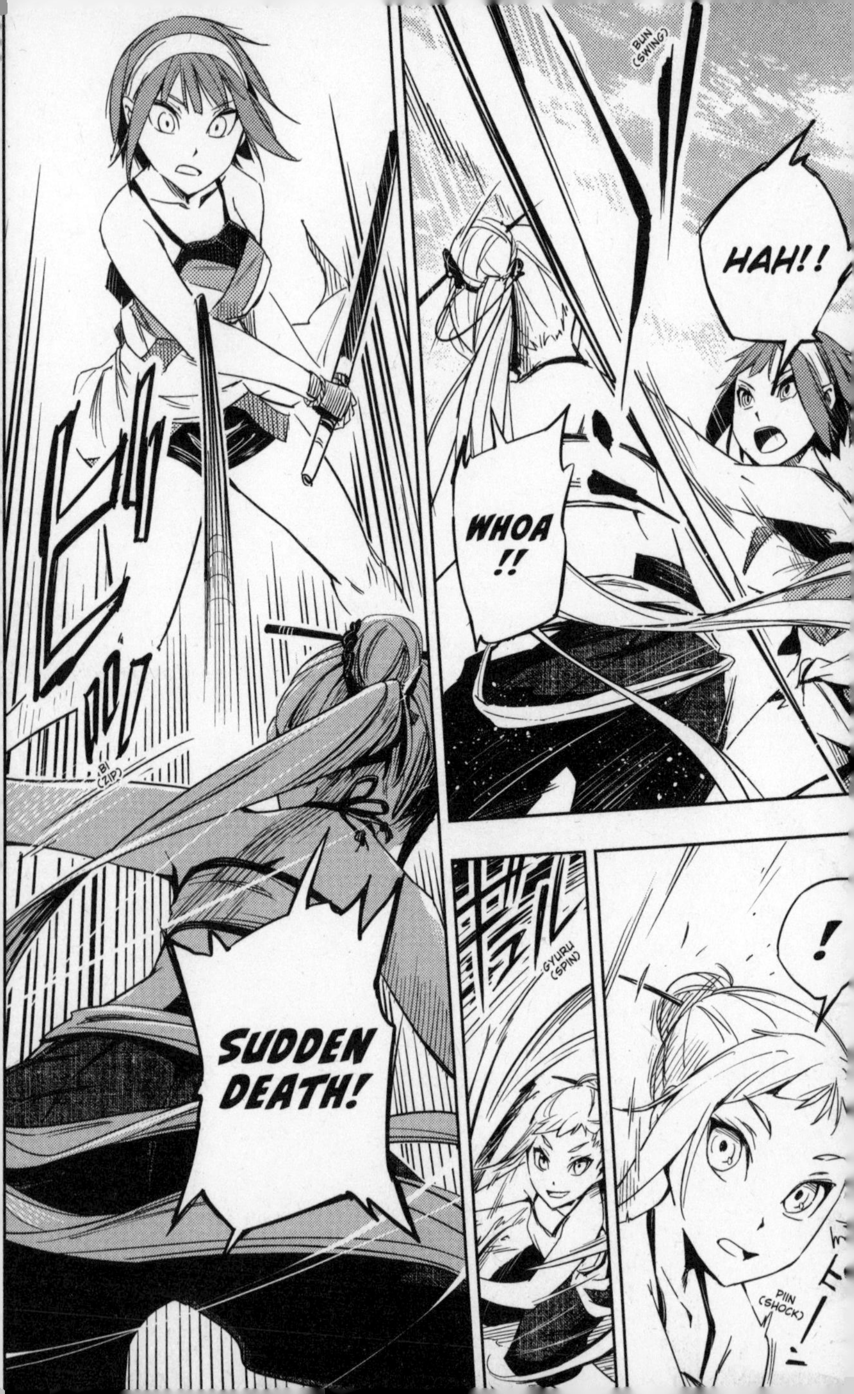
BUN (SWING)
HAH!!
WHOA!!
GYURU (SPIN)
!
PIIN (SHOCK)
BI (ZIP)
SUDDEN DEATH!

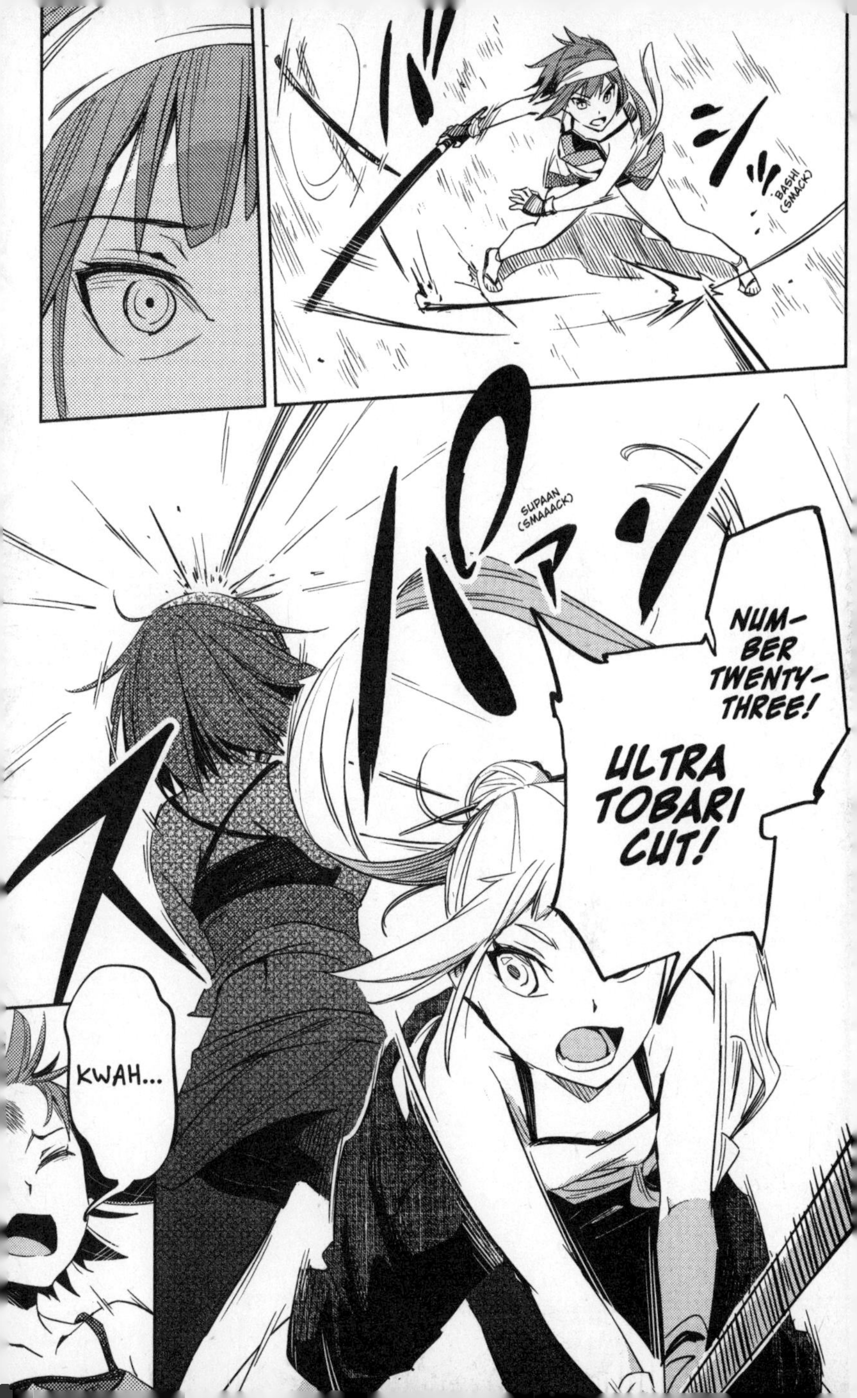
BASHI (SMACK)
SUPAAN (SMAAACK)
NUMBER TWENTY-THREE!
ULTRA TOBARI CUT!
KWAH...

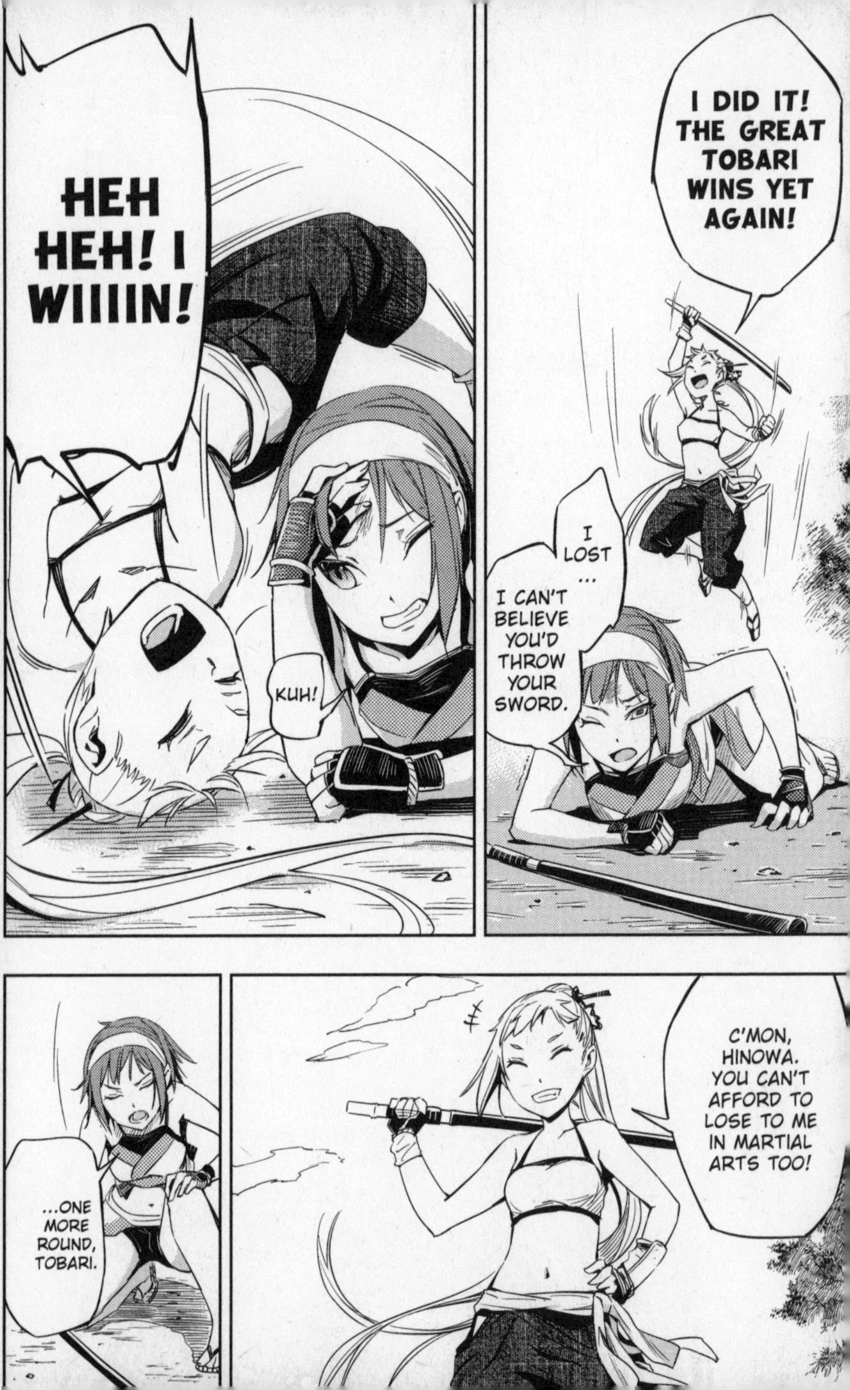
I DID IT! THE GREAT TOBARI WINS YET AGAIN!
I LOST ...
I CAN'T BELIEVE YOU'D THROW YOUR SWORD.
HEH HEH! I WIIIIN!
KUH!
C'MON, HINOWA. YOU CAN'T AFFORD TO LOSE TO ME IN MARTIAL ARTS TOO!
...ONE MORE ROUND, TOBARI.

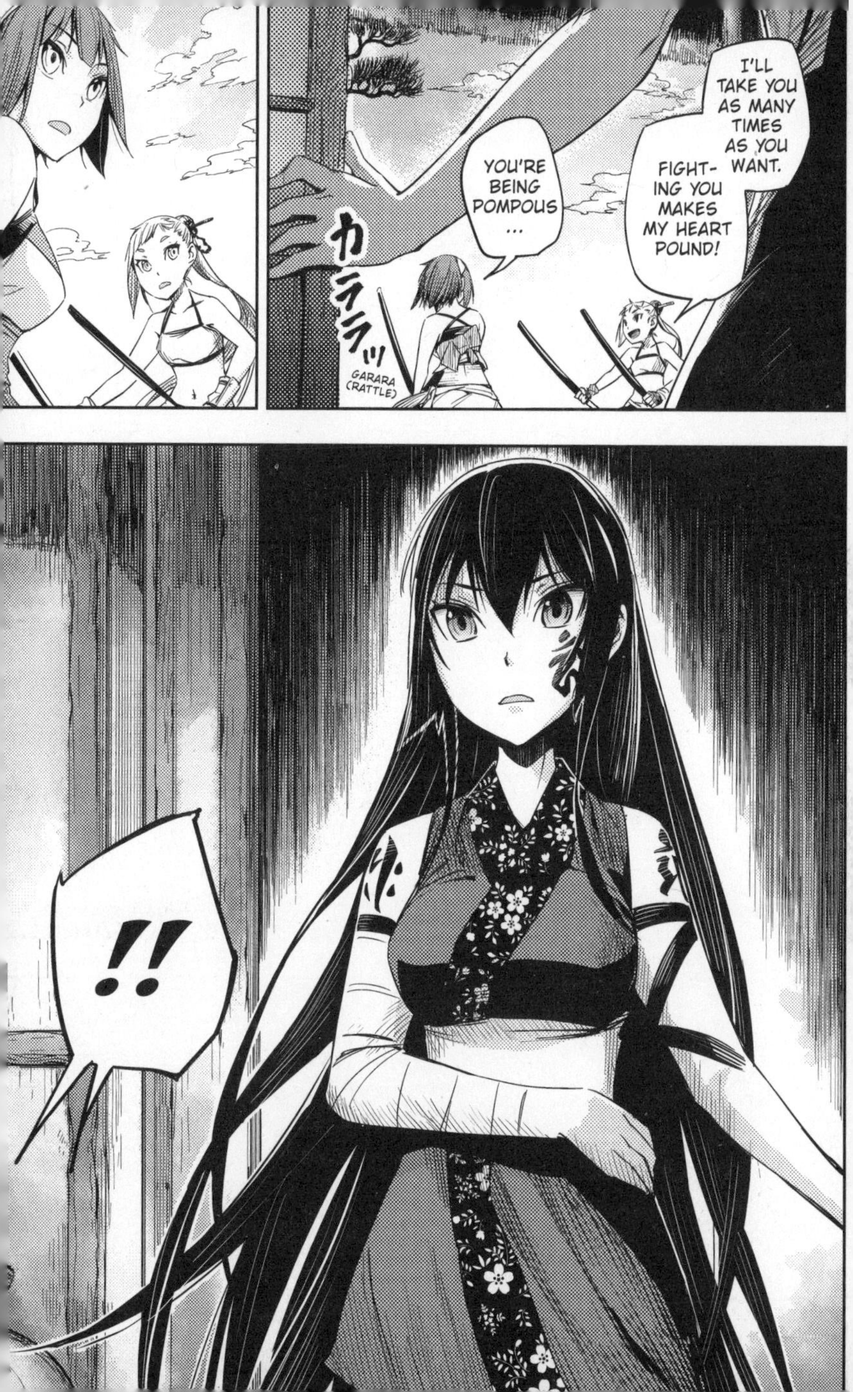
I'LL TAKE YOU AS MANY TIMES AS YOU WANT.
FIGHT-ING YOU MAKES MY HEART POUND!
YOU'RE BEING POMPOUS ...
カラララッ
GARARA (RATTLE)
!!

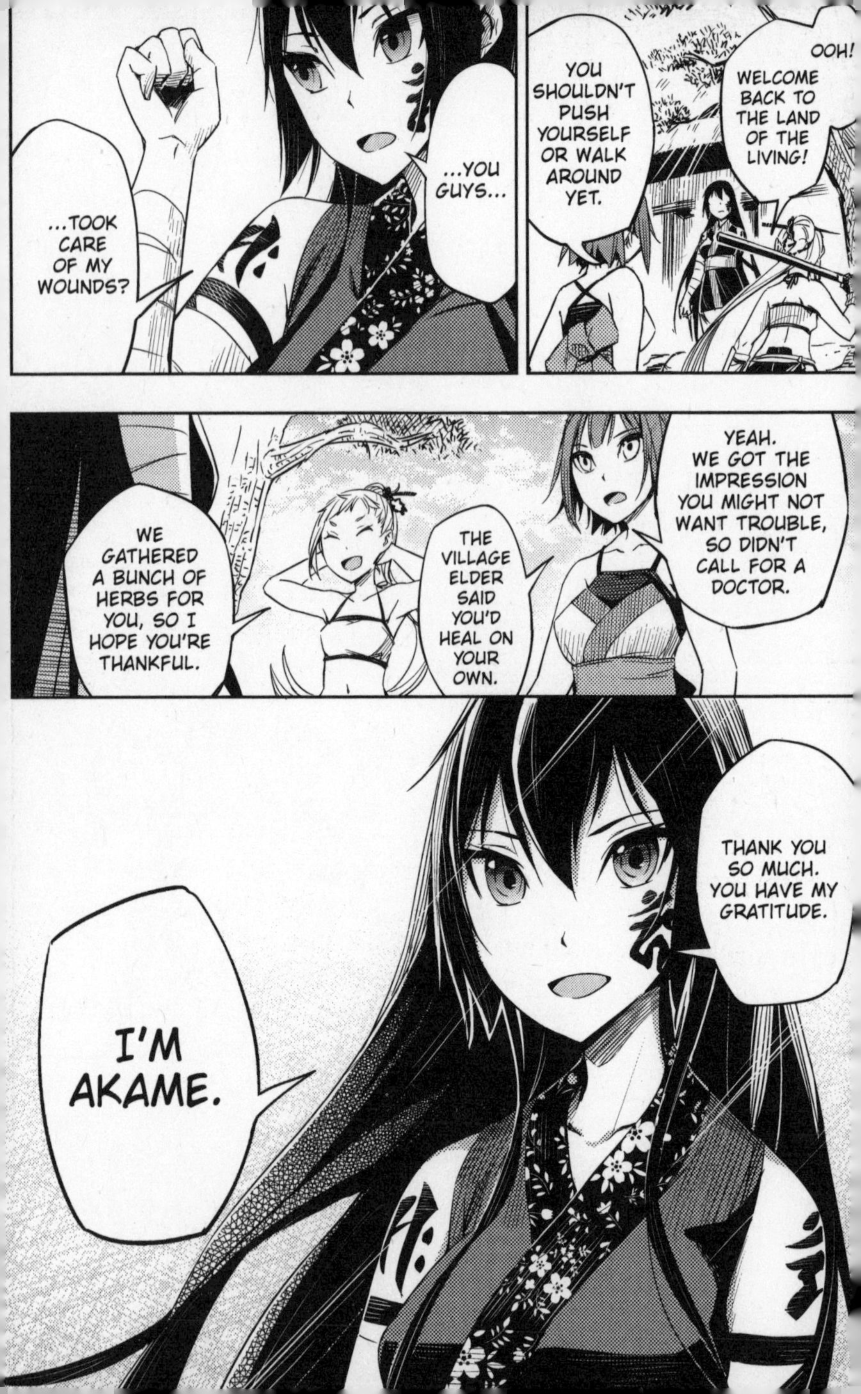
OOH! WELCOME BACK TO THE LAND OF THE LIVING!
YOU SHOULDN'T PUSH YOURSELF OR WALK AROUND YET.
...YOU GUYS...
...TOOK CARE OF MY WOUNDS?
YEAH. WE GOT THE IMPRESSION YOU MIGHT NOT WANT TROUBLE, SO DIDN'T CALL FOR A DOCTOR.
THE VILLAGE ELDER SAID YOU'D HEAL ON YOUR OWN.
WE GATHERED A BUNCH OF HERBS FOR YOU, SO I HOPE YOU'RE THANKFUL.
THANK YOU SO MUCH. YOU HAVE MY GRATITUDE.
I'M AKAME.

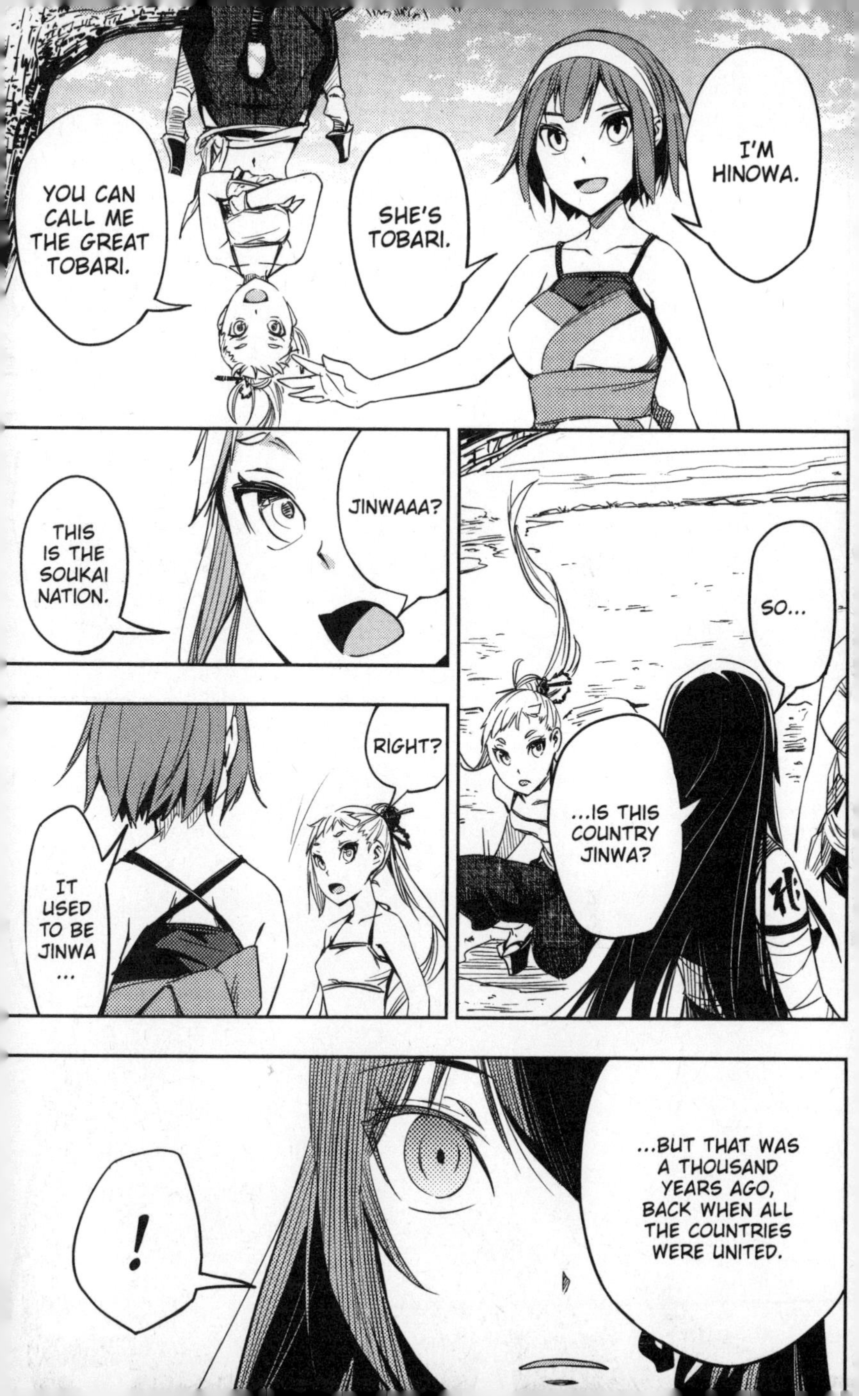
I'M HINOWA.
SHE'S TOBARI.
YOU CAN CALL ME THE GREAT TOBARI.
SO...
...IS THIS COUNTRY JINWA?
JINWAAA?
THIS IS THE SOUKAI NATION.
RIGHT?
IT USED TO BE JINWA...
...BUT THAT WAS A THOUSAND YEARS AGO, BACK WHEN ALL THE COUNTRIES WERE UNITED.
!

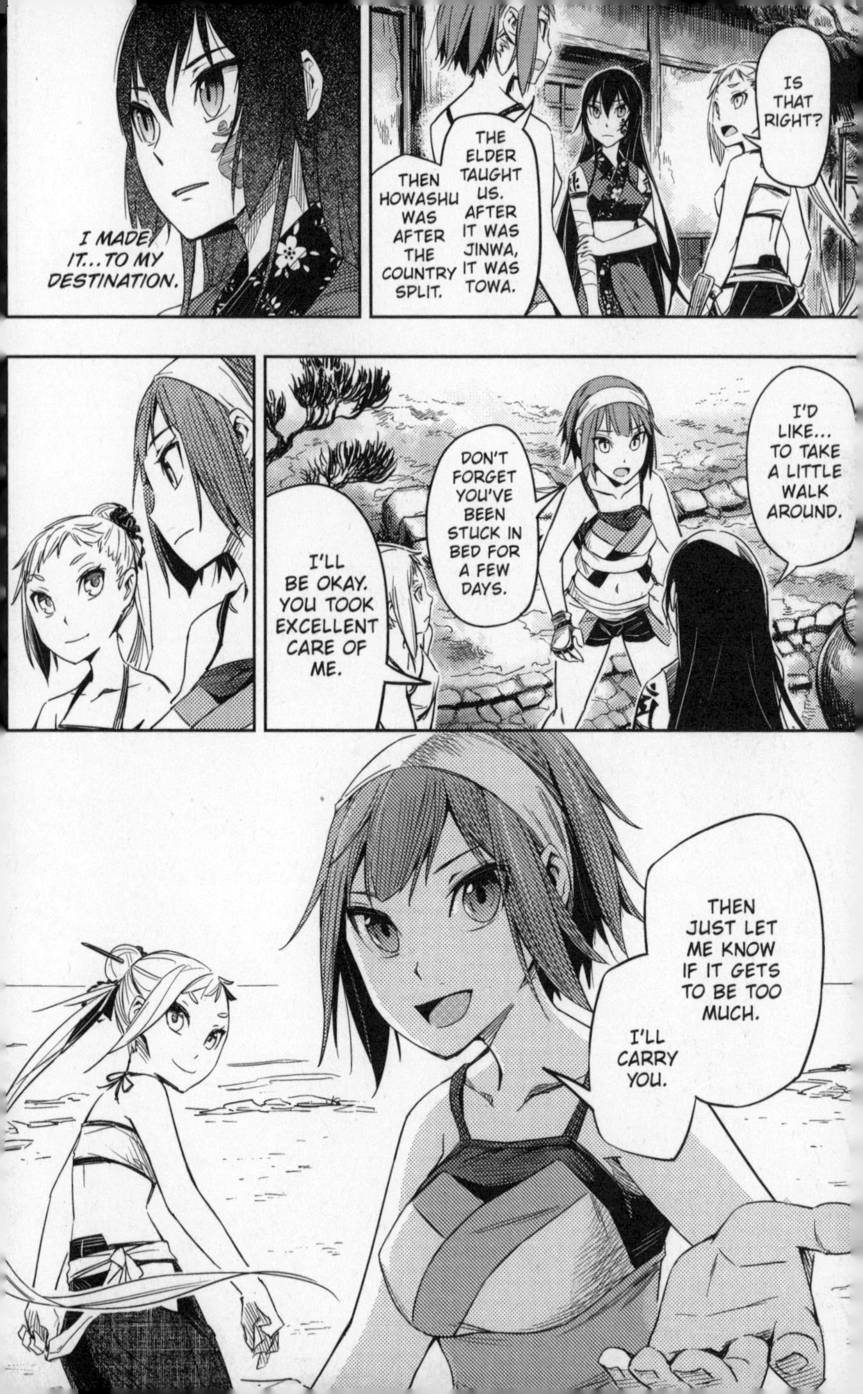
IS THAT RIGHT?
THE ELDER TAUGHT US. AFTER IT WAS JINWA, IT WAS TOWA.
THEN HOWASHU WAS AFTER THE COUNTRY SPLIT.
I MADE IT...TO MY DESTINATION.
I'D LIKE... TO TAKE A LITTLE WALK AROUND.
DON'T FORGET YOU'VE BEEN STUCK IN BED FOR A FEW DAYS.
I'LL BE OKAY. YOU TOOK EXCELLENT CARE OF ME.
THEN JUST LET ME KNOW IF IT GETS TO BE TOO MUCH.
I'LL CARRY YOU.

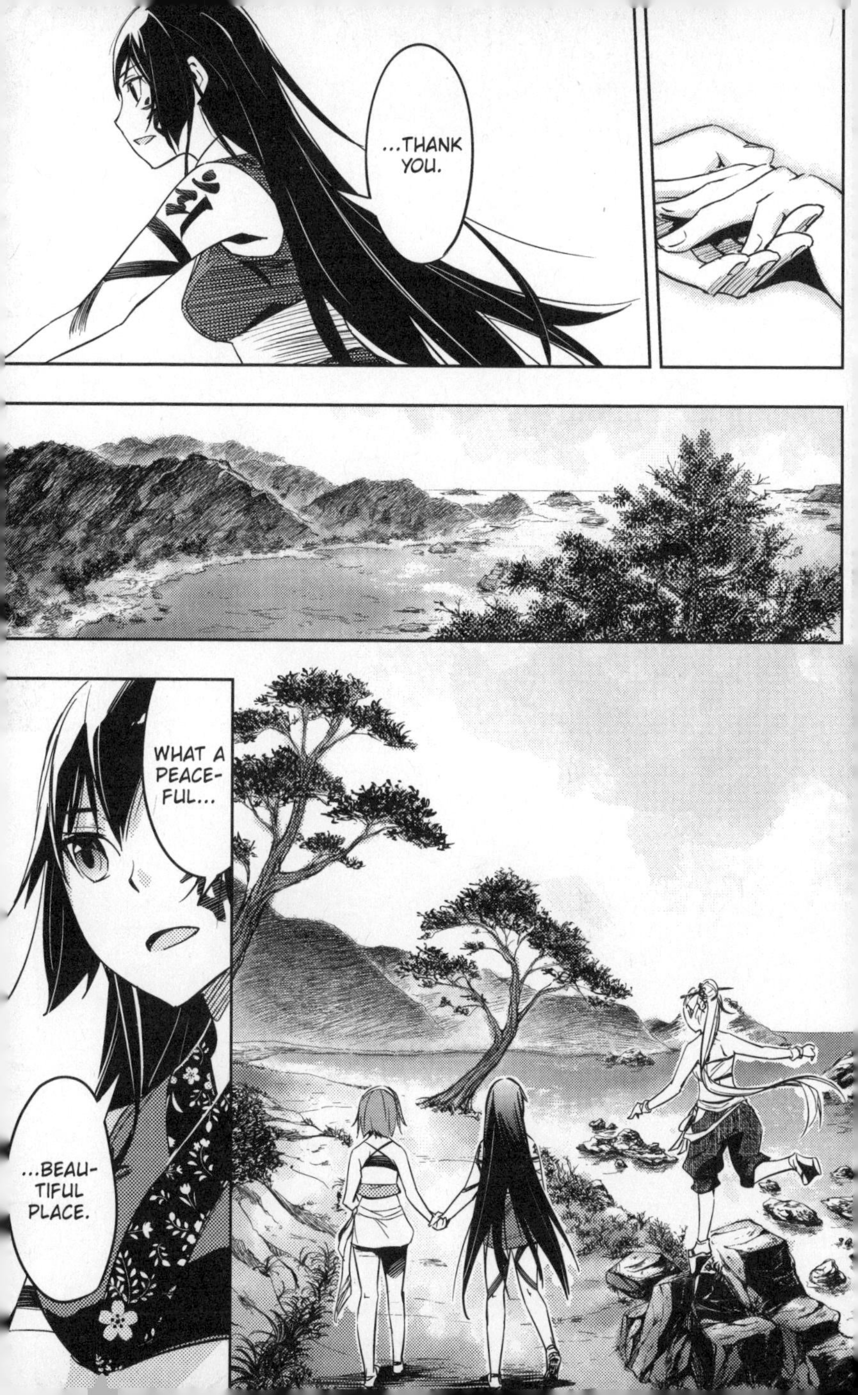
...THANK YOU.
WHAT A PEACE-FUL...
...BEAU-TIFUL PLACE.

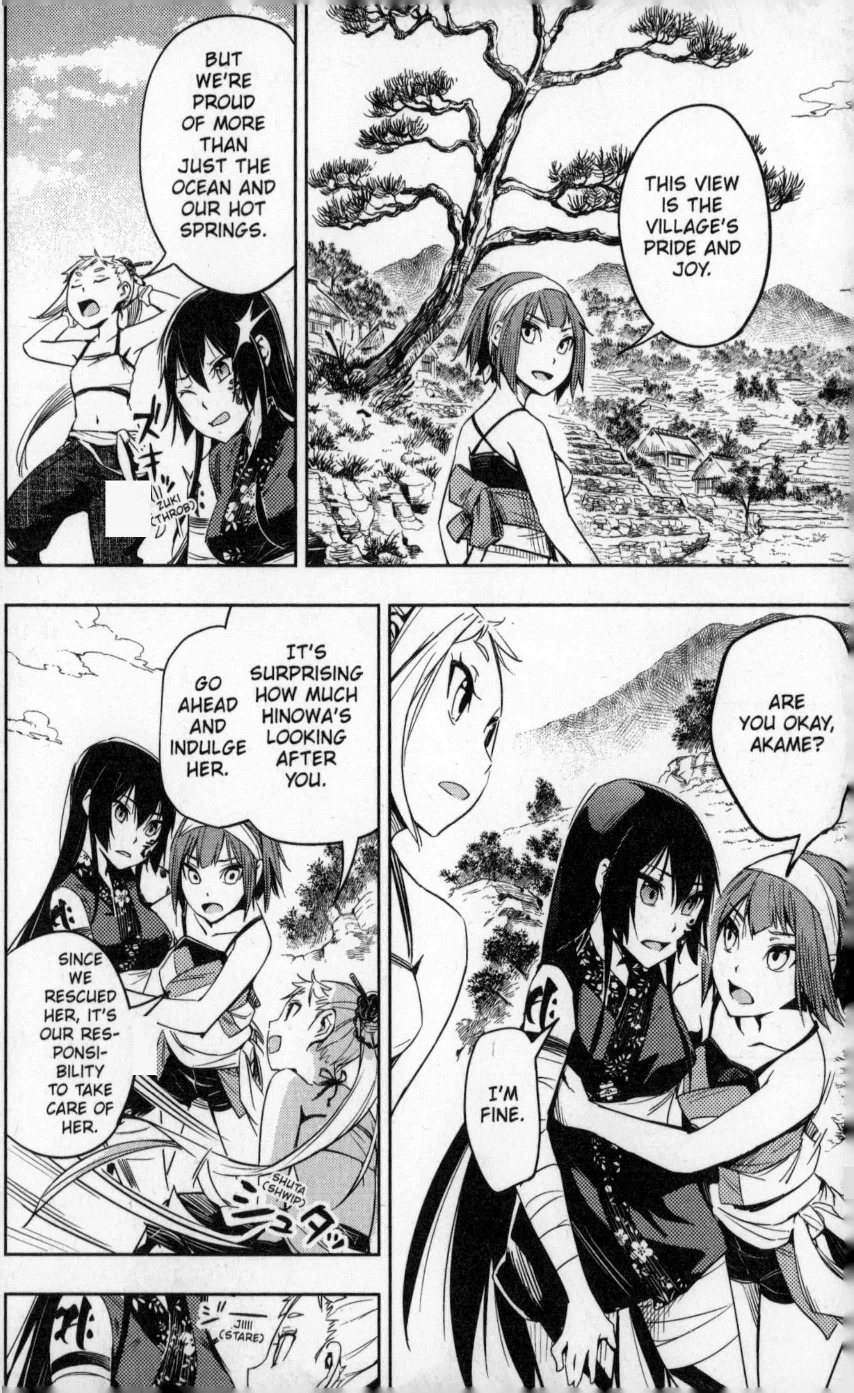
THIS VIEW IS THE VILLAGE'S PRIDE AND JOY.
BUT WE'RE PROUD OF MORE THAN JUST THE OCEAN AND OUR HOT SPRINGS.
ZUKI (THROB)
ARE YOU OKAY, AKAME?
I'M FINE.
IT'S SURPRISING HOW MUCH HINOWA'S LOOKING AFTER YOU.
GO AHEAD AND INDULGE HER.
SINCE WE RESCUED HER, IT'S OUR RES-PONSI-BILITY TO TAKE CARE OF HER.
SHUTA (SHWIP)
JIIII (STARE)

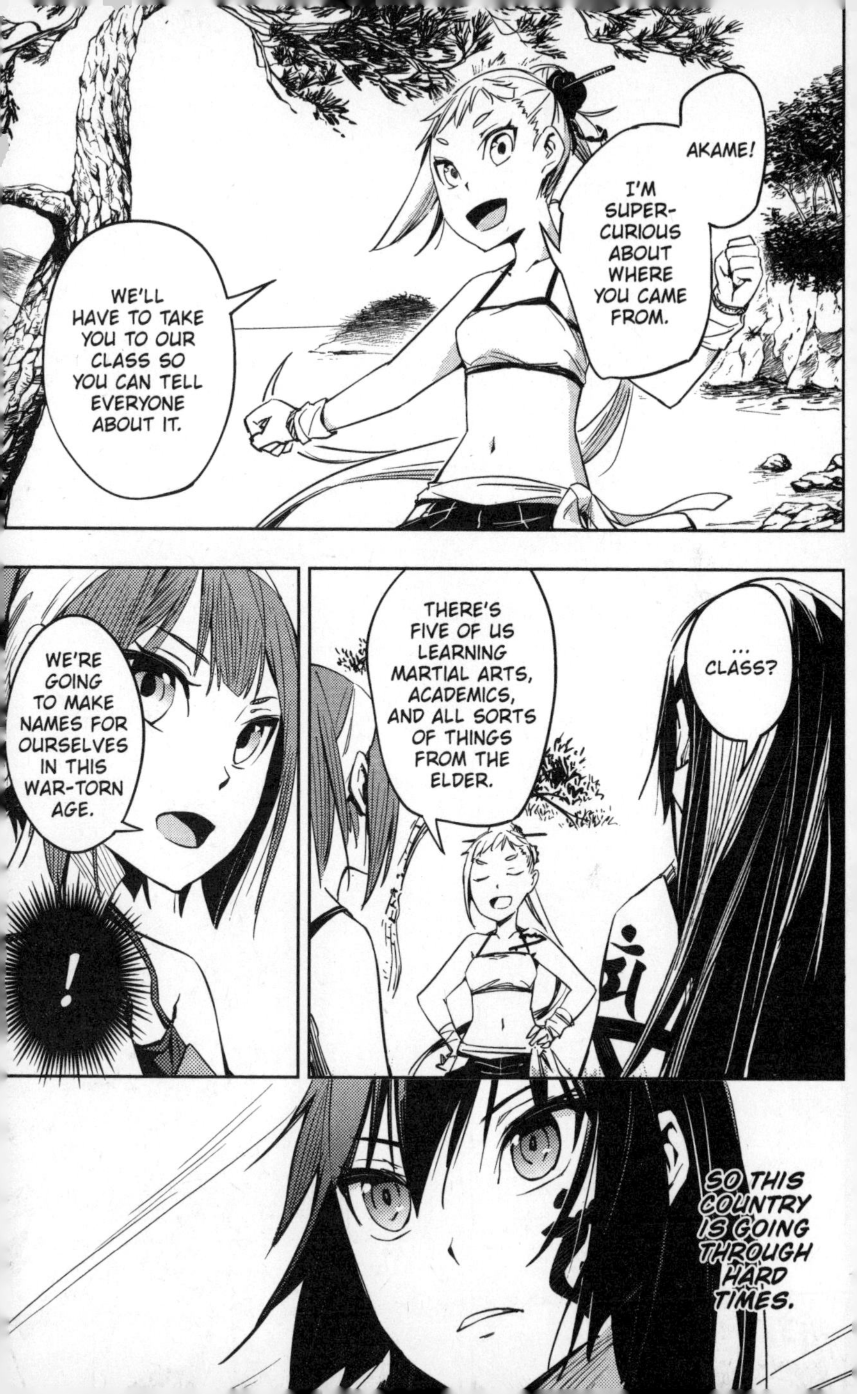
AKAME!
I'M SUPER-CURIOUS ABOUT WHERE YOU CAME FROM.
WE'LL HAVE TO TAKE YOU TO OUR CLASS SO YOU CAN TELL EVERYONE ABOUT IT.
... CLASS?
THERE'S FIVE OF US LEARNING MARTIAL ARTS, ACADEMICS, AND ALL SORTS OF THINGS FROM THE ELDER.
WE'RE GOING TO MAKE NAMES FOR OURSELVES IN THIS WAR-TORN AGE.
!
SO THIS COUNTRY IS GOING THROUGH HARD TIMES.

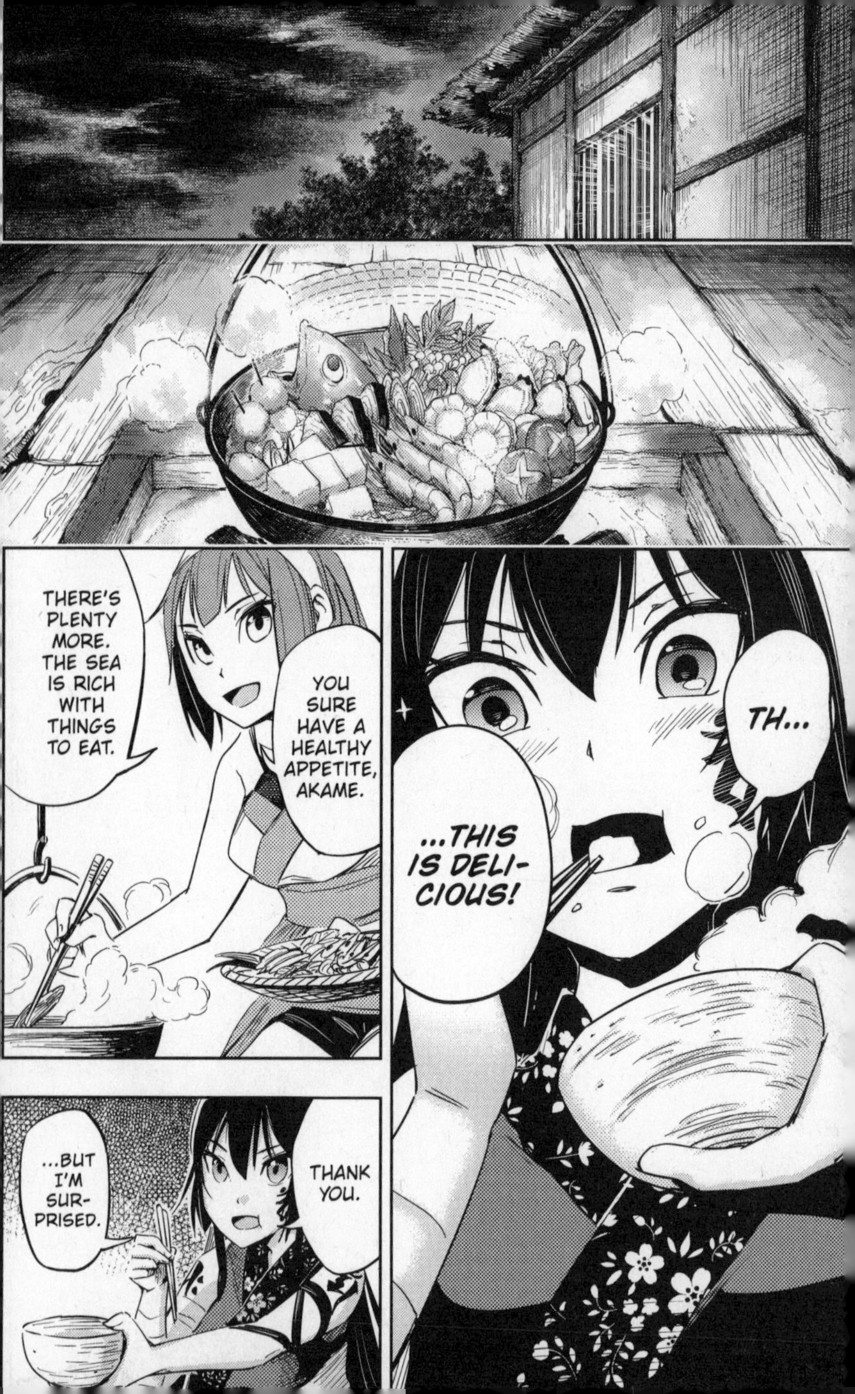
TH...
...THIS IS DELI-CIOUS!
YOU SURE HAVE A HEALTHY APPETITE, AKAME.
THERE'S PLENTY MORE. THE SEA IS RICH WITH THINGS TO EAT.
THANK YOU.
...BUT I'M SUR-PRISED.

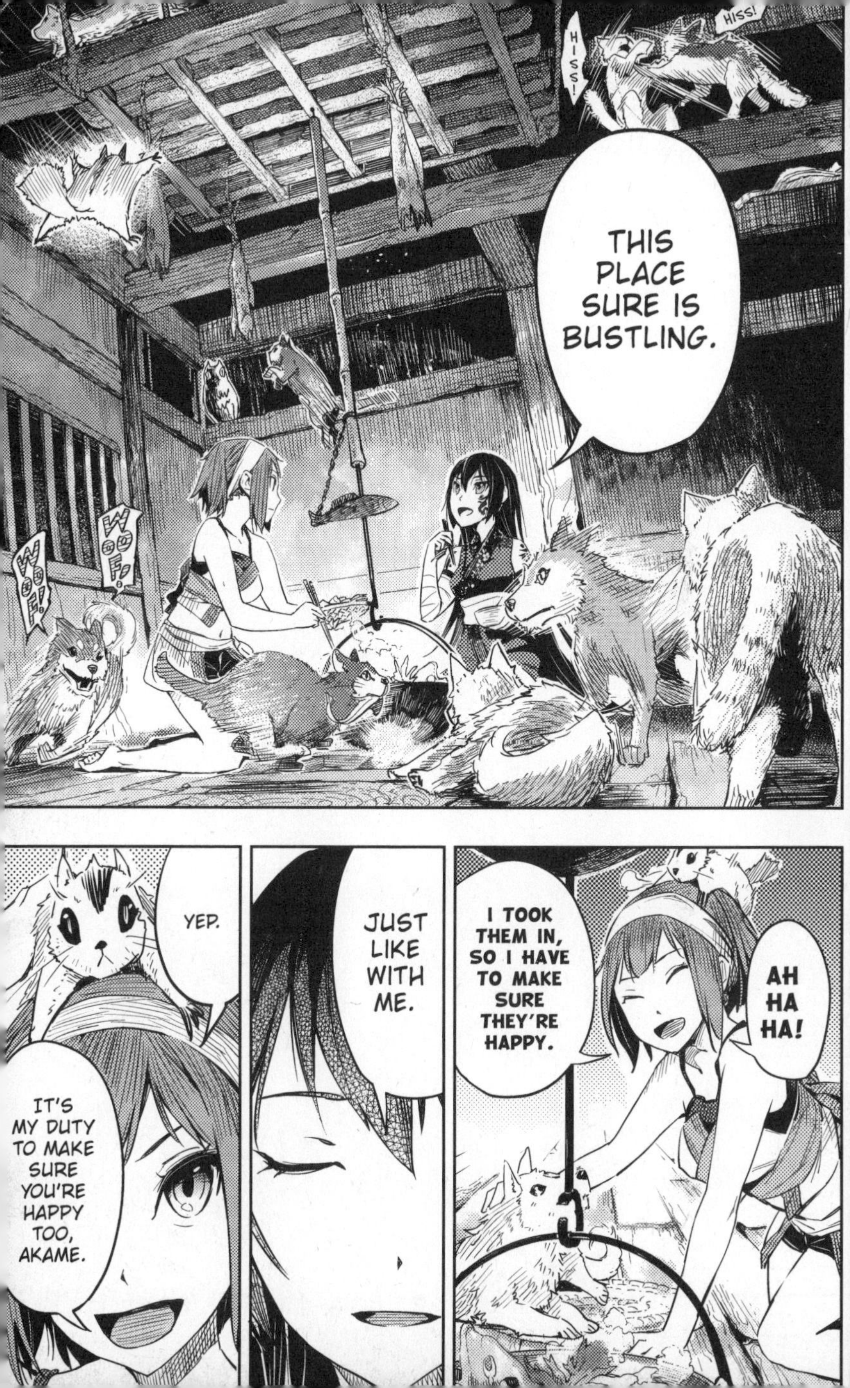
HISS!
HISS!
THIS PLACE SURE IS BUSTLING.
WOOF!
WOOF!
AH HA HA!
I TOOK THEM IN, SO I HAVE TO MAKE SURE THEY'RE HAPPY.
JUST LIKE WITH ME.
YEP.
IT'S MY DUTY TO MAKE SURE YOU'RE HAPPY TOO, AKAME.

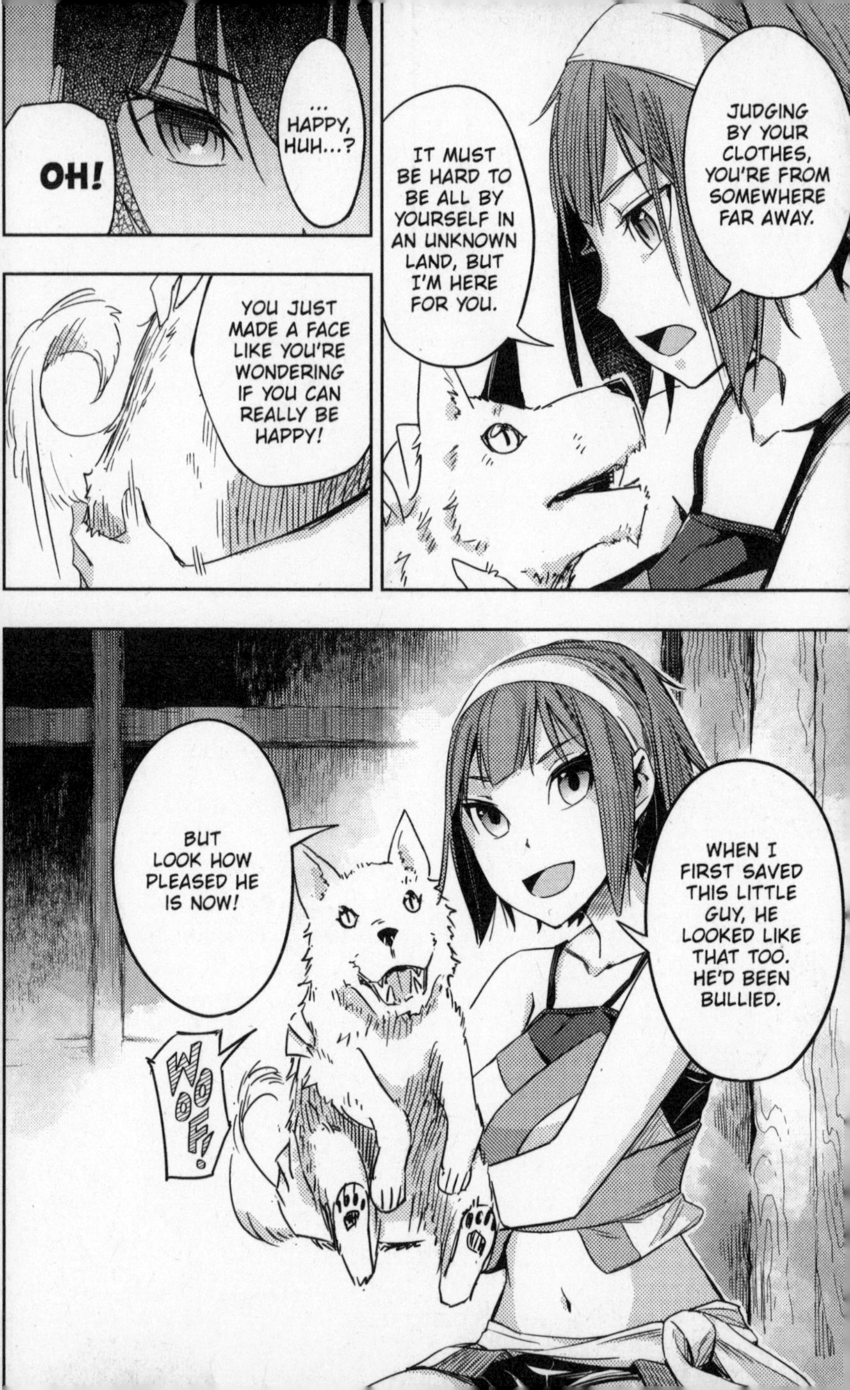
JUDGING BY YOUR CLOTHES, YOU'RE FROM SOMEWHERE FAR AWAY.
IT MUST BE HARD TO BE ALL BY YOURSELF IN AN UNKNOWN LAND, BUT I'M HERE FOR YOU.
... HAPPY, HUH...?
OH!
YOU JUST MADE A FACE LIKE YOU'RE WONDERING IF YOU CAN REALLY BE HAPPY!
WHEN I FIRST SAVED THIS LITTLE GUY, HE LOOKED LIKE THAT TOO. HE'D BEEN BULLIED.
BUT LOOK HOW PLEASED HE IS NOW!
WOOF!

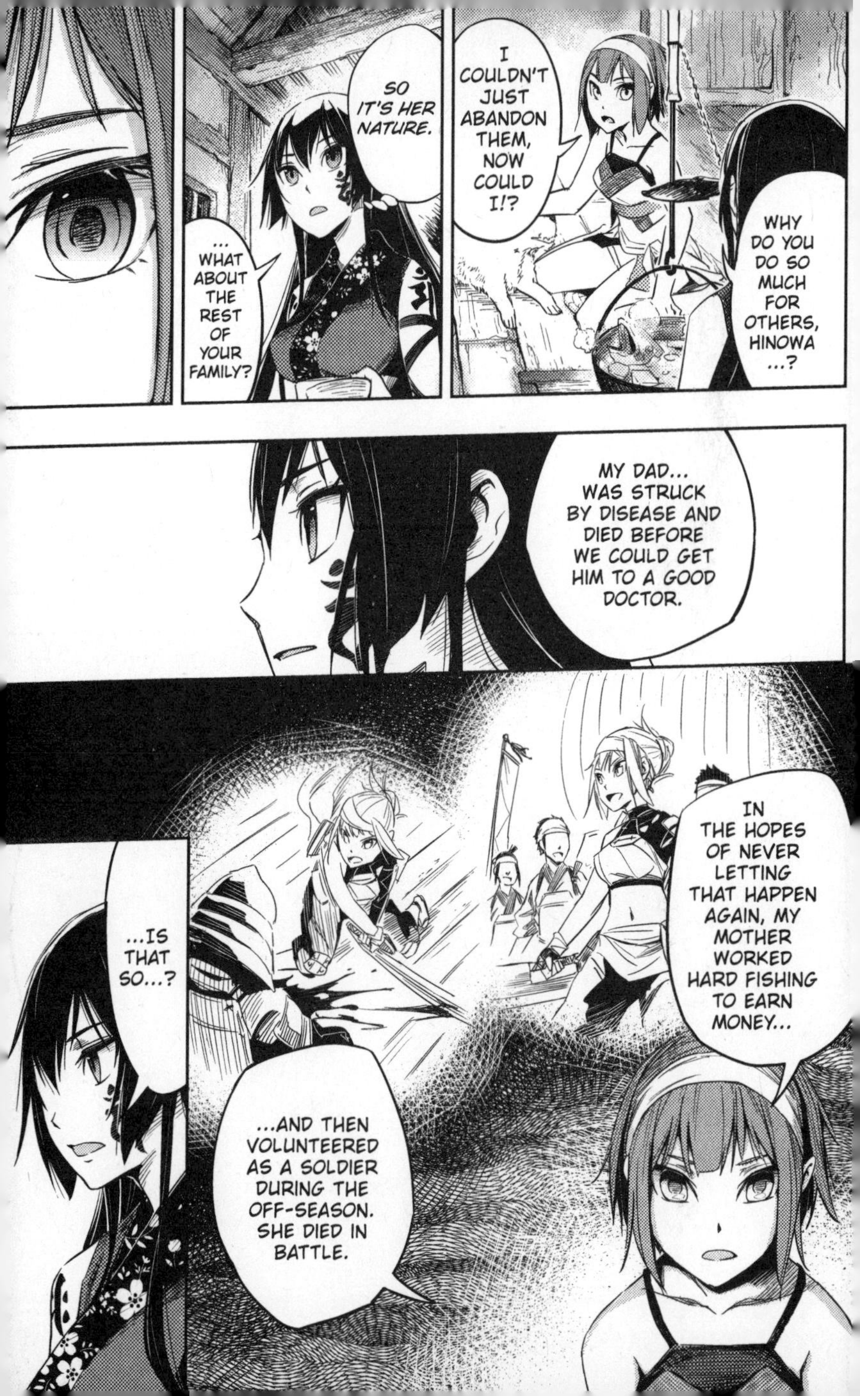
WHY DO YOU DO SO MUCH FOR OTHERS, HINOWA ...?
I COULDN'T JUST ABANDON THEM, NOW COULD I!?
SO IT'S HER NATURE.
... WHAT ABOUT THE REST OF YOUR FAMILY?
MY DAD... WAS STRUCK BY DISEASE AND DIED BEFORE WE COULD GET HIM TO A GOOD DOCTOR.
IN THE HOPES OF NEVER LETTING THAT HAPPEN AGAIN, MY MOTHER WORKED HARD FISHING TO EARN MONEY...
...AND THEN VOLUNTEERED AS A SOLDIER DURING THE OFF-SEASON. SHE DIED IN BATTLE.
...IS THAT SO...?

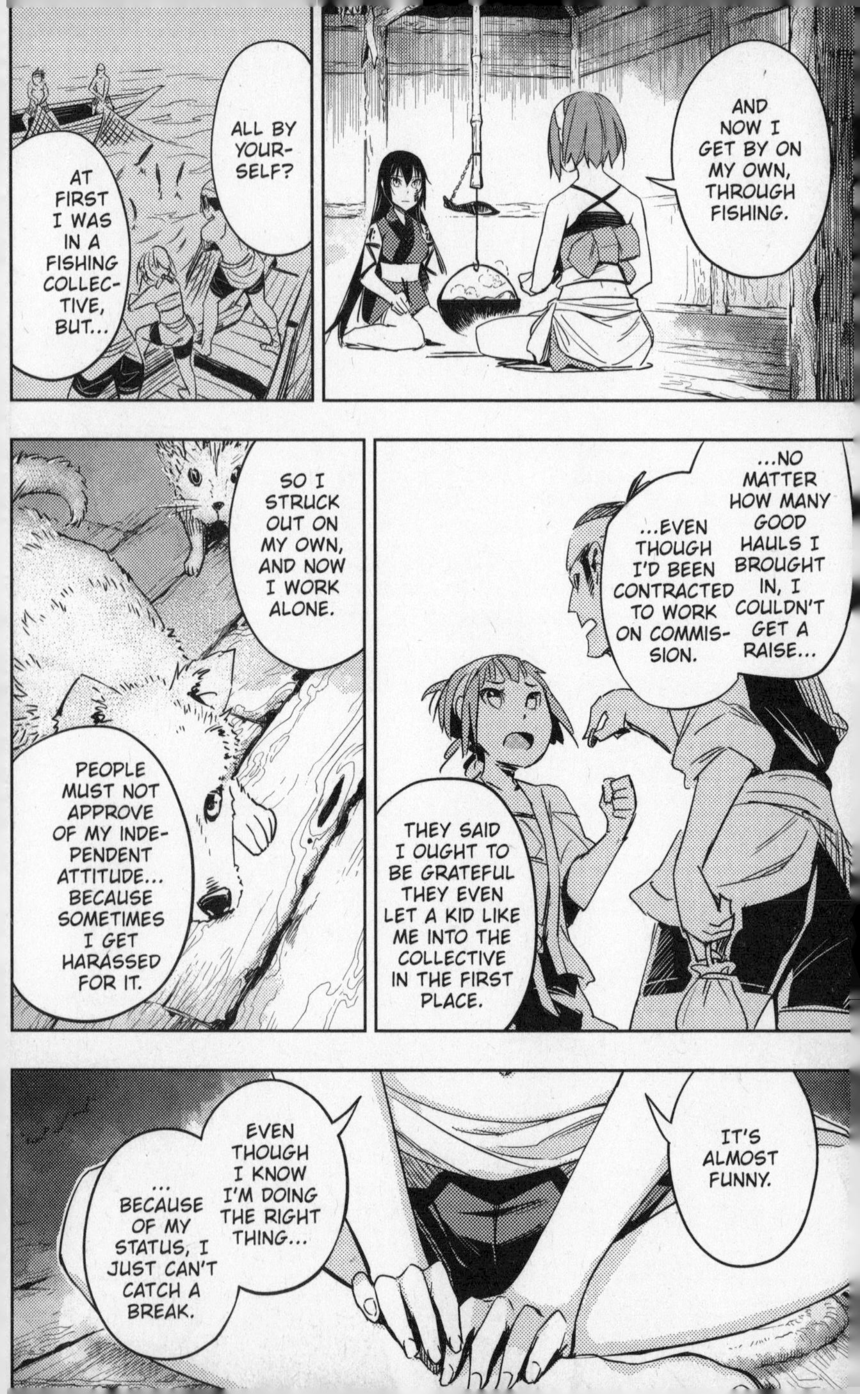
AND NOW I GET BY ON MY OWN, THROUGH FISHING.
ALL BY YOURSELF?
AT FIRST I WAS IN A FISHING COLLECTIVE, BUT...
...NO MATTER HOW MANY GOOD HAULS I BROUGHT IN, I COULDN'T GET A RAISE...
...EVEN THOUGH I'D BEEN CONTRACTED TO WORK ON COMMISSION.
THEY SAID I OUGHT TO BE GRATEFUL THEY EVEN LET A KID LIKE ME INTO THE COLLECTIVE IN THE FIRST PLACE.
SO I STRUCK OUT ON MY OWN, AND NOW I WORK ALONE.
PEOPLE MUST NOT APPROVE OF MY INDEPENDENT ATTITUDE... BECAUSE SOMETIMES I GET HARASSED FOR IT.
IT'S ALMOST FUNNY.
EVEN THOUGH I KNOW I'M DOING THE RIGHT THING...
...BECAUSE OF MY STATUS, I JUST CAN'T CATCH A BREAK.

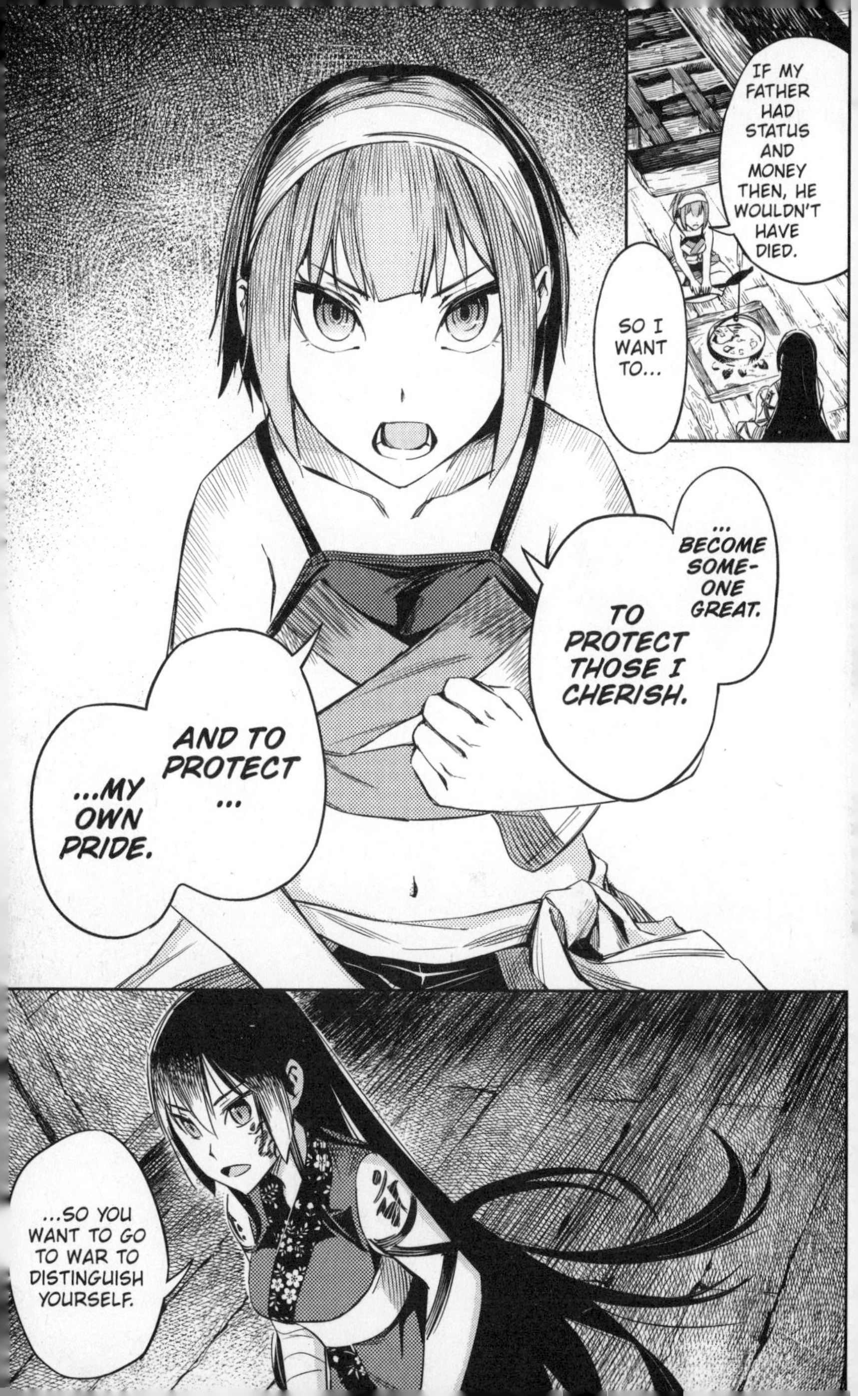
IF MY FATHER HAD STATUS AND MONEY THEN, HE WOULDN'T HAVE DIED.
SO I WANT TO...
... BECOME SOME-ONE GREAT.
TO PROTECT THOSE I CHERISH.
AND TO PROTECT ...
...MY OWN PRIDE.
...SO YOU WANT TO GO TO WAR TO DISTINGUISH YOURSELF.

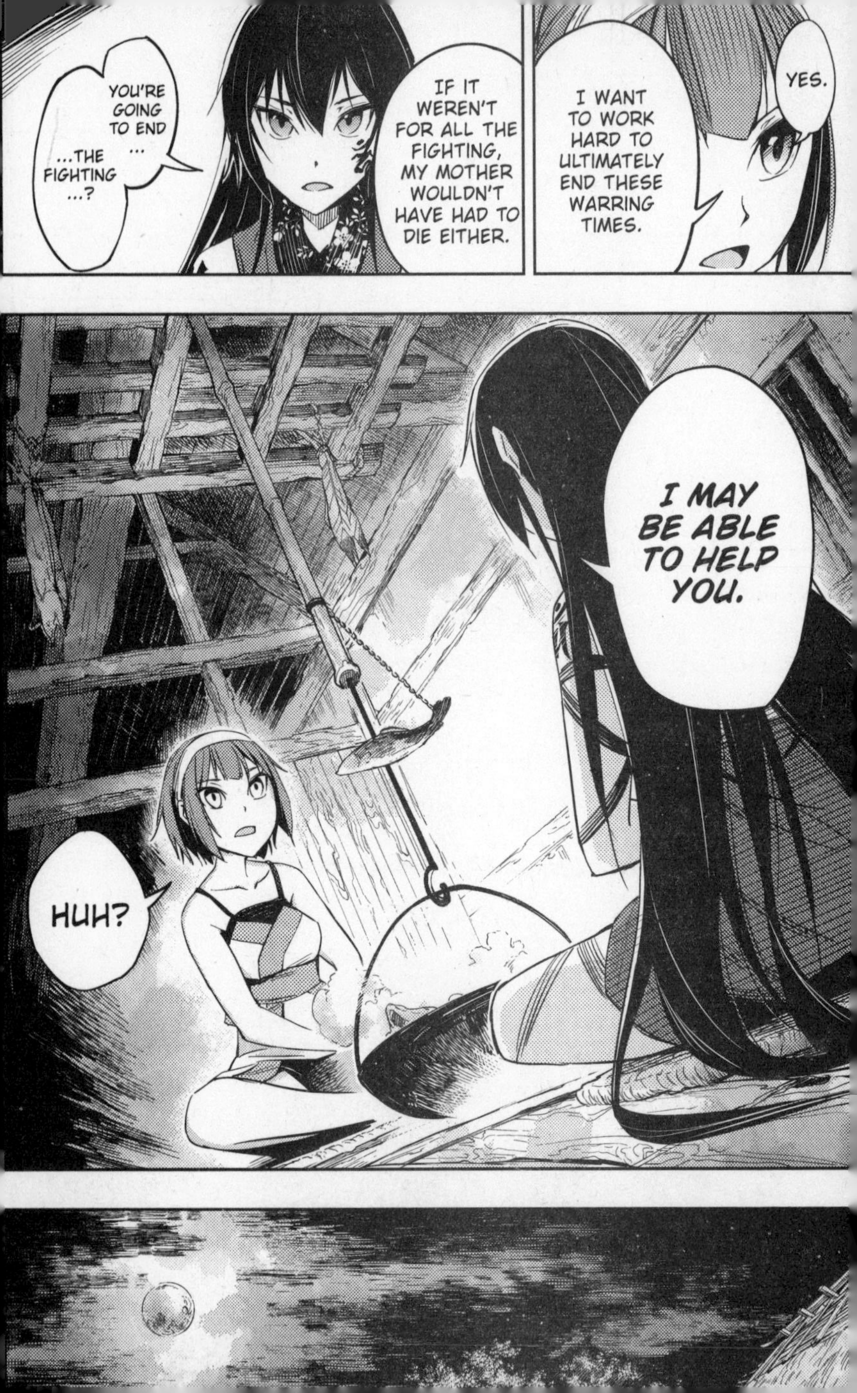
YES.
I WANT TO WORK HARD TO ULTIMATELY END THESE WARRING TIMES.
IF IT WEREN'T FOR ALL THE FIGHTING, MY MOTHER WOULDN'T HAVE HAD TO DIE EITHER.
YOU'RE GOING TO END ... ...THE FIGHTING ...?
I MAY BE ABLE TO HELP YOU.
HUH?

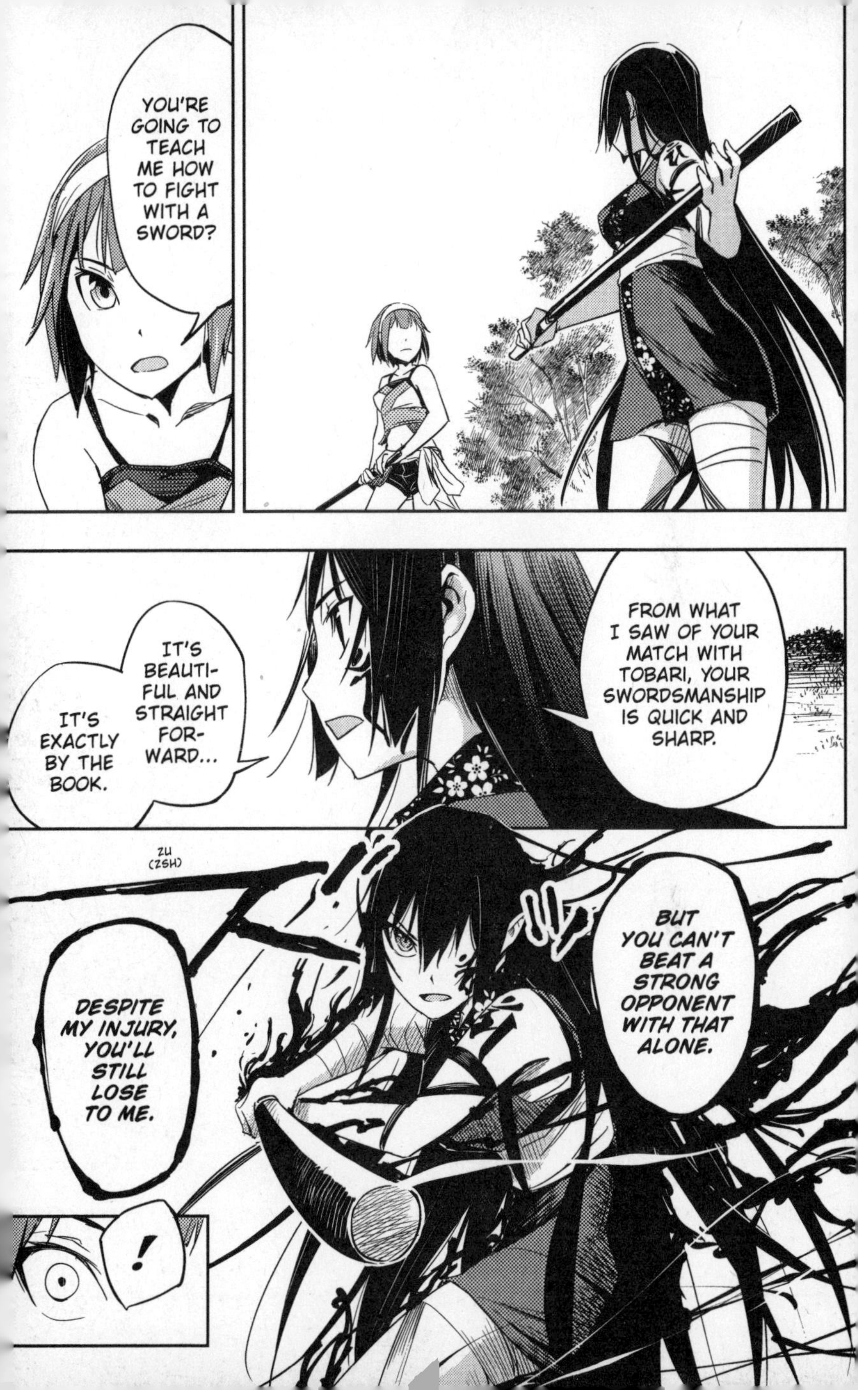
YOU'RE GOING TO TEACH ME HOW TO FIGHT WITH A SWORD?
FROM WHAT I SAW OF YOUR MATCH WITH TOBARI, YOUR SWORDSMANSHIP IS QUICK AND SHARP.
IT'S BEAUTI-FUL AND STRAIGHT FOR-WARD...
IT'S EXACTLY BY THE BOOK.
BUT YOU CAN'T BEAT A STRONG OPPONENT WITH THAT ALONE.
ZU (ZSH)
DESPITE MY INJURY, YOU'LL STILL LOSE TO ME.
!

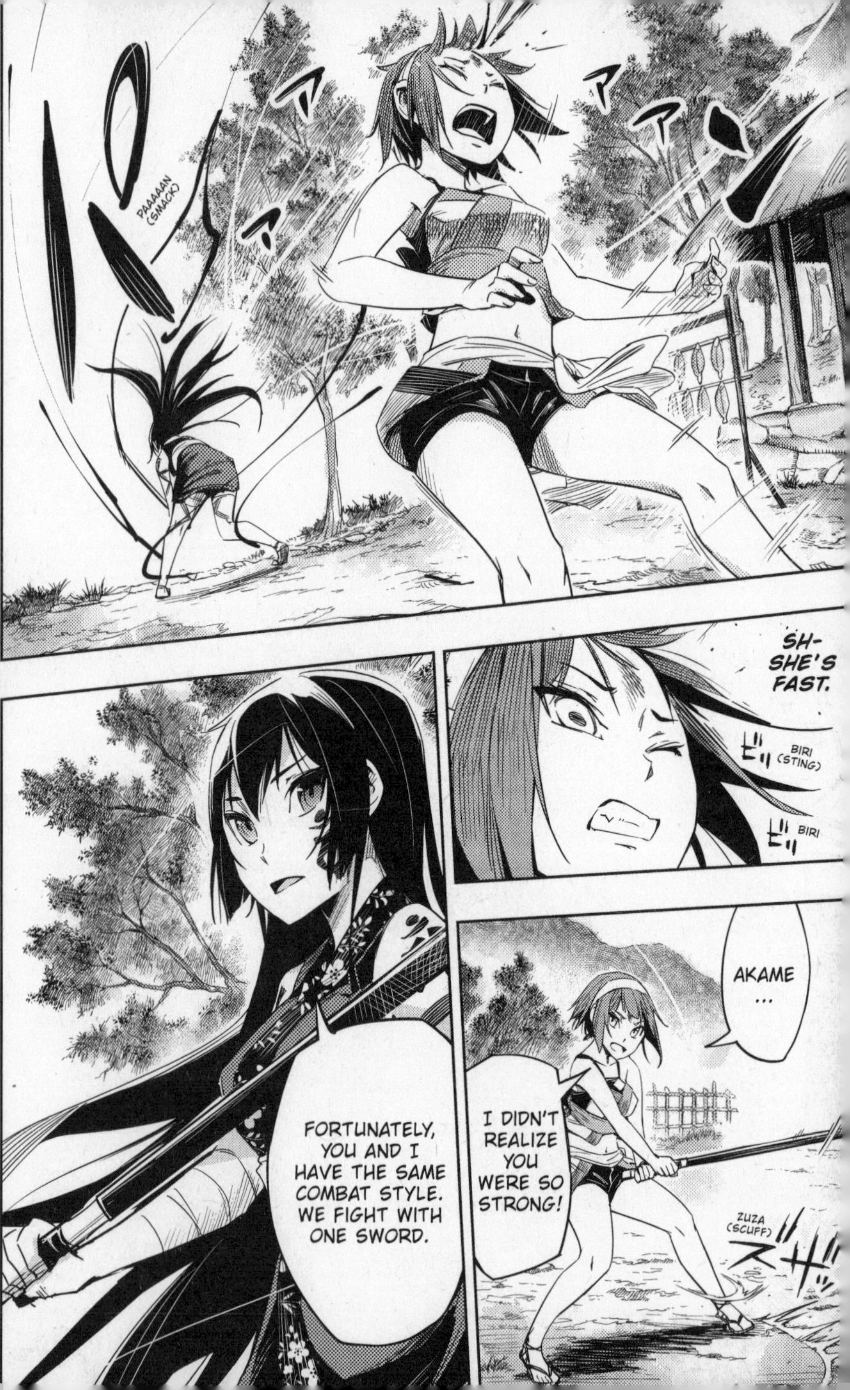
PAAAAAN (SMACK)
SH- SHE'S FAST.
BIRI (STING)
BIRI
AKAME ...
I DIDN'T REALIZE YOU WERE SO STRONG!
ZUZA (SCUFF)
FORTUNATELY, YOU AND I HAVE THE SAME COMBAT STYLE. WE FIGHT WITH ONE SWORD.

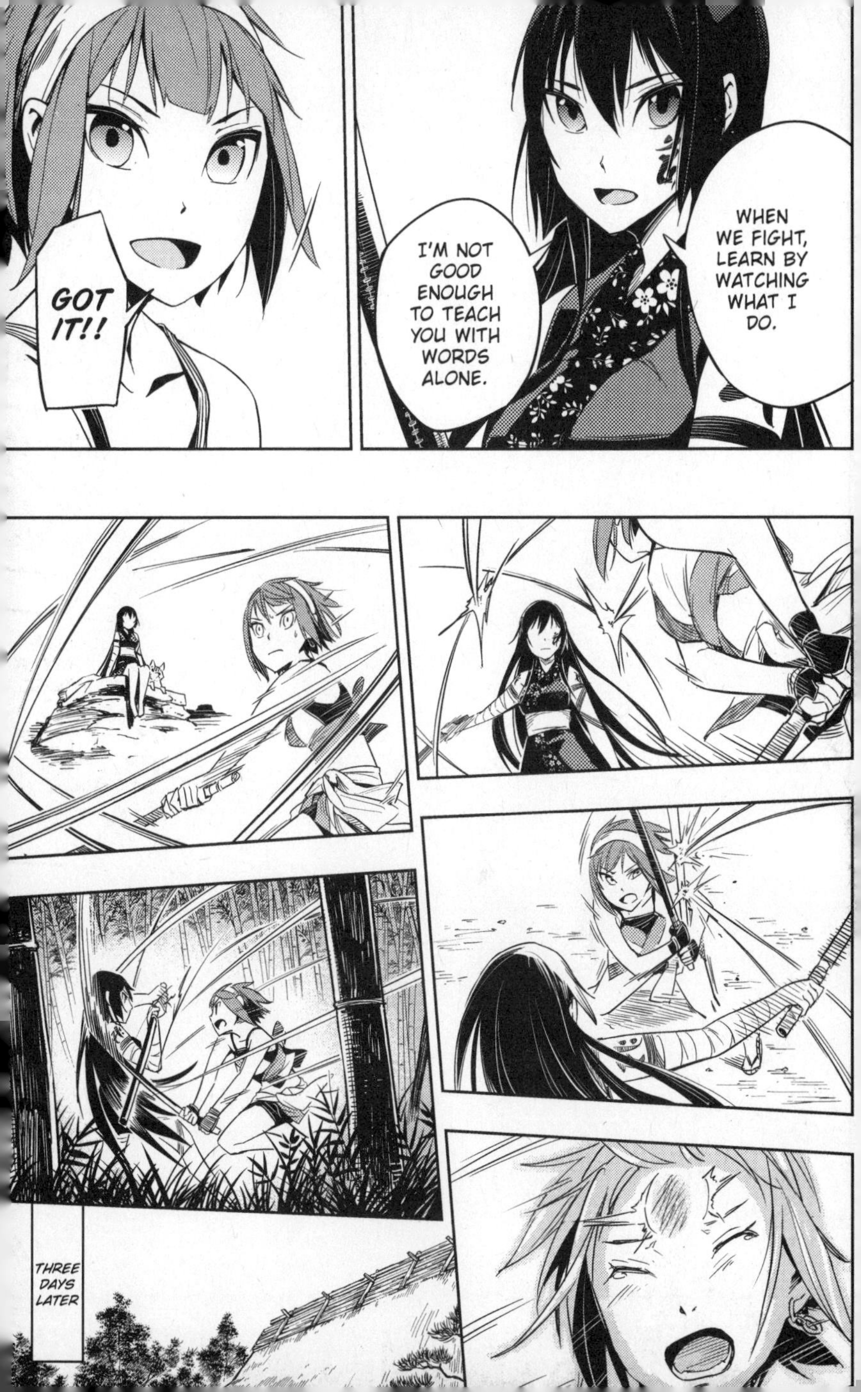
WHEN WE FIGHT, LEARN BY WATCHING WHAT I DO.
I'M NOT GOOD ENOUGH TO TEACH YOU WITH WORDS ALONE.
GOT IT!!
THREE DAYS LATER

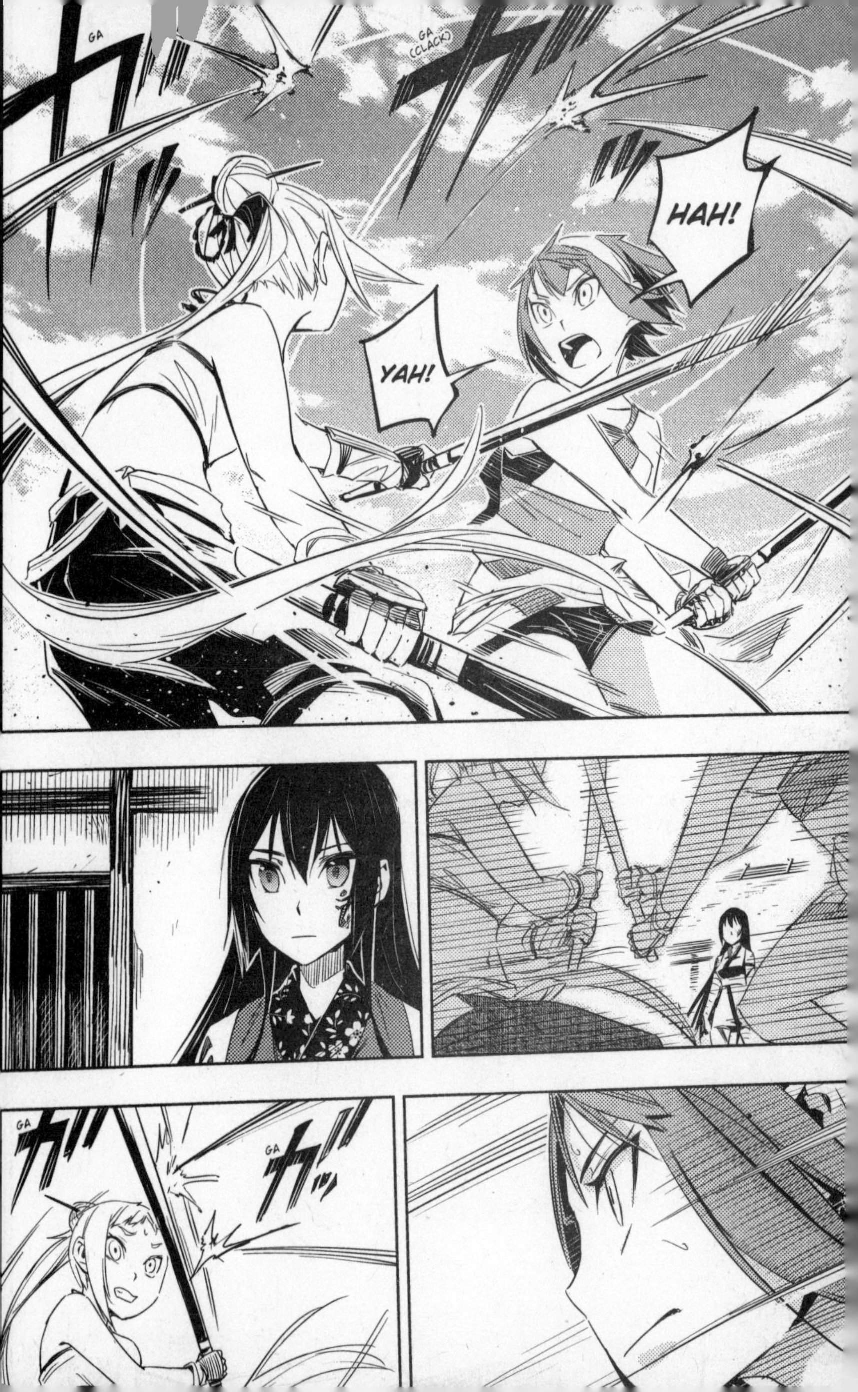
GA (CLACK)
GA
HAH!
YAH!
GA
GA

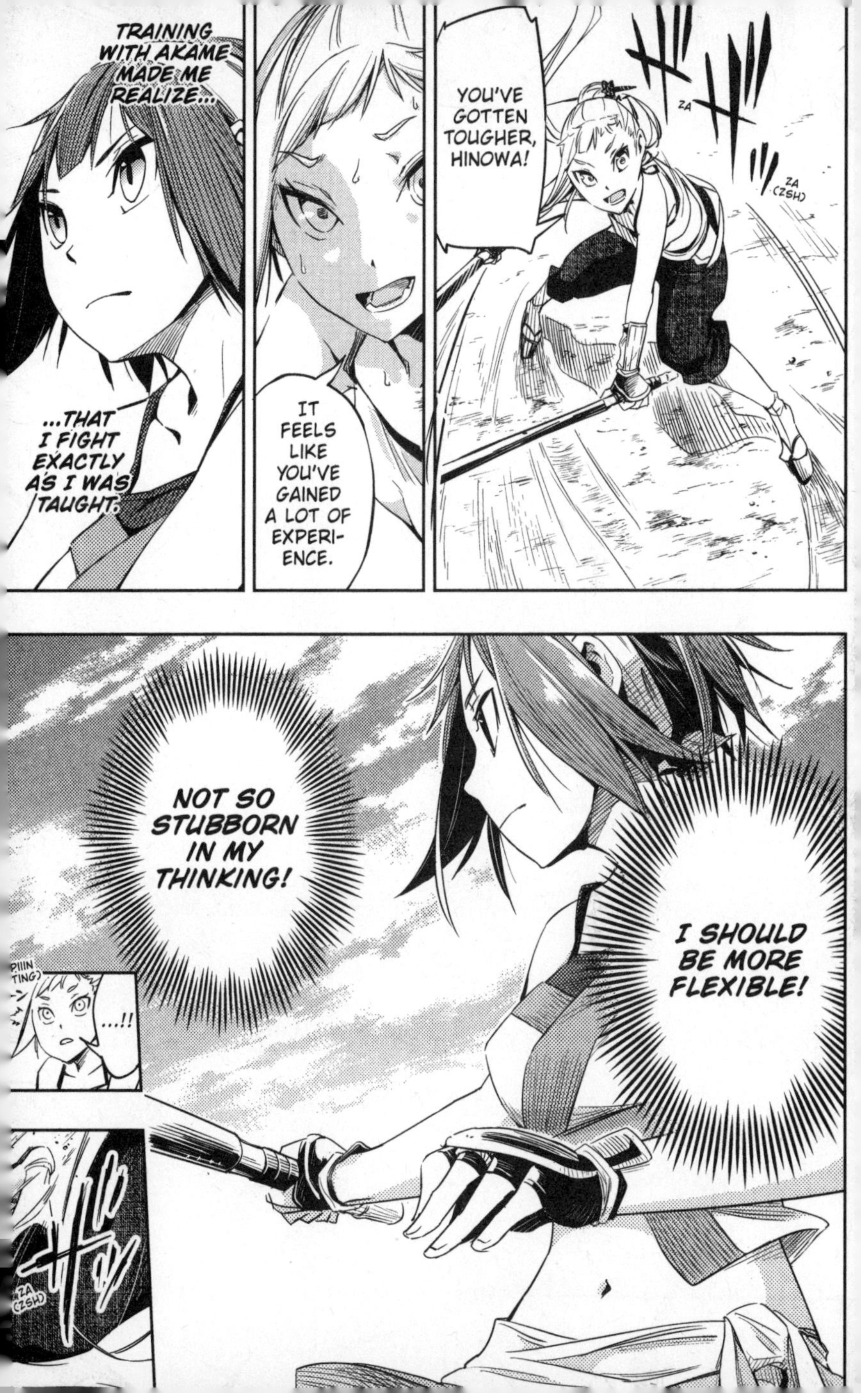
ZA
ZA (ZSH)
YOU'VE GOTTEN TOUGHER, HINOWA!
IT FEELS LIKE YOU'VE GAINED A LOT OF EXPERI-ENCE.
TRAINING WITH AKAME MADE ME REALIZE...
...THAT I FIGHT EXACTLY AS I WAS TAUGHT.
I SHOULD BE MORE FLEXIBLE!
NOT SO STUBBORN IN MY THINKING!
PIIIN (TING)
...!!
ZA (ZSH)

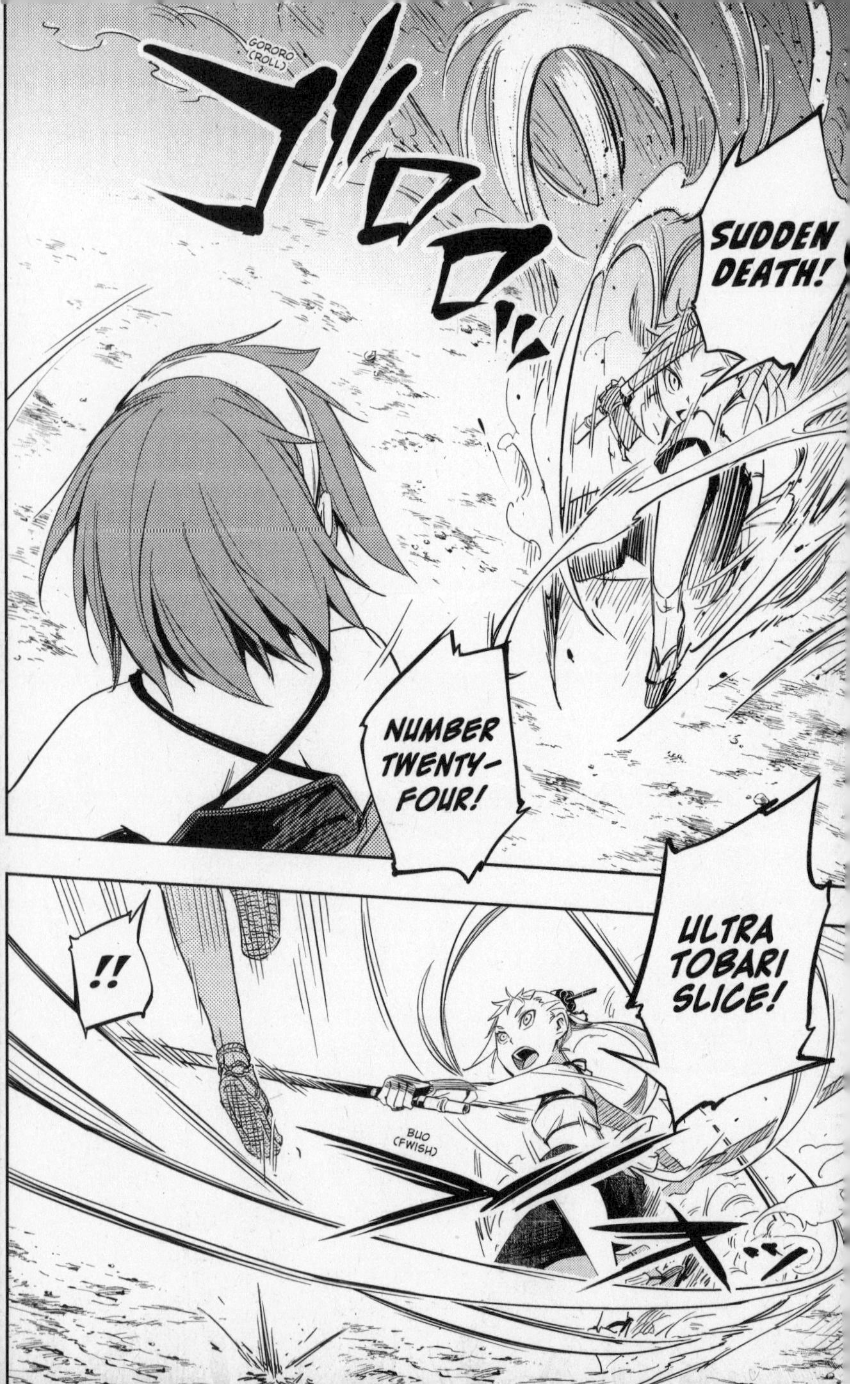
SUDDEN DEATH!
GORORO (ROLL)
NUMBER TWENTY-FOUR!
ULTRA TOBARI SLICE!
!!
BUO (FWISH)

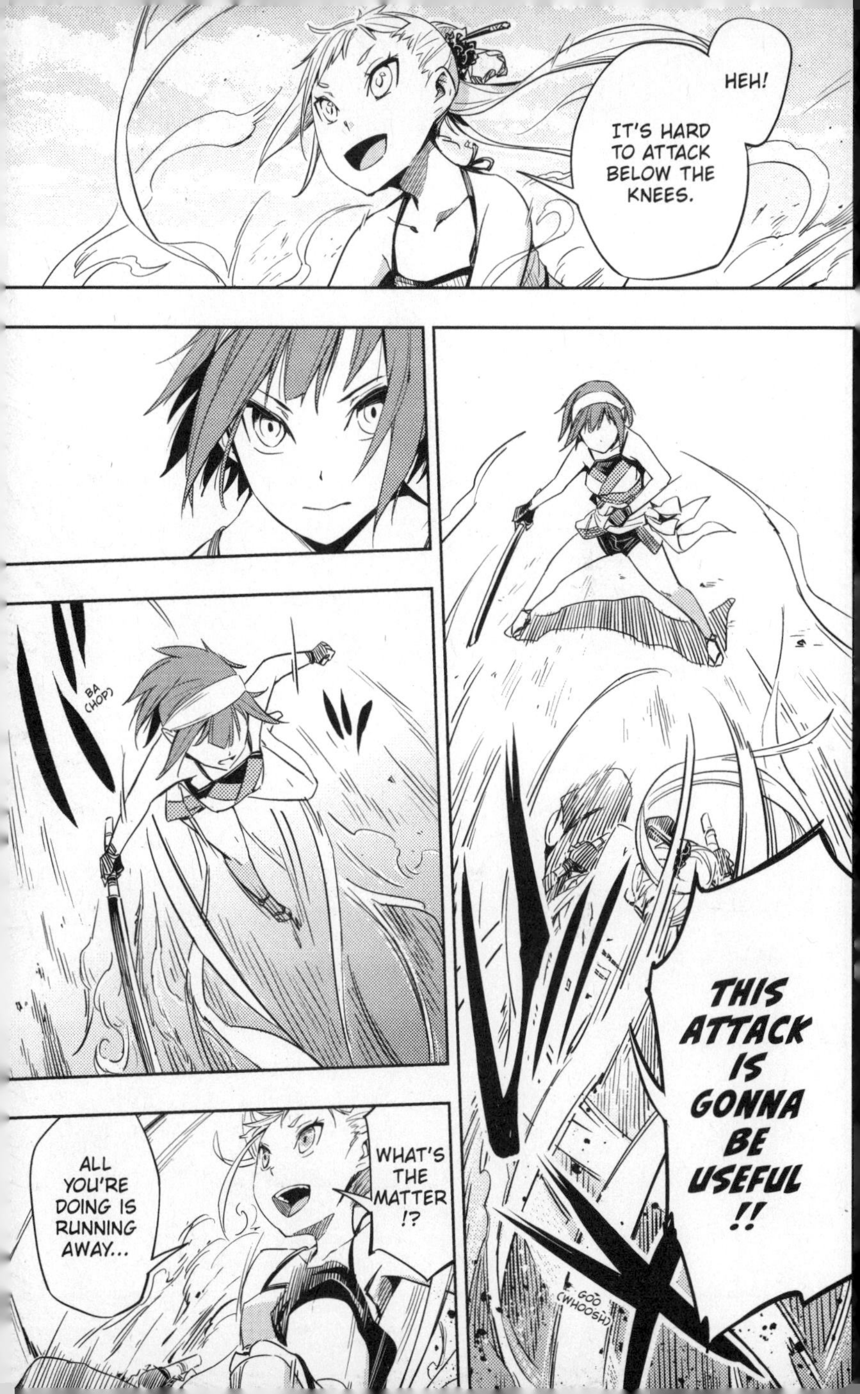
HEH!
IT'S HARD TO ATTACK BELOW THE KNEES.
THIS ATTACK IS GONNA BE USEFUL!!
GOO (WHOOSH)
BA (HOP)
WHAT'S THE MATTER!?
ALL YOU'RE DOING IS RUNNING AWAY...

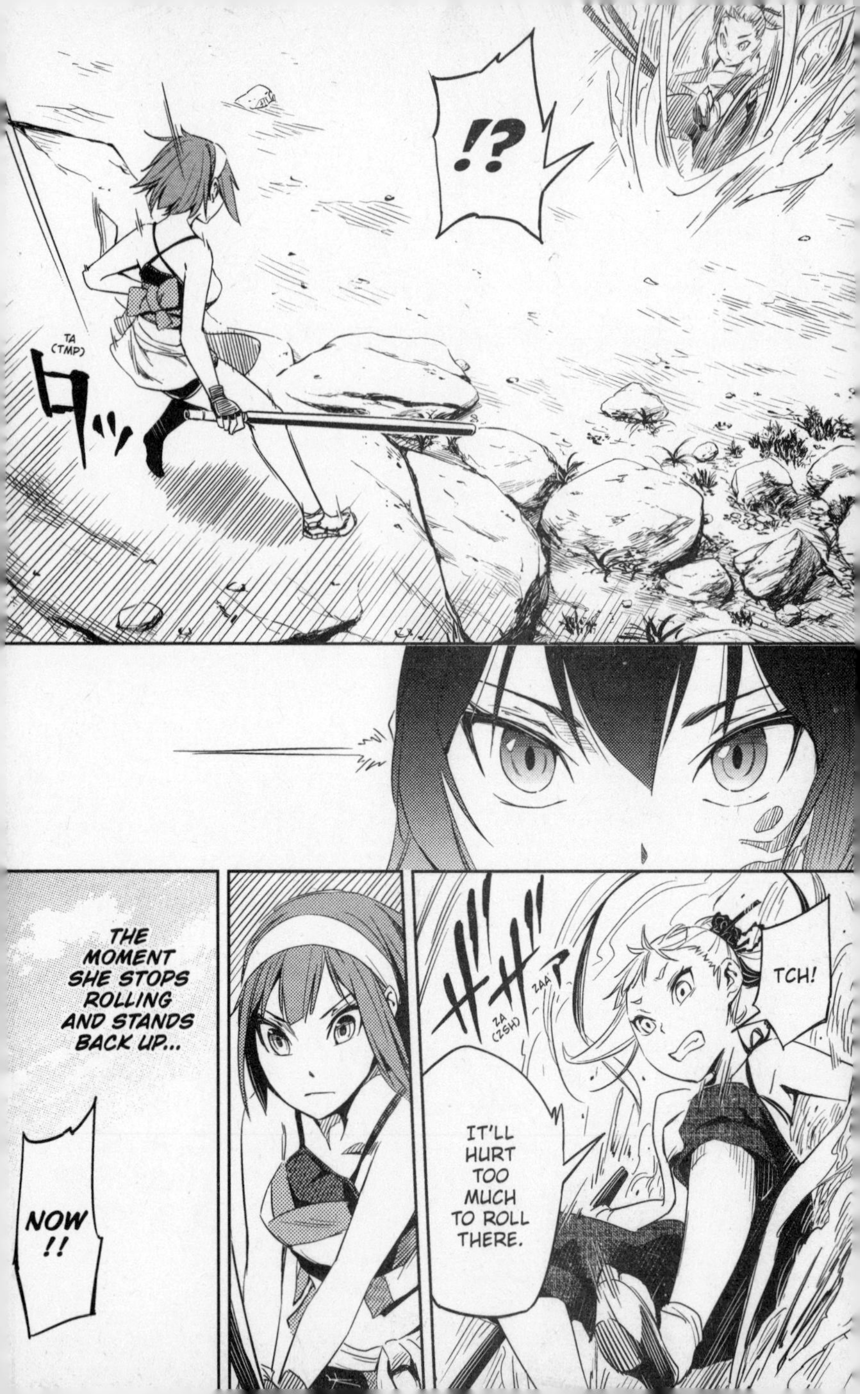
!?
TA (TMP)
TCH!
ZAA
ZA (ZSH)
IT'LL HURT TOO MUCH TO ROLL THERE.
THE MOMENT SHE STOPS ROLLING AND STANDS BACK UP...
NOW!!

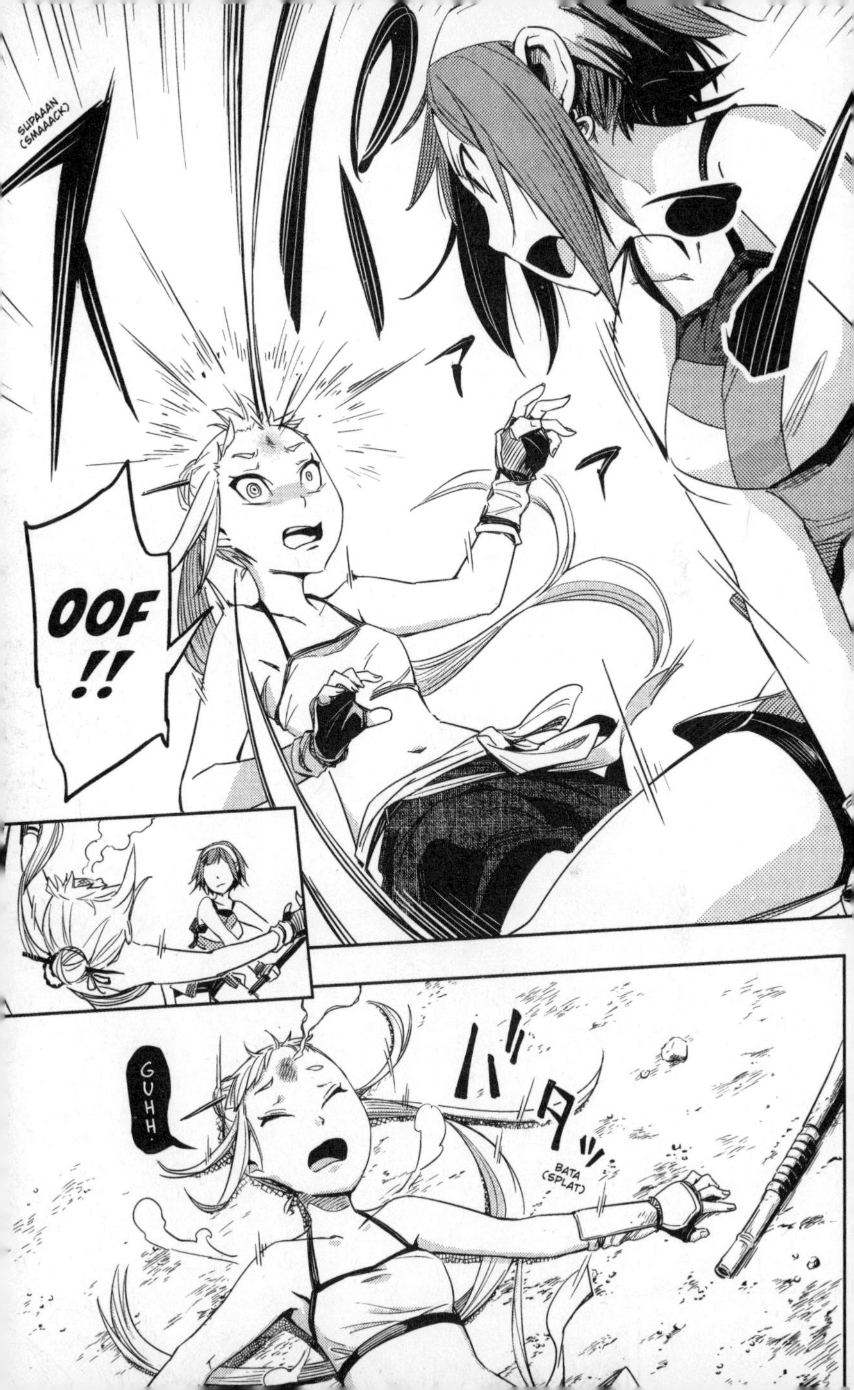
SUPAAAN (SMAAACK)
OOF!!
BATA (SPLAT)
GUHH.

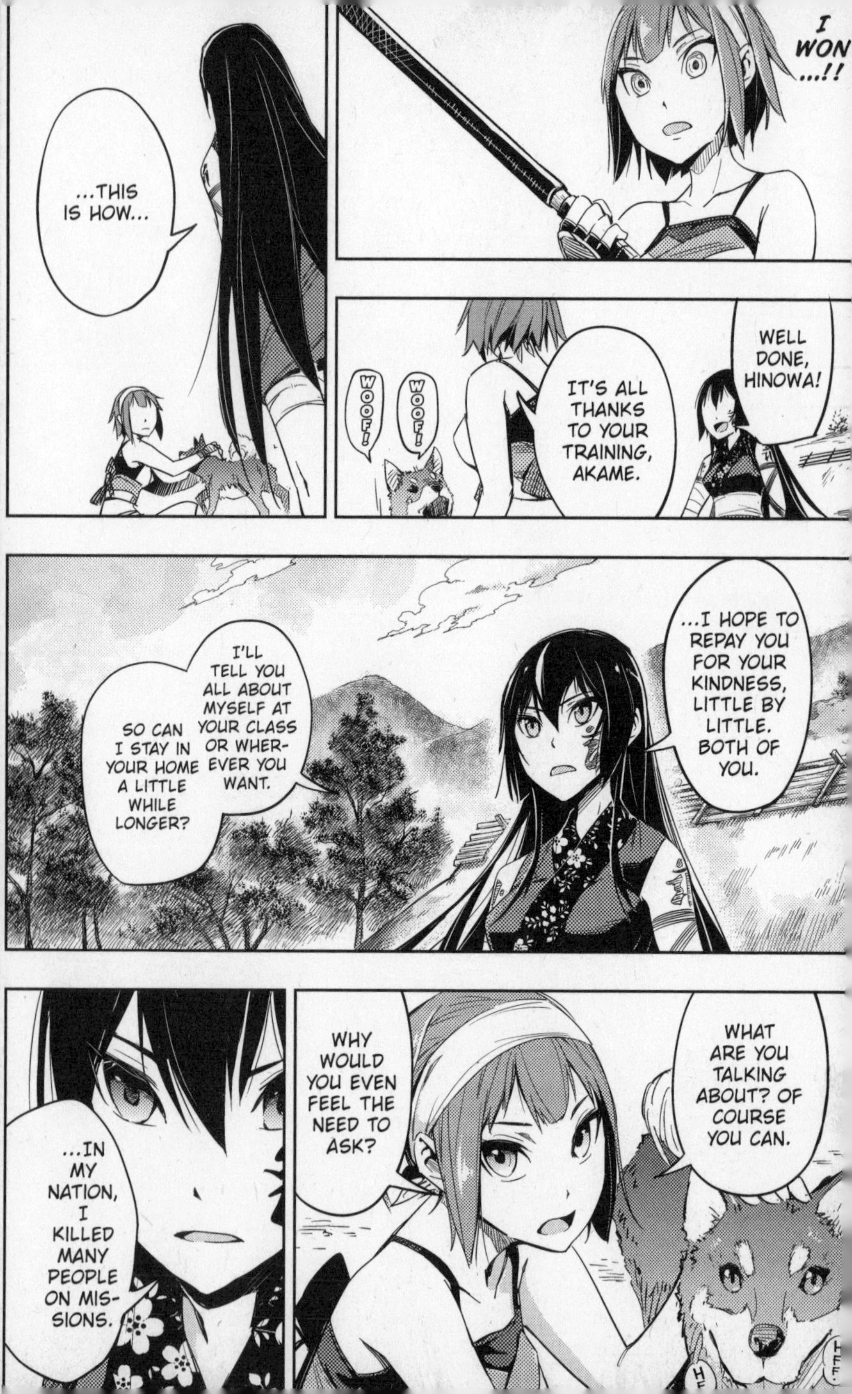
I WON ...!!
WELL DONE, HINOWA!
IT'S ALL THANKS TO YOUR TRAINING, AKAME.
WOOF!
WOOF!
...THIS IS HOW...
...I HOPE TO REPAY YOU FOR YOUR KINDNESS, LITTLE BY LITTLE. BOTH OF YOU.
I'LL TELL YOU ALL ABOUT MYSELF AT YOUR CLASS OR WHEREVER YOU WANT.
SO CAN I STAY IN YOUR HOME A LITTLE WHILE LONGER?
WHAT ARE YOU TALKING ABOUT? OF COURSE YOU CAN.
WHY WOULD YOU EVEN FEEL THE NEED TO ASK?
HFF
HF
...IN MY NATION, I KILLED MANY PEOPLE ON MISSIONS.

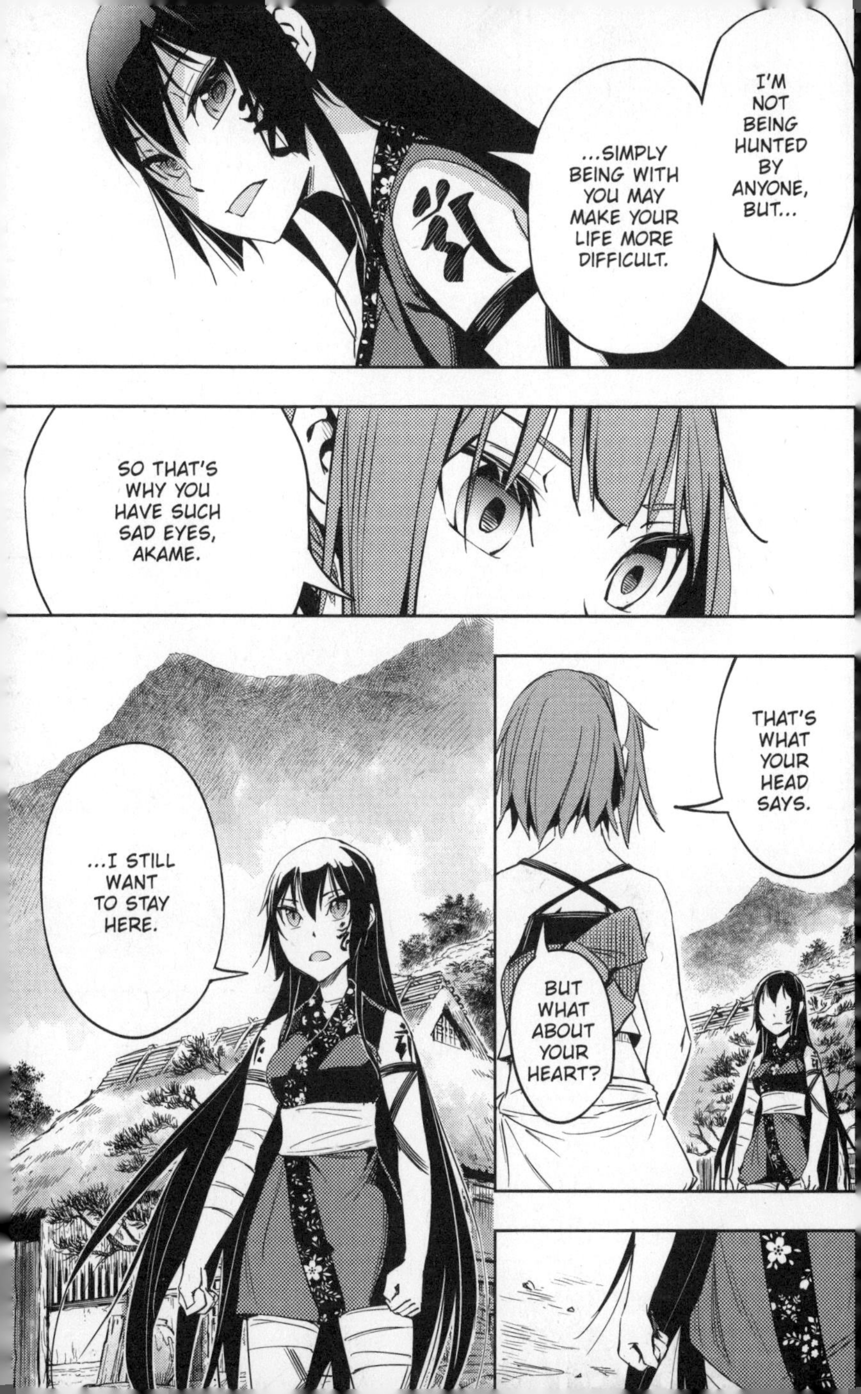
I'M NOT BEING HUNTED BY ANYONE, BUT...
...SIMPLY BEING WITH YOU MAY MAKE YOUR LIFE MORE DIFFICULT.
SO THAT'S WHY YOU HAVE SUCH SAD EYES, AKAME.
THAT'S WHAT YOUR HEAD SAYS.
BUT WHAT ABOUT YOUR HEART?
...I STILL WANT TO STAY HERE.

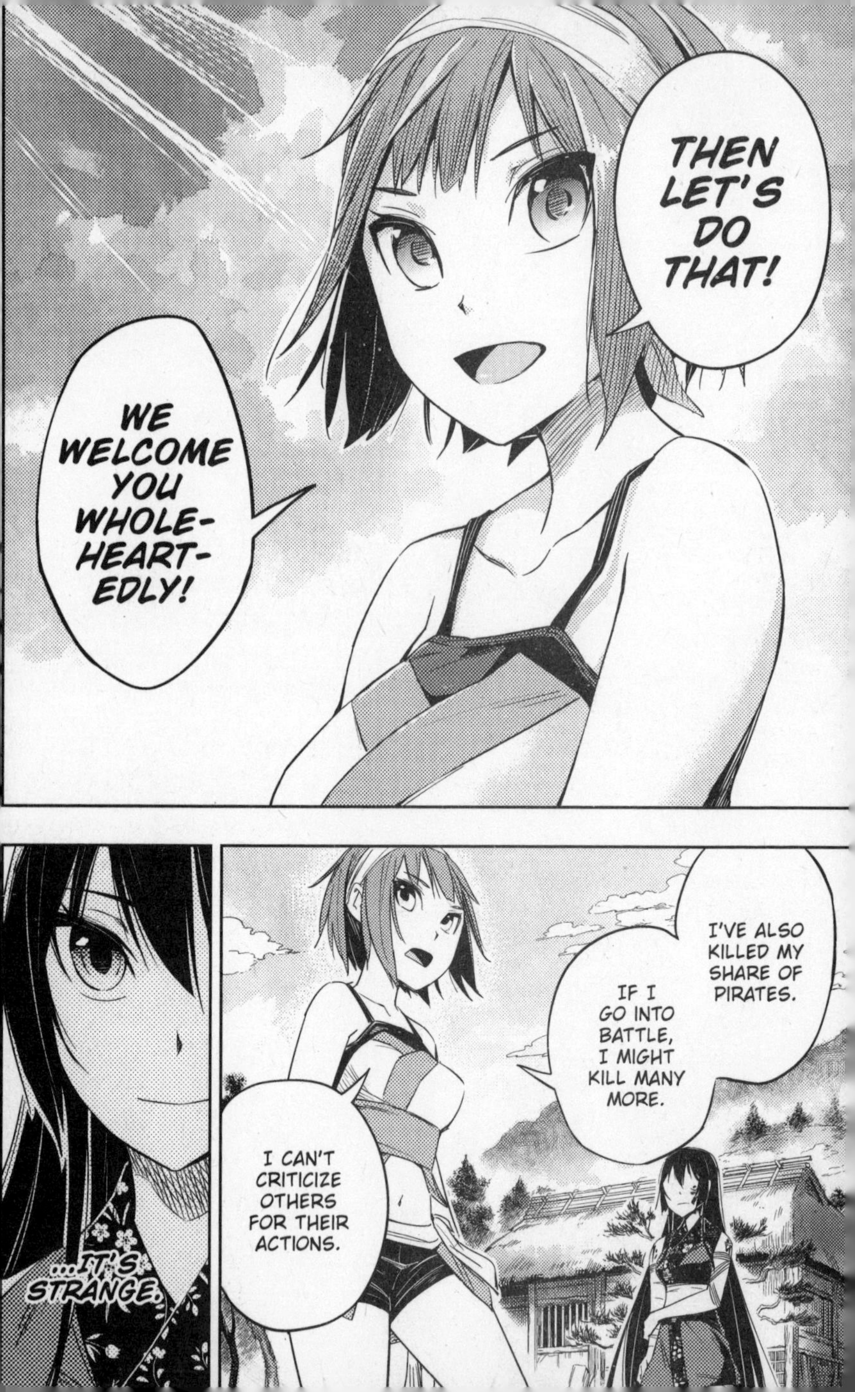
THEN LET'S DO THAT!
WE WELCOME YOU WHOLE-HEART-EDLY!
I'VE ALSO KILLED MY SHARE OF PIRATES.
IF I GO INTO BATTLE, I MIGHT KILL MANY MORE.
I CAN'T CRITICIZE OTHERS FOR THEIR ACTIONS.
...IT'S STRANGE.

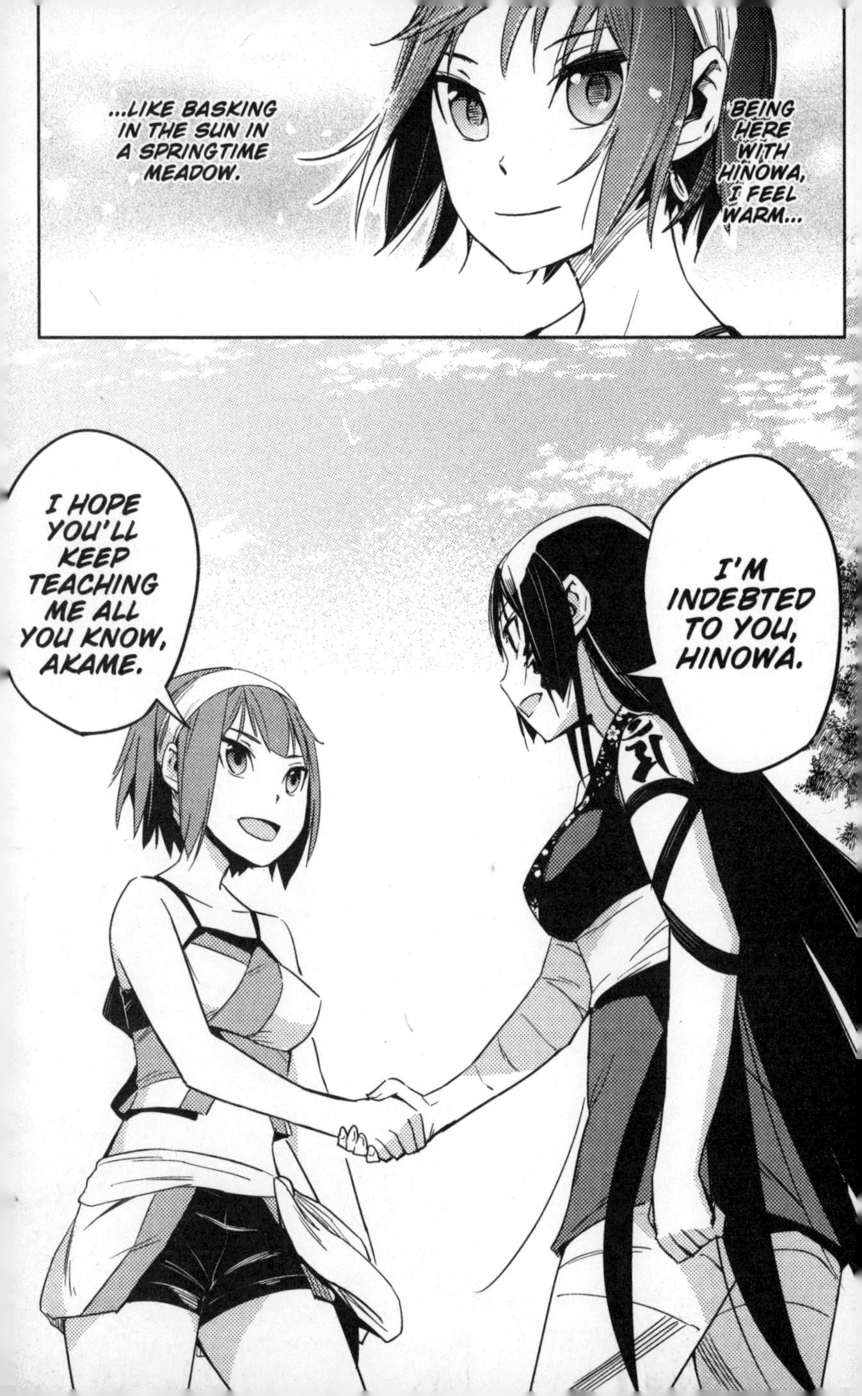
BEING HERE WITH HINOWA, I FEEL WARM...
...LIKE BASKING IN THE SUN IN A SPRINGTIME MEADOW.
I'M INDEBTED TO YOU, HINOWA.
I HOPE YOU'LL KEEP TEACHING ME ALL YOU KNOW, AKAME.

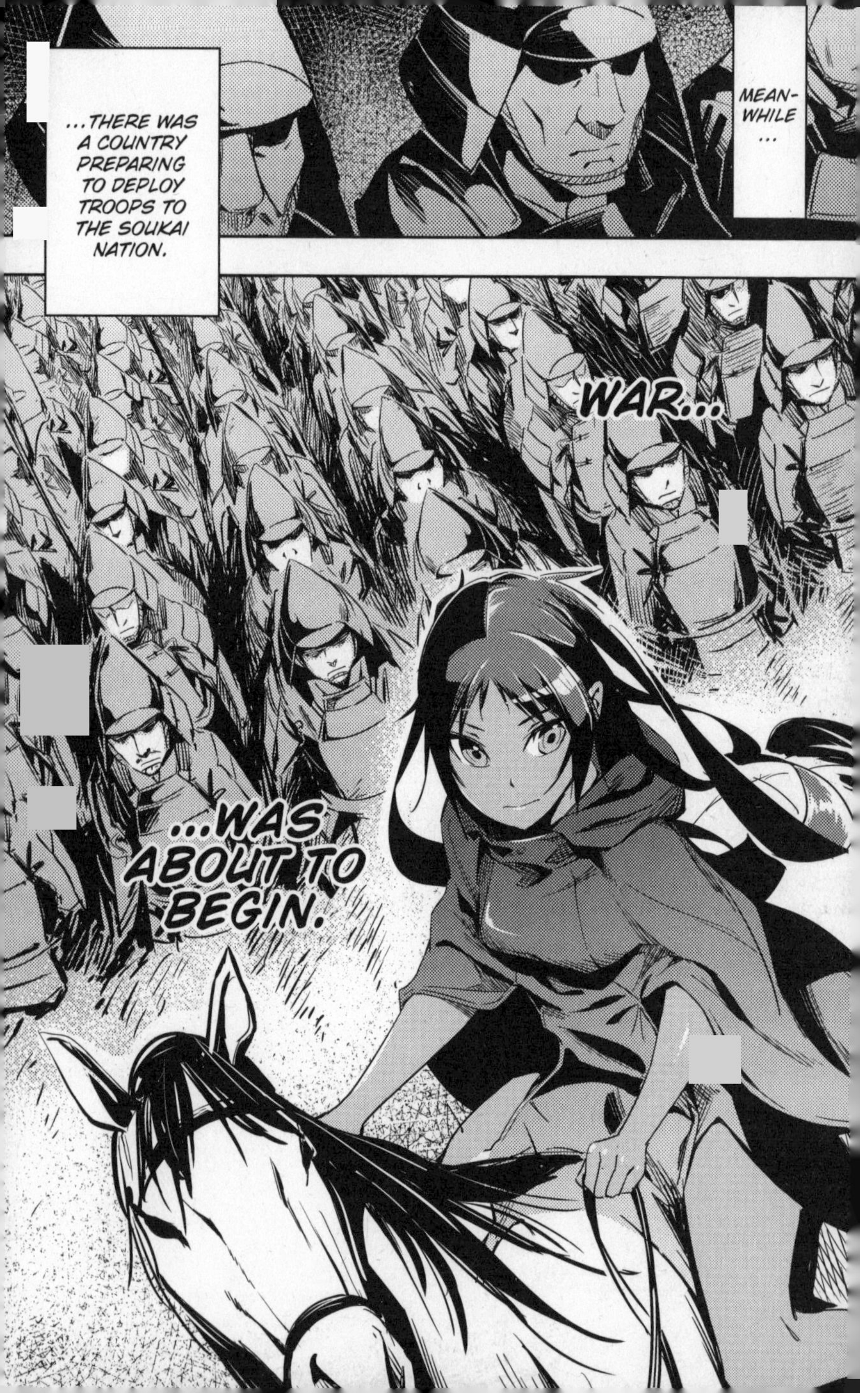
MEAN-WHILE ...
...THERE WAS A COUNTRY PREPARING TO DEPLOY TROOPS TO THE SOUKAI NATION.
WAR...
...WAS ABOUT TO BEGIN.

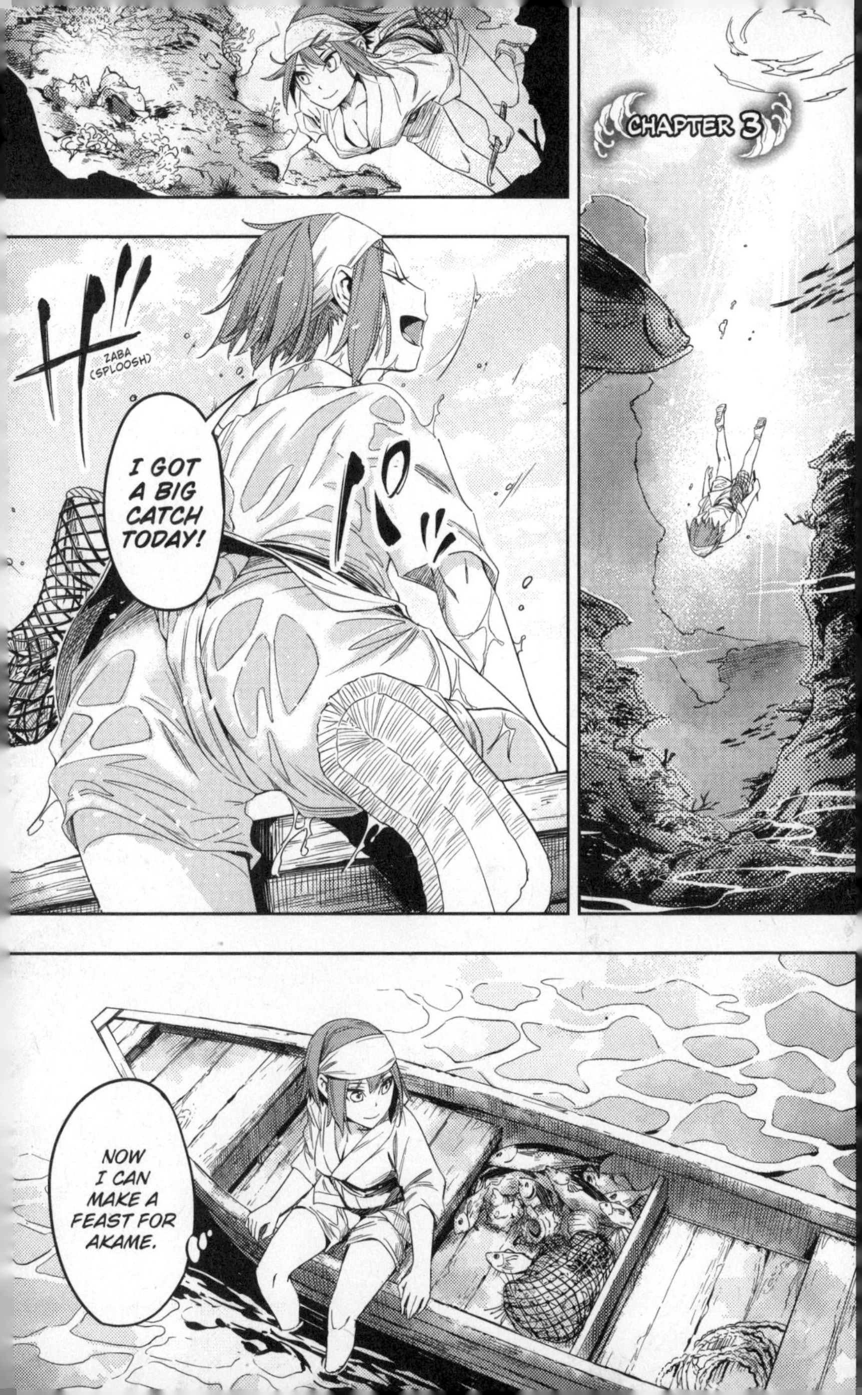
CHAPTER 3
ZABA (SPLOOSH)
I GOT A BIG CATCH TODAY!
NOW I CAN MAKE A FEAST FOR AKAME.

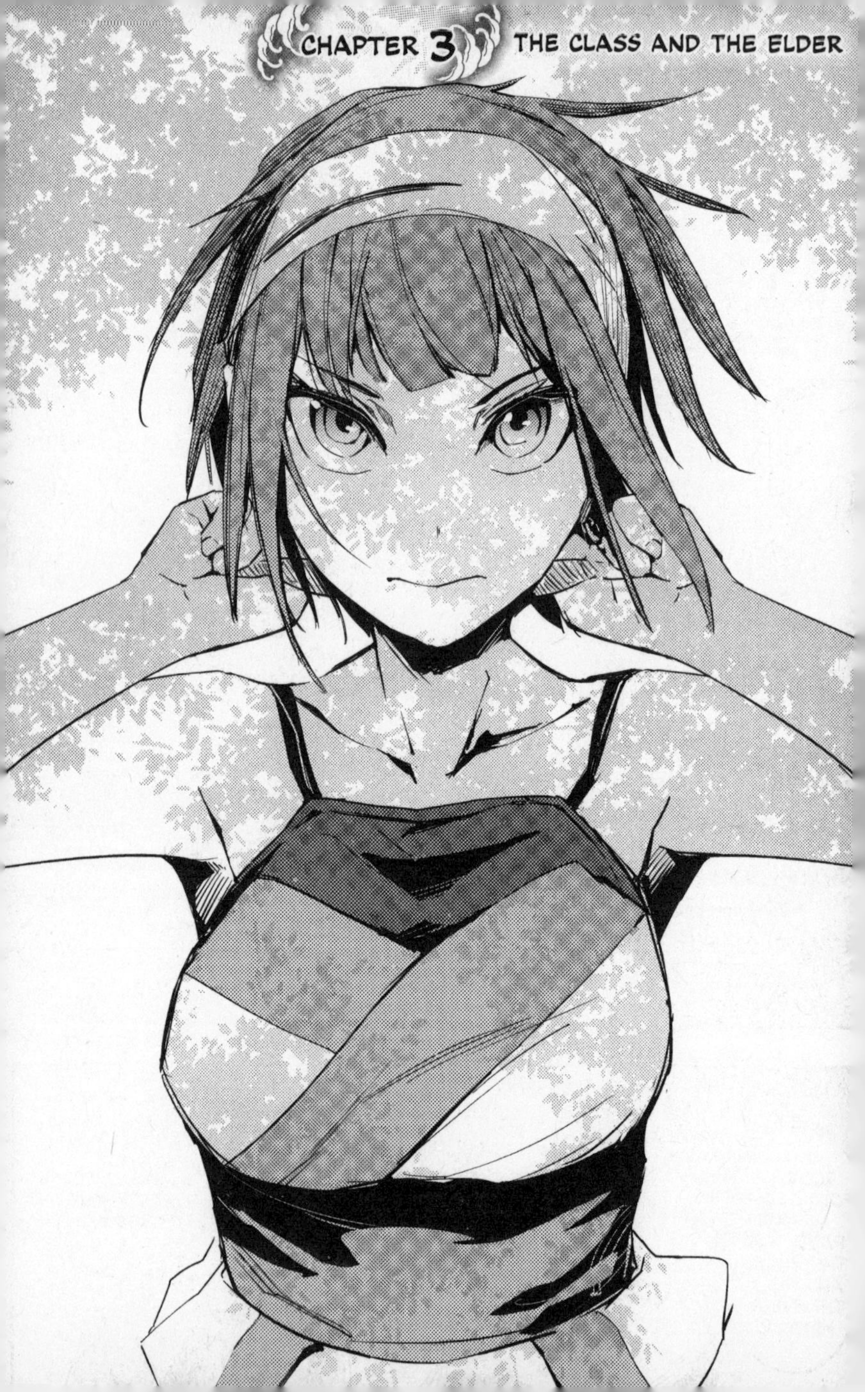
CHAPTER 3 THE CLASS AND THE ELDER

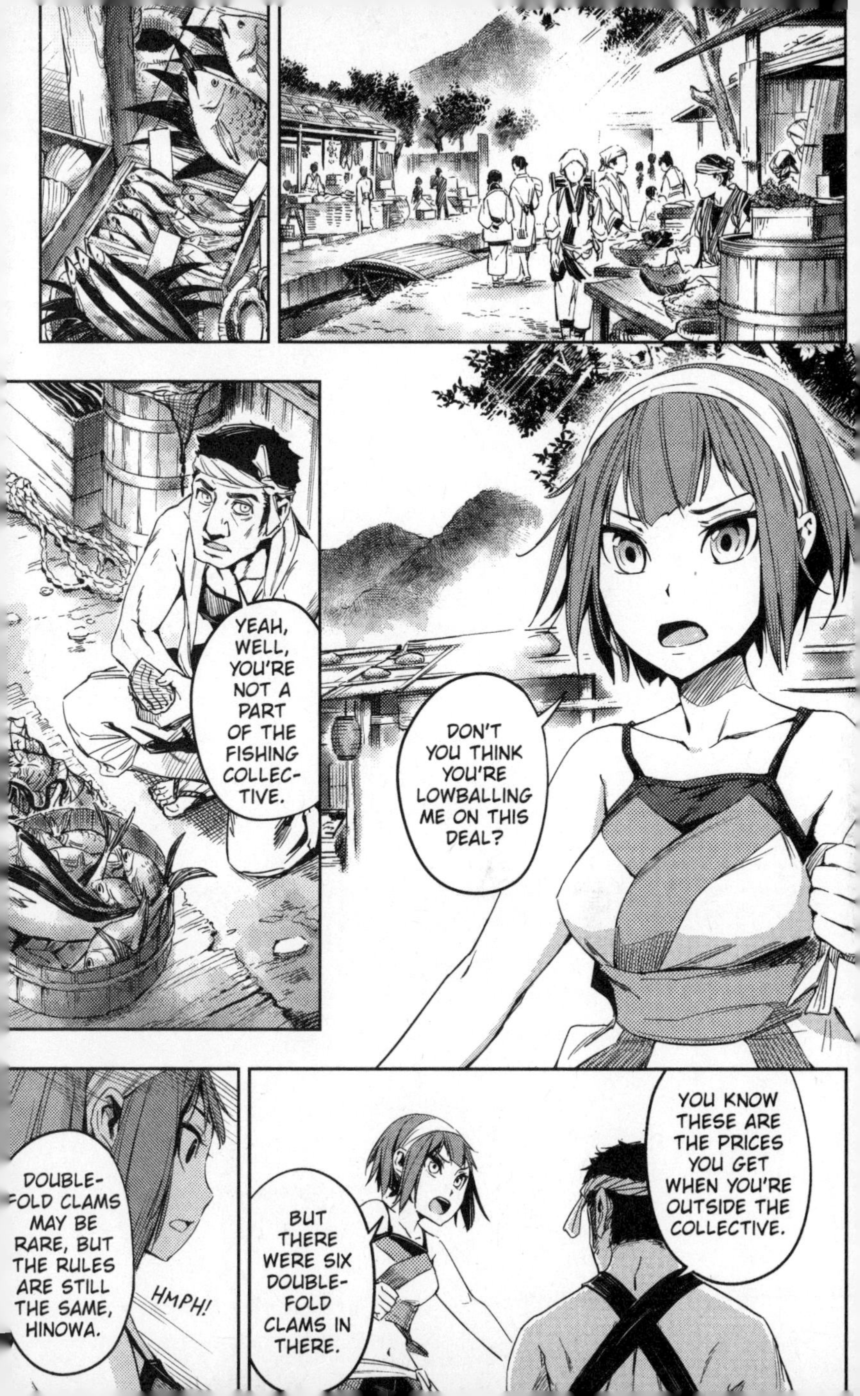
DON'T YOU THINK YOU'RE LOWBALLING ME ON THIS DEAL?
YEAH, WELL, YOU'RE NOT A PART OF THE FISHING COLLECTIVE.
YOU KNOW THESE ARE THE PRICES YOU GET WHEN YOU'RE OUTSIDE THE COLLECTIVE.
BUT THERE WERE SIX DOUBLE-FOLD CLAMS IN THERE.
DOUBLE-FOLD CLAMS MAY BE RARE, BUT THE RULES ARE STILL THE SAME, HINOWA.
HMPH!

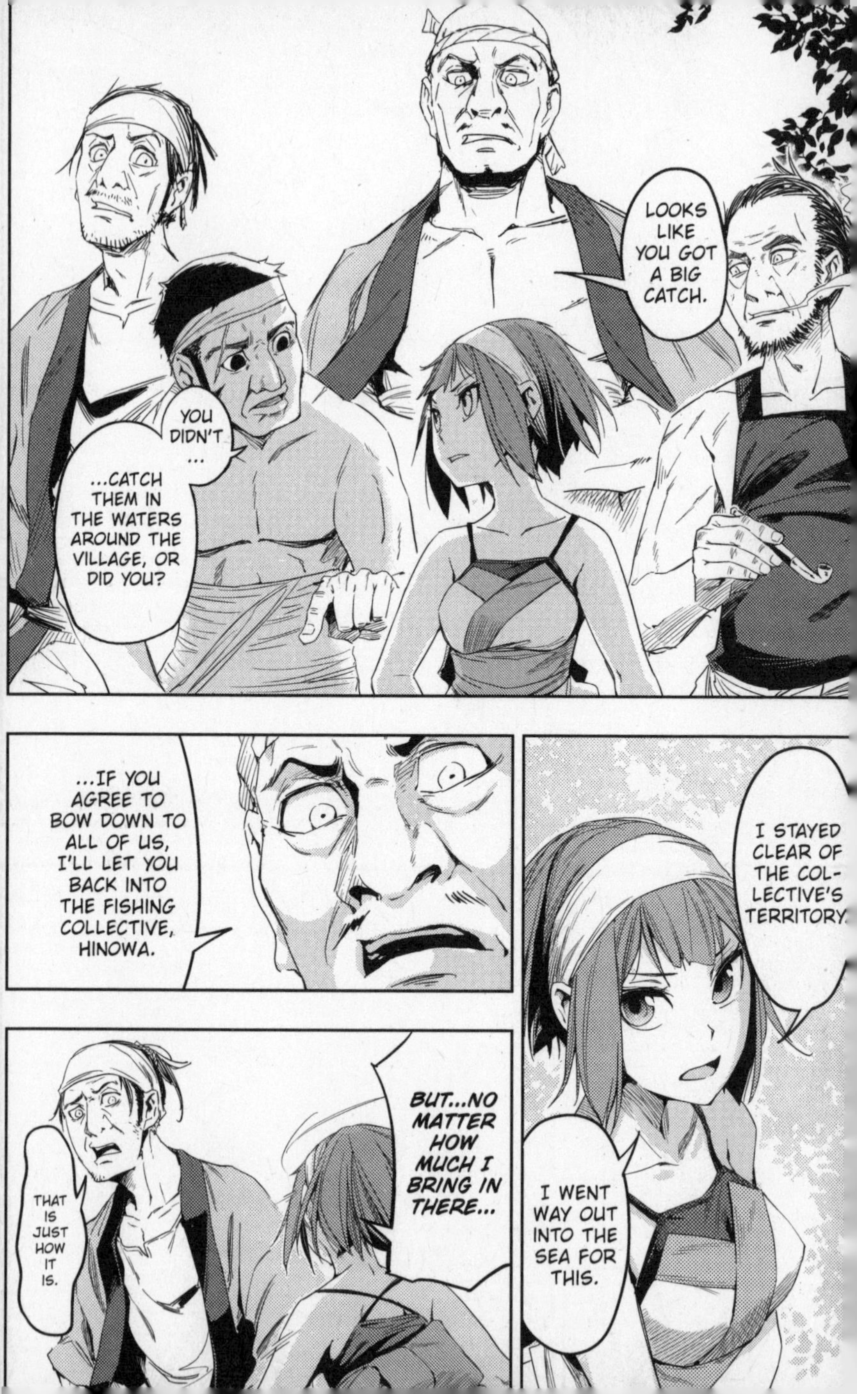
LOOKS LIKE YOU GOT A BIG CATCH.
YOU DIDN'T ...
...CATCH THEM IN THE WATERS AROUND THE VILLAGE, OR DID YOU?
I STAYED CLEAR OF THE COL-LECTIVE'S TERRITORY.
I WENT WAY OUT INTO THE SEA FOR THIS.
...IF YOU AGREE TO BOW DOWN TO ALL OF US, I'LL LET YOU BACK INTO THE FISHING COLLECTIVE, HINOWA.
BUT...NO MATTER HOW MUCH I BRING IN THERE...
THAT IS JUST HOW IT IS.

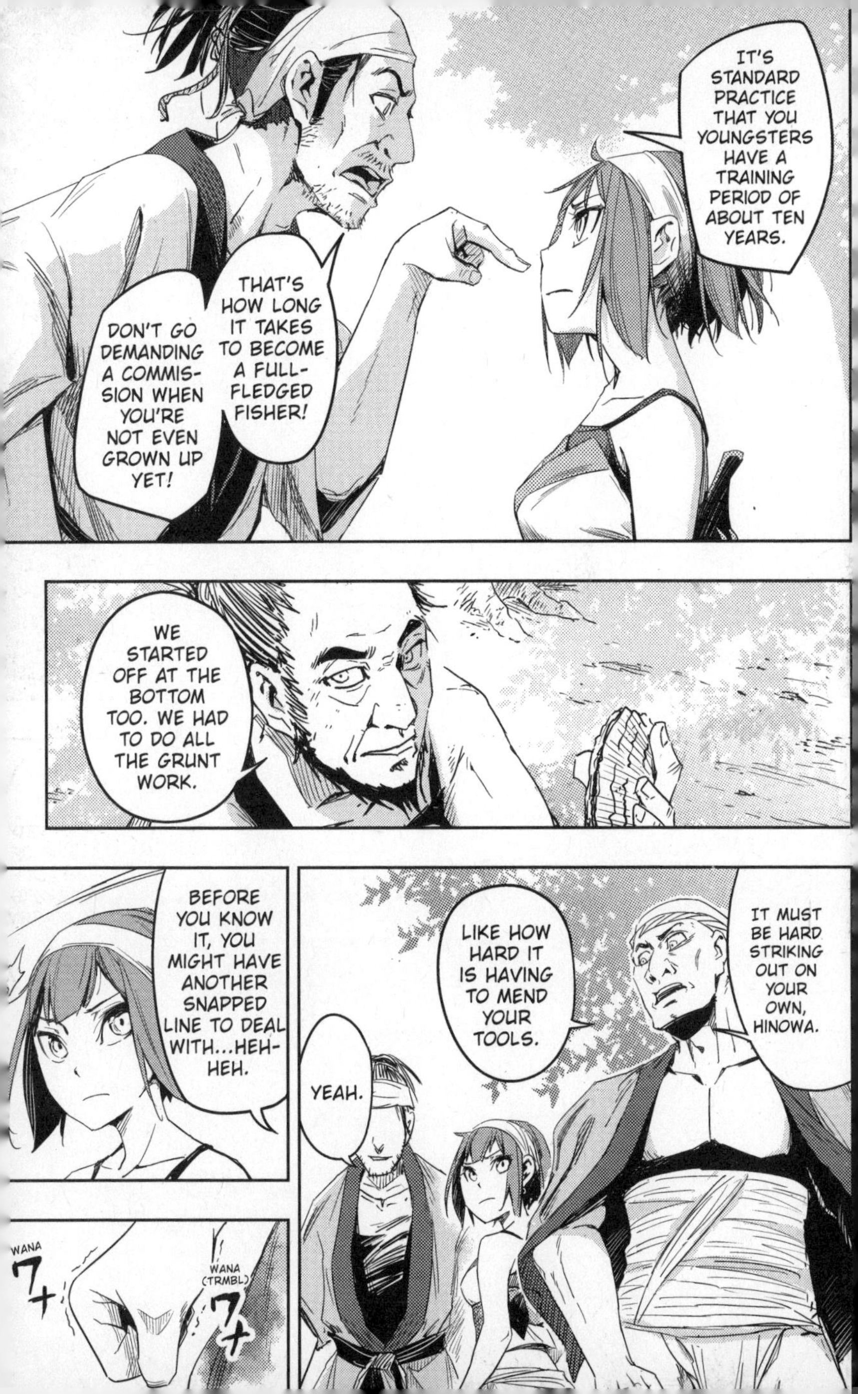
IT'S STANDARD PRACTICE THAT YOU YOUNGSTERS HAVE A TRAINING PERIOD OF ABOUT TEN YEARS.
THAT'S HOW LONG IT TAKES TO BECOME A FULL-FLEDGED FISHER!
DON'T GO DEMANDING A COMMISSION WHEN YOU'RE NOT EVEN GROWN UP YET!
WE STARTED OFF AT THE BOTTOM TOO. WE HAD TO DO ALL THE GRUNT WORK.
IT MUST BE HARD STRIKING OUT ON YOUR OWN, HINOWA.
LIKE HOW HARD IT IS HAVING TO MEND YOUR TOOLS.
YEAH.
BEFORE YOU KNOW IT, YOU MIGHT HAVE ANOTHER SNAPPED LINE TO DEAL WITH...HEH-HEH.
WANA (TRMBL) ワナ
WANA ワナ

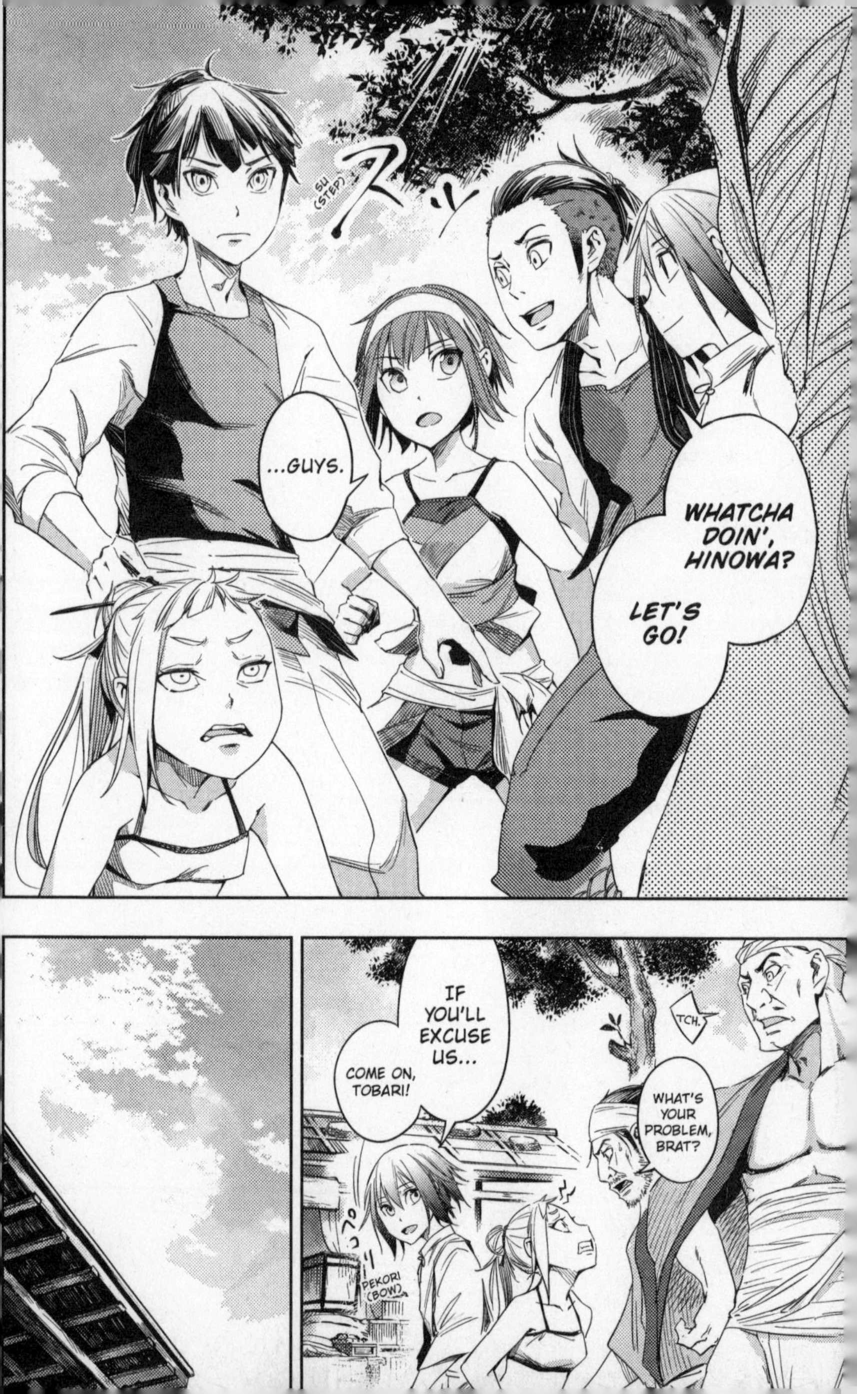
SU (STEP)
WHATCHA DOIN', HINOWA?
LET'S GO!
...GUYS.
TCH.
IF YOU'LL EXCUSE US...
WHAT'S YOUR PROBLEM, BRAT?
COME ON, TOBARI!
PEKORI (BOW)

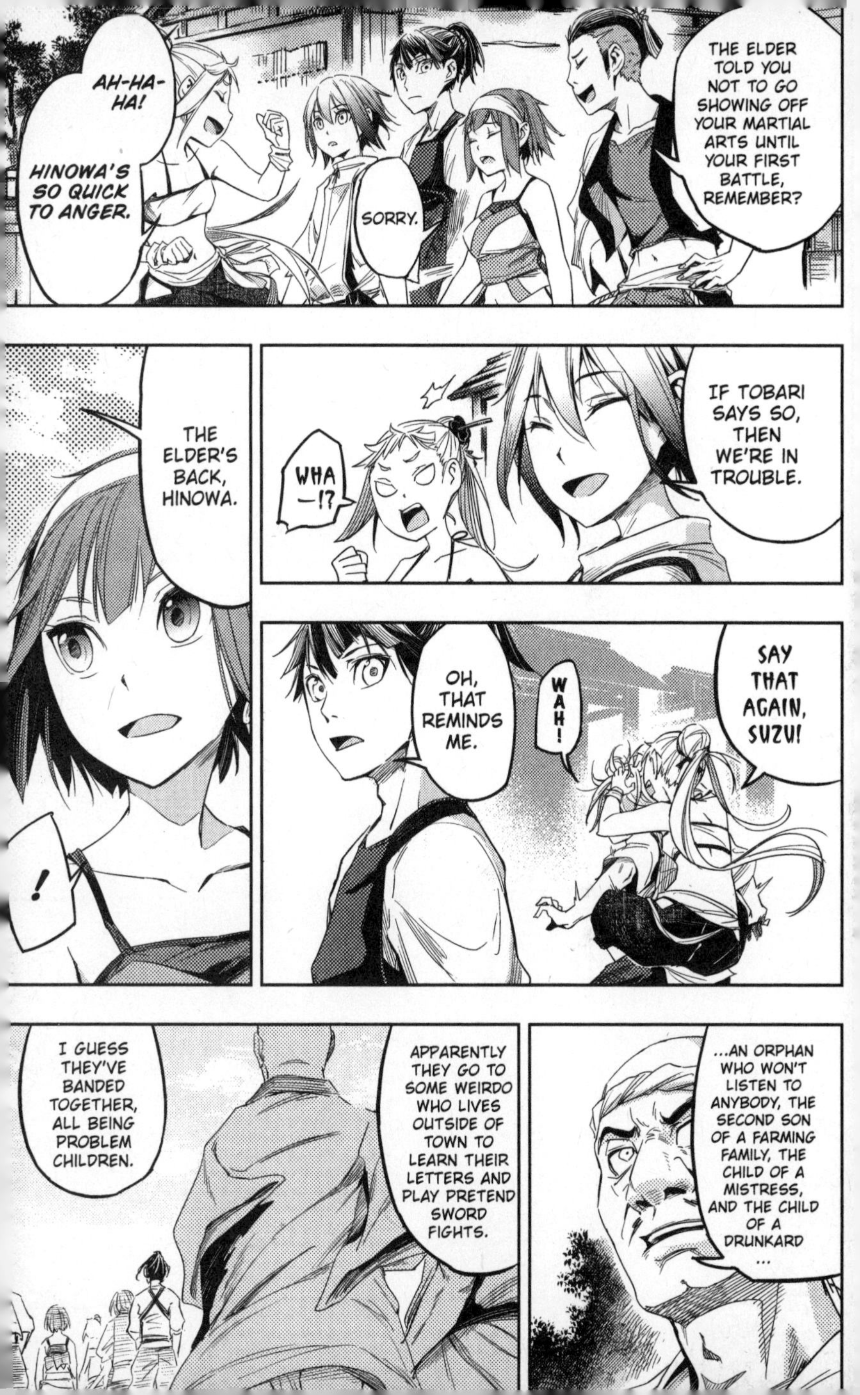
THE ELDER TOLD YOU NOT TO GO SHOWING OFF YOUR MARTIAL ARTS UNTIL YOUR FIRST BATTLE, REMEMBER?
SORRY.
AH-HA-HA! HINOWA'S SO QUICK TO ANGER.
IF TOBARI SAYS SO, THEN WE'RE IN TROUBLE.
WHA—!?
SAY THAT AGAIN, SUZU!
WAH!
OH, THAT REMINDS ME.
THE ELDER'S BACK, HINOWA.
!
...AN ORPHAN WHO WON'T LISTEN TO ANYBODY, THE SECOND SON OF A FARMING FAMILY, THE CHILD OF A MISTRESS, AND THE CHILD OF A DRUNKARD ...
APPARENTLY THEY GO TO SOME WEIRDO WHO LIVES OUTSIDE OF TOWN TO LEARN THEIR LETTERS AND PLAY PRETEND SWORD FIGHTS.
I GUESS THEY'VE BANDED TOGETHER, ALL BEING PROBLEM CHILDREN.

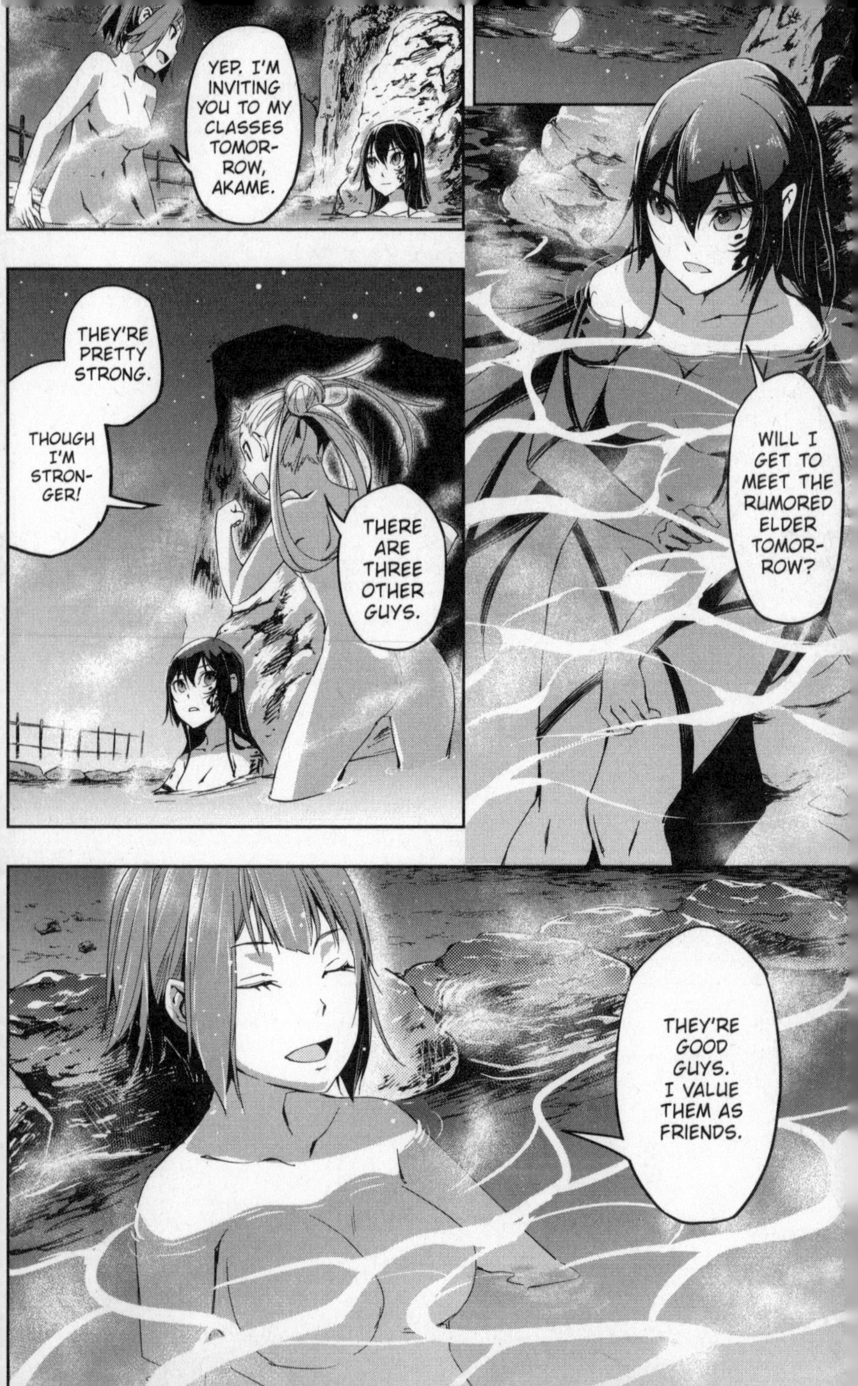
YEP. I'M INVITING YOU TO MY CLASSES TOMORROW, AKAME.
WILL I GET TO MEET THE RUMORED ELDER TOMORROW?
THERE ARE THREE OTHER GUYS.
THEY'RE PRETTY STRONG.
THOUGH I'M STRONGER!
THEY'RE GOOD GUYS. I VALUE THEM AS FRIENDS.

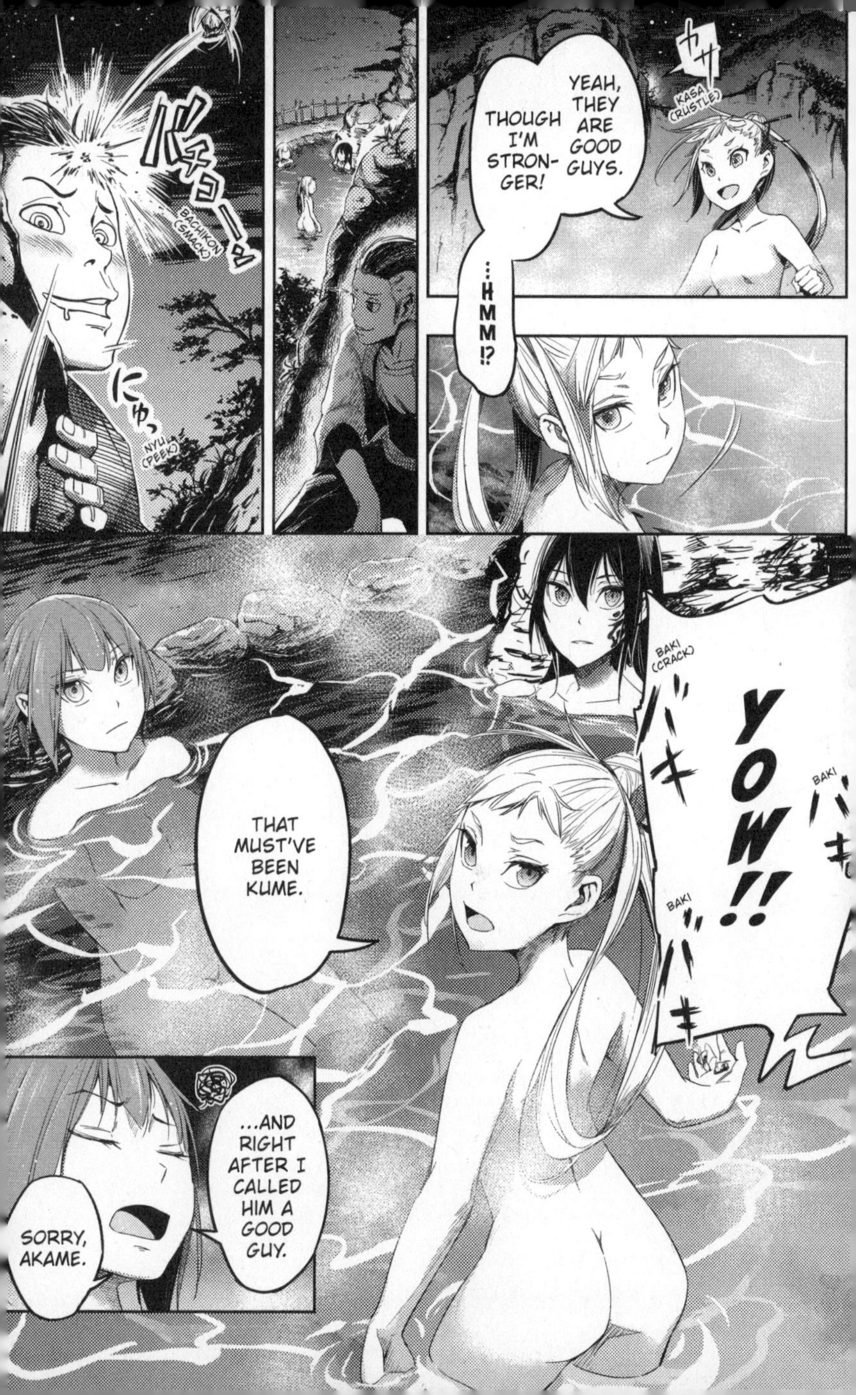

カサ
KASA (RUSTLE)
YEAH, THEY ARE GOOD GUYS.
THOUGH I'M STRONGER!
...HMM!?
バチコーン
BACHIKON (SMACK)
にゅっ
NYU (PEEK)
バキ
BAKI (CRACK)
YOW!!
バキ
BAKI
バキ
BAKI
THAT MUST'VE BEEN KUME.
...AND RIGHT AFTER I CALLED HIM A GOOD GUY.
SORRY, AKAME.

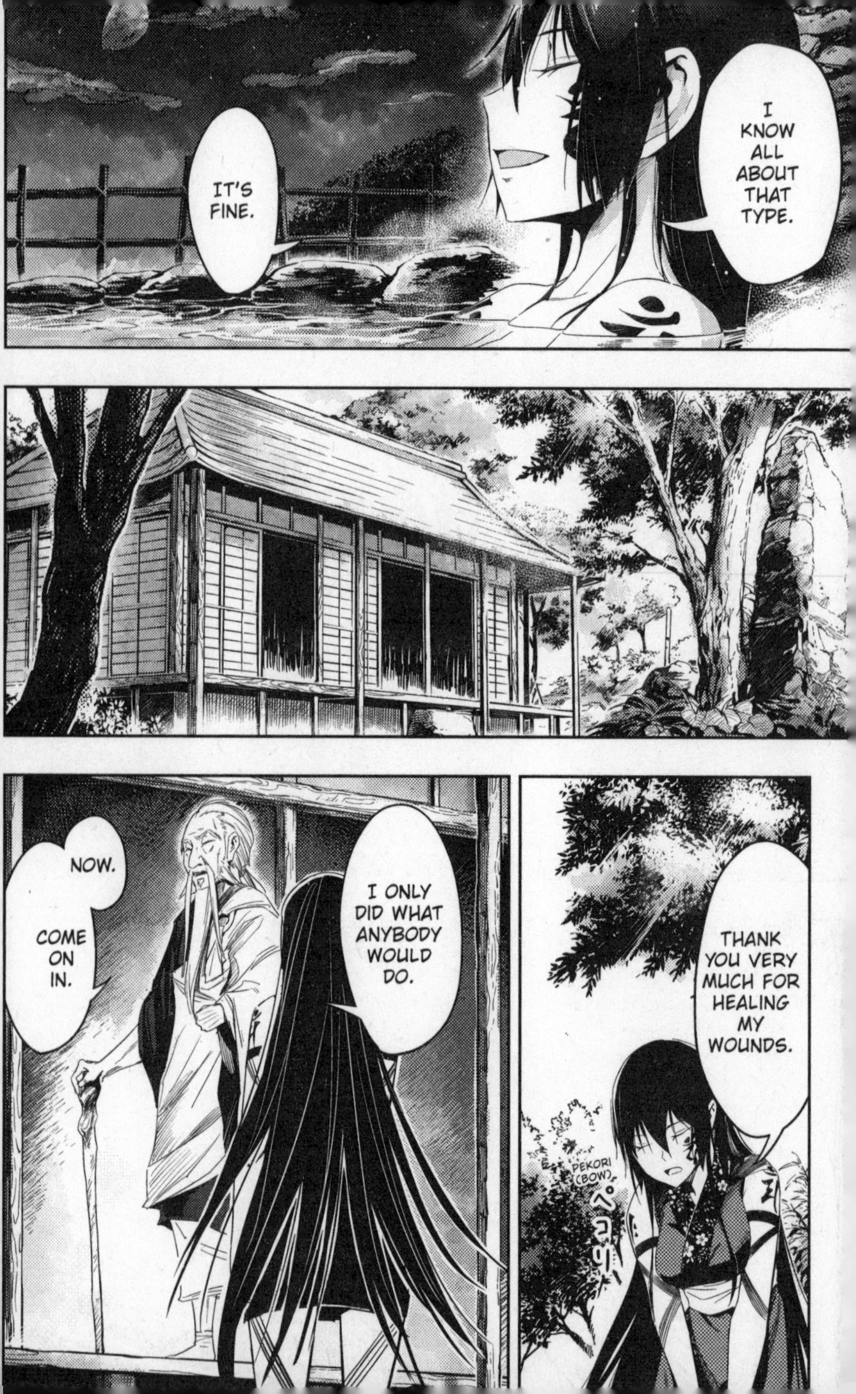

I KNOW ALL ABOUT THAT TYPE.
IT'S FINE.
THANK YOU VERY MUCH FOR HEALING MY WOUNDS.
PEKORI (BOW)
ペコリ
I ONLY DID WHAT ANYBODY WOULD DO.
NOW.
COME ON IN.

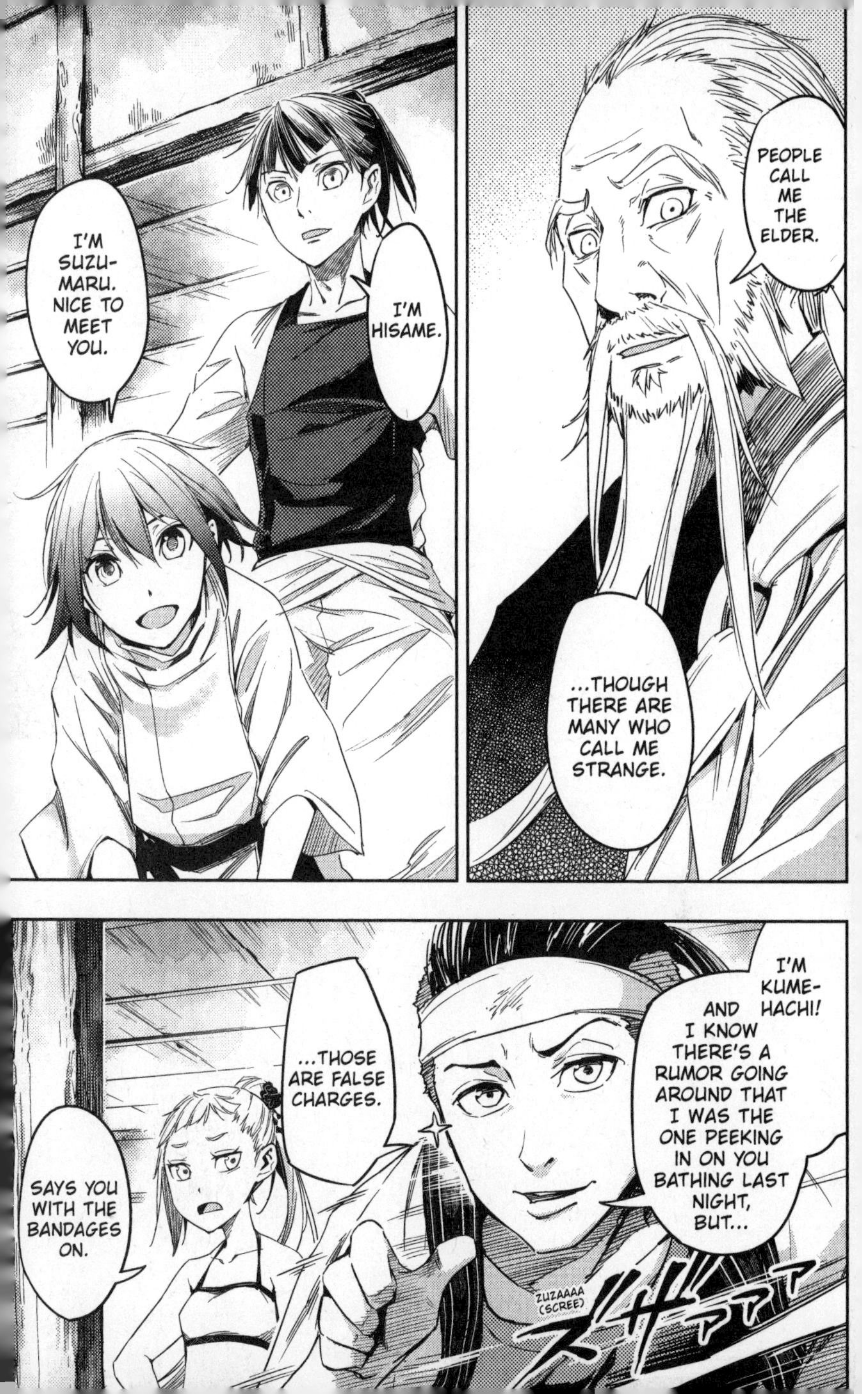
PEOPLE CALL ME THE ELDER.
...THOUGH THERE ARE MANY WHO CALL ME STRANGE.
I'M HISAME.
I'M SUZU-MARU. NICE TO MEET YOU.
I'M KUME-HACHI! AND I KNOW THERE'S A RUMOR GOING AROUND THAT I WAS THE ONE PEEKING IN ON YOU BATHING LAST NIGHT, BUT...
...THOSE ARE FALSE CHARGES.
SAYS YOU WITH THE BANDAGES ON.
ZUZAAAA (SCREE)

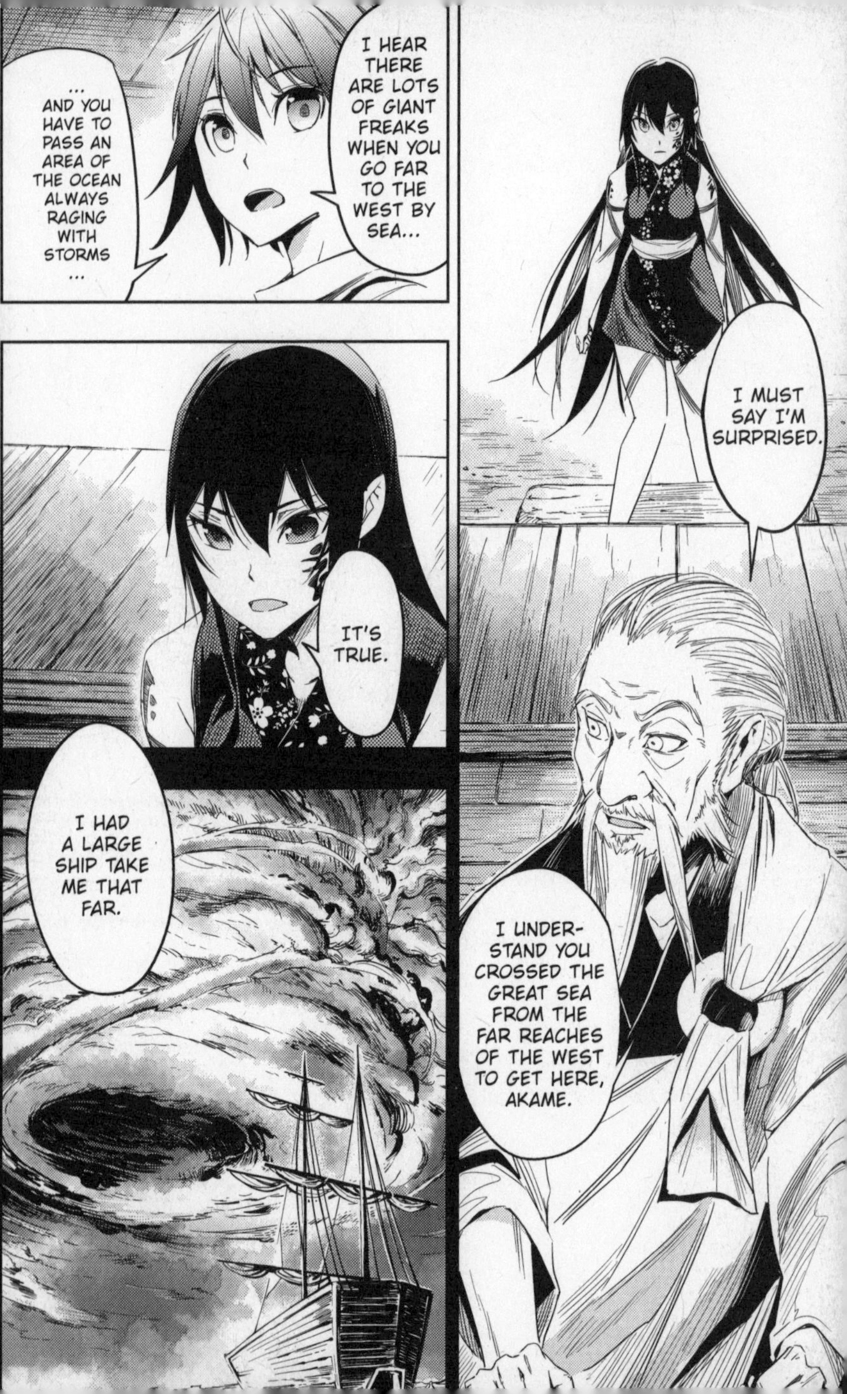
I UNDER-STAND YOU CROSSED THE GREAT SEA FROM THE FAR REACHES OF THE WEST TO GET HERE, AKAME.
I MUST SAY I'M SURPRISED.
IT'S TRUE.
I HAD A LARGE SHIP TAKE ME THAT FAR.
I HEAR THERE ARE LOTS OF GIANT FREAKS WHEN YOU GO FAR TO THE WEST BY SEA...
... AND YOU HAVE TO PASS AN AREA OF THE OCEAN ALWAYS RAGING WITH STORMS ...

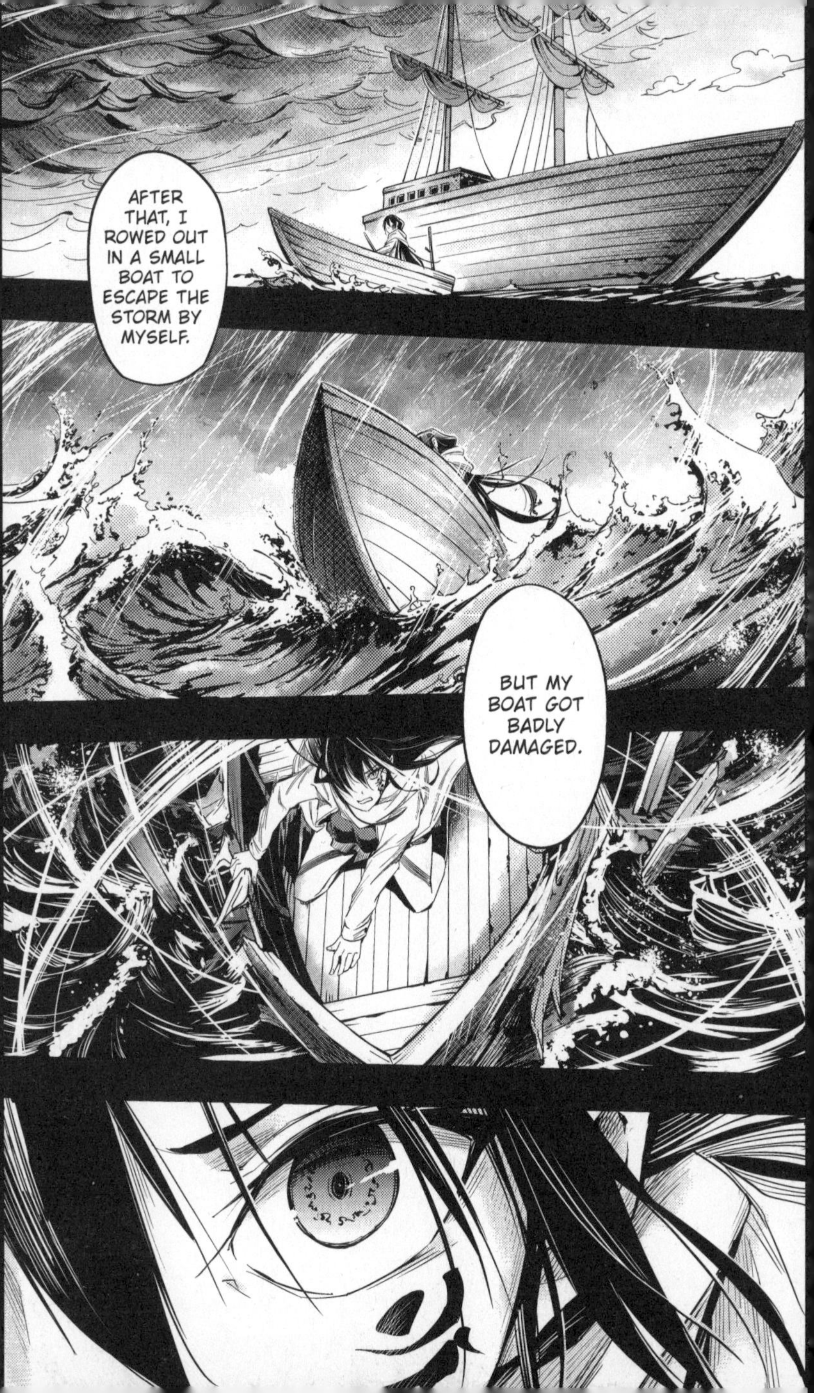
AFTER THAT, I ROWED OUT IN A SMALL BOAT TO ESCAPE THE STORM BY MYSELF.
BUT MY BOAT GOT BADLY DAMAGED.

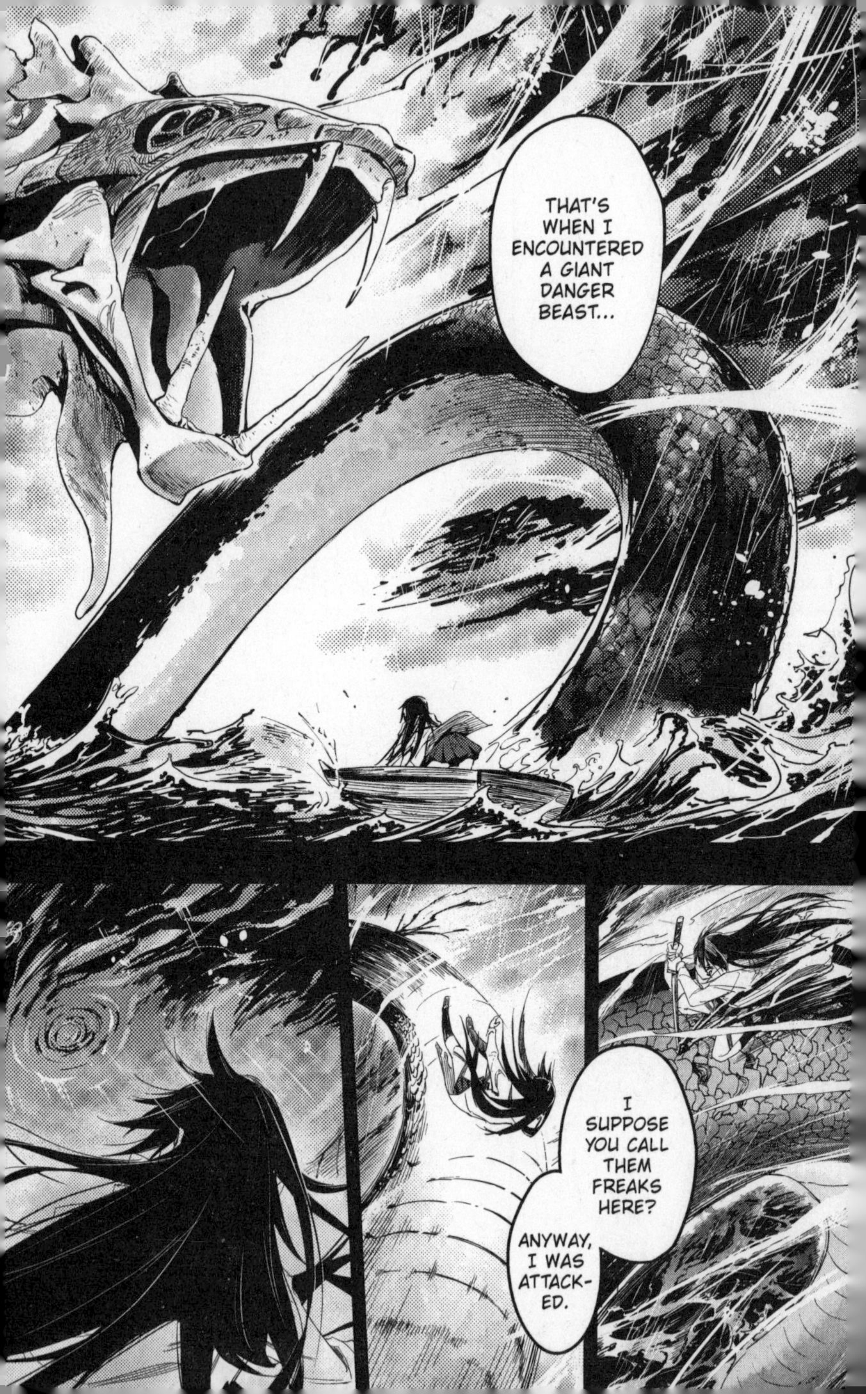
THAT'S WHEN I ENCOUNTERED A GIANT DANGER BEAST...
I SUPPOSE YOU CALL THEM FREAKS HERE?
ANYWAY, I WAS ATTACK-ED.

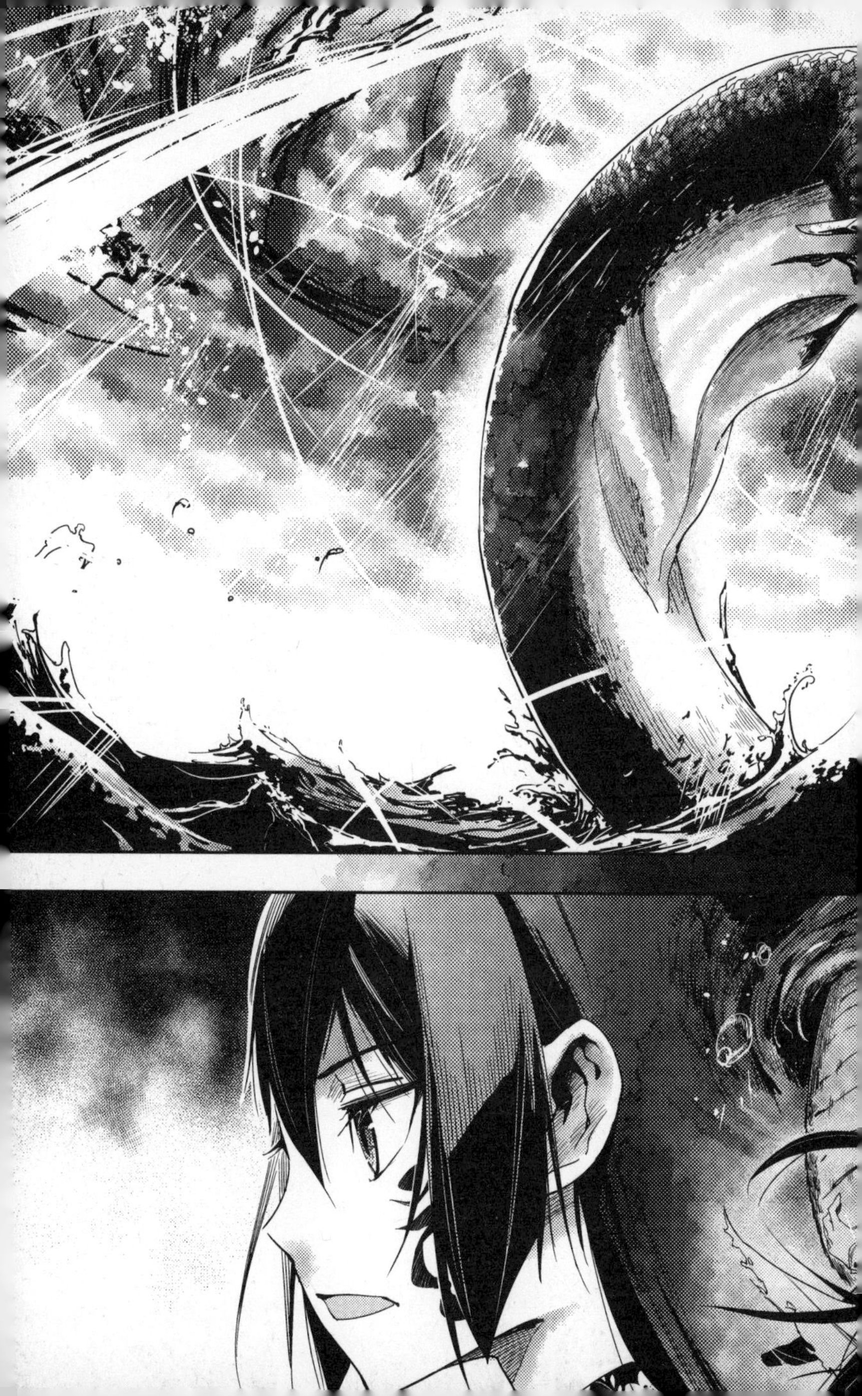

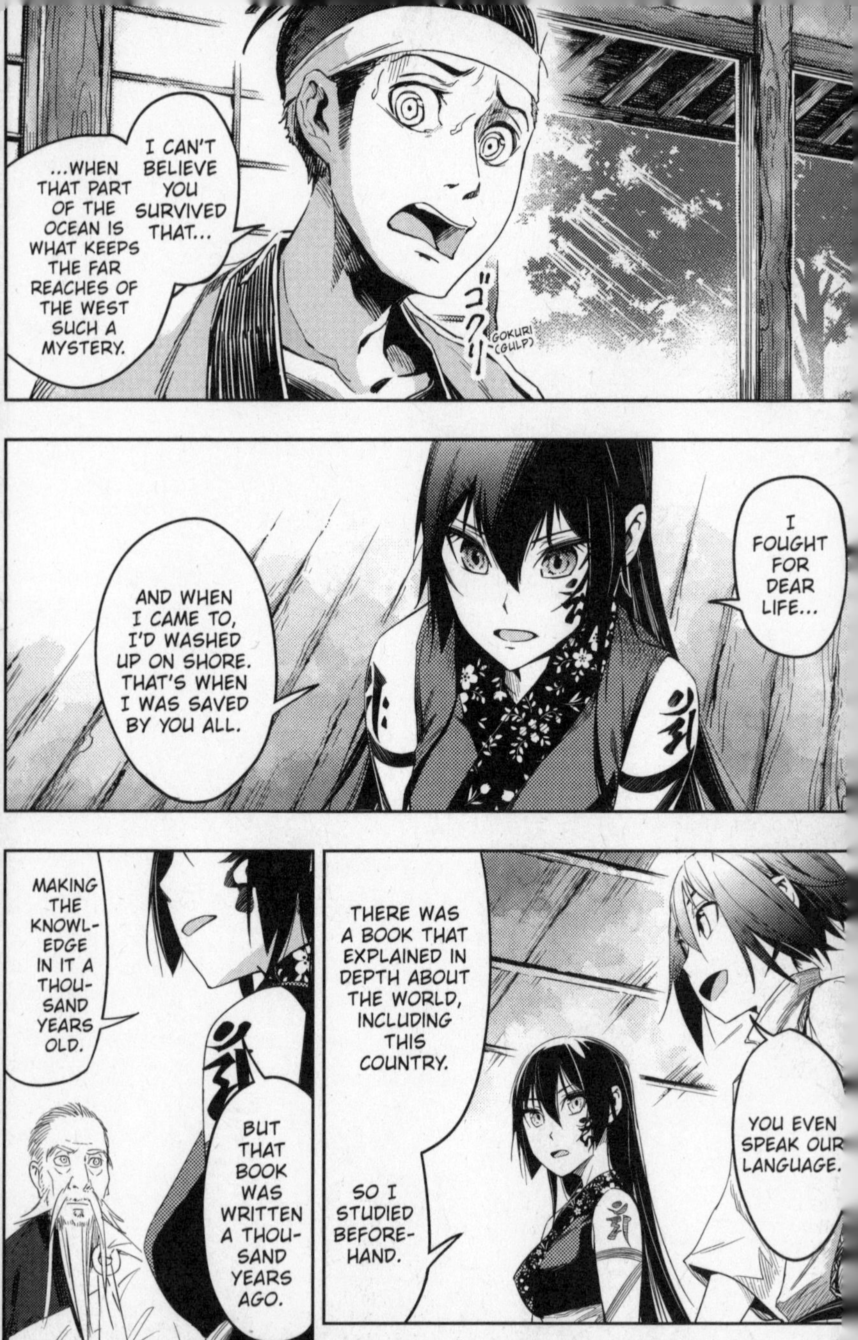
I CAN'T BELIEVE YOU SURVIVED THAT...
...WHEN THAT PART OF THE OCEAN IS WHAT KEEPS THE FAR REACHES OF THE WEST SUCH A MYSTERY.
GOKURI (GULP)
I FOUGHT FOR DEAR LIFE...
AND WHEN I CAME TO, I'D WASHED UP ON SHORE. THAT'S WHEN I WAS SAVED BY YOU ALL.
YOU EVEN SPEAK OUR LANGUAGE.
THERE WAS A BOOK THAT EXPLAINED IN DEPTH ABOUT THE WORLD, INCLUDING THIS COUNTRY.
SO I STUDIED BEFOREHAND.
BUT THAT BOOK WAS WRITTEN A THOUSAND YEARS AGO.
MAKING THE KNOWLEDGE IN IT A THOUSAND YEARS OLD.

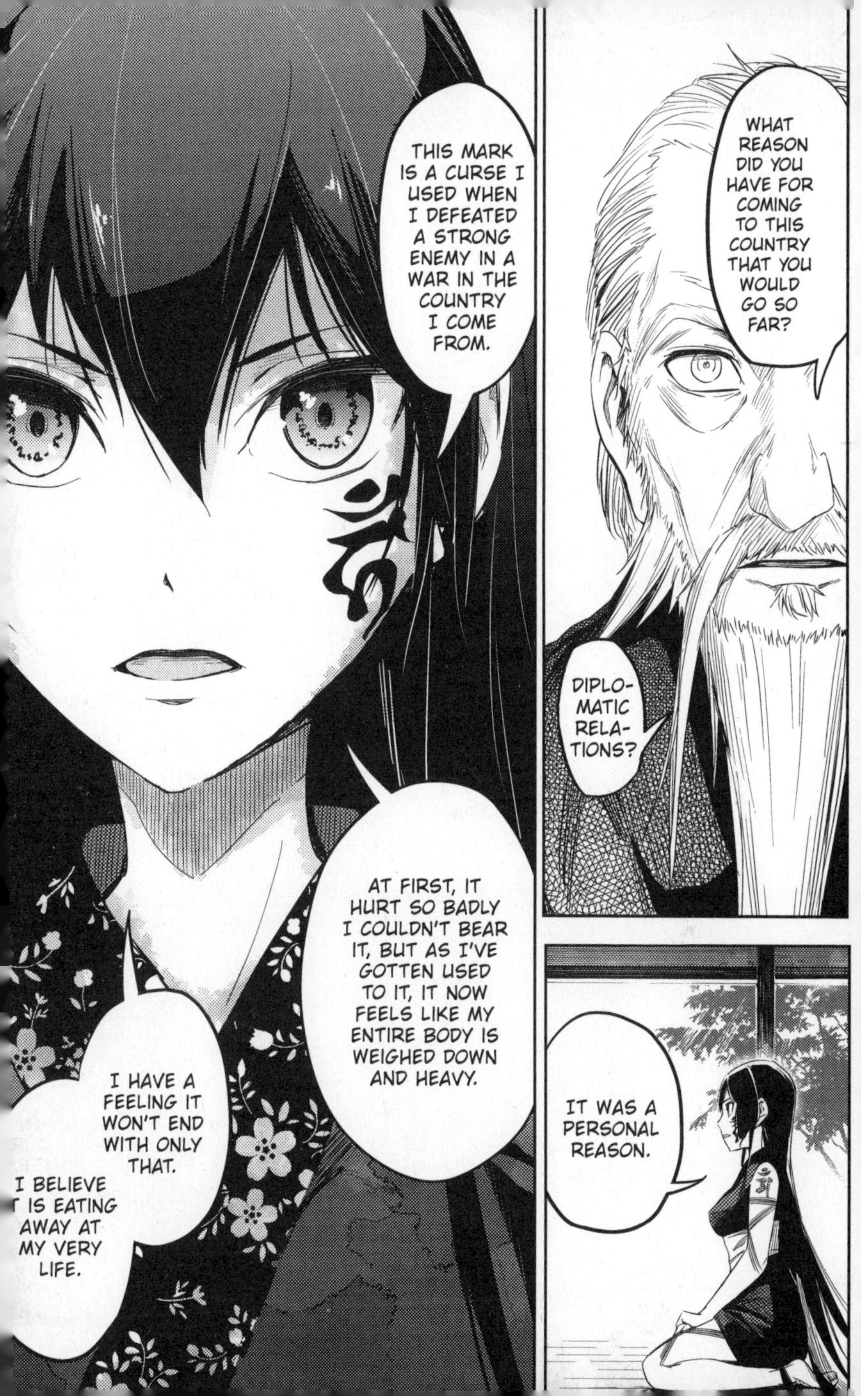
WHAT REASON DID YOU HAVE FOR COMING TO THIS COUNTRY THAT YOU WOULD GO SO FAR?
DIPLO-MATIC RELA-TIONS?
IT WAS A PERSONAL REASON.
THIS MARK IS A CURSE I USED WHEN I DEFEATED A STRONG ENEMY IN A WAR IN THE COUNTRY I COME FROM.
AT FIRST, IT HURT SO BADLY I COULDN'T BEAR IT, BUT AS I'VE GOTTEN USED TO IT, IT NOW FEELS LIKE MY ENTIRE BODY IS WEIGHED DOWN AND HEAVY.
I HAVE A FEELING IT WON'T END WITH ONLY THAT.
I BELIEVE T IS EATING AWAY AT MY VERY LIFE.

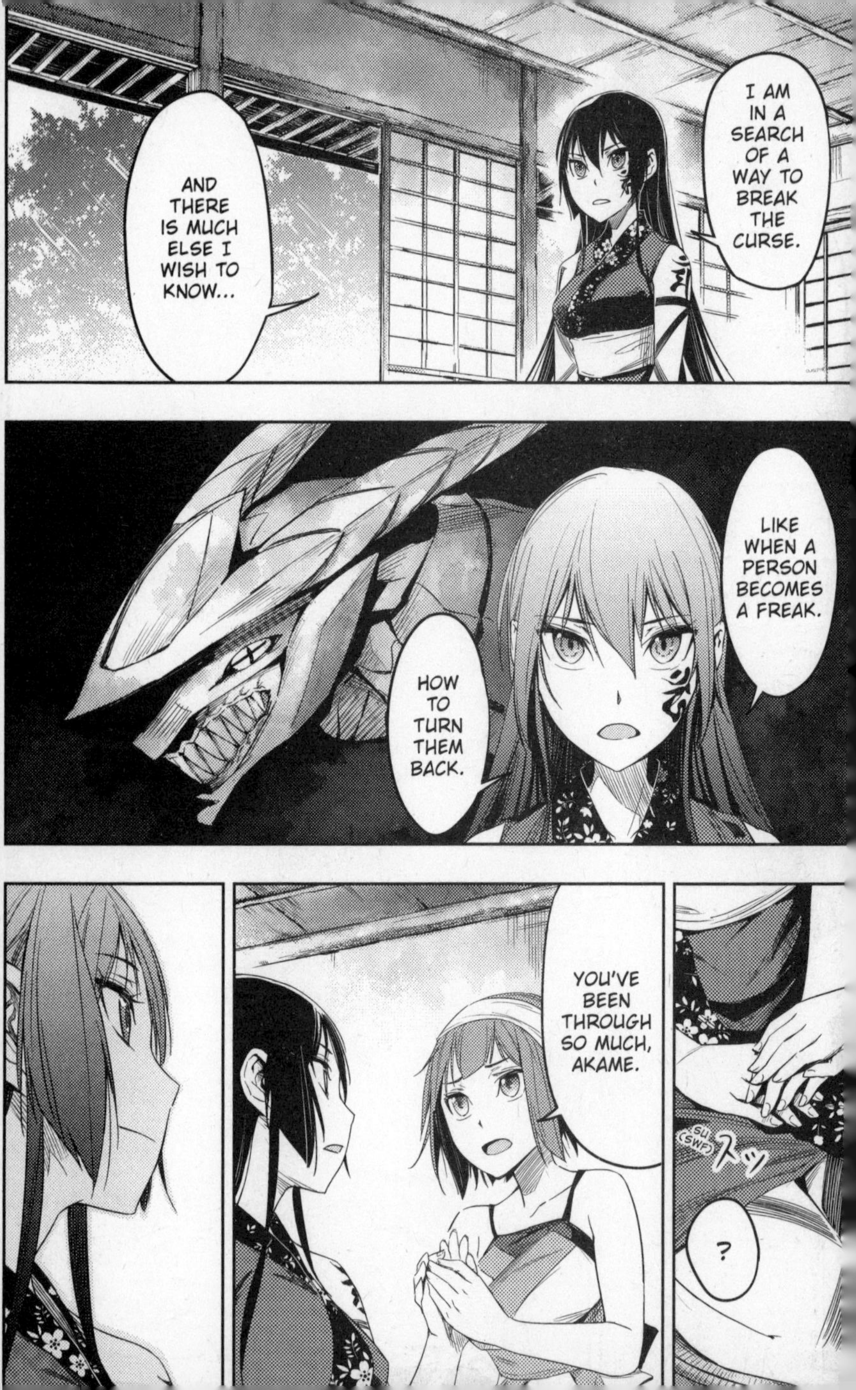
I AM IN A SEARCH OF A WAY TO BREAK THE CURSE.
AND THERE IS MUCH ELSE I WISH TO KNOW...
LIKE WHEN A PERSON BECOMES A FREAK.
HOW TO TURN THEM BACK.
SU (SWF) スッ
?
YOU'VE BEEN THROUGH SO MUCH, AKAME.

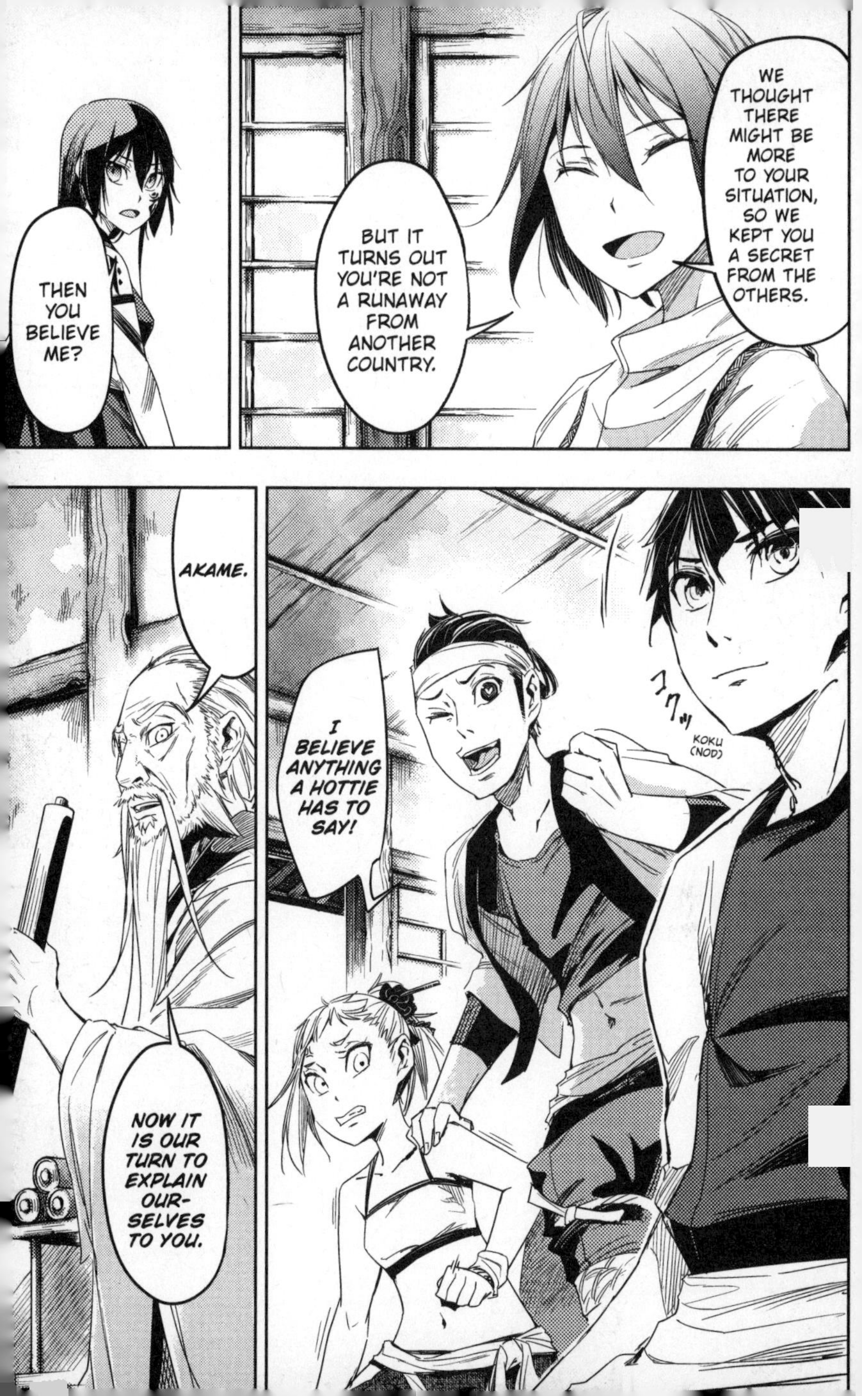
WE THOUGHT THERE MIGHT BE MORE TO YOUR SITUATION, SO WE KEPT YOU A SECRET FROM THE OTHERS.
BUT IT TURNS OUT YOU'RE NOT A RUNAWAY FROM ANOTHER COUNTRY.
THEN YOU BELIEVE ME?
コクッ
KOKU (NOD)
I BELIEVE ANYTHING A HOTTIE HAS TO SAY!
AKAME.
NOW IT IS OUR TURN TO EXPLAIN OUR-SELVES TO YOU.

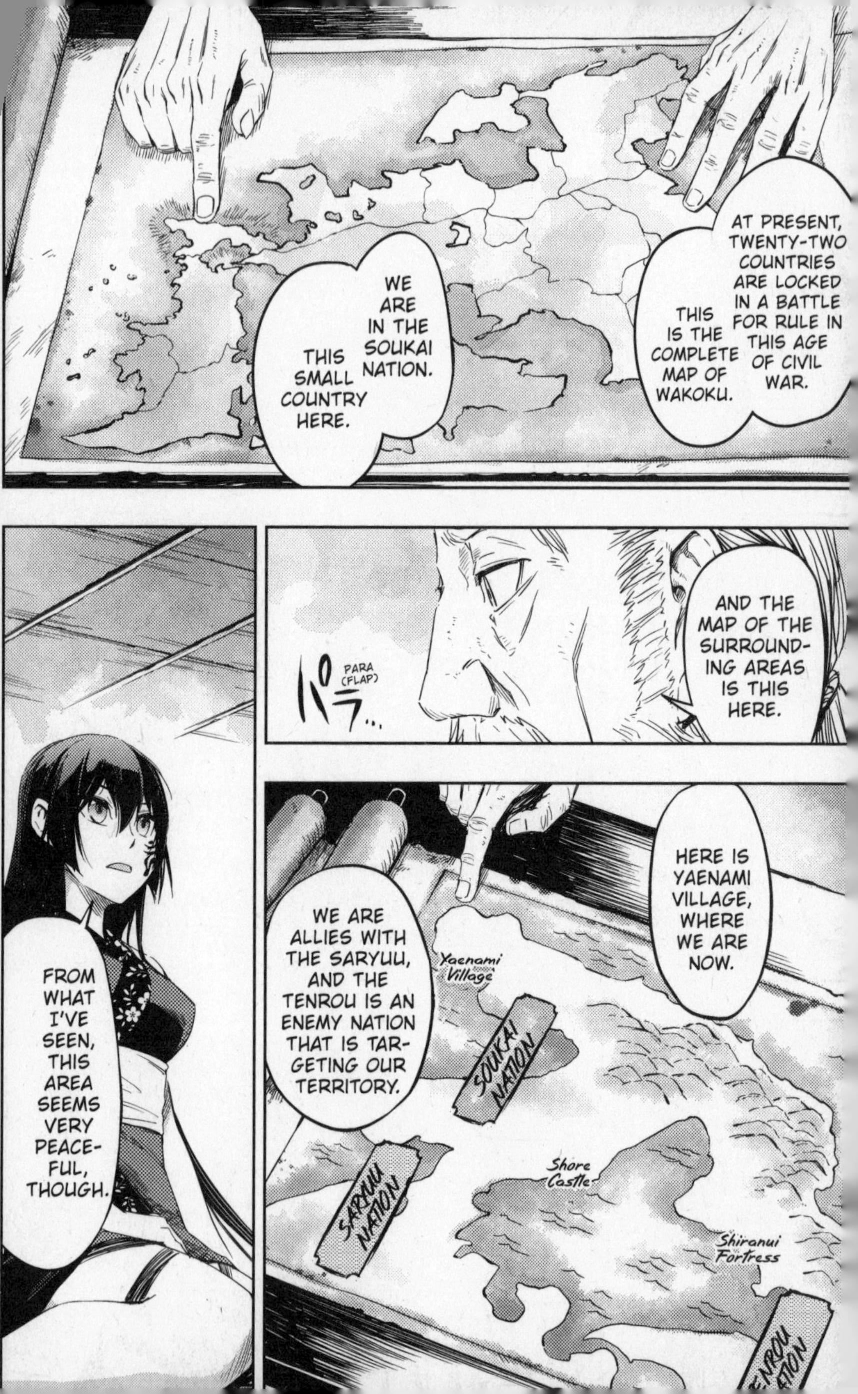

AT PRESENT, TWENTY-TWO COUNTRIES ARE LOCKED IN A BATTLE FOR RULE IN THIS AGE OF CIVIL WAR.
THIS IS THE COMPLETE MAP OF WAKOKU.
WE ARE IN THE SOUKAI NATION.
THIS SMALL COUNTRY HERE.
AND THE MAP OF THE SURROUND-ING AREAS IS THIS HERE.
パラ..
PARA (FLAP)
HERE IS YAENAMI VILLAGE, WHERE WE ARE NOW.
WE ARE ALLIES WITH THE SARYUU, AND THE TENROU IS AN ENEMY NATION THAT IS TAR-GETING OUR TERRITORY.
Yaenami Village
SOUKAI NATION
Shore Castle
Shiranui Fortress
SARYUU NATION
TENROU NATION
FROM WHAT I'VE SEEN, THIS AREA SEEMS VERY PEACE-FUL, THOUGH.

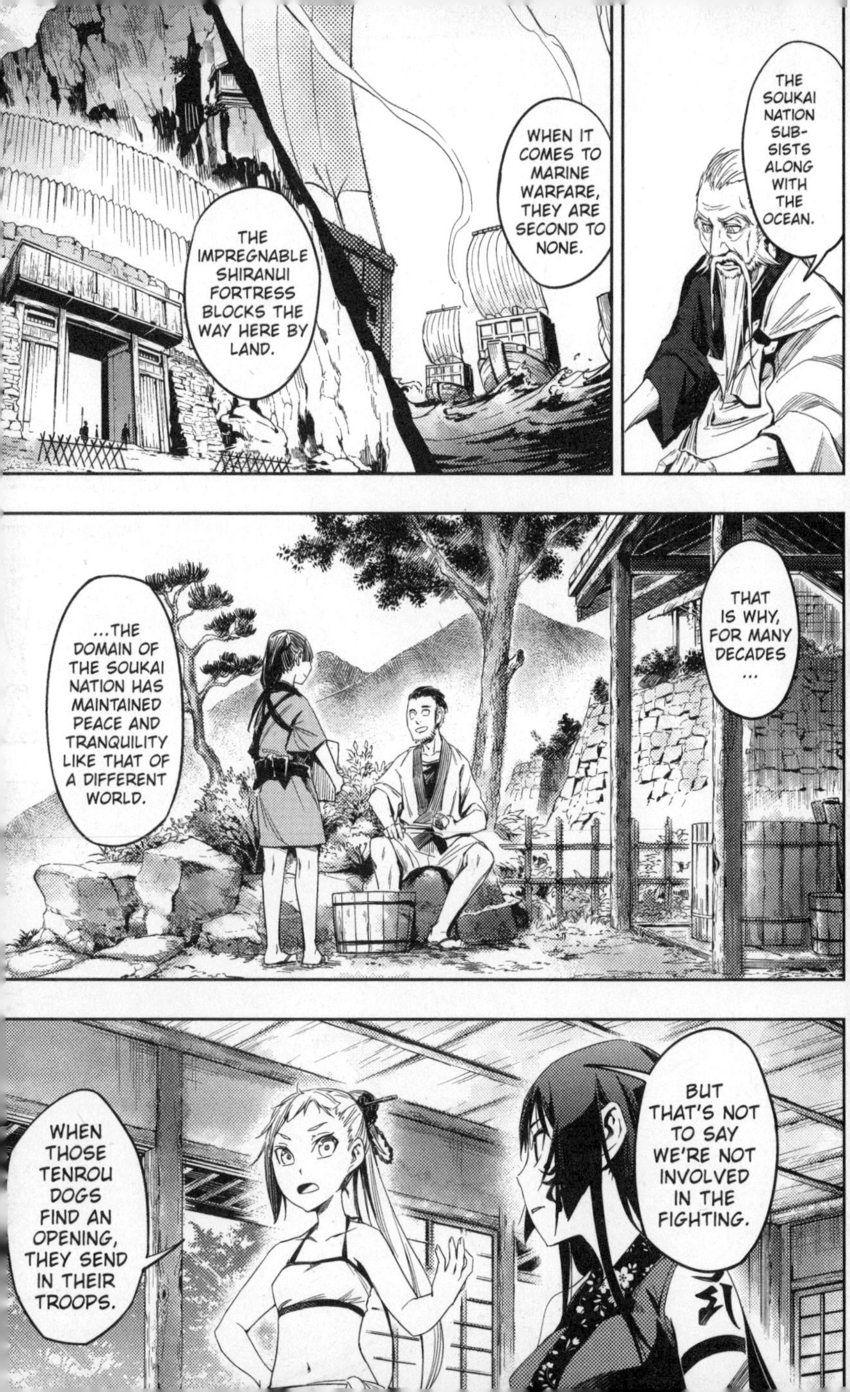
THE SOUKAI NATION SUB-SISTS ALONG WITH THE OCEAN.
WHEN IT COMES TO MARINE WARFARE, THEY ARE SECOND TO NONE.
THE IMPREGNABLE SHIRANUI FORTRESS BLOCKS THE WAY HERE BY LAND.
THAT IS WHY, FOR MANY DECADES...
...THE DOMAIN OF THE SOUKAI NATION HAS MAINTAINED PEACE AND TRANQUILITY LIKE THAT OF A DIFFERENT WORLD.
BUT THAT'S NOT TO SAY WE'RE NOT INVOLVED IN THE FIGHTING.
WHEN THOSE TENROU DOGS FIND AN OPENING, THEY SEND IN THEIR TROOPS.

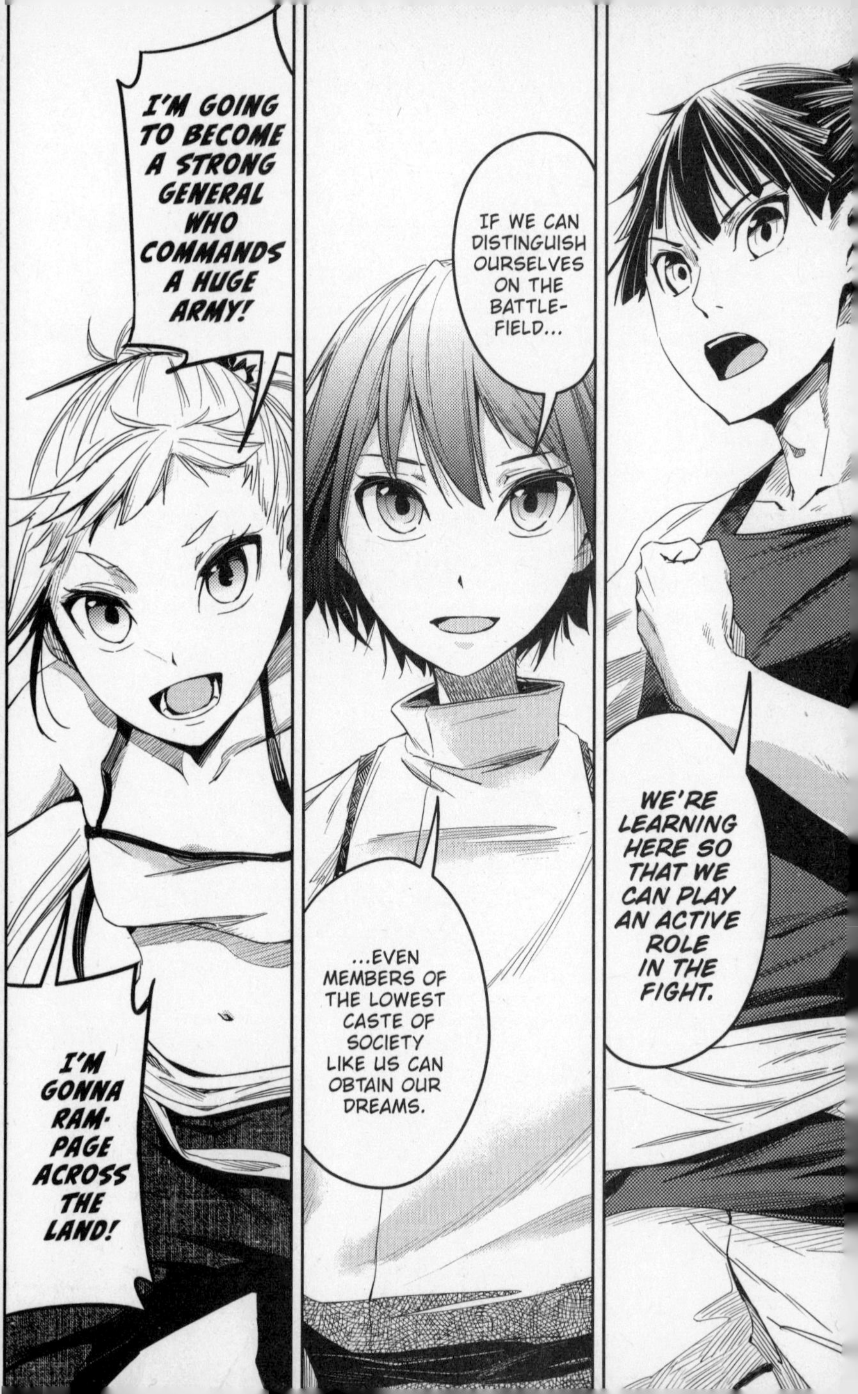
WE'RE LEARNING HERE SO THAT WE CAN PLAY AN ACTIVE ROLE IN THE FIGHT.
IF WE CAN DISTINGUISH OURSELVES ON THE BATTLE-FIELD...
...EVEN MEMBERS OF THE LOWEST CASTE OF SOCIETY LIKE US CAN OBTAIN OUR DREAMS.
I'M GOING TO BECOME A STRONG GENERAL WHO COMMANDS A HUGE ARMY!
I'M GONNA RAM-PAGE ACROSS THE LAND!

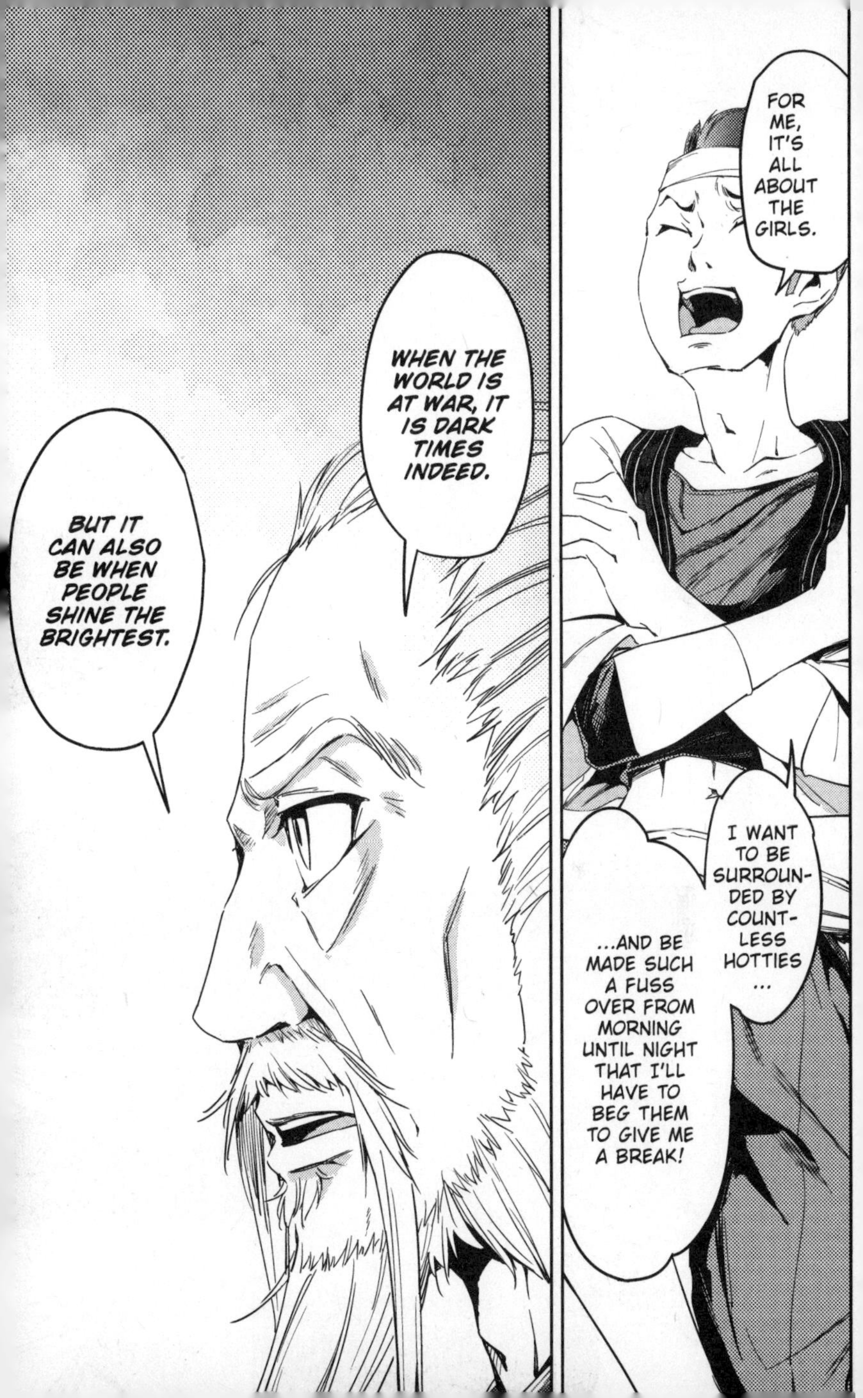
FOR ME, IT'S ALL ABOUT THE GIRLS.
I WANT TO BE SURROUNDED BY COUNTLESS HOTTIES...
...AND BE MADE SUCH A FUSS OVER FROM MORNING UNTIL NIGHT THAT I'LL HAVE TO BEG THEM TO GIVE ME A BREAK!
WHEN THE WORLD IS AT WAR, IT IS DARK TIMES INDEED.
BUT IT CAN ALSO BE WHEN PEOPLE SHINE THE BRIGHTEST.

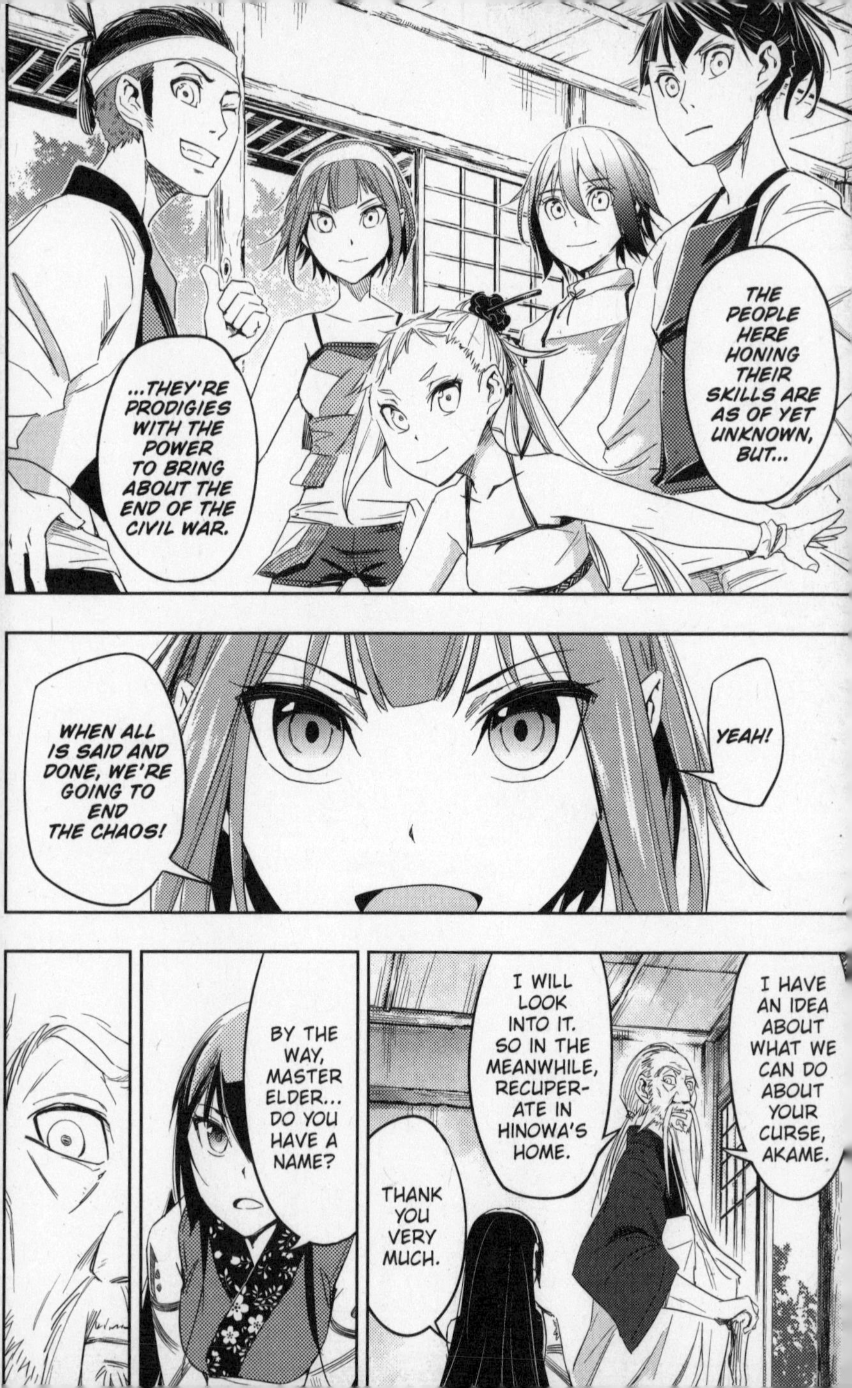
THE PEOPLE HERE HONING THEIR SKILLS ARE AS OF YET UNKNOWN, BUT...
...THEY'RE PRODIGIES WITH THE POWER TO BRING ABOUT THE END OF THE CIVIL WAR.
YEAH!
WHEN ALL IS SAID AND DONE, WE'RE GOING TO END THE CHAOS!
I HAVE AN IDEA ABOUT WHAT WE CAN DO ABOUT YOUR CURSE, AKAME.
I WILL LOOK INTO IT. SO IN THE MEANWHILE, RECUPERATE IN HINOWA'S HOME.
THANK YOU VERY MUCH.
BY THE WAY, MASTER ELDER... DO YOU HAVE A NAME?

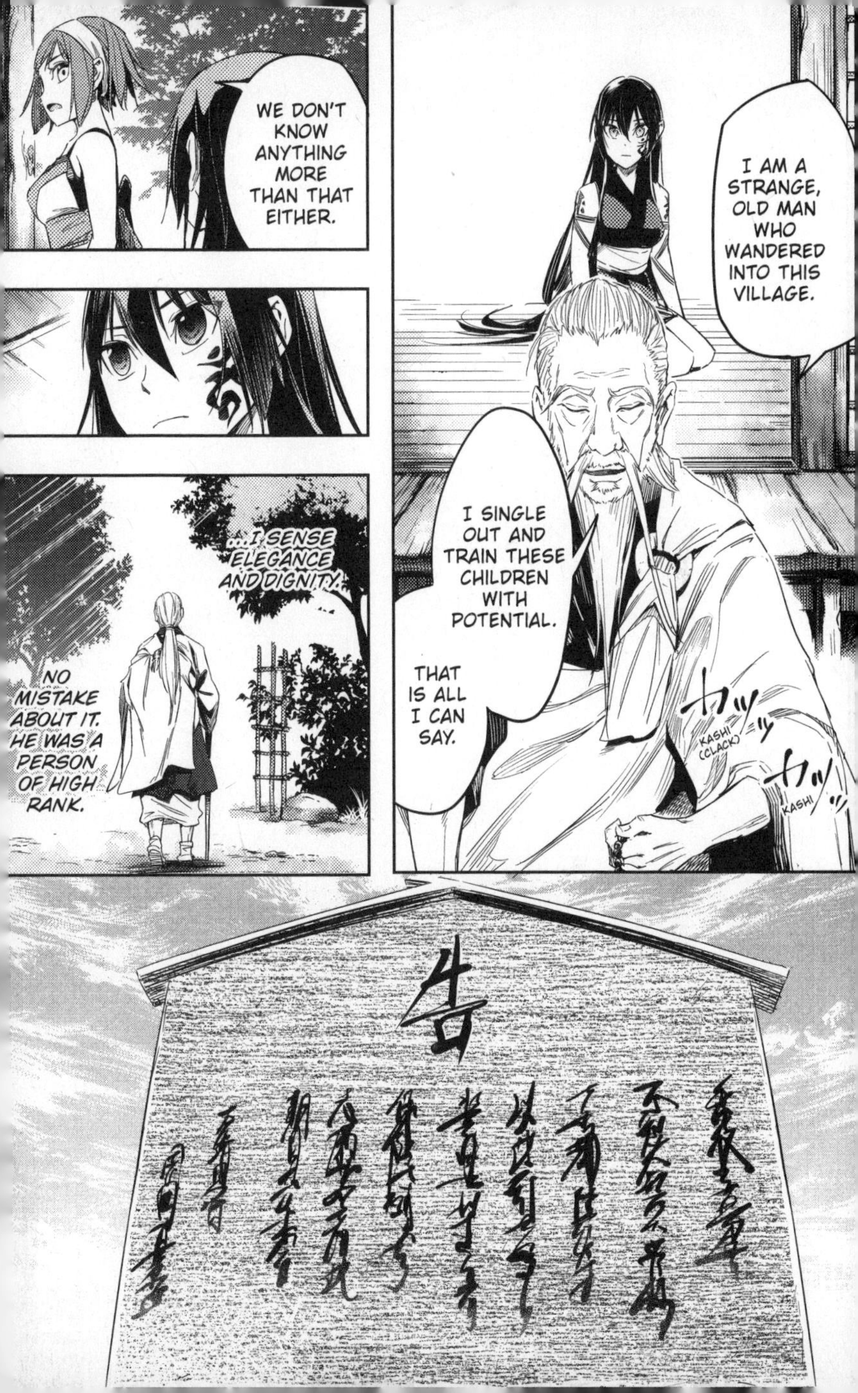
I AM A STRANGE, OLD MAN WHO WANDERED INTO THIS VILLAGE.
I SINGLE OUT AND TRAIN THESE CHILDREN WITH POTENTIAL.
THAT IS ALL I CAN SAY.
カッ
KASHI (CLACK)
カッ
KASHI
WE DON'T KNOW ANYTHING MORE THAN THAT EITHER.
...I SENSE ELEGANCE AND DIGNITY.
NO MISTAKE ABOUT IT. HE WAS A PERSON OF HIGH RANK.
告

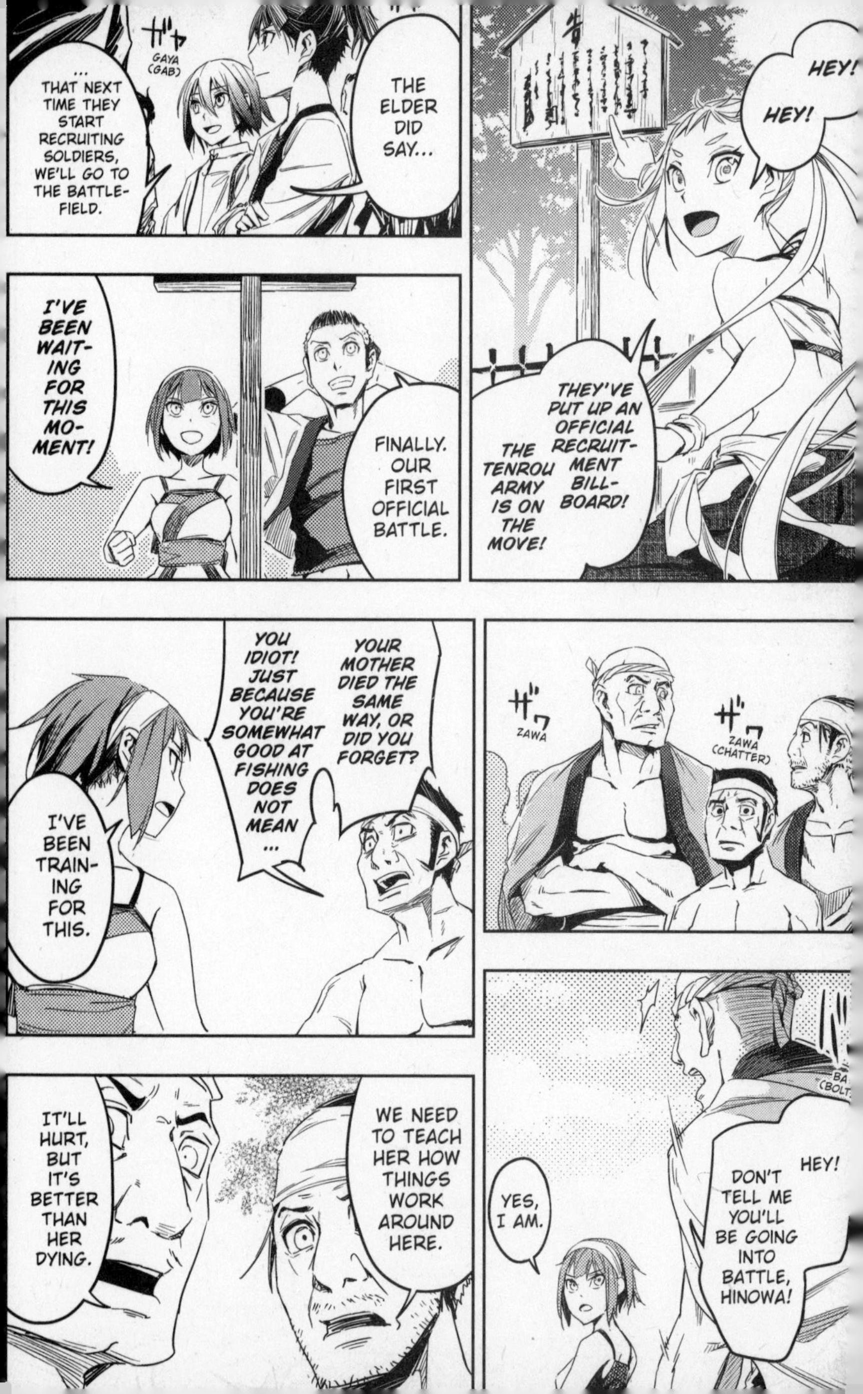
HEY!
HEY!
THEY'VE PUT UP AN OFFICIAL RECRUITMENT BILLBOARD!
THE TENROU ARMY IS ON THE MOVE!
ガヤ
GAYA (GAB)
THE ELDER DID SAY...
... THAT NEXT TIME THEY START RECRUITING SOLDIERS, WE'LL GO TO THE BATTLEFIELD.
FINALLY. OUR FIRST OFFICIAL BATTLE.
I'VE BEEN WAITING FOR THIS MOMENT!
ザワ
ZAWA (CHATTER)
ザワ
ZAWA
YOUR MOTHER DIED THE SAME WAY, OR DID YOU FORGET?
YOU IDIOT! JUST BECAUSE YOU'RE SOMEWHAT GOOD AT FISHING DOES NOT MEAN ...
I'VE BEEN TRAINING FOR THIS.
HEY!
DON'T TELL ME YOU'LL BE GOING INTO BATTLE, HINOWA!
YES, I AM.
WE NEED TO TEACH HER HOW THINGS WORK AROUND HERE.
IT'LL HURT, BUT IT'S BETTER THAN HER DYING.

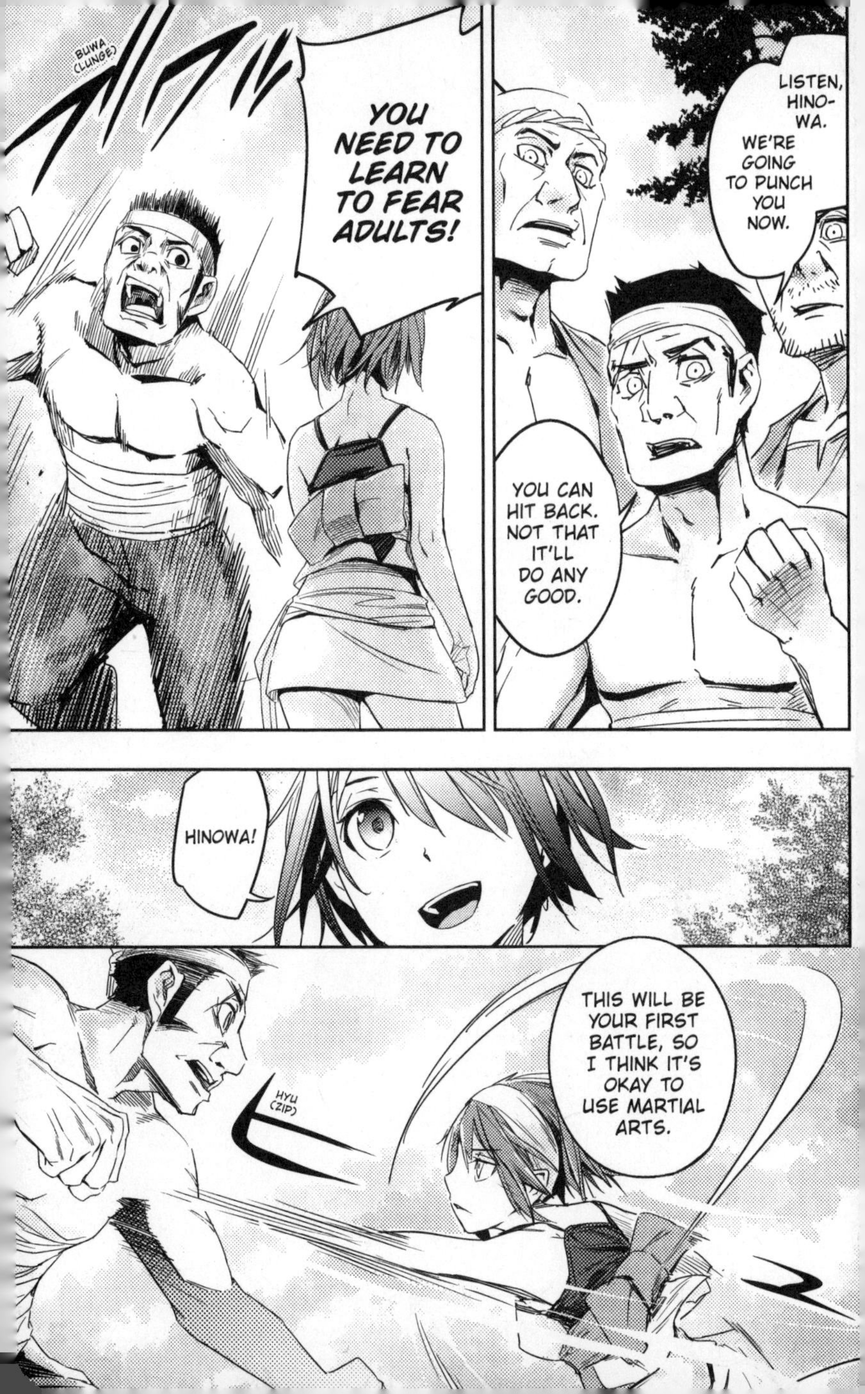
LISTEN, HINOWA.
WE'RE GOING TO PUNCH YOU NOW.
YOU CAN HIT BACK. NOT THAT IT'LL DO ANY GOOD.
YOU NEED TO LEARN TO FEAR ADULTS!
BUWA (LUNGE)
HINOWA!
THIS WILL BE YOUR FIRST BATTLE, SO I THINK IT'S OKAY TO USE MARTIAL ARTS.
HYU (ZIP)

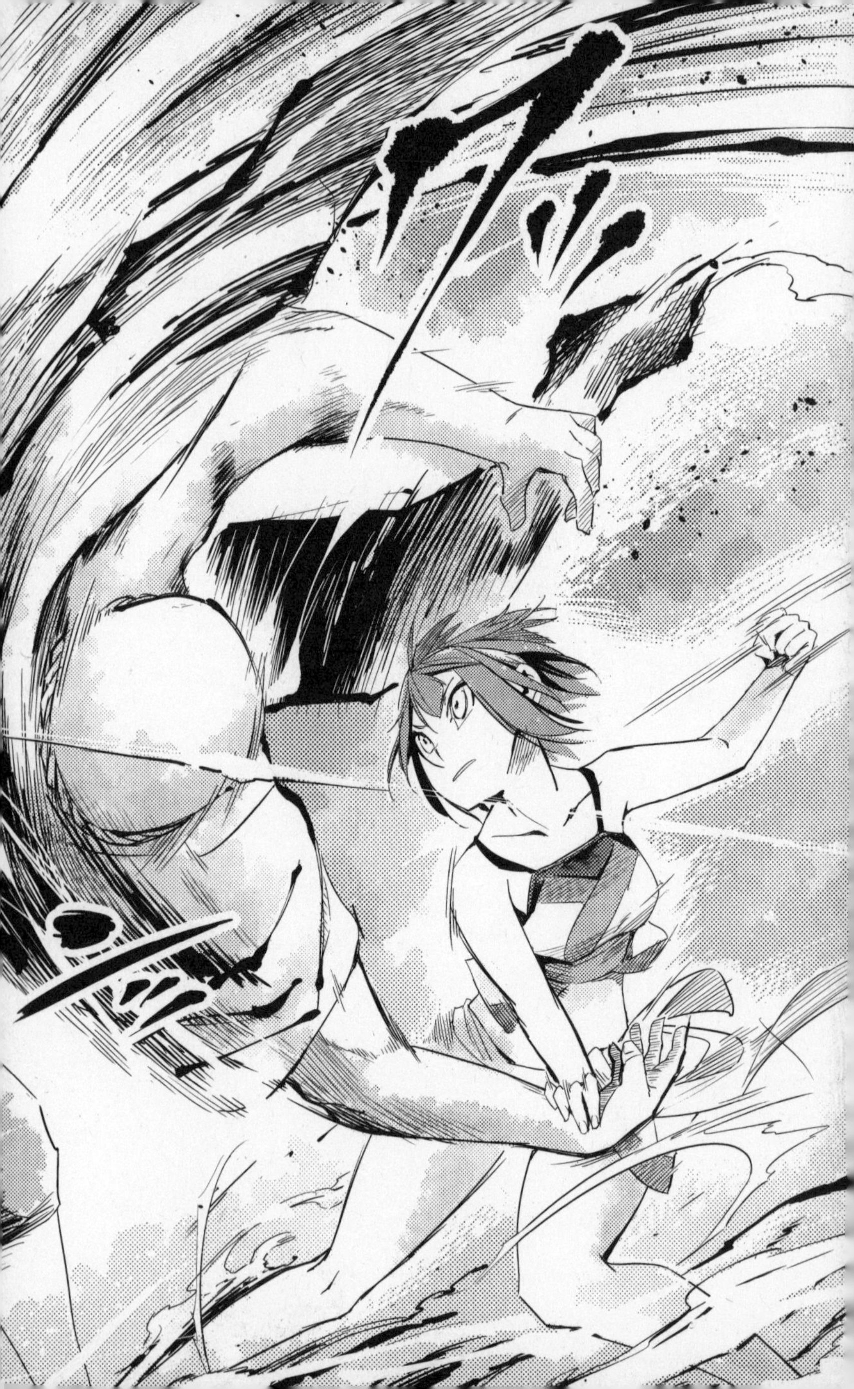

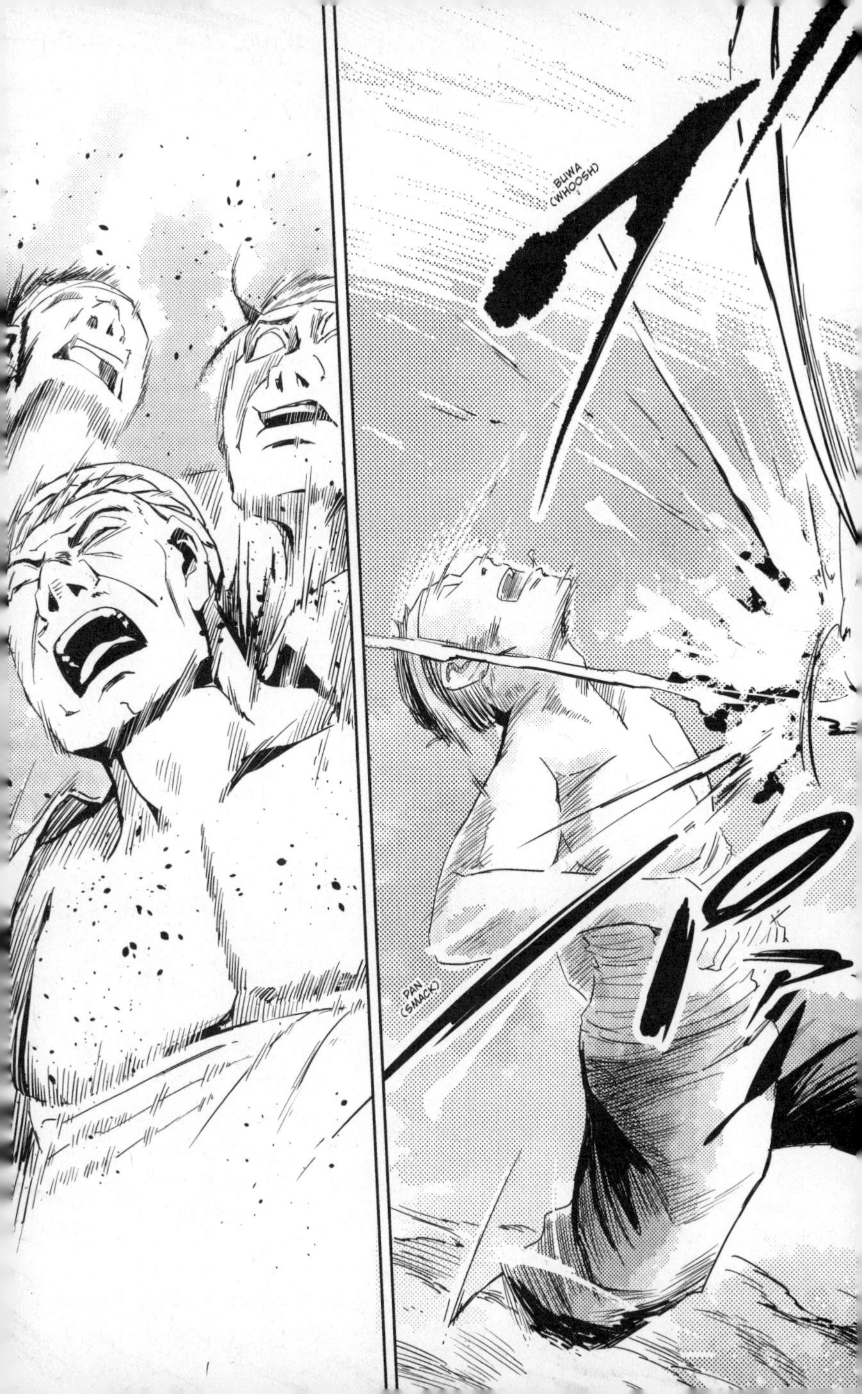
BUWA (WHOOSH)
PAN (SMACK)

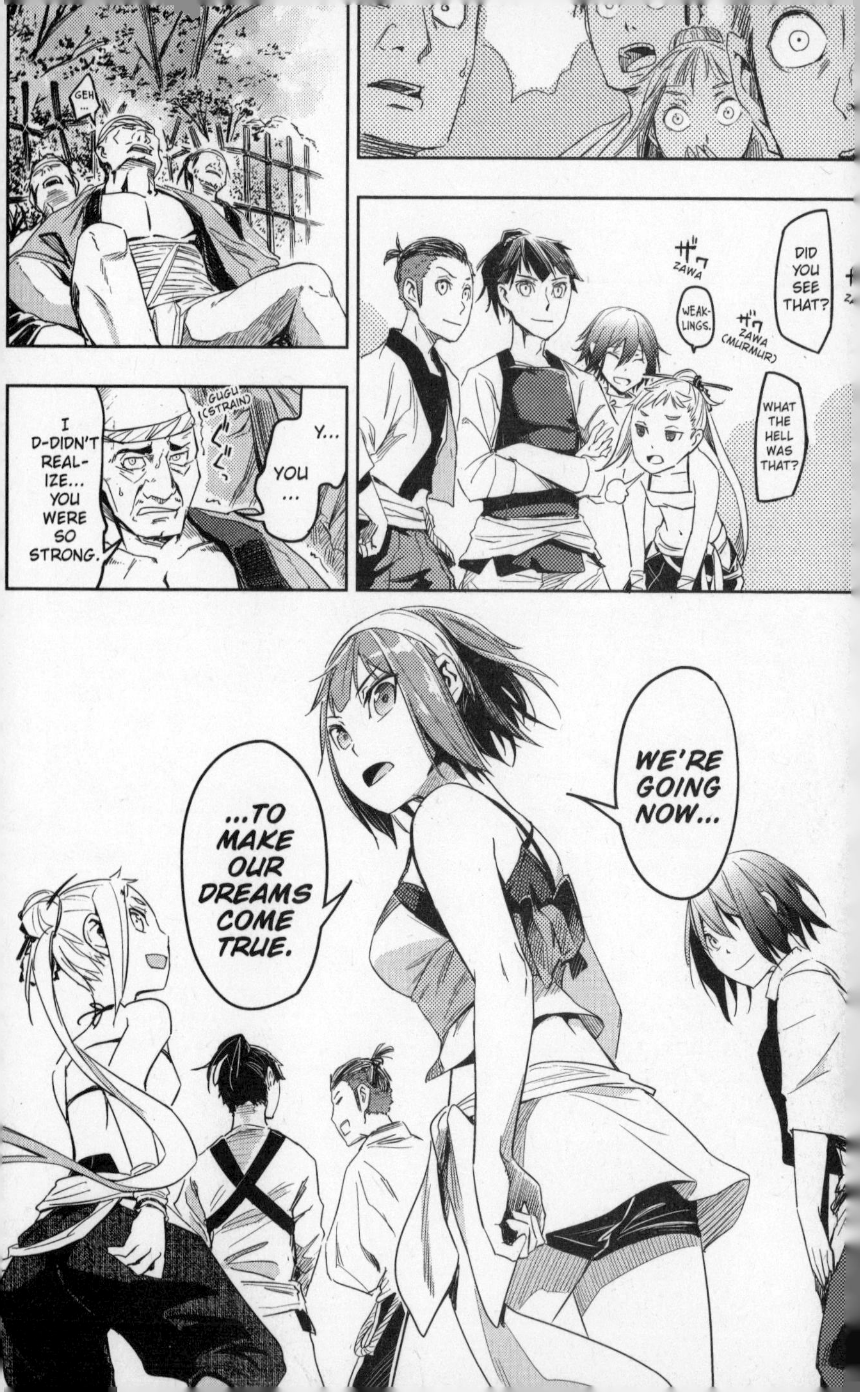
GEH...
DID YOU SEE THAT?
ザワ ZAWA
ザワ ZAWA (MURMUR)
WEAK-LINGS.
WHAT THE HELL WAS THAT?
Y... YOU...
GUGU (STRAIN)
I D-DIDN'T REAL-IZE... YOU WERE SO STRONG.
WE'RE GOING NOW...
...TO MAKE OUR DREAMS COME TRUE.

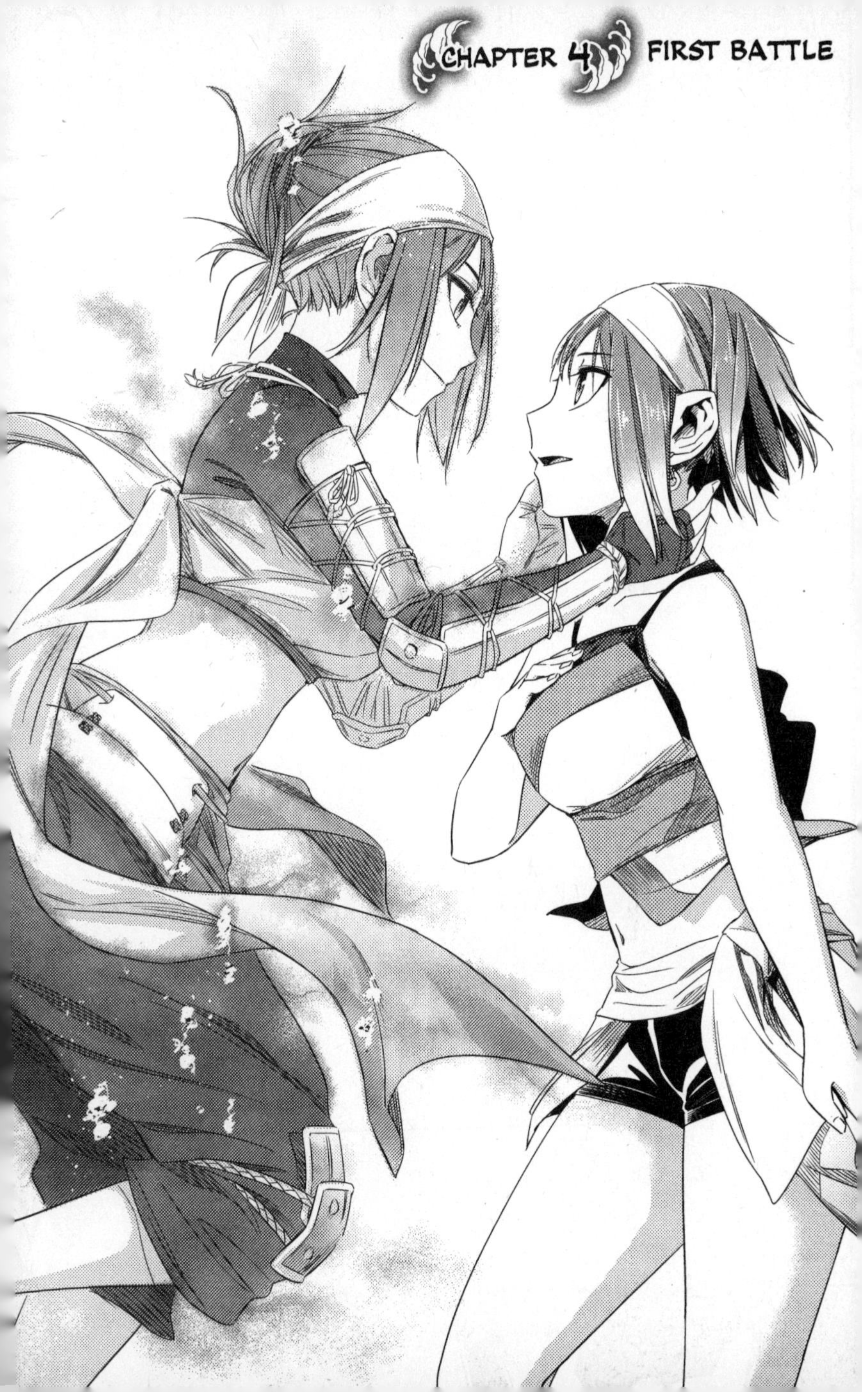
CHAPTER 4 FIRST BATTLE

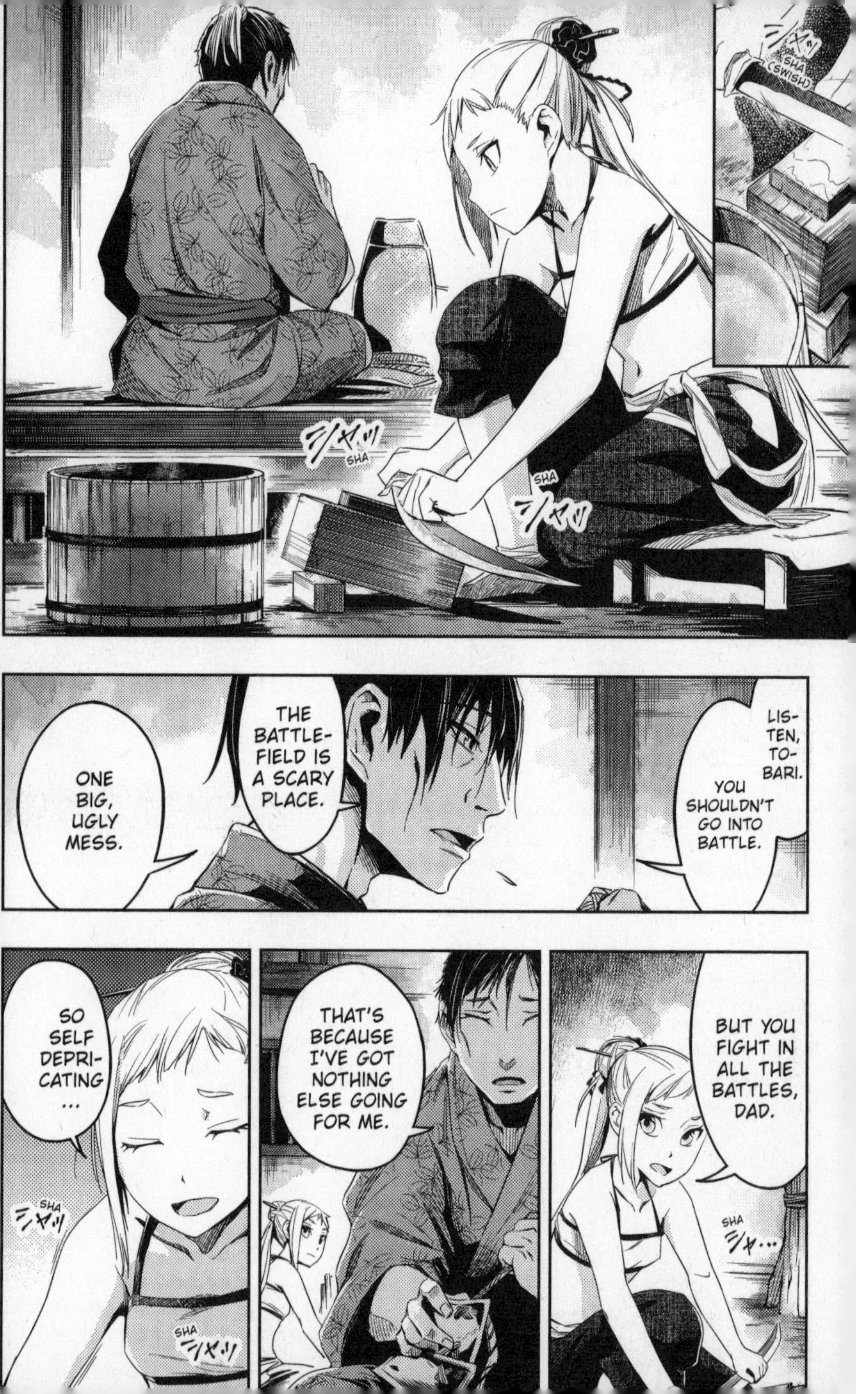
シャッ SHA (SWISH)
シャッ SHA
SHA シャッ
LISTEN, TOBARI.
YOU SHOULDN'T GO INTO BATTLE.
THE BATTLEFIELD IS A SCARY PLACE.
ONE BIG, UGLY MESS.
BUT YOU FIGHT IN ALL THE BATTLES, DAD.
SHA シャ…
THAT'S BECAUSE I'VE GOT NOTHING ELSE GOING FOR ME.
SO SELF DEPRICATING ...
SHA シャッ
SHA シャッ

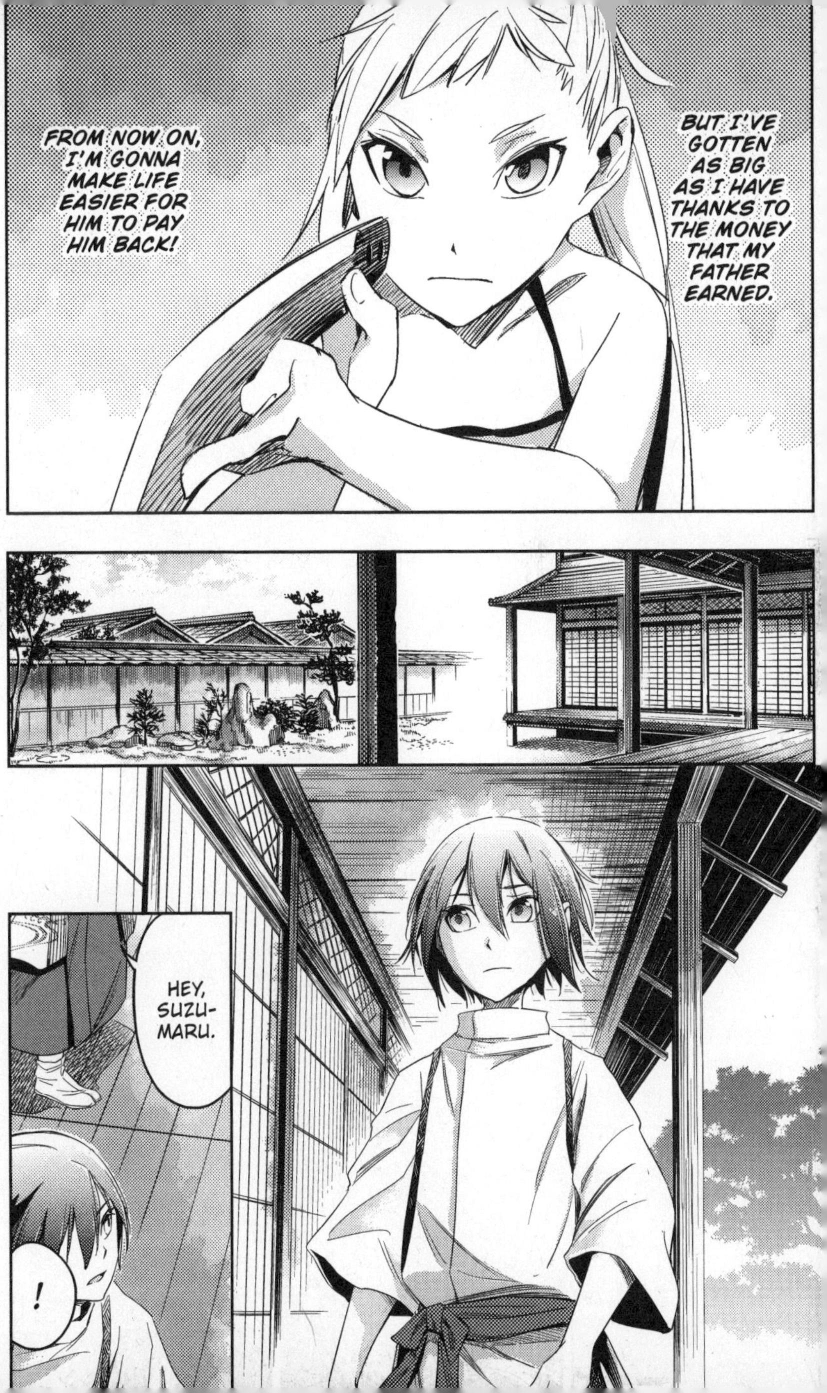
BUT I'VE GOTTEN AS BIG AS I HAVE THANKS TO THE MONEY THAT MY FATHER EARNED.
FROM NOW ON, I'M GONNA MAKE LIFE EASIER FOR HIM TO PAY HIM BACK!
HEY, SUZU-MARU.
!

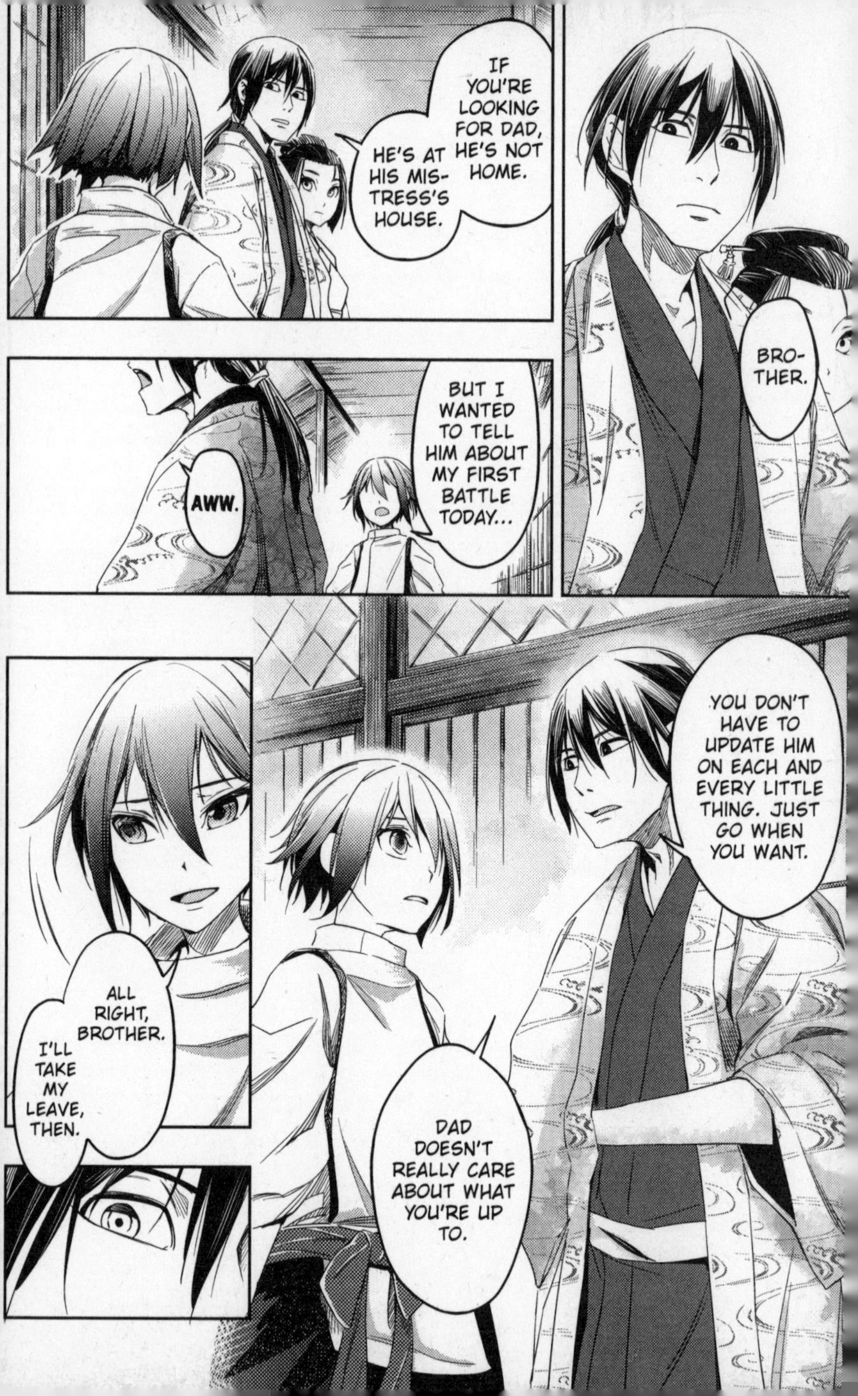
BROTHER.
IF YOU'RE LOOKING FOR DAD, HE'S NOT HOME.
HE'S AT HIS MISTRESS'S HOUSE.
BUT I WANTED TO TELL HIM ABOUT MY FIRST BATTLE TODAY...
AWW.
YOU DON'T HAVE TO UPDATE HIM ON EACH AND EVERY LITTLE THING. JUST GO WHEN YOU WANT.
DAD DOESN'T REALLY CARE ABOUT WHAT YOU'RE UP TO.
ALL RIGHT, BROTHER.
I'LL TAKE MY LEAVE, THEN.

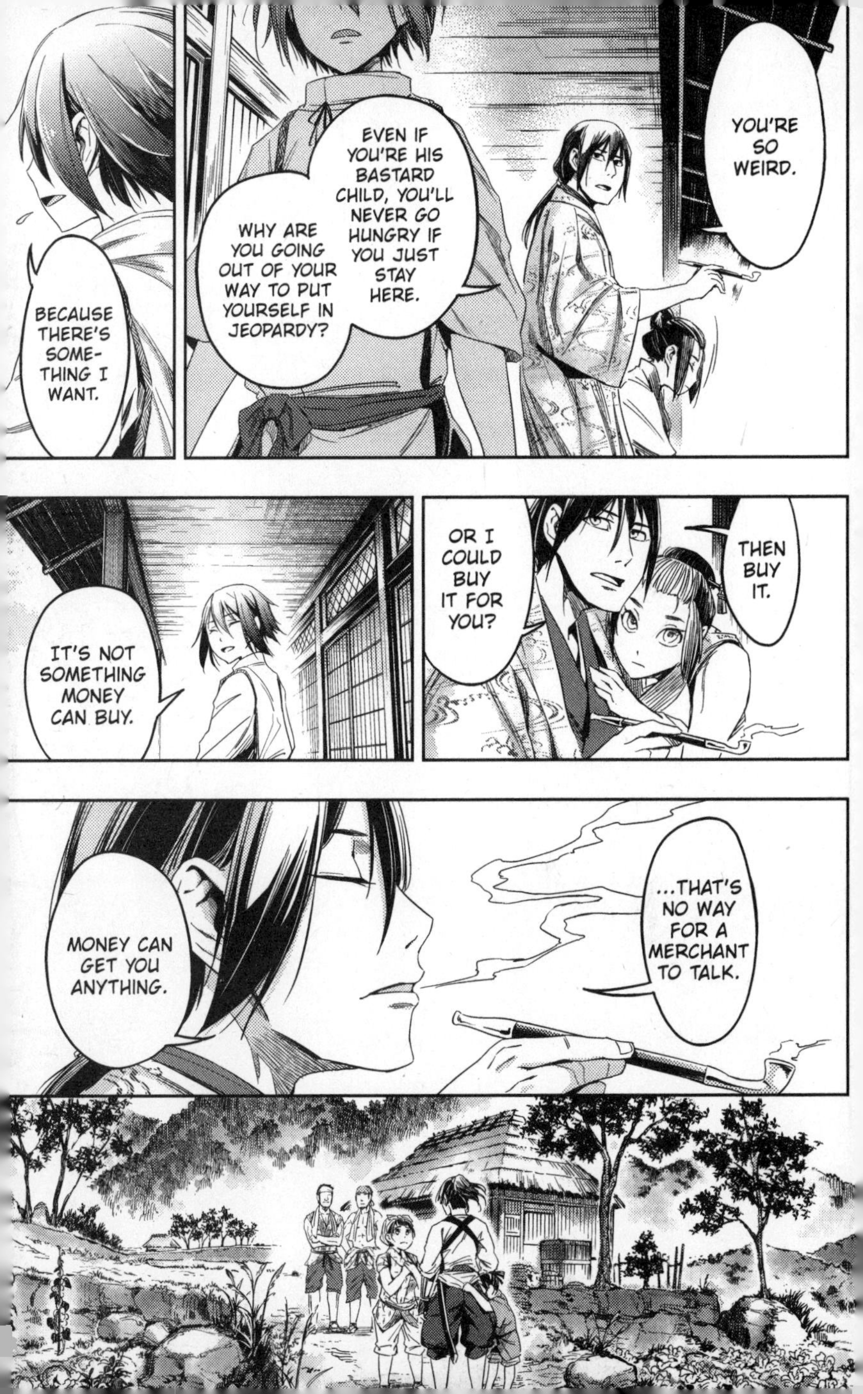
YOU'RE SO WEIRD.
EVEN IF YOU'RE HIS BASTARD CHILD, YOU'LL NEVER GO HUNGRY IF YOU JUST STAY HERE.
WHY ARE YOU GOING OUT OF YOUR WAY TO PUT YOURSELF IN JEOPARDY?
BECAUSE THERE'S SOME-THING I WANT.
THEN BUY IT.
OR I COULD BUY IT FOR YOU?
IT'S NOT SOMETHING MONEY CAN BUY.
...THAT'S NO WAY FOR A MERCHANT TO TALK.
MONEY CAN GET YOU ANYTHING.

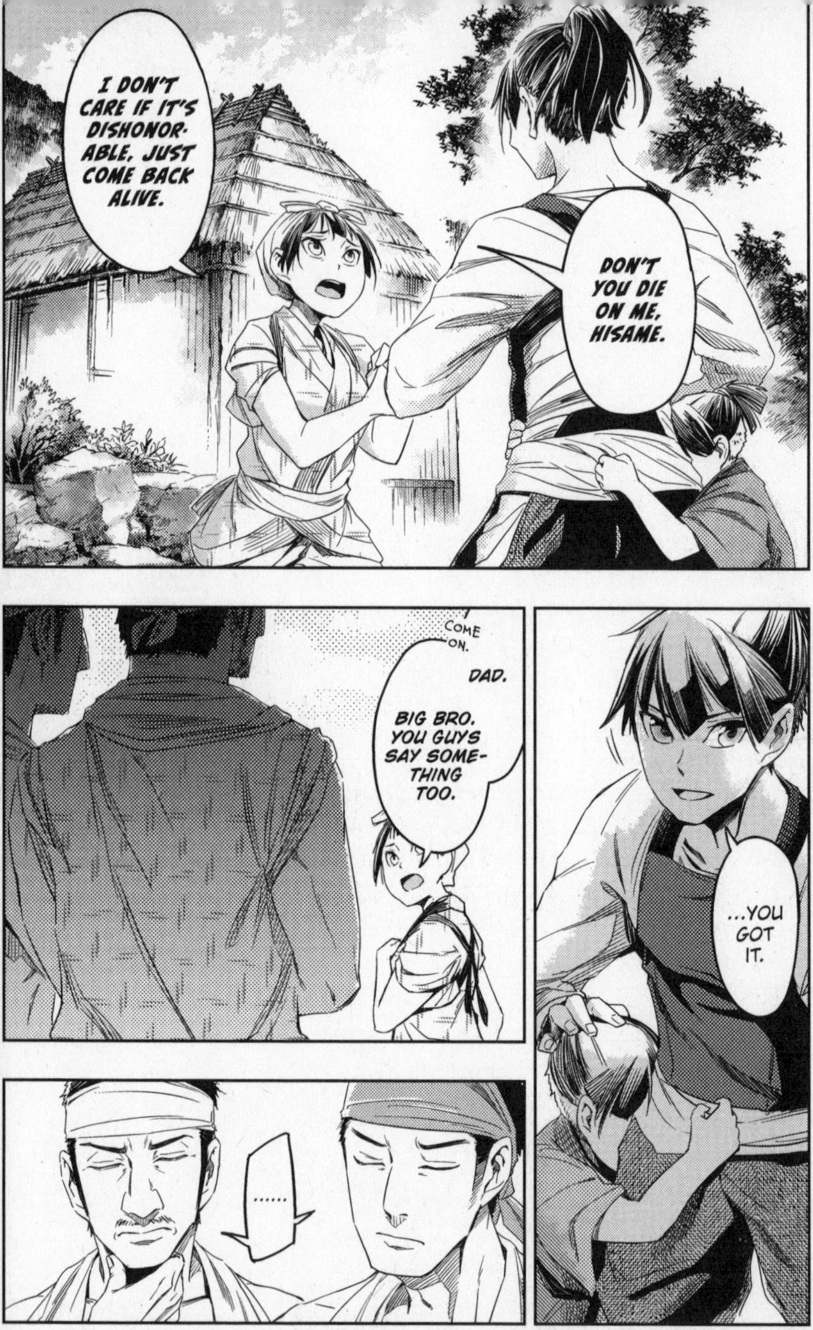
DON'T YOU DIE ON ME, HISAME.
I DON'T CARE IF IT'S DISHONORABLE. JUST COME BACK ALIVE.
...YOU GOT IT.
COME ON.
DAD.
BIG BRO. YOU GUYS SAY SOMETHING TOO.
......

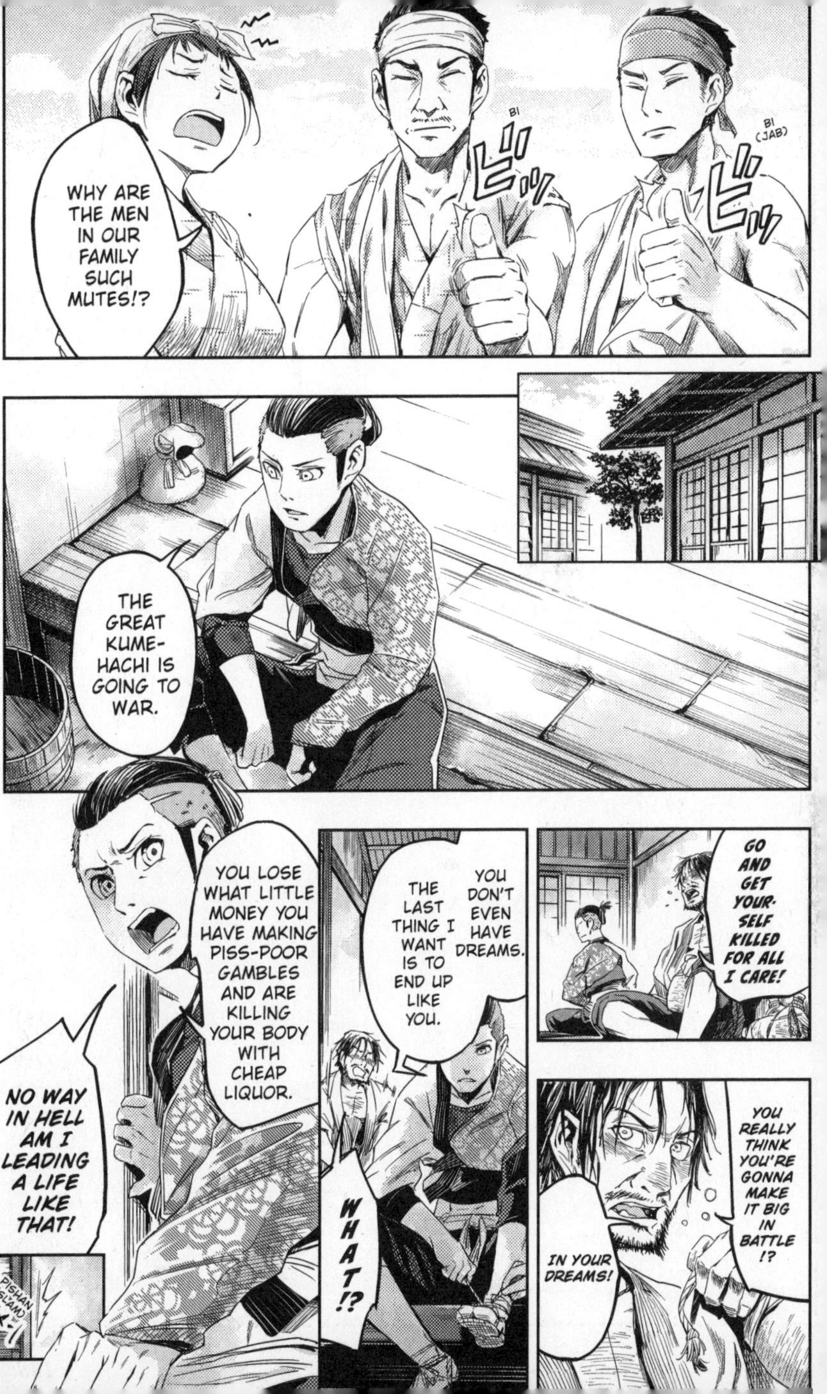
BI (JAB)
BI
WHY ARE THE MEN IN OUR FAMILY SUCH MUTES!?
THE GREAT KUME-HACHI IS GOING TO WAR.
GO AND GET YOURSELF KILLED FOR ALL I CARE!
YOU REALLY THINK YOU'RE GONNA MAKE IT BIG IN BATTLE!?
IN YOUR DREAMS!
YOU DON'T EVEN HAVE DREAMS.
THE LAST THING I WANT IS TO END UP LIKE YOU.
WHAT!?
YOU LOSE WHAT LITTLE MONEY YOU HAVE MAKING PISS-POOR GAMBLES AND ARE KILLING YOUR BODY WITH CHEAP LIQUOR.
NO WAY IN HELL AM I LEADING A LIFE LIKE THAT!
PISHAN (SLAM)

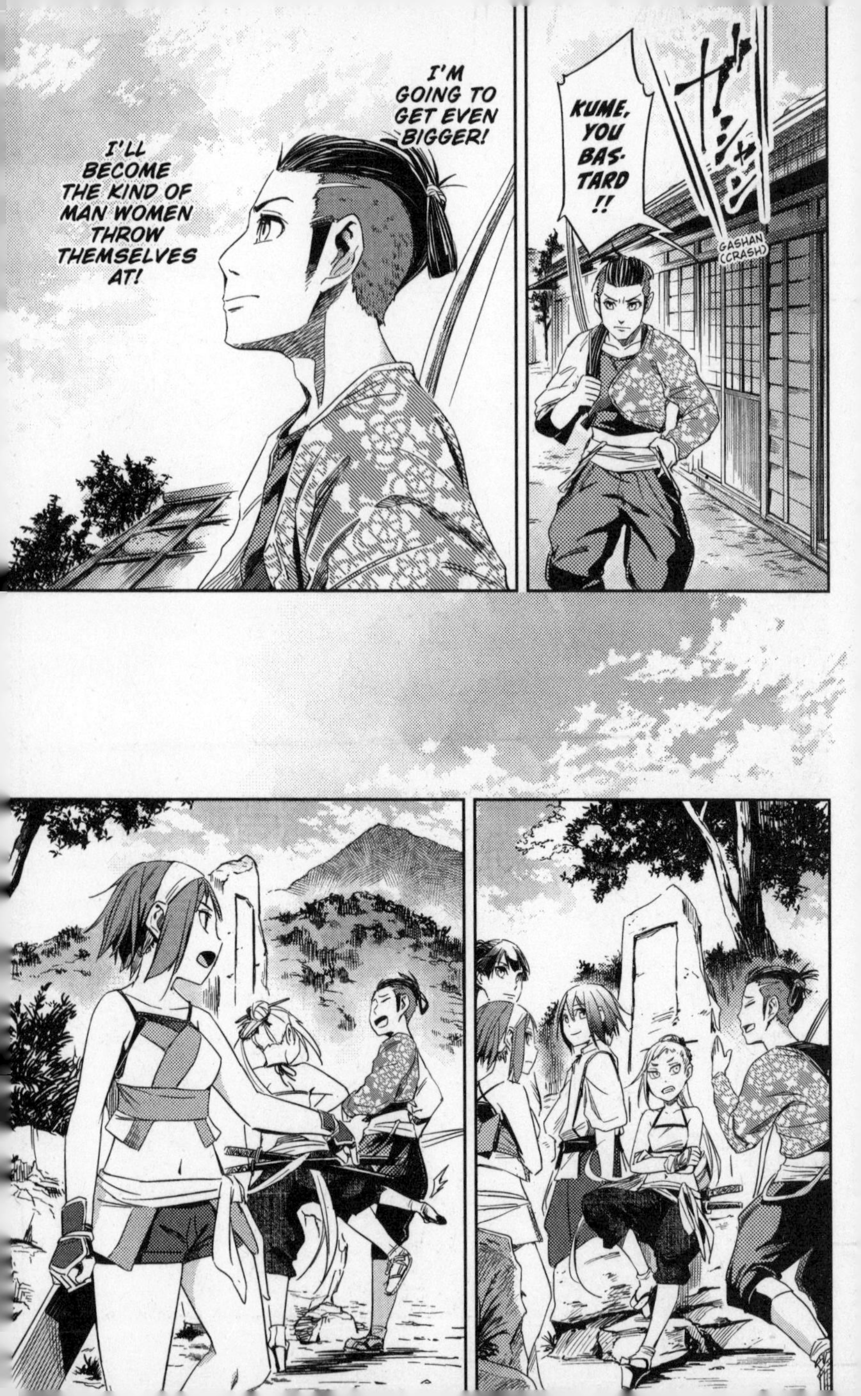
KUME, YOU BAS-TARD!!
GASHAN (CRASH)
I'M GOING TO GET EVEN BIGGER!
I'LL BECOME THE KIND OF MAN WOMEN THROW THEMSELVES AT!

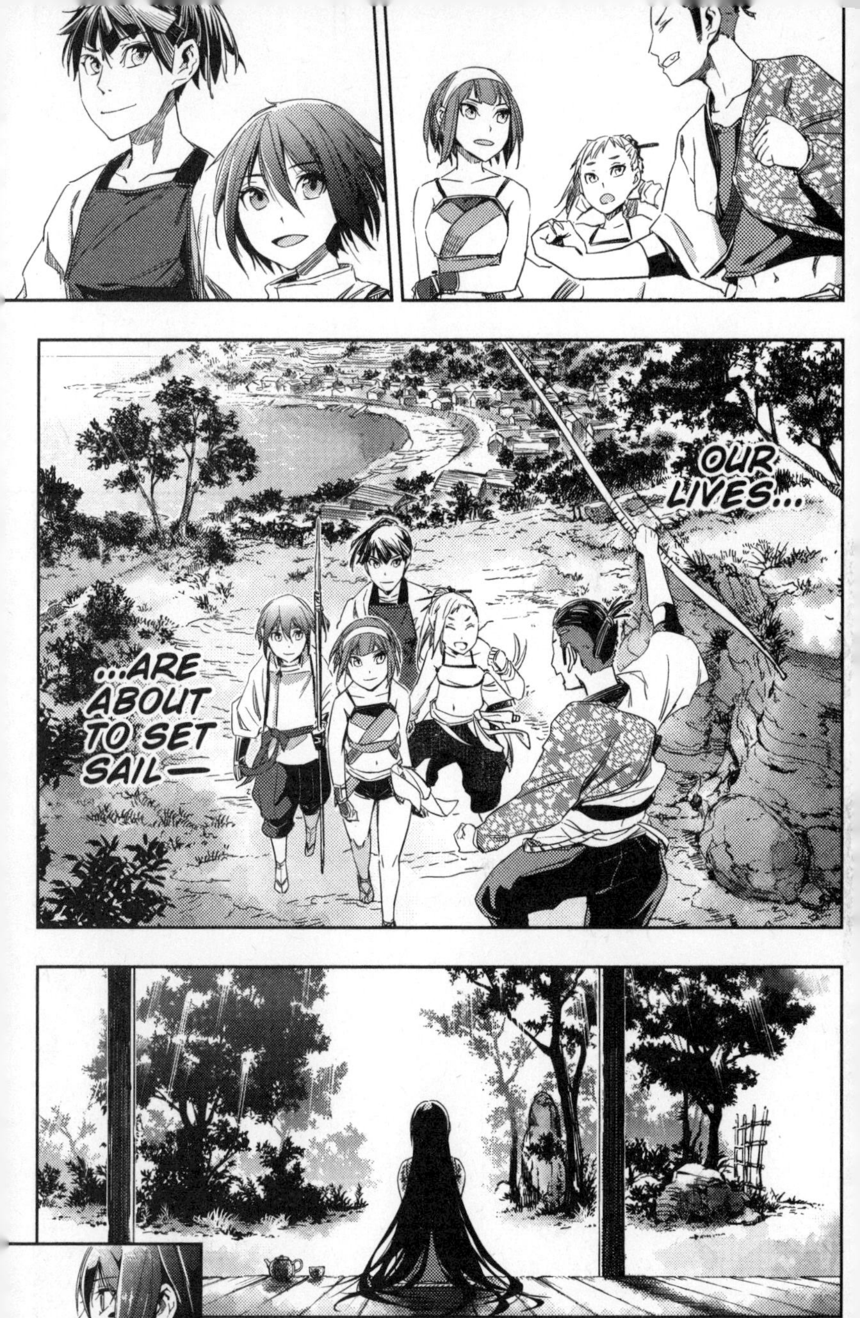
OUR LIVES...
...ARE ABOUT TO SET SAIL—

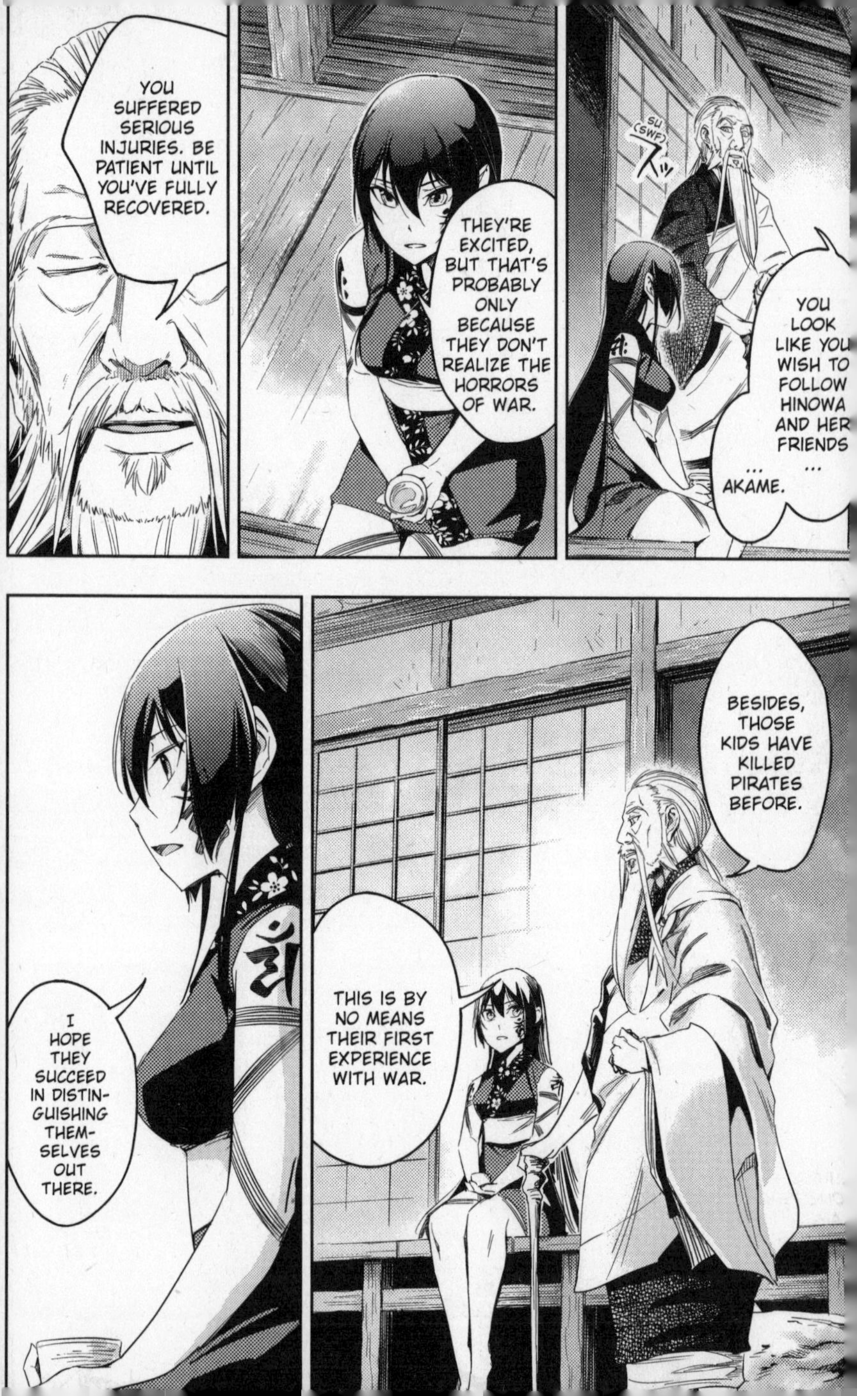
SU (SWF) スッ
YOU LOOK LIKE YOU WISH TO FOLLOW HINOWA AND HER FRIENDS... ...AKAME.
THEY'RE EXCITED, BUT THAT'S PROBABLY ONLY BECAUSE THEY DON'T REALIZE THE HORRORS OF WAR.
YOU SUFFERED SERIOUS INJURIES. BE PATIENT UNTIL YOU'VE FULLY RECOVERED.
BESIDES, THOSE KIDS HAVE KILLED PIRATES BEFORE.
THIS IS BY NO MEANS THEIR FIRST EXPERIENCE WITH WAR.
I HOPE THEY SUCCEED IN DISTIN-GUISHING THEM-SELVES OUT THERE.

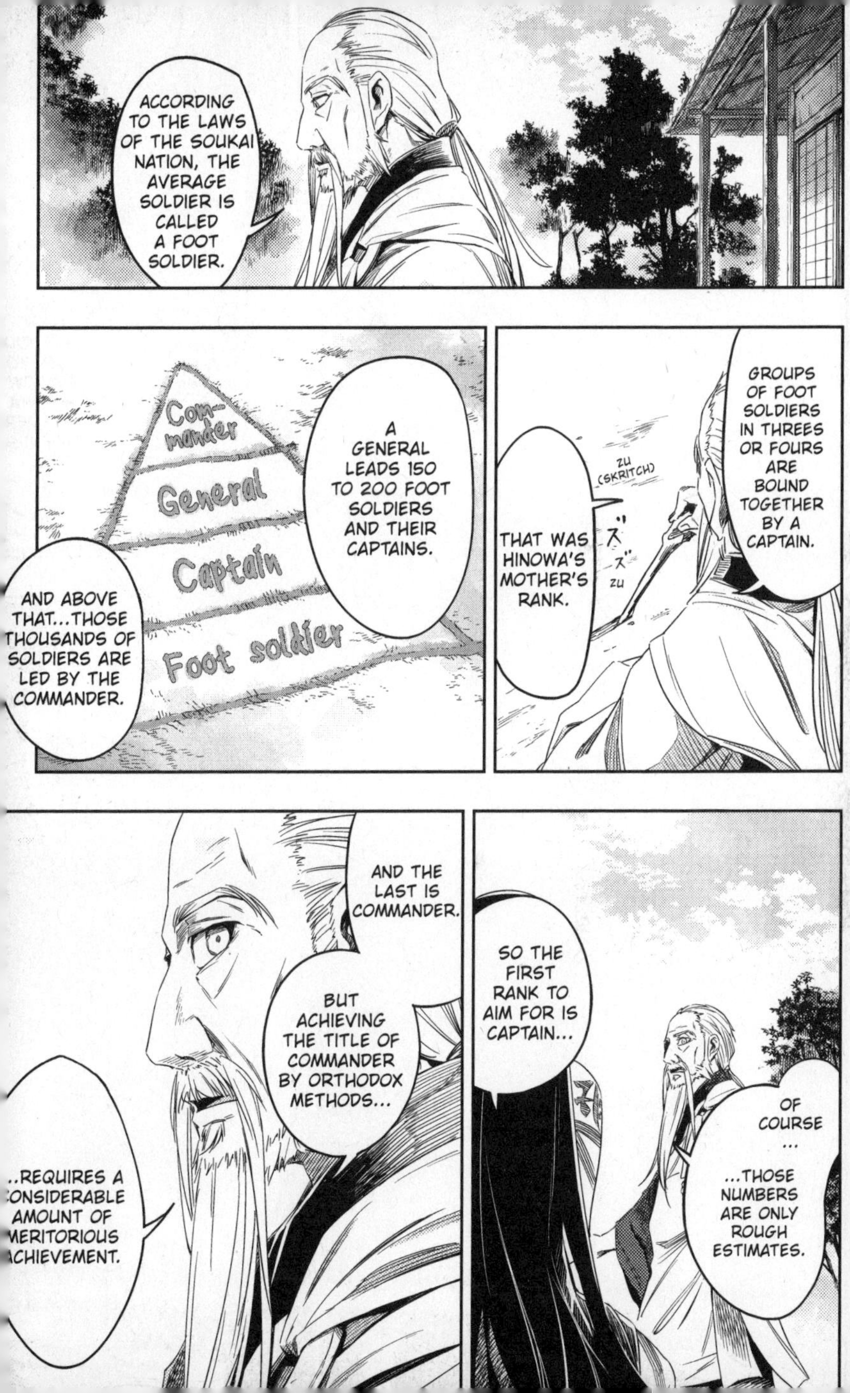
ACCORDING TO THE LAWS OF THE SOUKAI NATION, THE AVERAGE SOLDIER IS CALLED A FOOT SOLDIER.
GROUPS OF FOOT SOLDIERS IN THREES OR FOURS ARE BOUND TOGETHER BY A CAPTAIN.
ZU (SKRITCH)
ズズ
ZU
THAT WAS HINOWA'S MOTHER'S RANK.
A GENERAL LEADS 150 TO 200 FOOT SOLDIERS AND THEIR CAPTAINS.
Com-mander
General
Captain
Foot soldier
AND ABOVE THAT...THOSE THOUSANDS OF SOLDIERS ARE LED BY THE COMMANDER.
SO THE FIRST RANK TO AIM FOR IS CAPTAIN...
OF COURSE...
...THOSE NUMBERS ARE ONLY ROUGH ESTIMATES.
AND THE LAST IS COMMANDER.
BUT ACHIEVING THE TITLE OF COMMANDER BY ORTHODOX METHODS...
..REQUIRES A CONSIDERABLE AMOUNT OF MERITORIOUS ACHIEVEMENT.

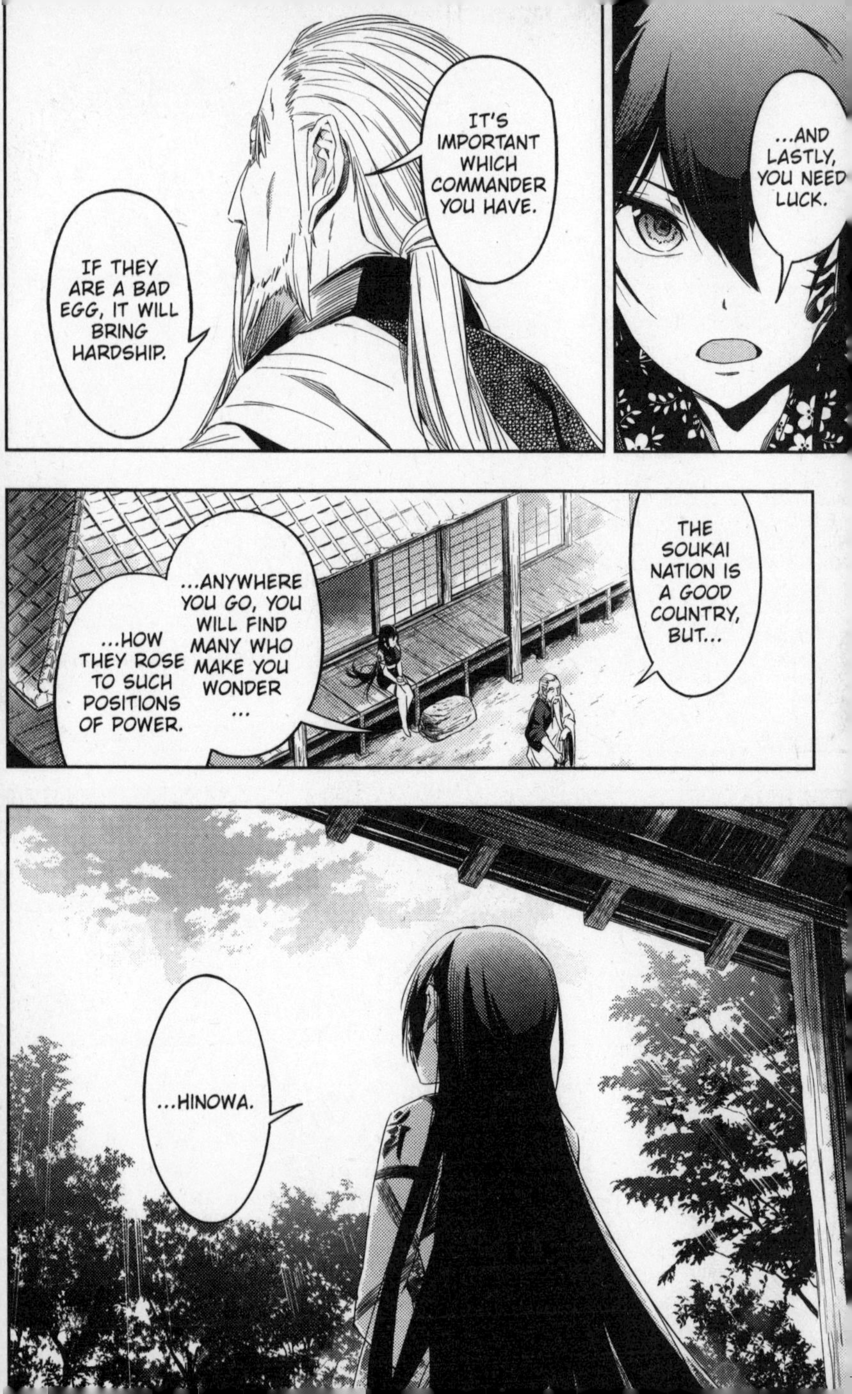
...AND LASTLY, YOU NEED LUCK.
IT'S IMPORTANT WHICH COMMANDER YOU HAVE.
IF THEY ARE A BAD EGG, IT WILL BRING HARDSHIP.
THE SOUKAI NATION IS A GOOD COUNTRY, BUT...
...ANYWHERE YOU GO, YOU WILL FIND MANY WHO MAKE YOU WONDER ...
...HOW THEY ROSE TO SUCH POSITIONS OF POWER.
...HINOWA.

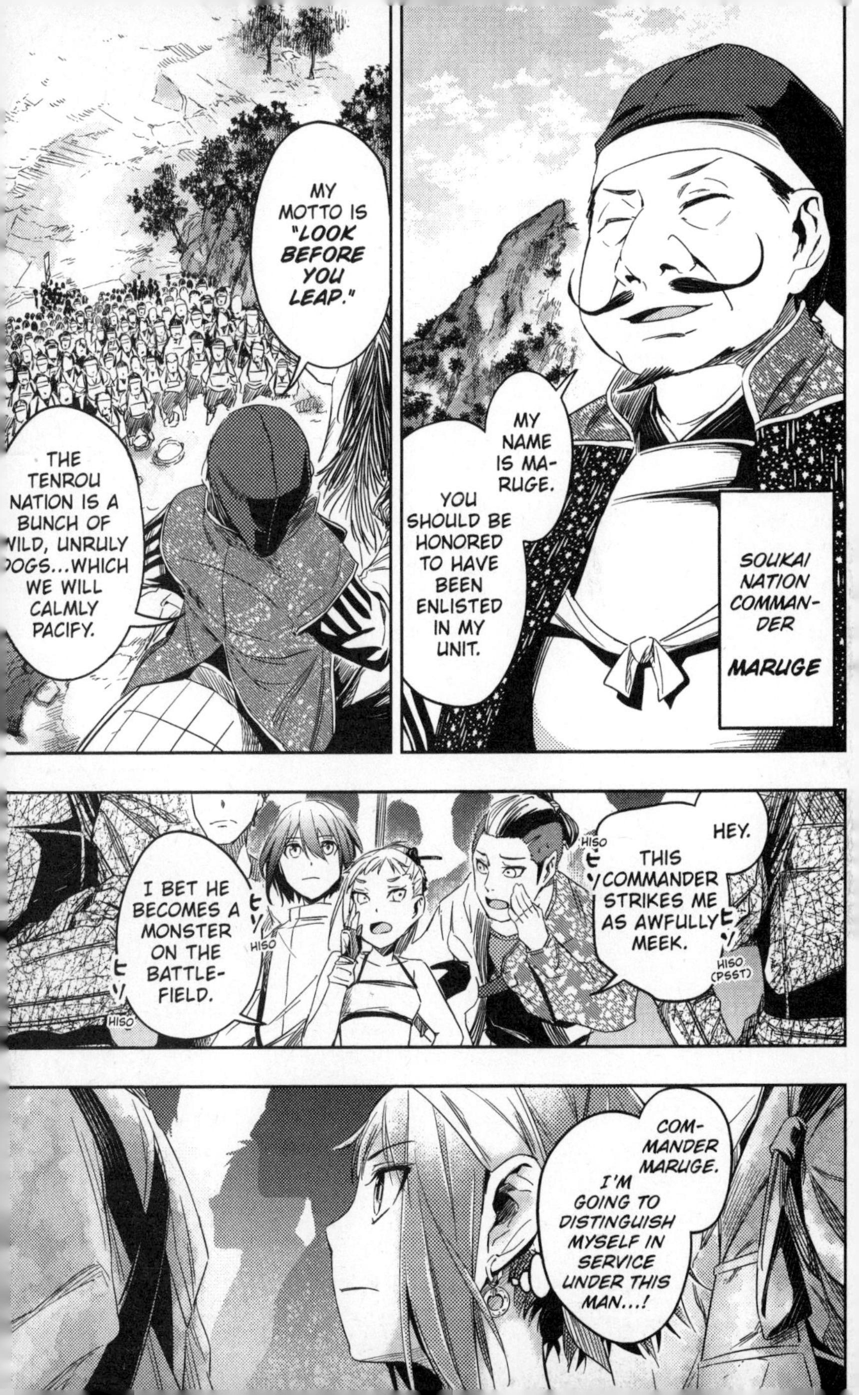
SOUKAI NATION COMMANDER MARUGE
MY NAME IS MARUGE.
YOU SHOULD BE HONORED TO HAVE BEEN ENLISTED IN MY UNIT.
MY MOTTO IS *"LOOK BEFORE YOU LEAP."*
THE TENROU NATION IS A BUNCH OF WILD, UNRULY DOGS...WHICH WE WILL CALMLY PACIFY.
HEY.
THIS COMMANDER STRIKES ME AS AWFULLY MEEK.
HISO (PSST)
HISO
I BET HE BECOMES A MONSTER ON THE BATTLEFIELD.
HISO
HISO
COMMANDER MARUGE.
I'M GOING TO DISTINGUISH MYSELF IN SERVICE UNDER THIS MAN...!

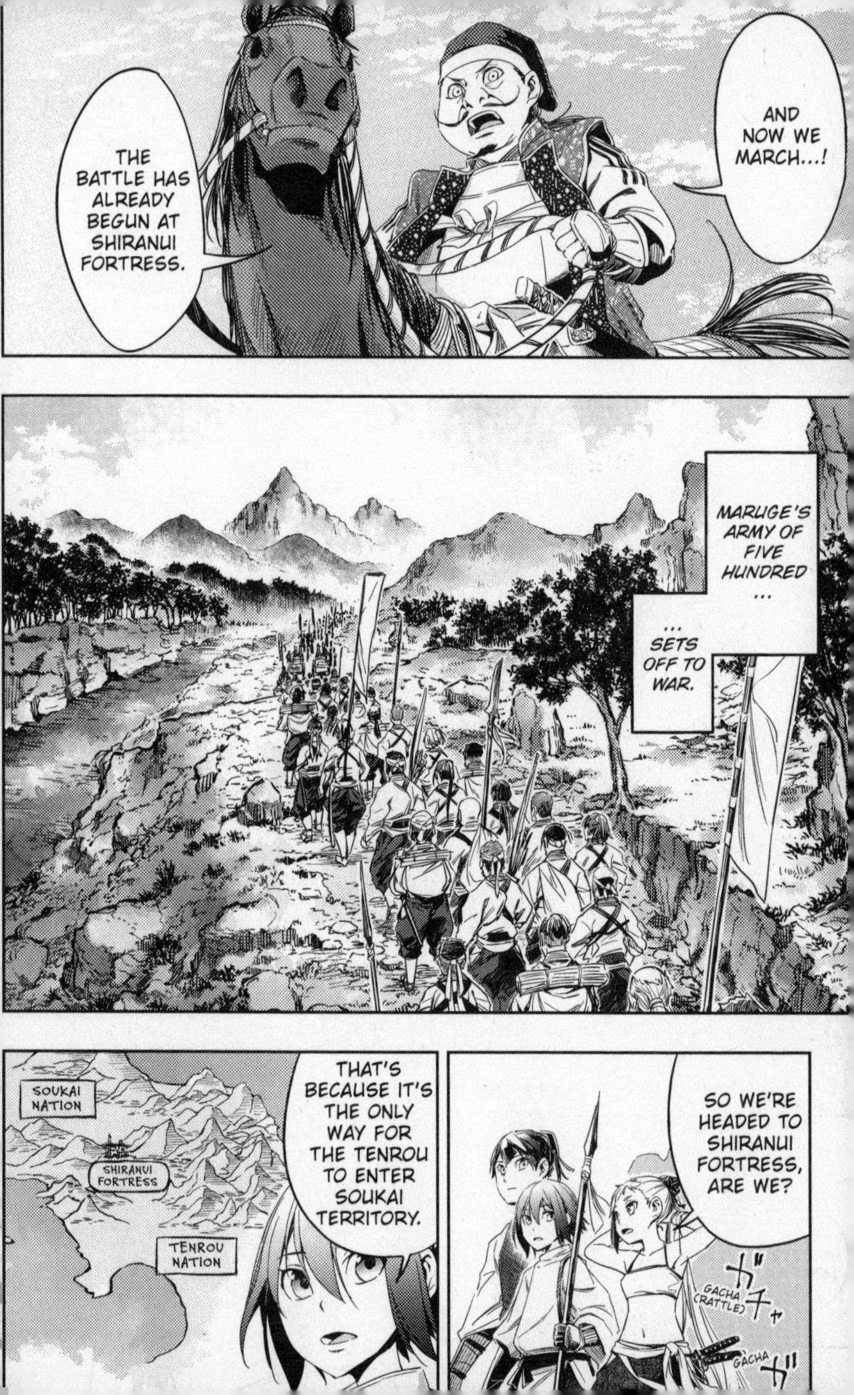
AND NOW WE MARCH...!
THE BATTLE HAS ALREADY BEGUN AT SHIRANUI FORTRESS.
MARUGE'S ARMY OF FIVE HUNDRED...
...SETS OFF TO WAR.
SO WE'RE HEADED TO SHIRANUI FORTRESS, ARE WE?
GACHA (RATTLE)
GACHA
THAT'S BECAUSE IT'S THE ONLY WAY FOR THE TENROU TO ENTER SOUKAI TERRITORY.
SOUKAI NATION
SHIRANUI FORTRESS
TENROU NATION

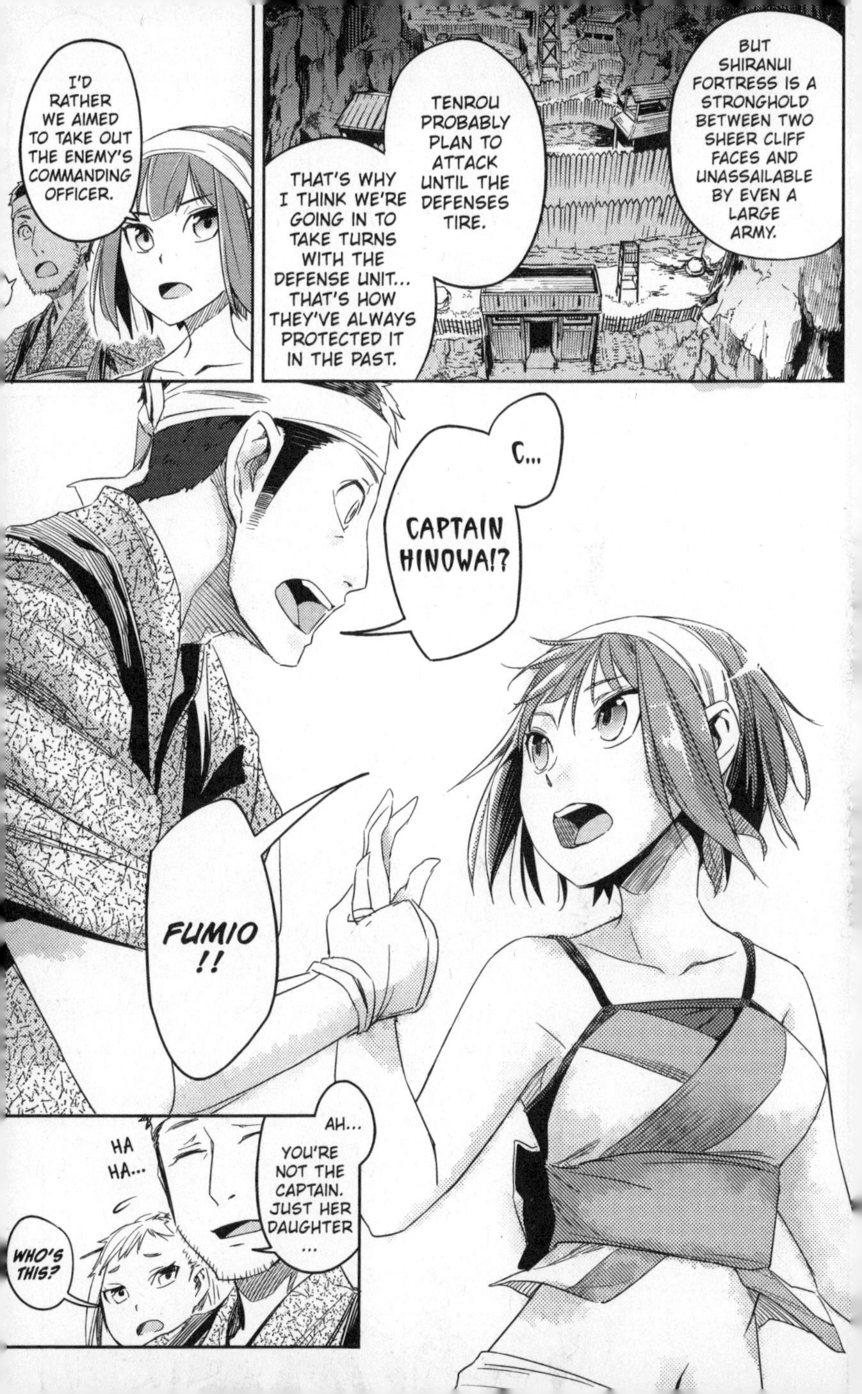
BUT SHIRANUI FORTRESS IS A STRONGHOLD BETWEEN TWO SHEER CLIFF FACES AND UNASSAILABLE BY EVEN A LARGE ARMY.
TENROU PROBABLY PLAN TO ATTACK UNTIL THE DEFENSES TIRE.
THAT'S WHY I THINK WE'RE GOING IN TO TAKE TURNS WITH THE DEFENSE UNIT... THAT'S HOW THEY'VE ALWAYS PROTECTED IT IN THE PAST.
I'D RATHER WE AIMED TO TAKE OUT THE ENEMY'S COMMANDING OFFICER.
C...
CAPTAIN HINOWA!?
FUMIO!!
AH... YOU'RE NOT THE CAPTAIN. JUST HER DAUGHTER...
HA HA...
WHO'S THIS?

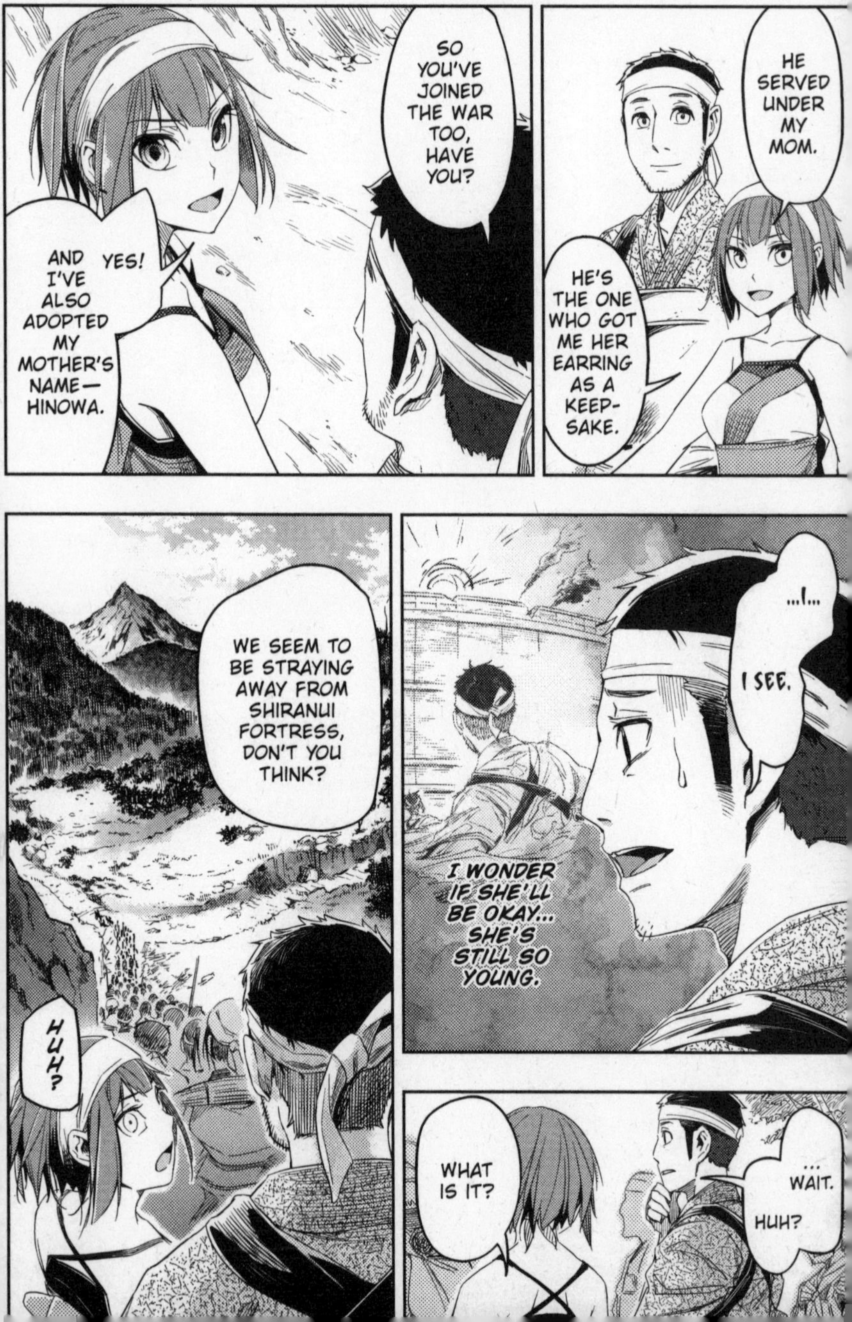
HE SERVED UNDER MY MOM.
HE'S THE ONE WHO GOT ME HER EARRING AS A KEEP-SAKE.
SO YOU'VE JOINED THE WAR TOO, HAVE YOU?
YES!
AND I'VE ALSO ADOPTED MY MOTHER'S NAME—HINOWA.
...I...
I SEE.
I WONDER IF SHE'LL BE OKAY... SHE'S STILL SO YOUNG.
...WAIT.
HUH?
WHAT IS IT?
WE SEEM TO BE STRAYING AWAY FROM SHIRANUI FORTRESS, DON'T YOU THINK?
HUH?

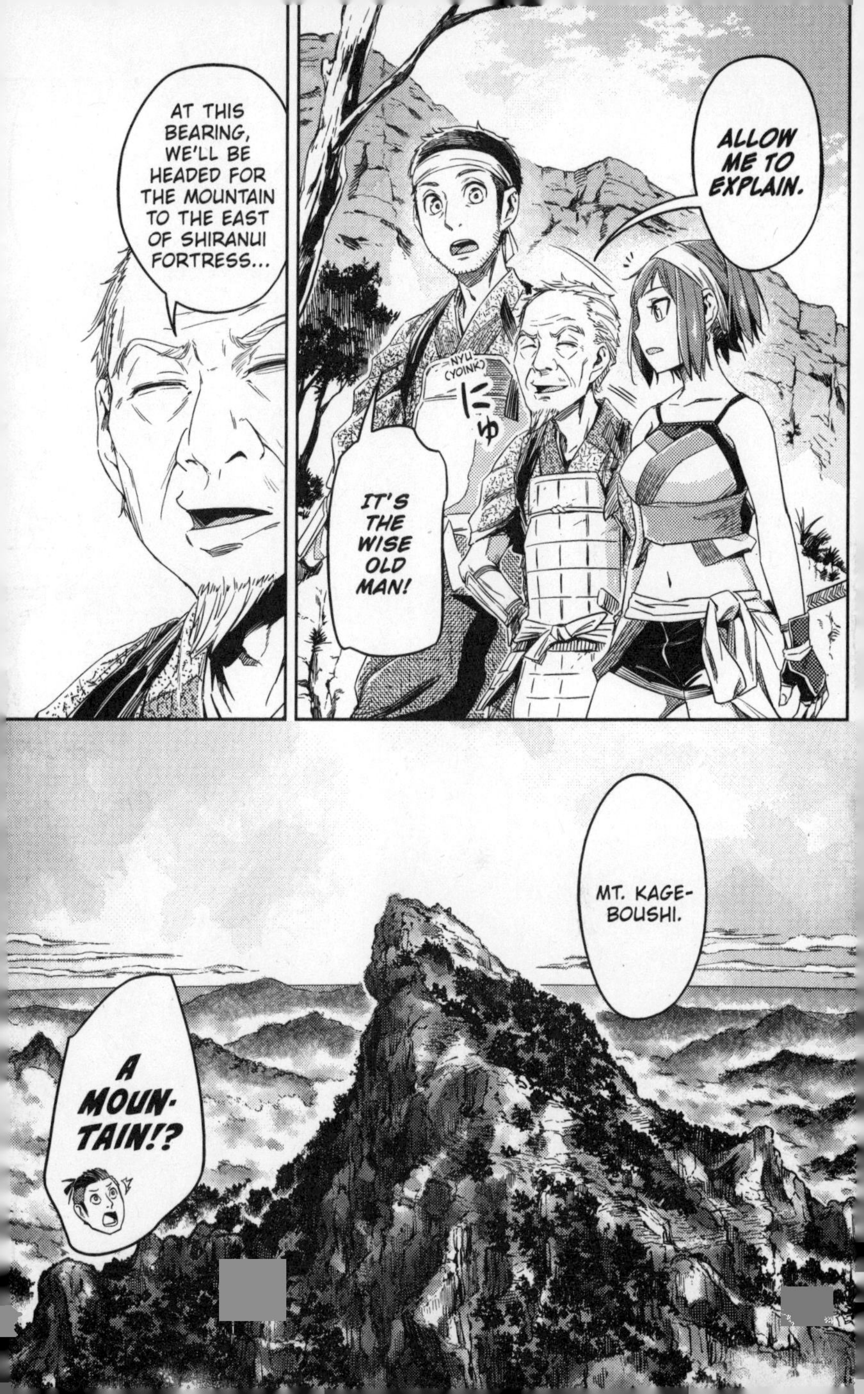
ALLOW ME TO EXPLAIN.
NYU (YOINK)
にゅ
IT'S THE WISE OLD MAN!
AT THIS BEARING, WE'LL BE HEADED FOR THE MOUNTAIN TO THE EAST OF SHIRANUI FORTRESS...
MT. KAGE-BOUSHI.
A MOUN-TAIN!?

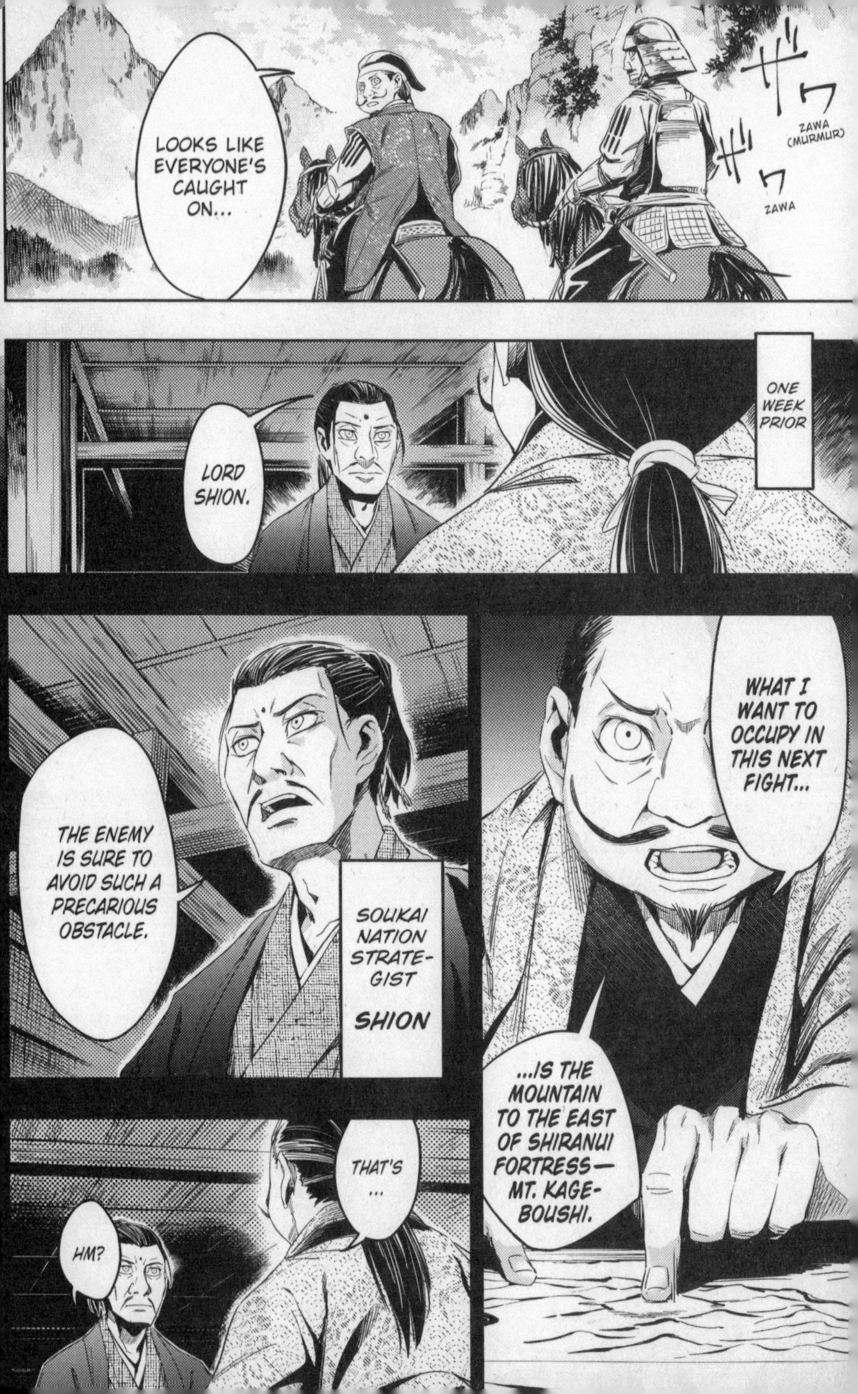
ザワ
ZAWA (MURMUR)
ザワ
ZAWA
LOOKS LIKE EVERYONE'S CAUGHT ON...
ONE WEEK PRIOR
LORD SHION.
WHAT I WANT TO OCCUPY IN THIS NEXT FIGHT...
...IS THE MOUNTAIN TO THE EAST OF SHIRANUI FORTRESS—MT. KAGE-BOUSHI.
SOUKAI NATION STRATE-GIST
SHION
THE ENEMY IS SURE TO AVOID SUCH A PRECARIOUS OBSTACLE.
THAT'S ...
HM?

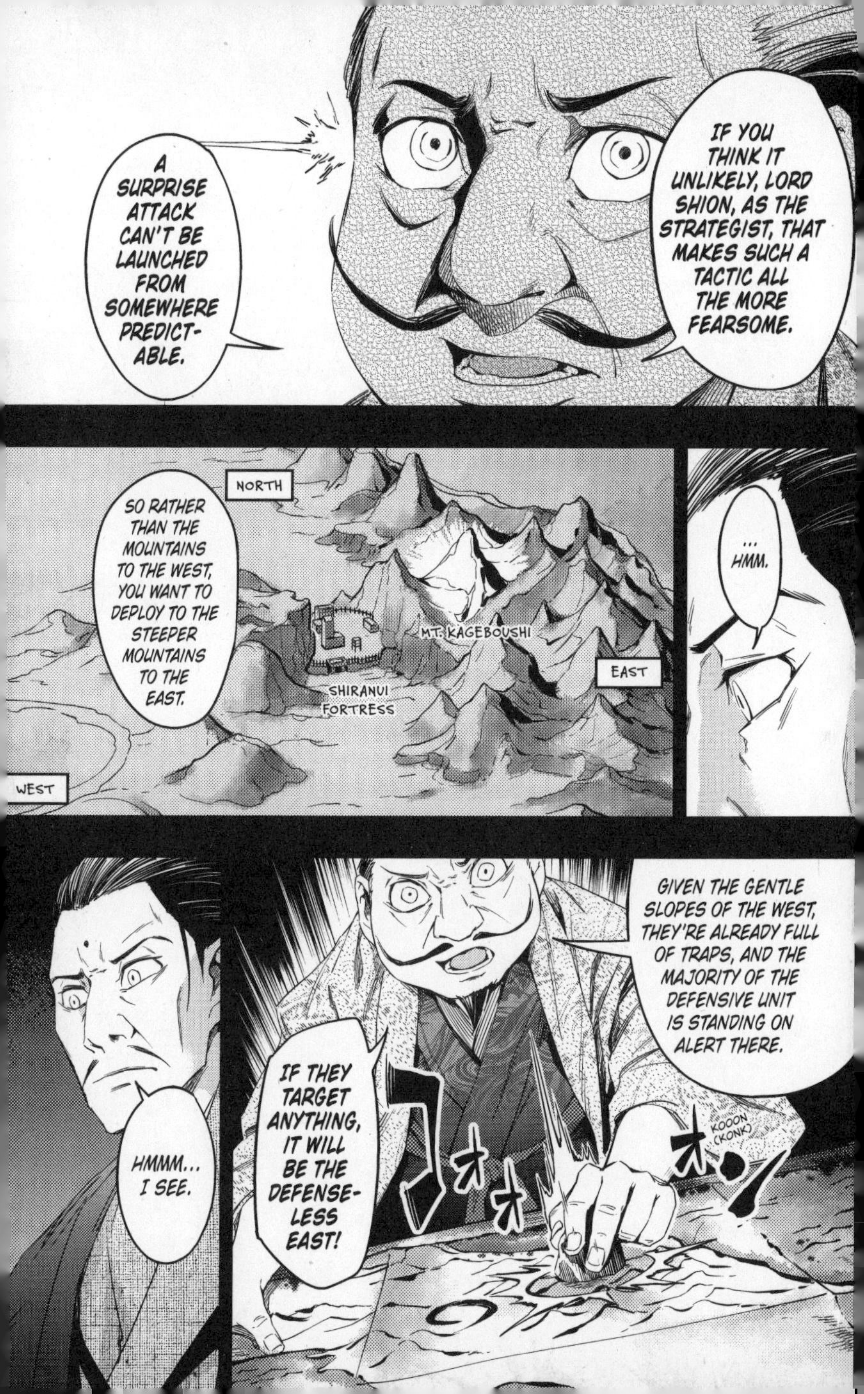
IF YOU THINK IT UNLIKELY, LORD SHION, AS THE STRATEGIST, THAT MAKES SUCH A TACTIC ALL THE MORE FEARSOME.
A SURPRISE ATTACK CAN'T BE LAUNCHED FROM SOMEWHERE PREDICT-ABLE.
... HMM.
NORTH
SO RATHER THAN THE MOUNTAINS TO THE WEST, YOU WANT TO DEPLOY TO THE STEEPER MOUNTAINS TO THE EAST.
MT. KAGEBOUSHI
EAST
SHIRANUI FORTRESS
WEST
GIVEN THE GENTLE SLOPES OF THE WEST, THEY'RE ALREADY FULL OF TRAPS, AND THE MAJORITY OF THE DEFENSIVE UNIT IS STANDING ON ALERT THERE.
KOOON (KONK)
IF THEY TARGET ANYTHING, IT WILL BE THE DEFENSE-LESS EAST!
HMMM... I SEE.

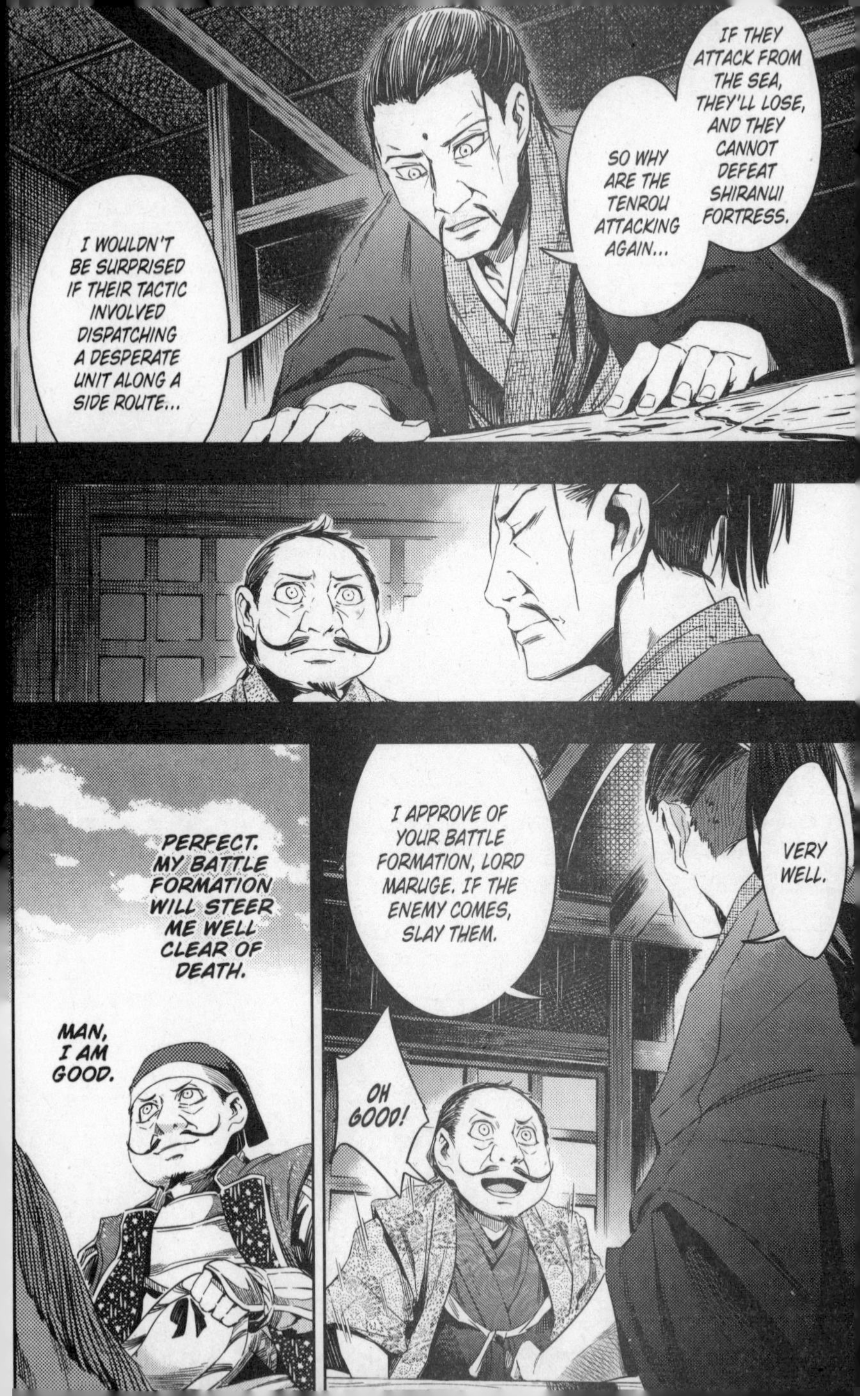
IF THEY ATTACK FROM THE SEA, THEY'LL LOSE, AND THEY CANNOT DEFEAT SHIRANUI FORTRESS.
SO WHY ARE THE TENROU ATTACKING AGAIN...
I WOULDN'T BE SURPRISED IF THEIR TACTIC INVOLVED DISPATCHING A DESPERATE UNIT ALONG A SIDE ROUTE...
VERY WELL.
I APPROVE OF YOUR BATTLE FORMATION, LORD MARUGE. IF THE ENEMY COMES, SLAY THEM.
OH GOOD!
PERFECT. MY BATTLE FORMATION WILL STEER ME WELL CLEAR OF DEATH.
MAN, I AM GOOD.

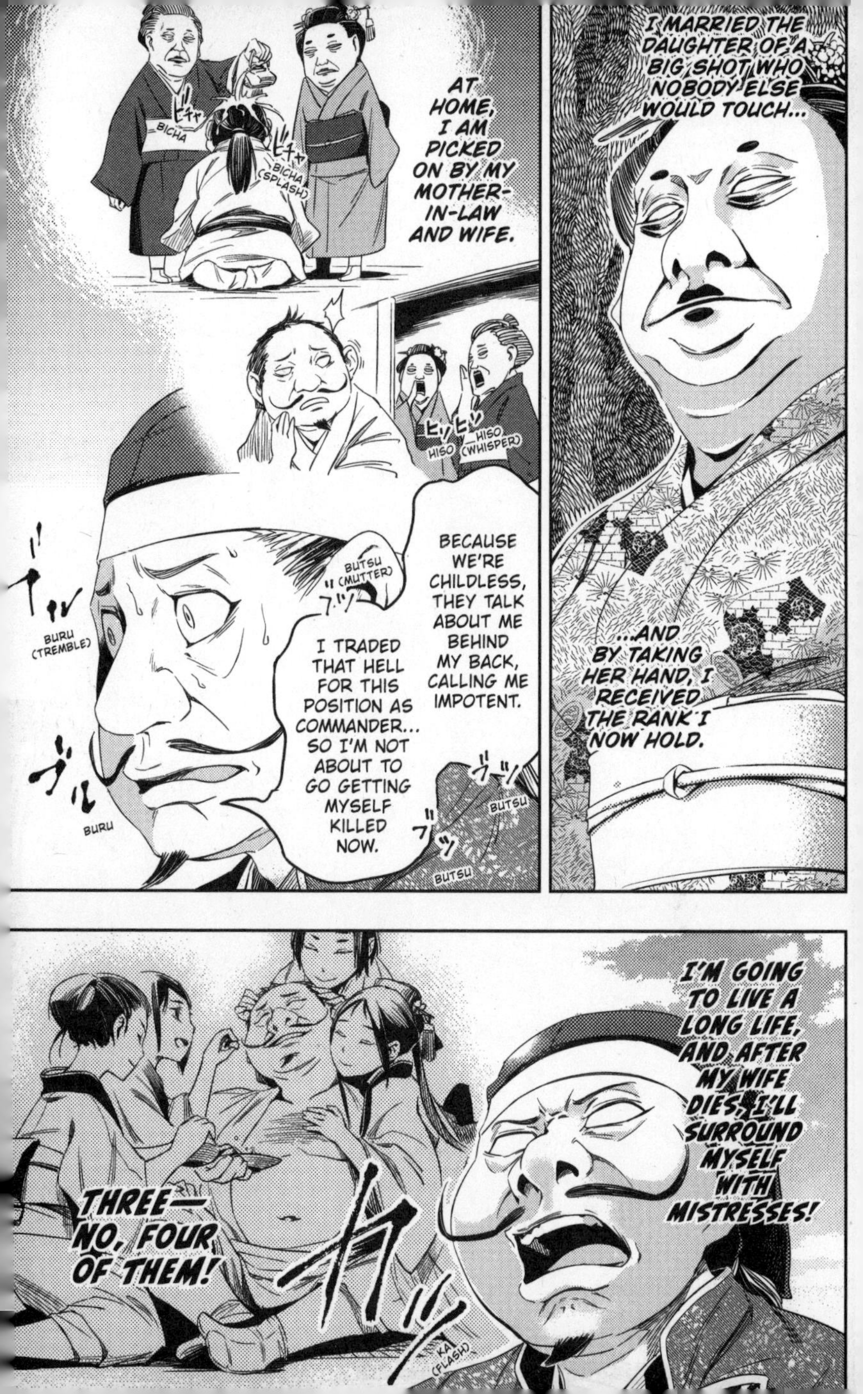
I MARRIED THE DAUGHTER OF A BIG SHOT WHO NOBODY ELSE WOULD TOUCH...
...AND BY TAKING HER HAND, I RECEIVED THE RANK I NOW HOLD.
AT HOME, I AM PICKED ON BY MY MOTHER-IN-LAW AND WIFE.
BICHA
BICHA (SPLASH)
HISO
HISO (WHISPER)
BECAUSE WE'RE CHILDLESS, THEY TALK ABOUT ME BEHIND MY BACK, CALLING ME IMPOTENT.
BUTSU (MUTTER)
I TRADED THAT HELL FOR THIS POSITION AS COMMANDER... SO I'M NOT ABOUT TO GO GETTING MYSELF KILLED NOW.
BUTSU
BUTSU
BURU (TREMBLE)
BURU
I'M GOING TO LIVE A LONG LIFE, AND AFTER MY WIFE DIES, I'LL SURROUND MYSELF WITH MISTRESSES!
THREE—NO, FOUR OF THEM!
KA (FLASH)

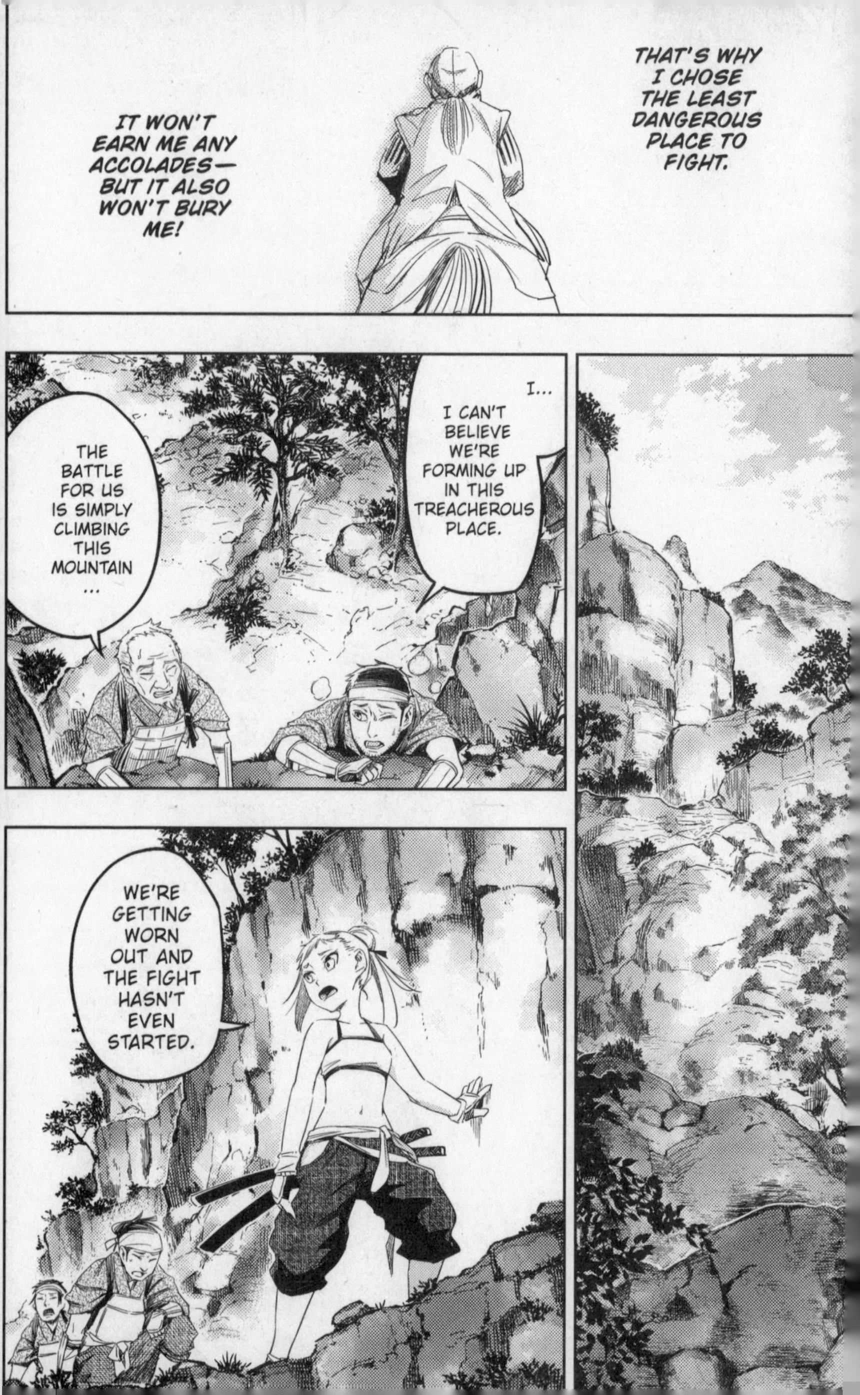
THAT'S WHY I CHOSE THE LEAST DANGEROUS PLACE TO FIGHT.
IT WON'T EARN ME ANY ACCOLADES—BUT IT ALSO WON'T BURY ME!
I... I CAN'T BELIEVE WE'RE FORMING UP IN THIS TREACHEROUS PLACE.
THE BATTLE FOR US IS SIMPLY CLIMBING THIS MOUNTAIN...
WE'RE GETTING WORN OUT AND THE FIGHT HASN'T EVEN STARTED.

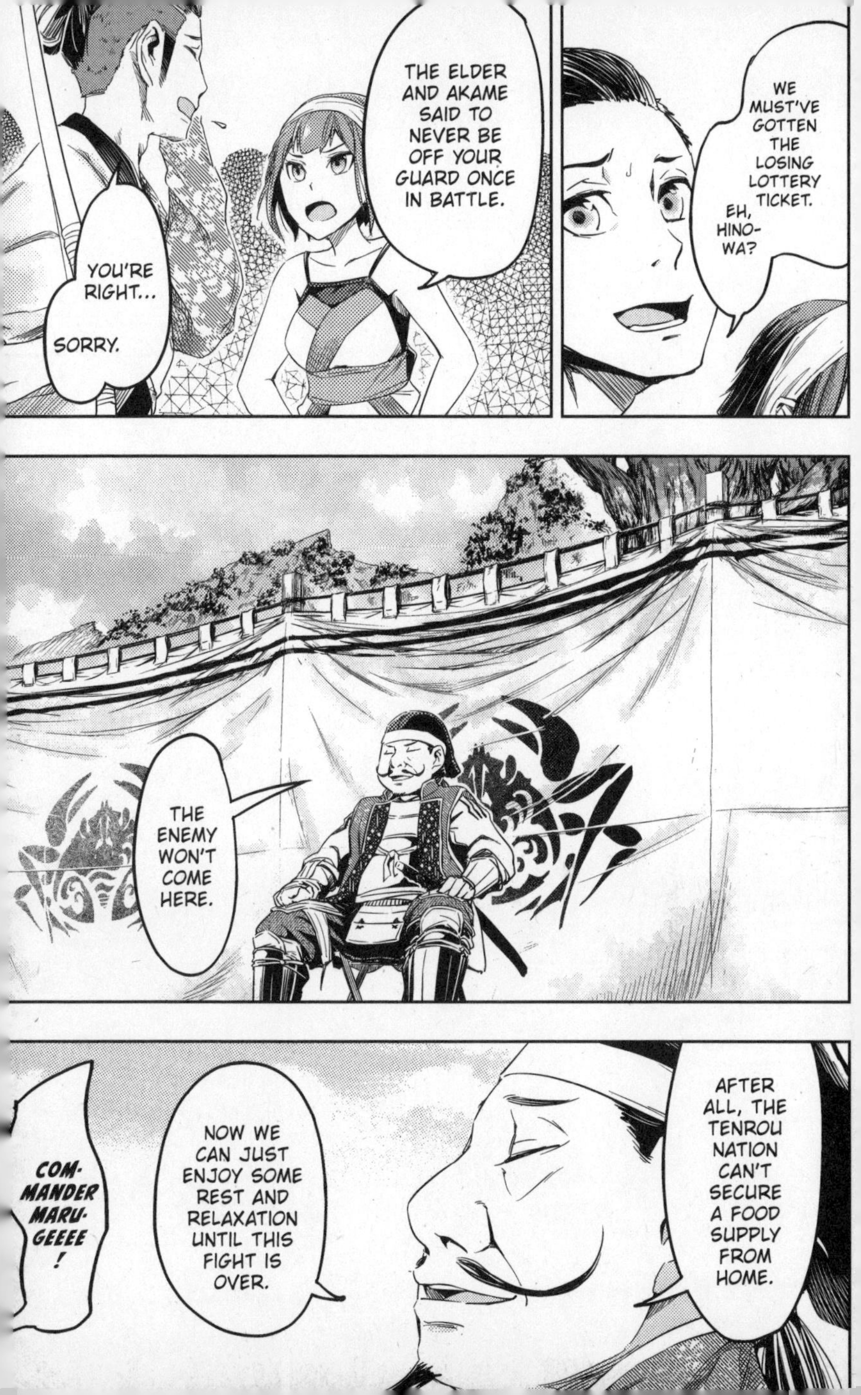
WE MUST'VE GOTTEN THE LOSING LOTTERY TICKET.
EH, HINO-WA?
THE ELDER AND AKAME SAID TO NEVER BE OFF YOUR GUARD ONCE IN BATTLE.
YOU'RE RIGHT...
SORRY.
THE ENEMY WON'T COME HERE.
AFTER ALL, THE TENROU NATION CAN'T SECURE A FOOD SUPPLY FROM HOME.
NOW WE CAN JUST ENJOY SOME REST AND RELAXATION UNTIL THIS FIGHT IS OVER.
COM-MANDER MARU-GEEEE!

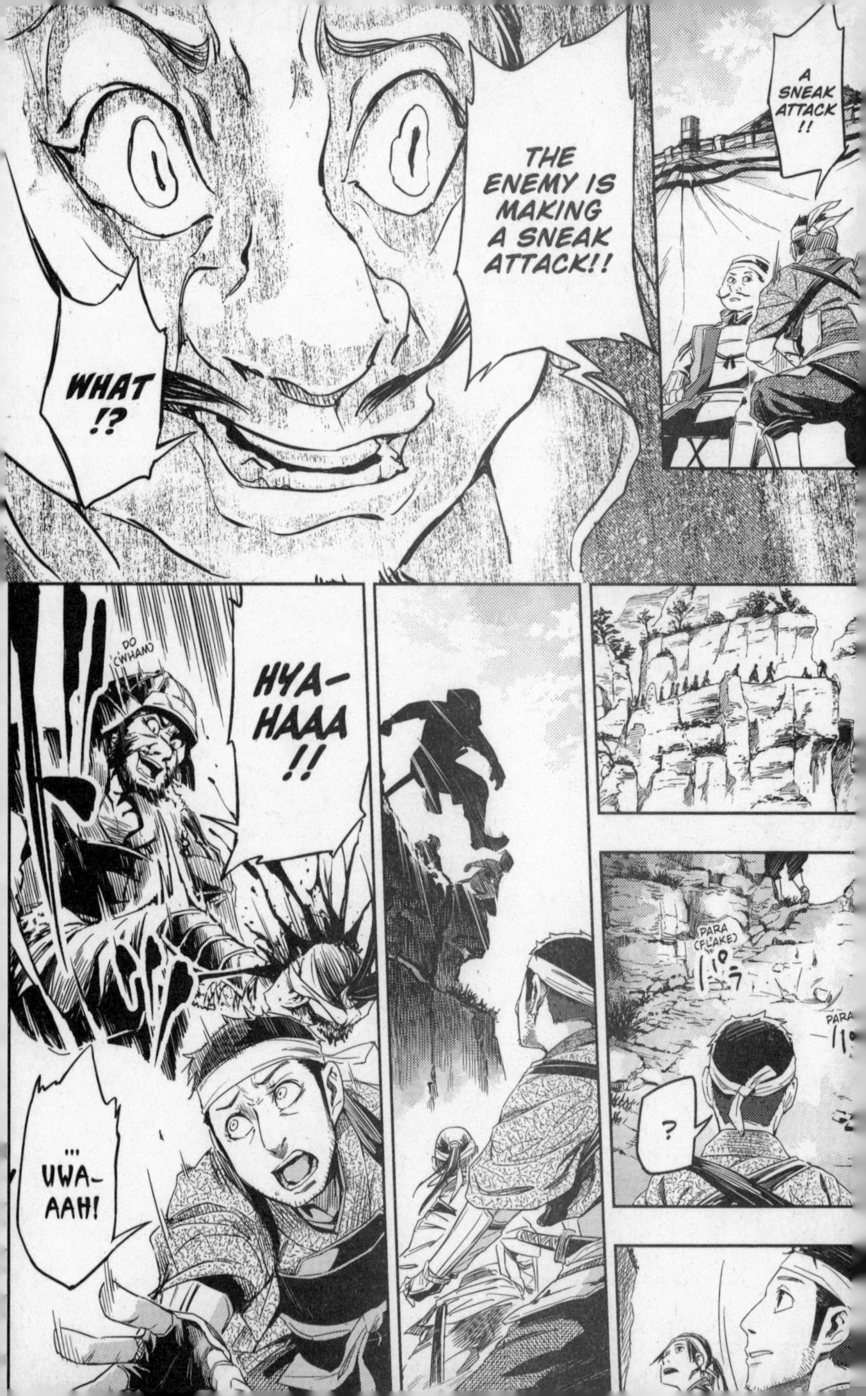
A SNEAK ATTACK!!
THE ENEMY IS MAKING A SNEAK ATTACK!!
WHAT!?
PARA (FLAKE)
PARA
?
DO (WHAM)
HYA-HAAA!!
...UWA-AAH!

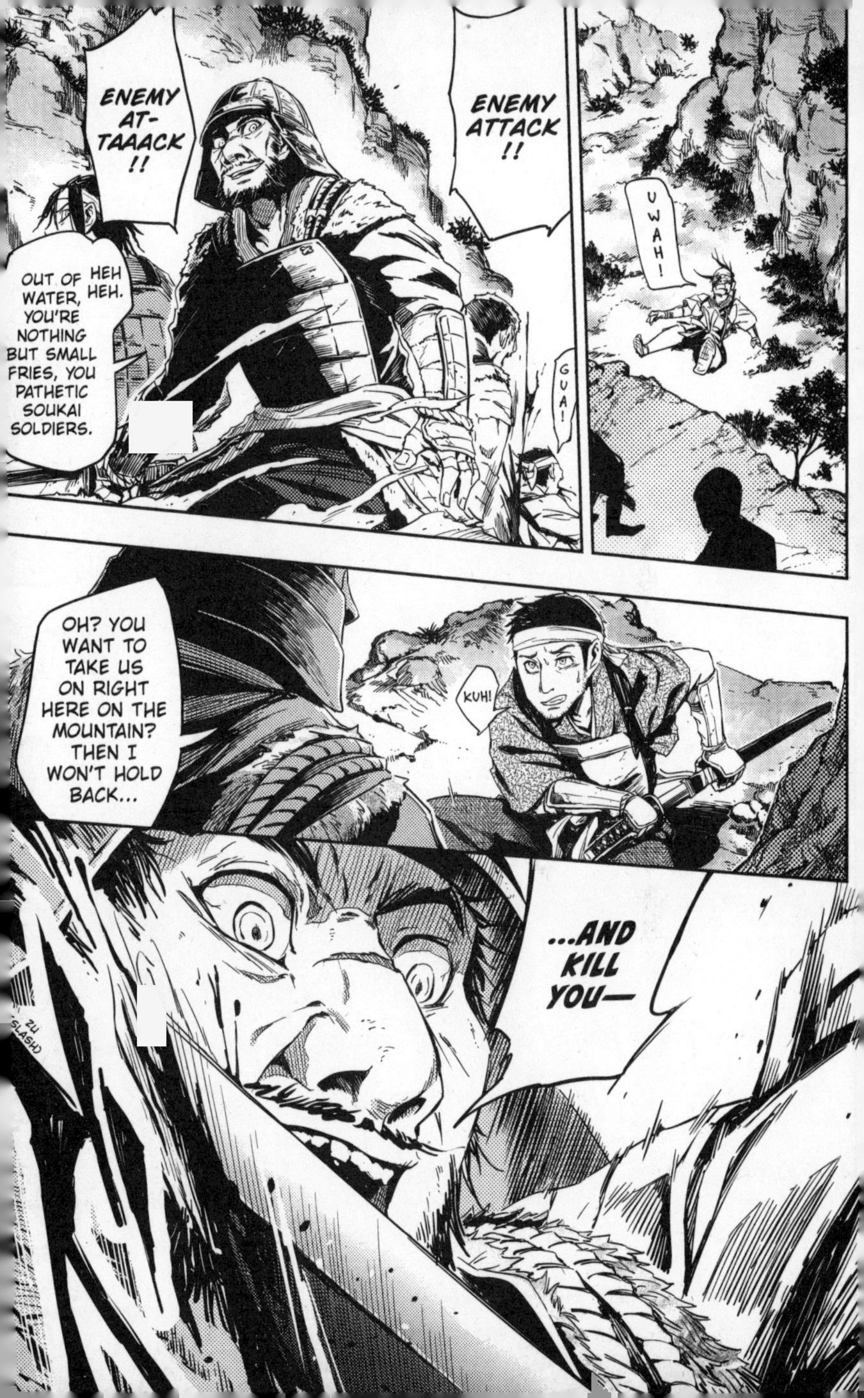
UWAH!
ENEMY ATTACK!!
ENEMY AT-TAAACK!!
GUA!
HEH HEH.
OUT OF WATER, YOU'RE NOTHING BUT SMALL FRIES, YOU PATHETIC SOUKAI SOLDIERS.
OH? YOU WANT TO TAKE US ON RIGHT HERE ON THE MOUNTAIN? THEN I WON'T HOLD BACK...
KUH!
...AND KILL YOU—
ZU
SLASH)

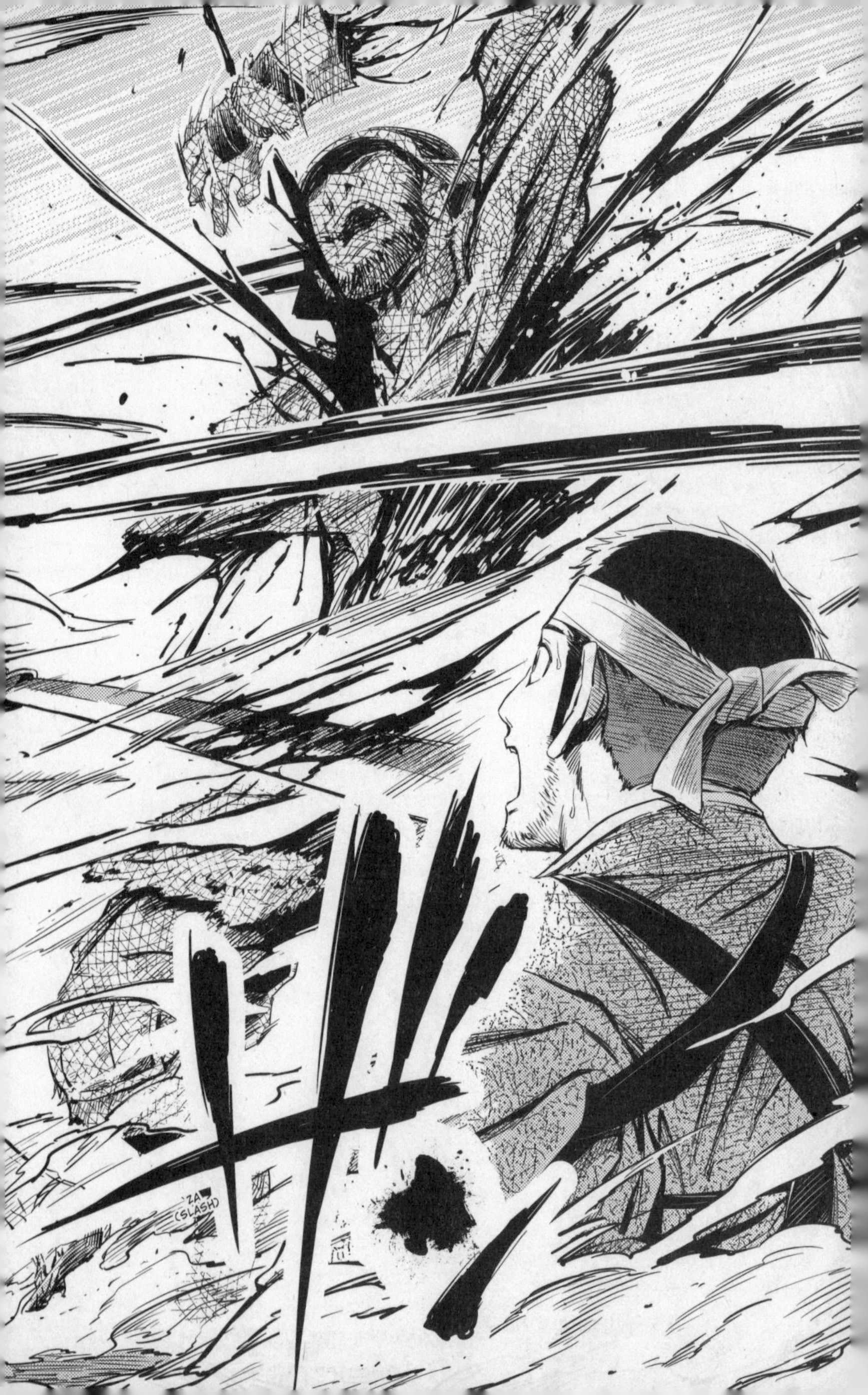
ZA
(SLASH)

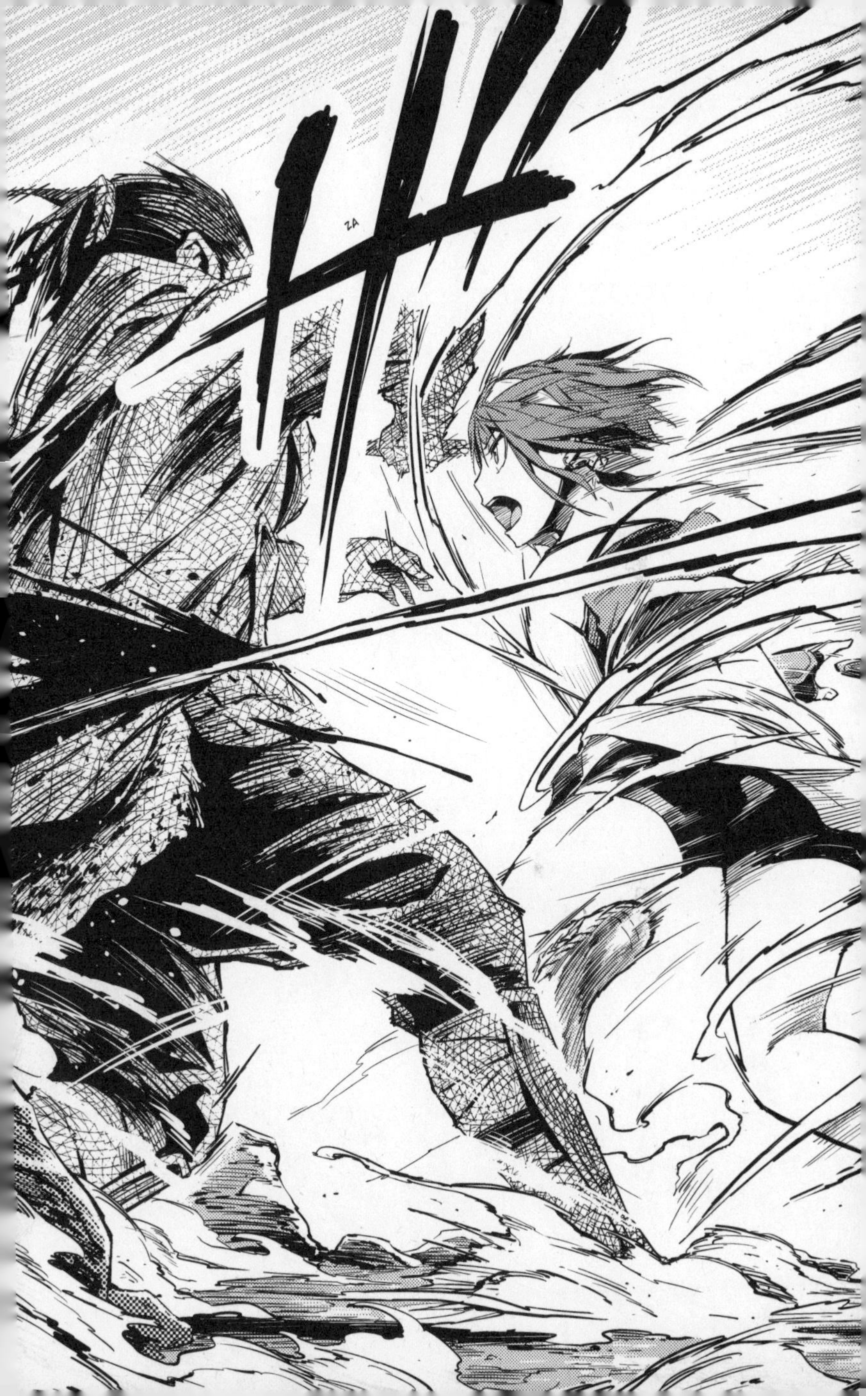
ZA

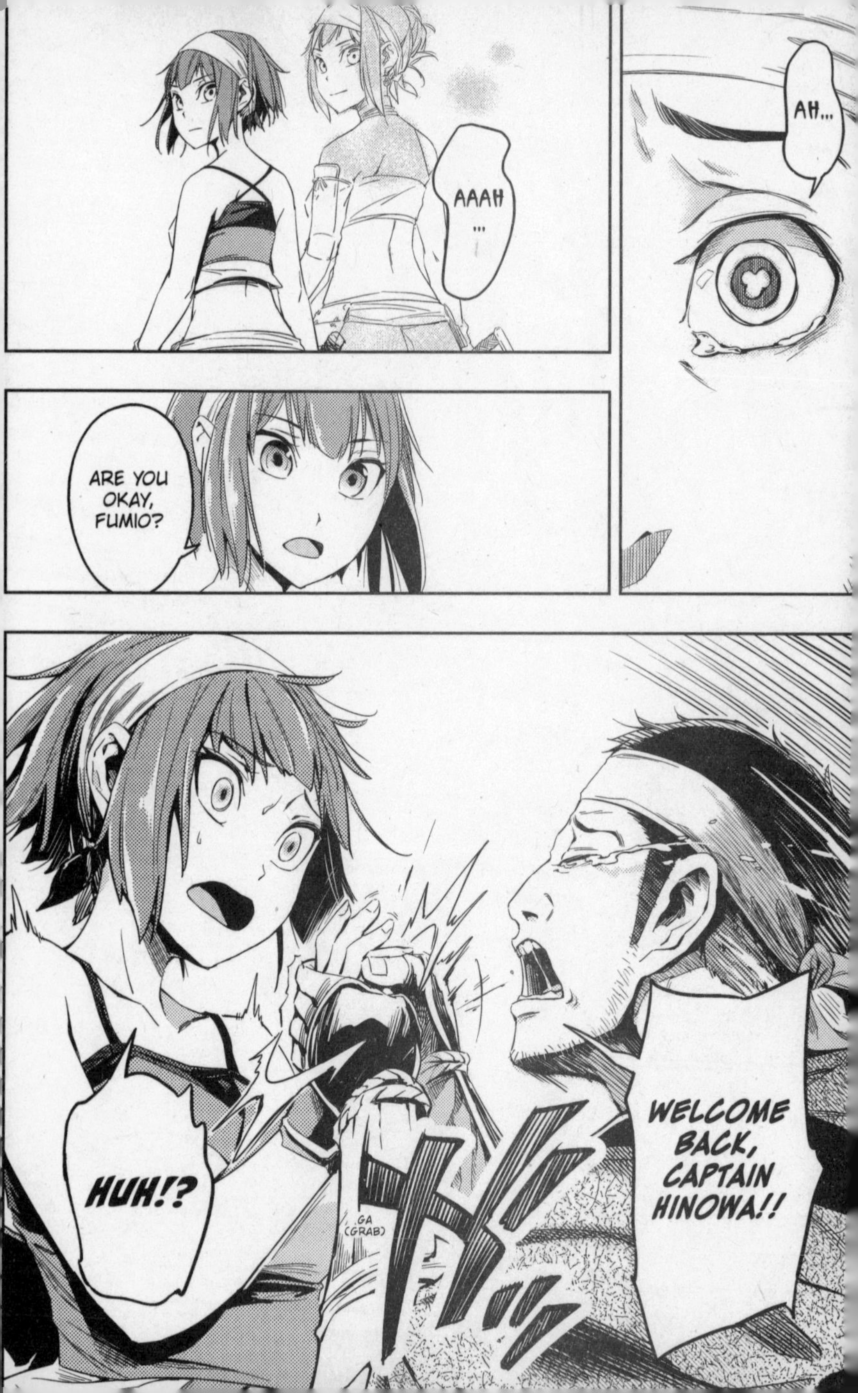
AH...
AAAH ...
ARE YOU OKAY, FUMIO?
WELCOME BACK, CAPTAIN HINOWA!!
GA (GRAB)
HUH!?

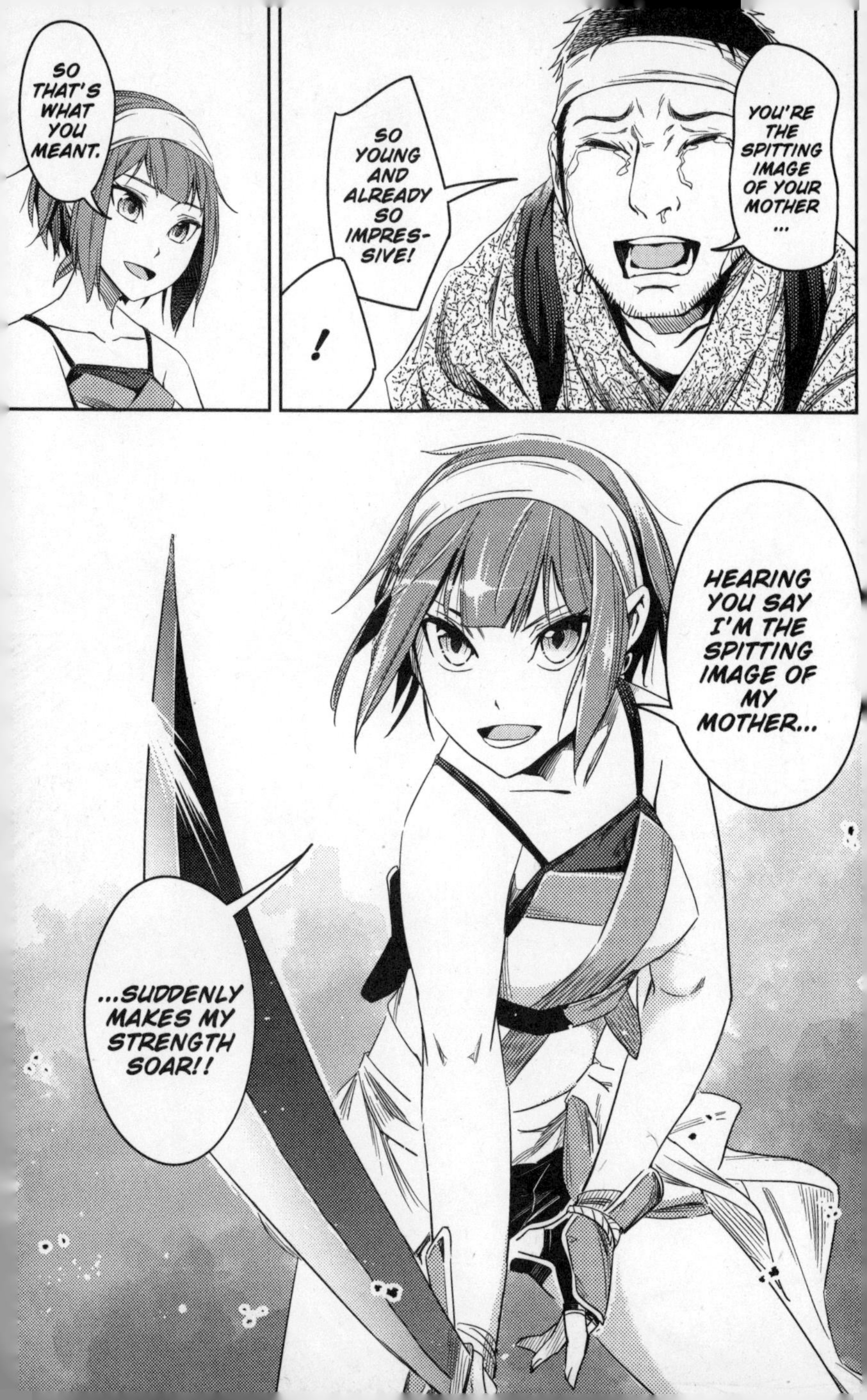
YOU'RE THE SPITTING IMAGE OF YOUR MOTHER ...
SO YOUNG AND ALREADY SO IMPRES-SIVE!
!
SO THAT'S WHAT YOU MEANT.
HEARING YOU SAY I'M THE SPITTING IMAGE OF MY MOTHER...
...SUDDENLY MAKES MY STRENGTH SOAR!!

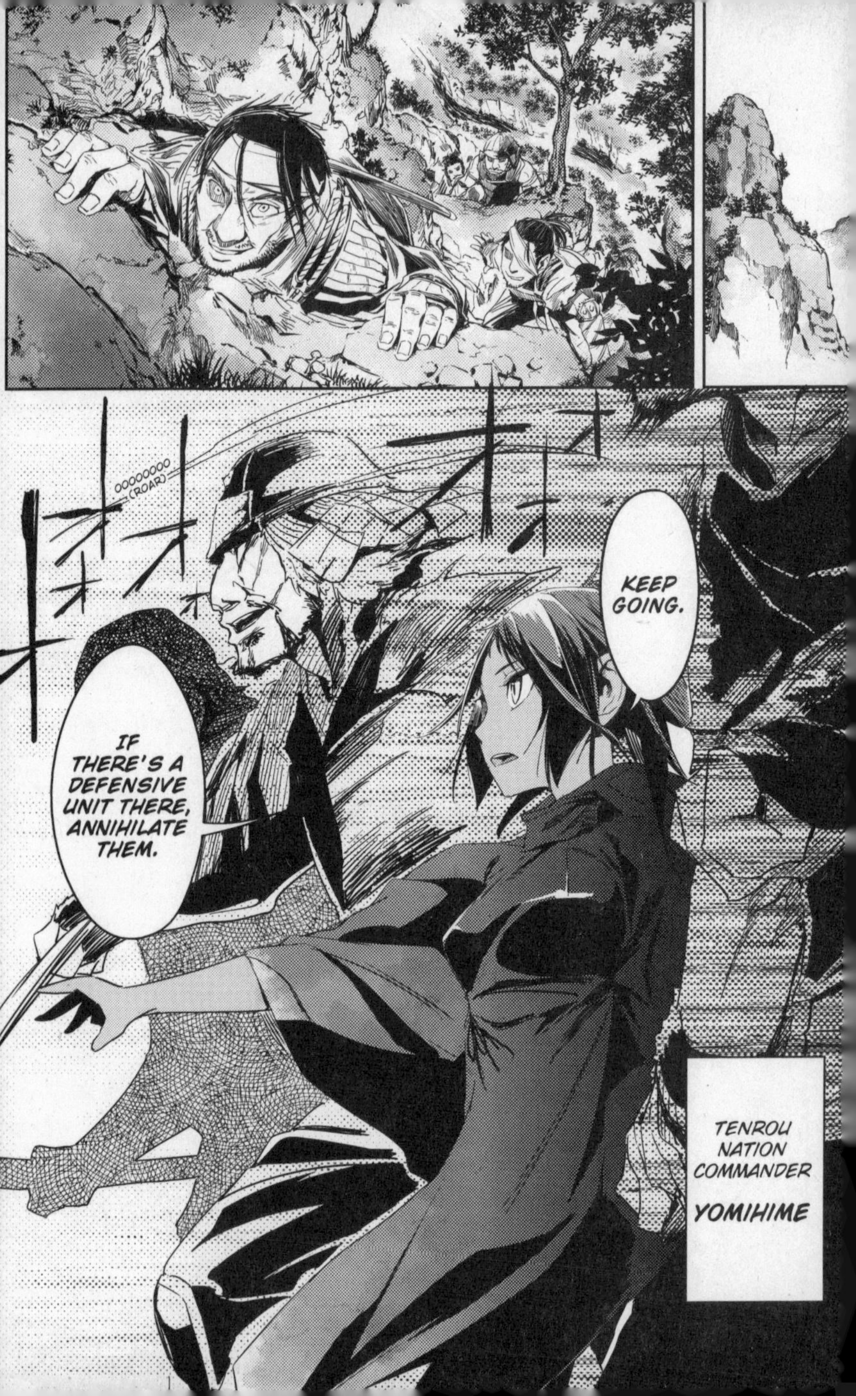
KEEP GOING.
OOOOOOOO (ROAR)
IF THERE'S A DEFENSIVE UNIT THERE, ANNIHILATE THEM.
TENROU NATION COMMANDER YOMIHIME

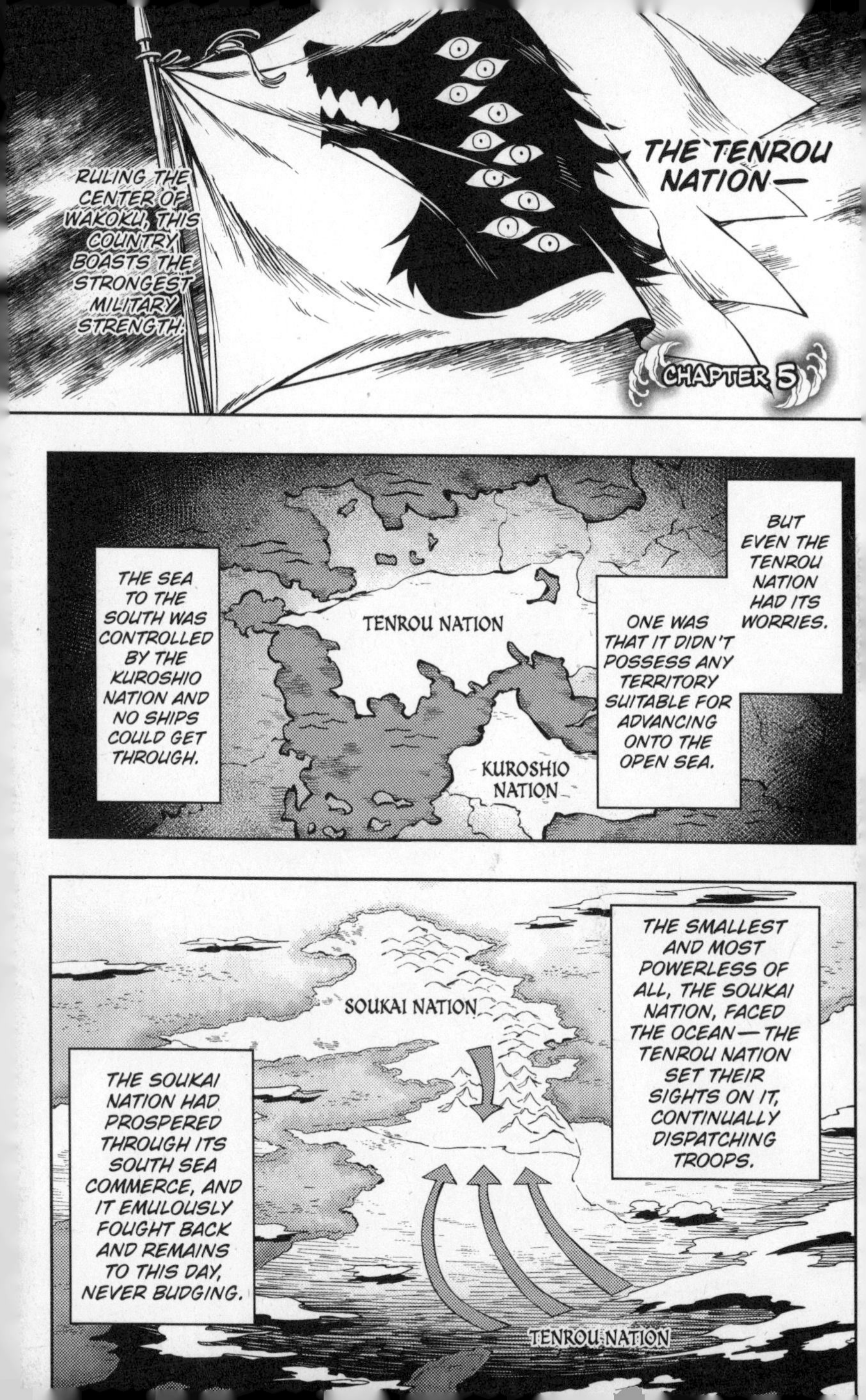
THE TENROU NATION—
RULING THE CENTER OF WAKOKU, THIS COUNTRY BOASTS THE STRONGEST MILITARY STRENGTH.
CHAPTER 5
BUT EVEN THE TENROU NATION HAD ITS WORRIES.
ONE WAS THAT IT DIDN'T POSSESS ANY TERRITORY SUITABLE FOR ADVANCING ONTO THE OPEN SEA.
TENROU NATION
THE SEA TO THE SOUTH WAS CONTROLLED BY THE KUROSHIO NATION AND NO SHIPS COULD GET THROUGH.
KUROSHIO NATION
THE SMALLEST AND MOST POWERLESS OF ALL, THE SOUKAI NATION, FACED THE OCEAN—THE TENROU NATION SET THEIR SIGHTS ON IT, CONTINUALLY DISPATCHING TROOPS.
SOUKAI NATION
THE SOUKAI NATION HAD PROSPERED THROUGH ITS SOUTH SEA COMMERCE, AND IT EMULOUSLY FOUGHT BACK AND REMAINS TO THIS DAY, NEVER BUDGING.
TENROU NATION

# CHAPTER 5 THE FIGHT ON MT. KAGEBOUSHI

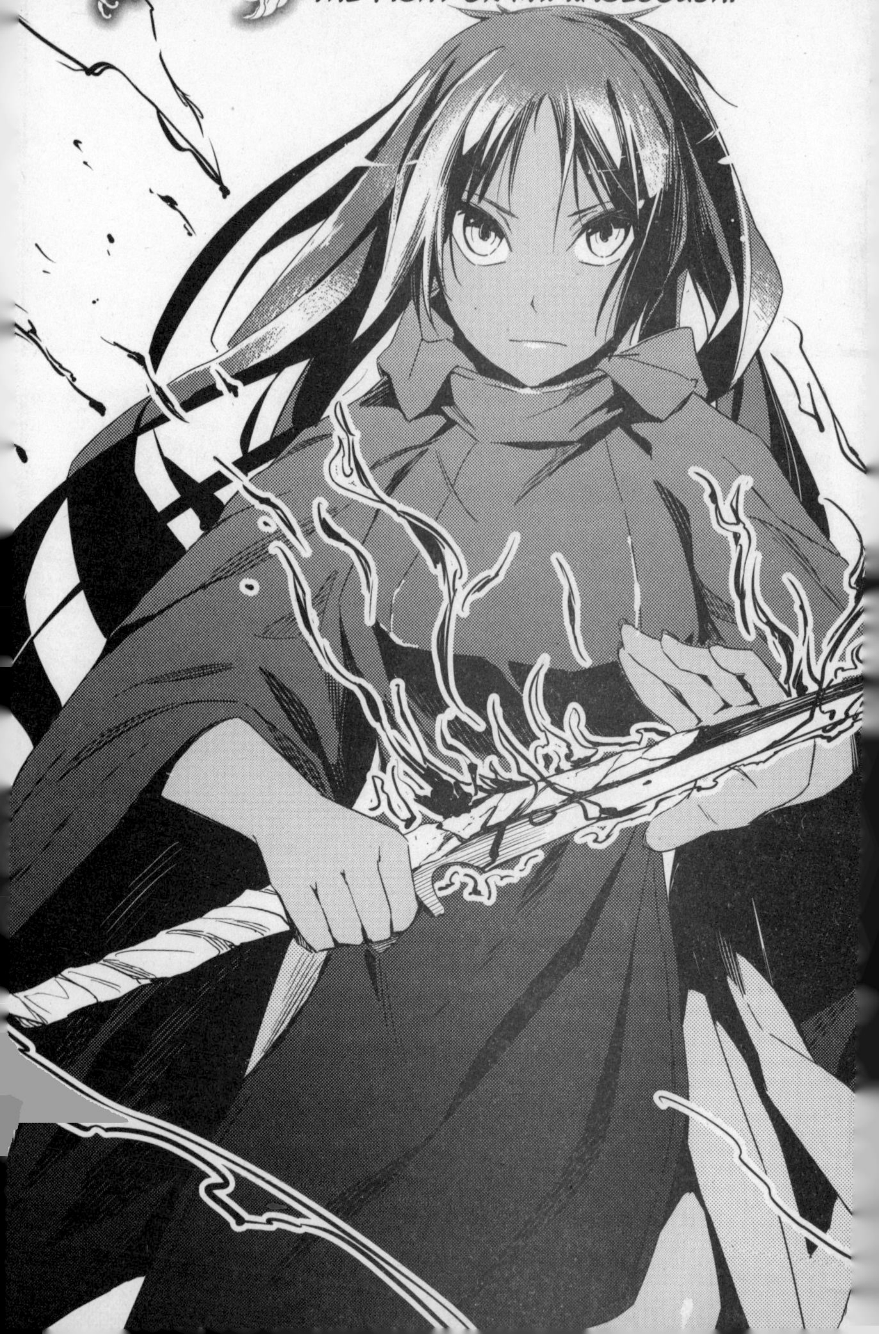

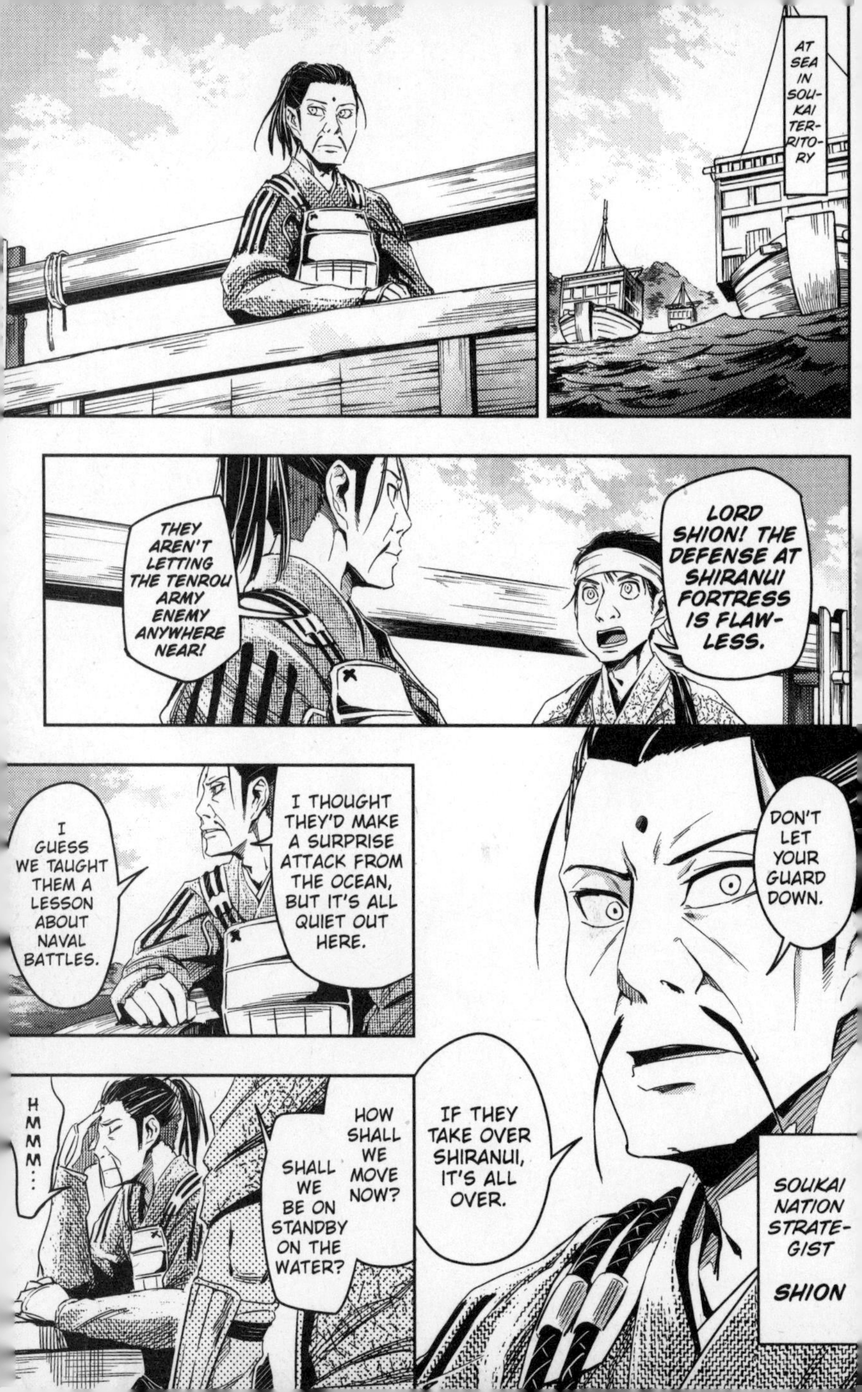
AT SEA IN SOU-KAI TER-RITO-RY
LORD SHION! THE DEFENSE AT SHIRANUI FORTRESS IS FLAW-LESS.
THEY AREN'T LETTING THE TENROU ARMY ENEMY ANYWHERE NEAR!
DON'T LET YOUR GUARD DOWN.
IF THEY TAKE OVER SHIRANUI, IT'S ALL OVER.
SOUKAI NATION STRATE-GIST
SHION
I THOUGHT THEY'D MAKE A SURPRISE ATTACK FROM THE OCEAN, BUT IT'S ALL QUIET OUT HERE.
I GUESS WE TAUGHT THEM A LESSON ABOUT NAVAL BATTLES.
HOW SHALL WE MOVE NOW?
SHALL WE BE ON STANDBY ON THE WATER?
HMMM...

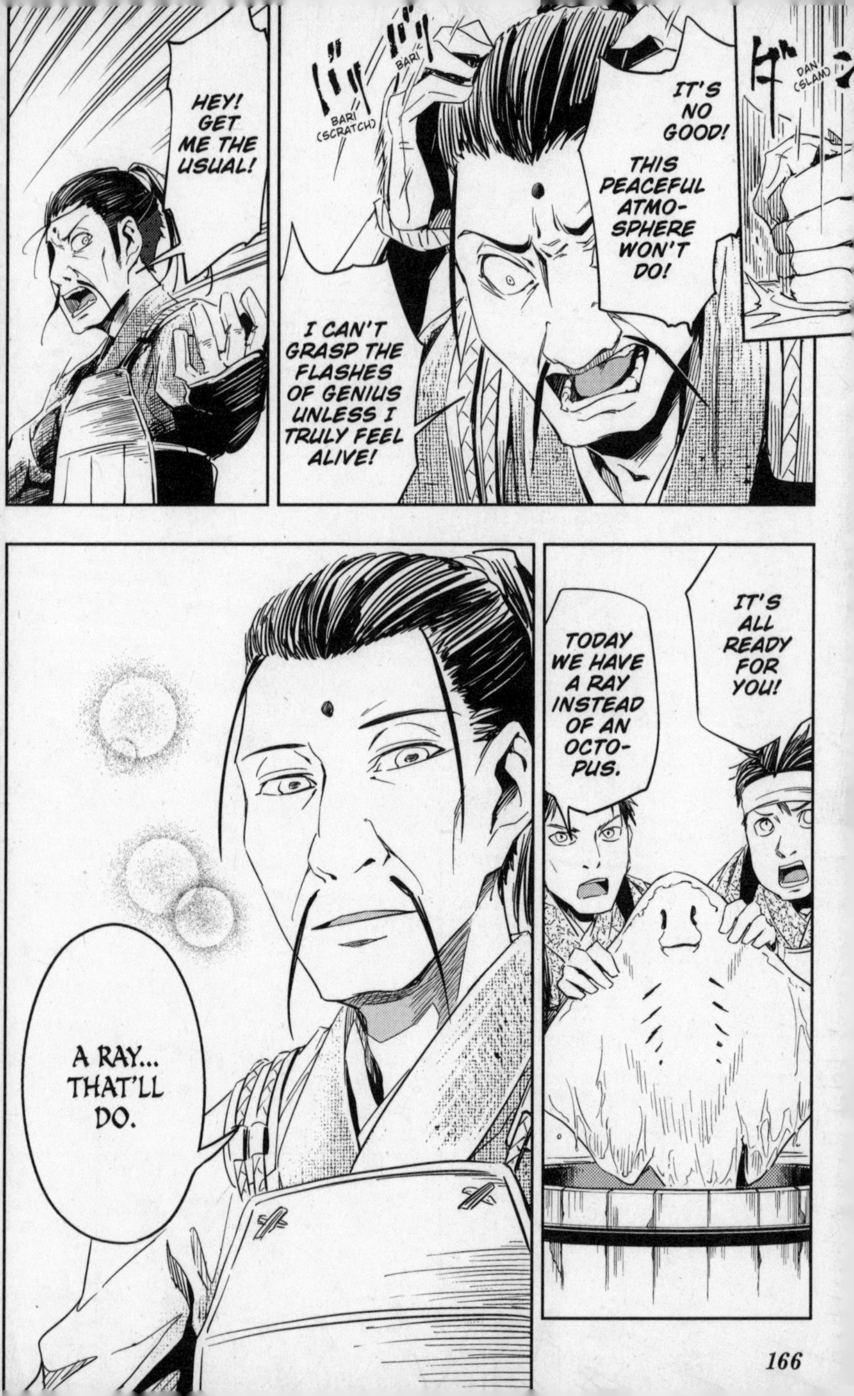
DAN (SLAM)
BARI
BARI (SCRATCH)
IT'S NO GOOD!
THIS PEACEFUL ATMOSPHERE WON'T DO!
I CAN'T GRASP THE FLASHES OF GENIUS UNLESS I TRULY FEEL ALIVE!
HEY! GET ME THE USUAL!
IT'S ALL READY FOR YOU!
TODAY WE HAVE A RAY INSTEAD OF AN OCTOPUS.
A RAY... THAT'LL DO.

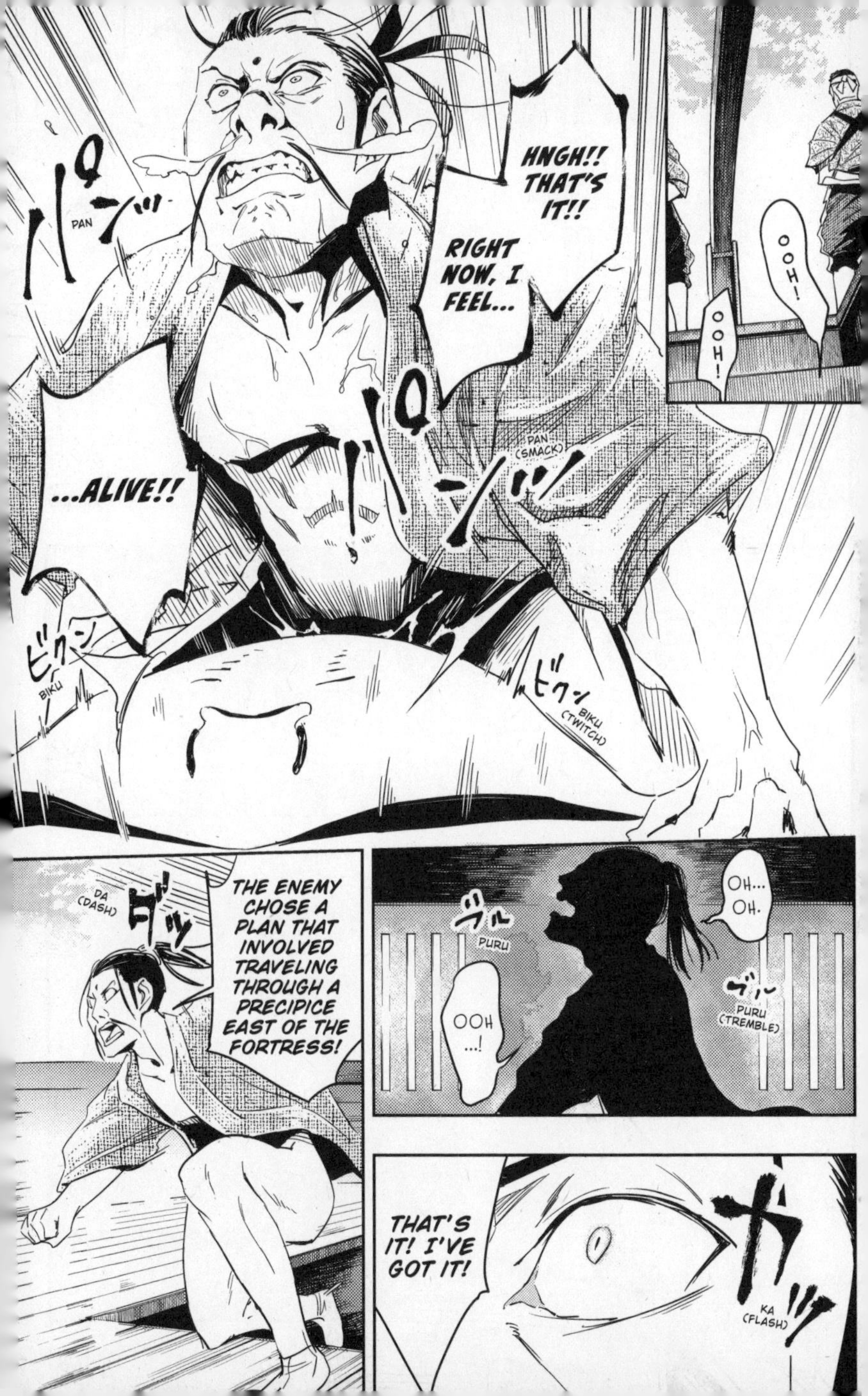
OOH!
OOH!
HNGH!! THAT'S IT!!
PAN
RIGHT NOW, I FEEL...
PAN (SMACK)
...ALIVE!!
BIKU
BIKU (TWITCH)
OH... OH.
PURU
OOH ...!
PURU (TREMBLE)
THAT'S IT! I'VE GOT IT!
KA (FLASH)
DA (DASH)
THE ENEMY CHOSE A PLAN THAT INVOLVED TRAVELING THROUGH A PRECIPICE EAST OF THE FORTRESS!

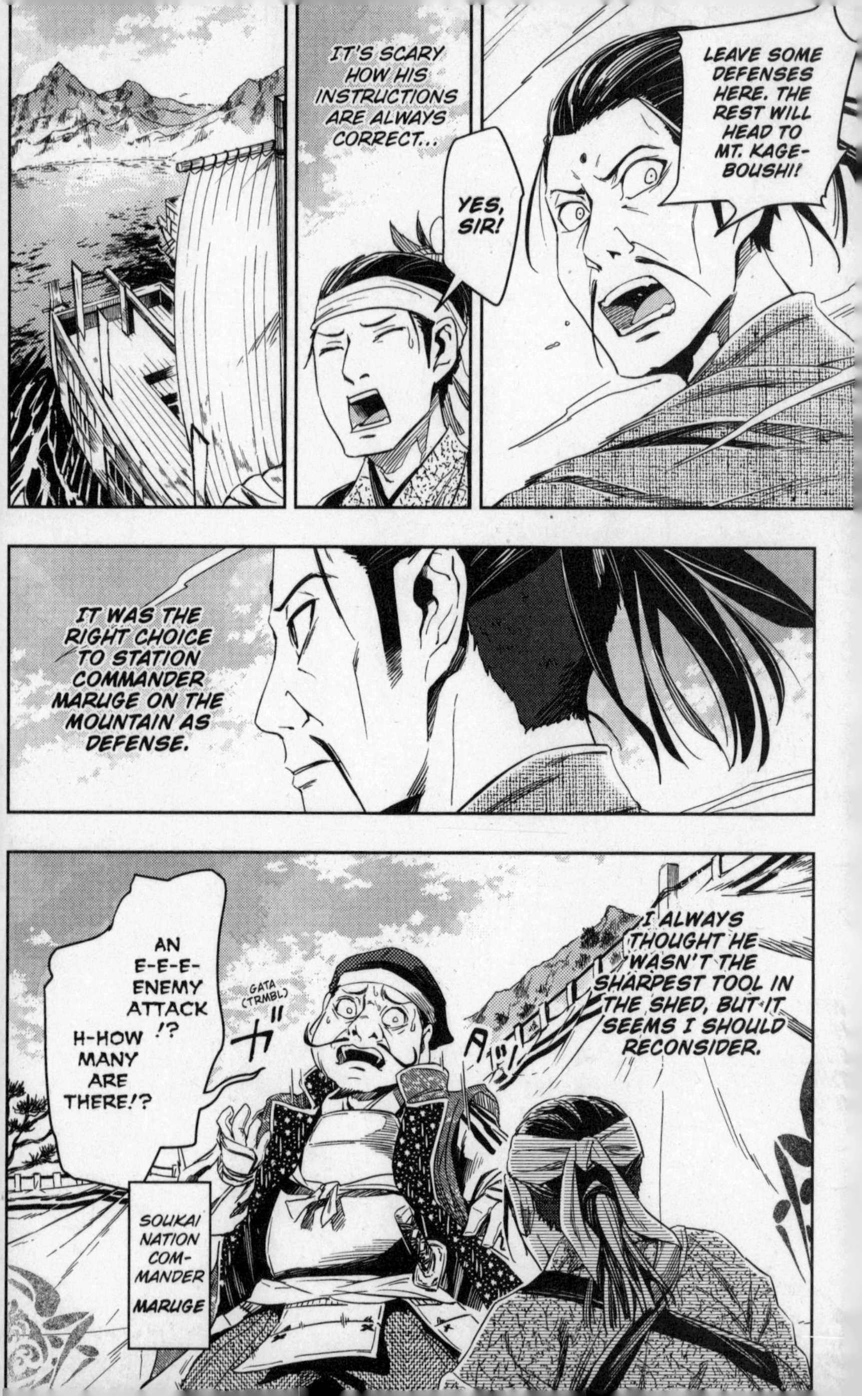
LEAVE SOME DEFENSES HERE. THE REST WILL HEAD TO MT. KAGE-BOUSHI!
YES, SIR!
IT'S SCARY HOW HIS INSTRUCTIONS ARE ALWAYS CORRECT...
IT WAS THE RIGHT CHOICE TO STATION COMMANDER MARUGE ON THE MOUNTAIN AS DEFENSE.
I ALWAYS THOUGHT HE WASN'T THE SHARPEST TOOL IN THE SHED, BUT IT SEEMS I SHOULD RECONSIDER.
GATA (TRMBL)
AN E-E-E-ENEMY ATTACK!? H-HOW MANY ARE THERE!?
SOUKAI NATION COMMANDER MARUGE

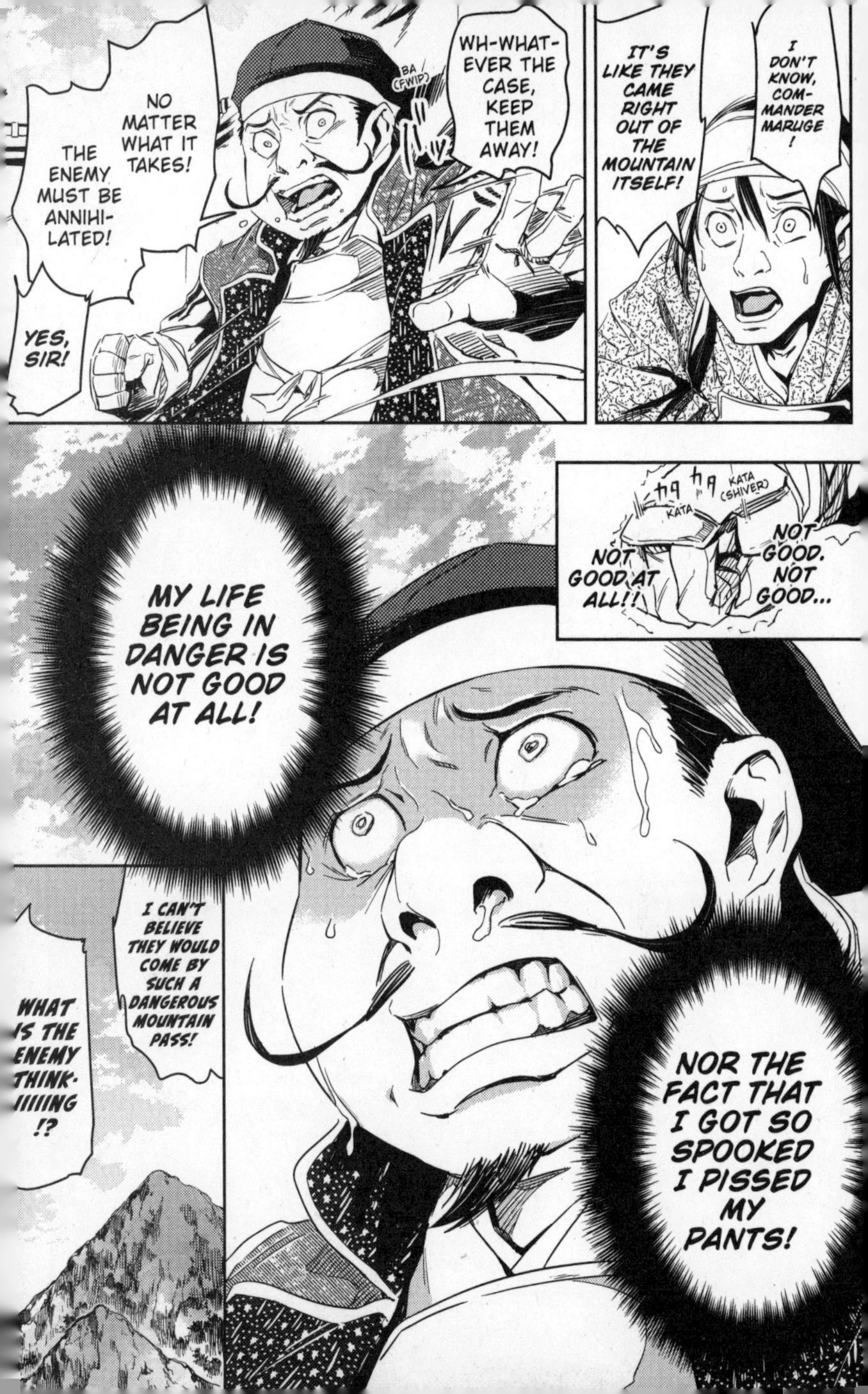
I DON'T KNOW, COMMANDER MARUGE!
IT'S LIKE THEY CAME RIGHT OUT OF THE MOUNTAIN ITSELF!
WH-WHATEVER THE CASE, KEEP THEM AWAY!
BA (FWIP)
NO MATTER WHAT IT TAKES!
THE ENEMY MUST BE ANNIHILATED!
YES, SIR!
カタ カタ
KATA (SHIVER)
KATA
NOT GOOD. NOT GOOD...
NOT GOOD AT ALL!!
MY LIFE BEING IN DANGER IS NOT GOOD AT ALL!
NOR THE FACT THAT I GOT SO SPOOKED I PISSED MY PANTS!
I CAN'T BELIEVE THEY WOULD COME BY SUCH A DANGEROUS MOUNTAIN PASS!
WHAT IS THE ENEMY THINKIIIIING!?

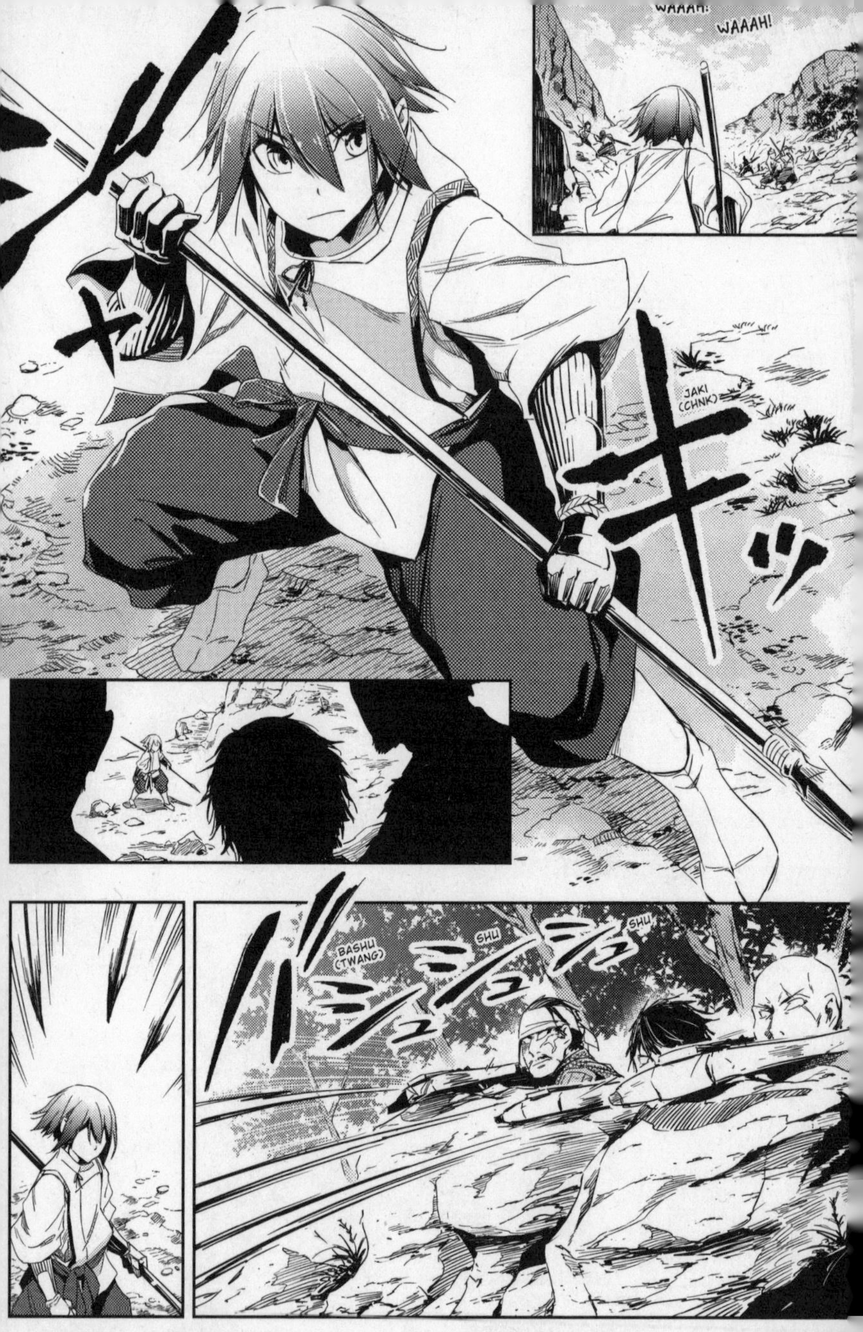
WAAAH!
WAAAH!
JAKI (CHNK)
BASHU (TWANG)
SHU
SHU

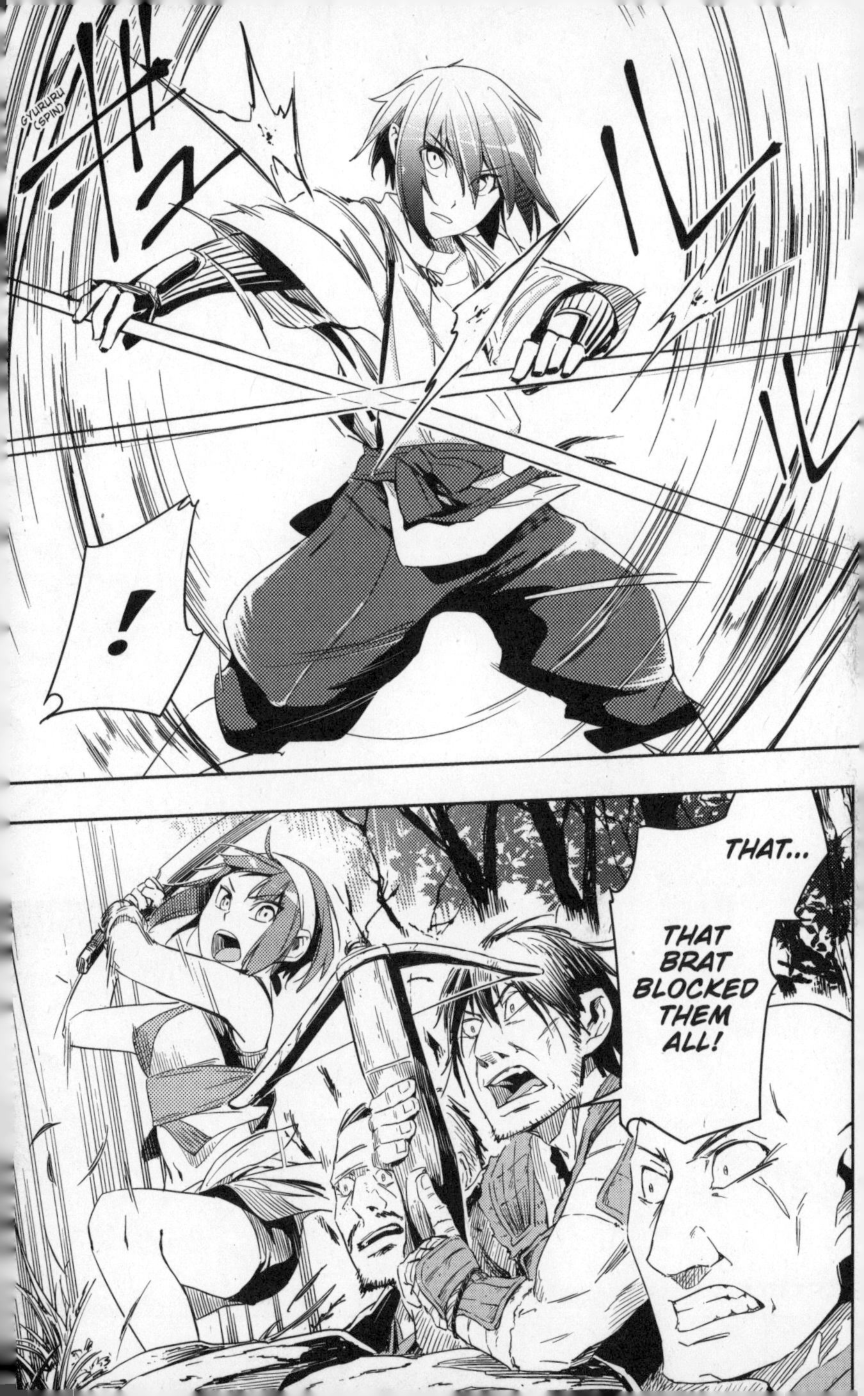
GYURURU (SPIN)
!
THAT...
THAT BRAT BLOCKED THEM ALL!

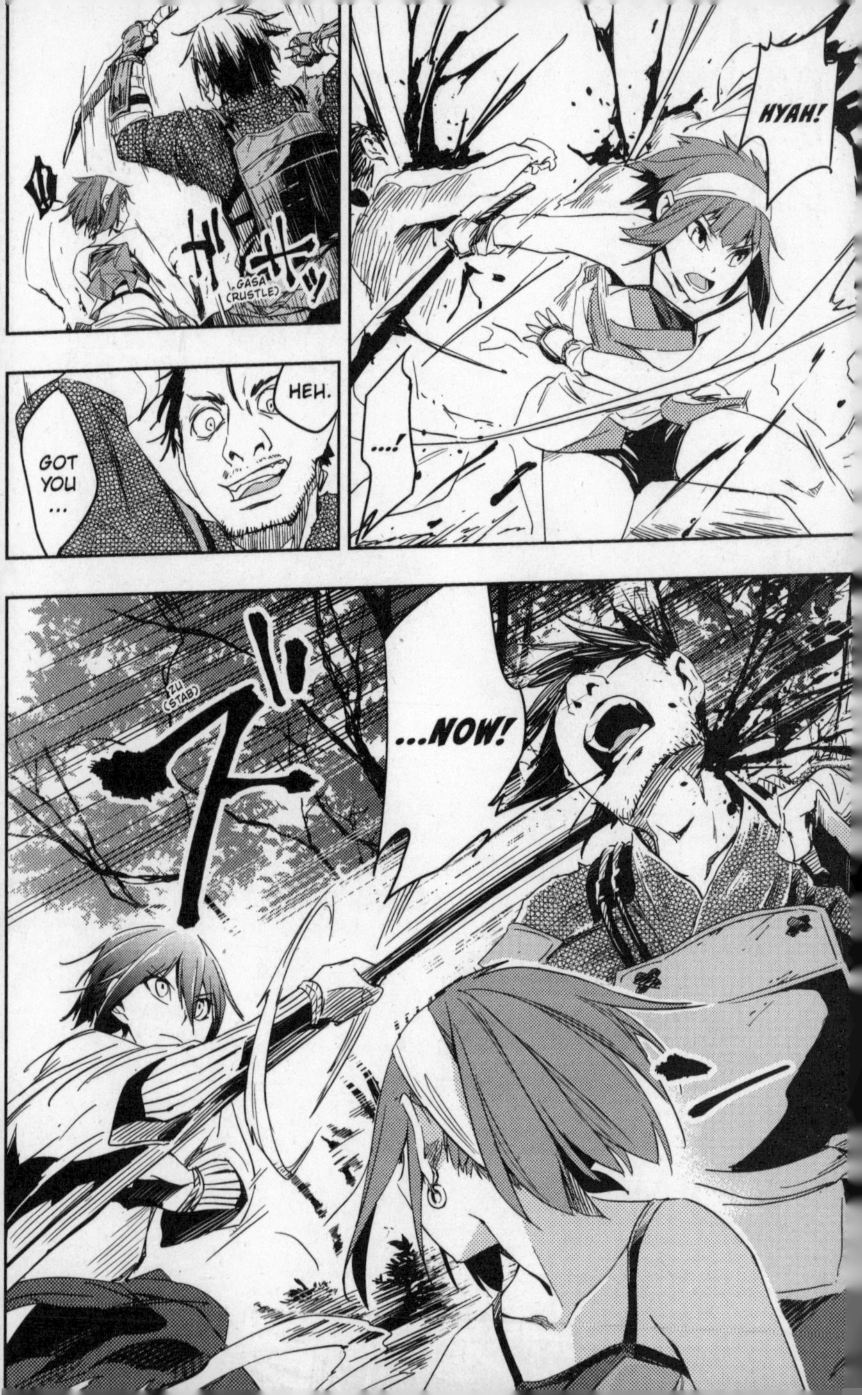
HYAH!
...!
ガサッ
GASA (RUSTLE)
HEH.
GOT YOU ...
...NOW!
ズッ
ZU (STAB)

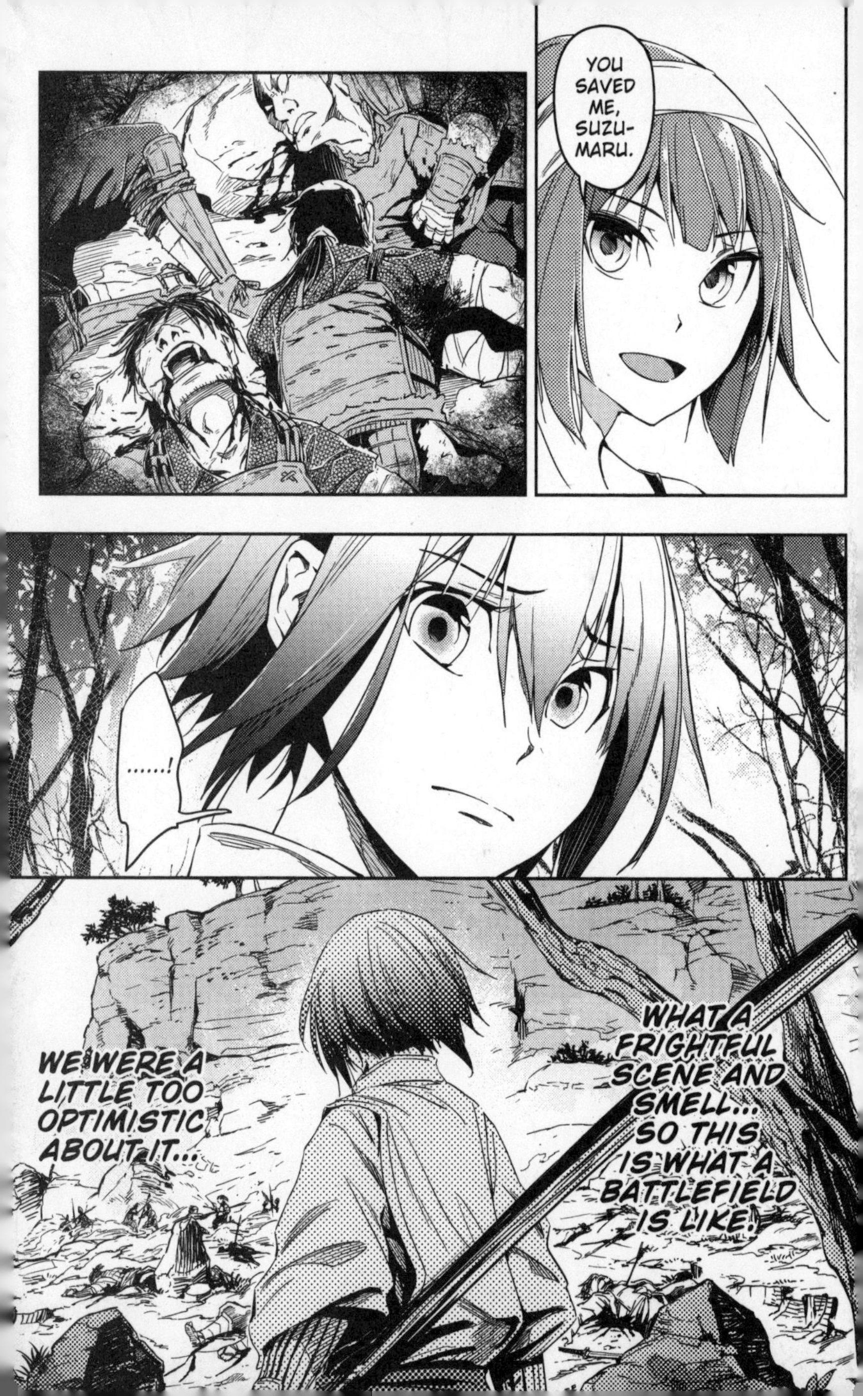
YOU SAVED ME, SUZU-MARU.
......!
WHAT A FRIGHTFUL SCENE AND SMELL... SO THIS IS WHAT A BATTLEFIELD IS LIKE.
WE WERE A LITTLE TOO OPTIMISTIC ABOUT IT...

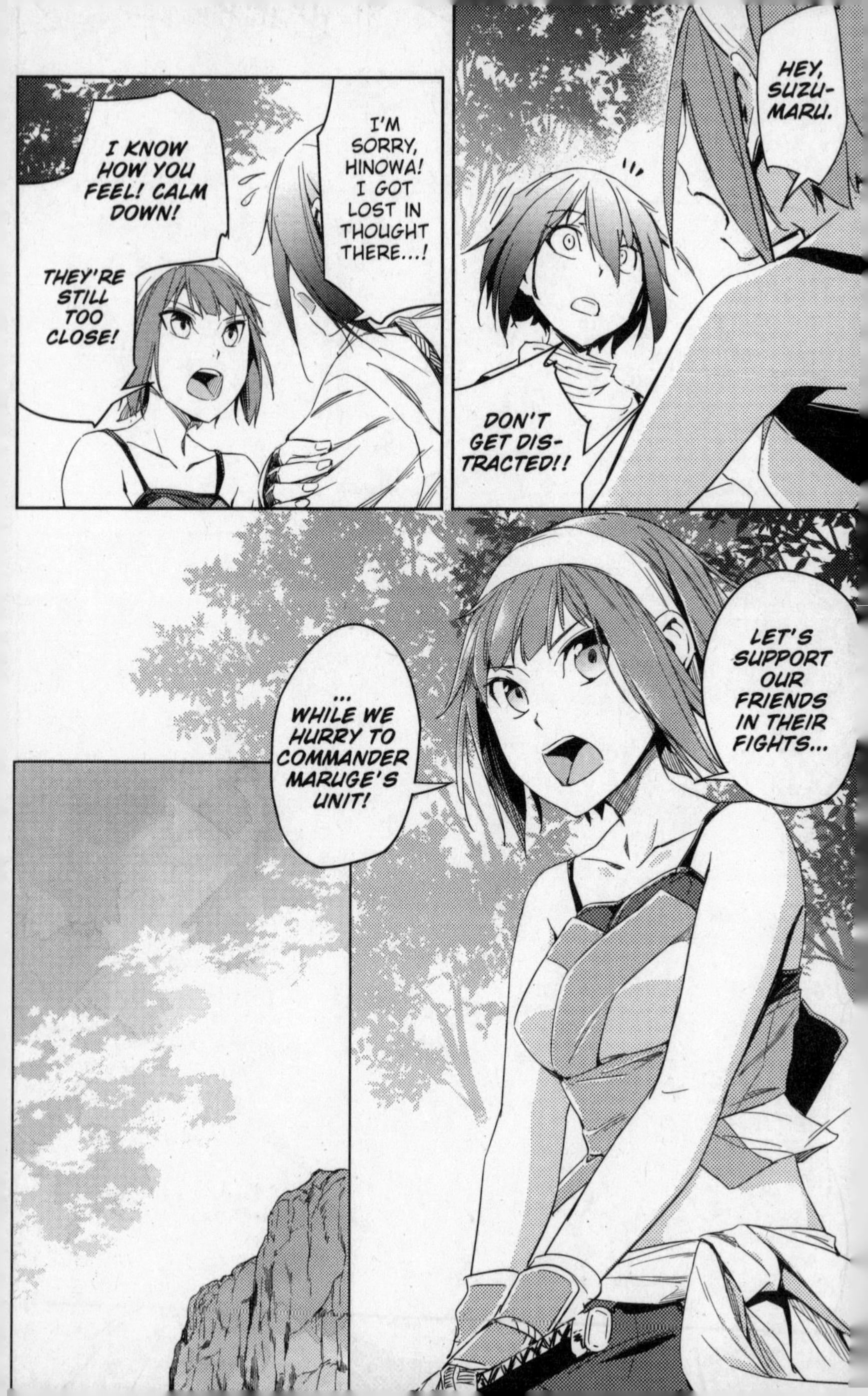
HEY, SUZU-MARU.
DON'T GET DIS-TRACTED!!
I'M SORRY, HINOWA! I GOT LOST IN THOUGHT THERE...!
I KNOW HOW YOU FEEL! CALM DOWN!
THEY'RE STILL TOO CLOSE!
LET'S SUPPORT OUR FRIENDS IN THEIR FIGHTS...
...WHILE WE HURRY TO COMMANDER MARUGE'S UNIT!

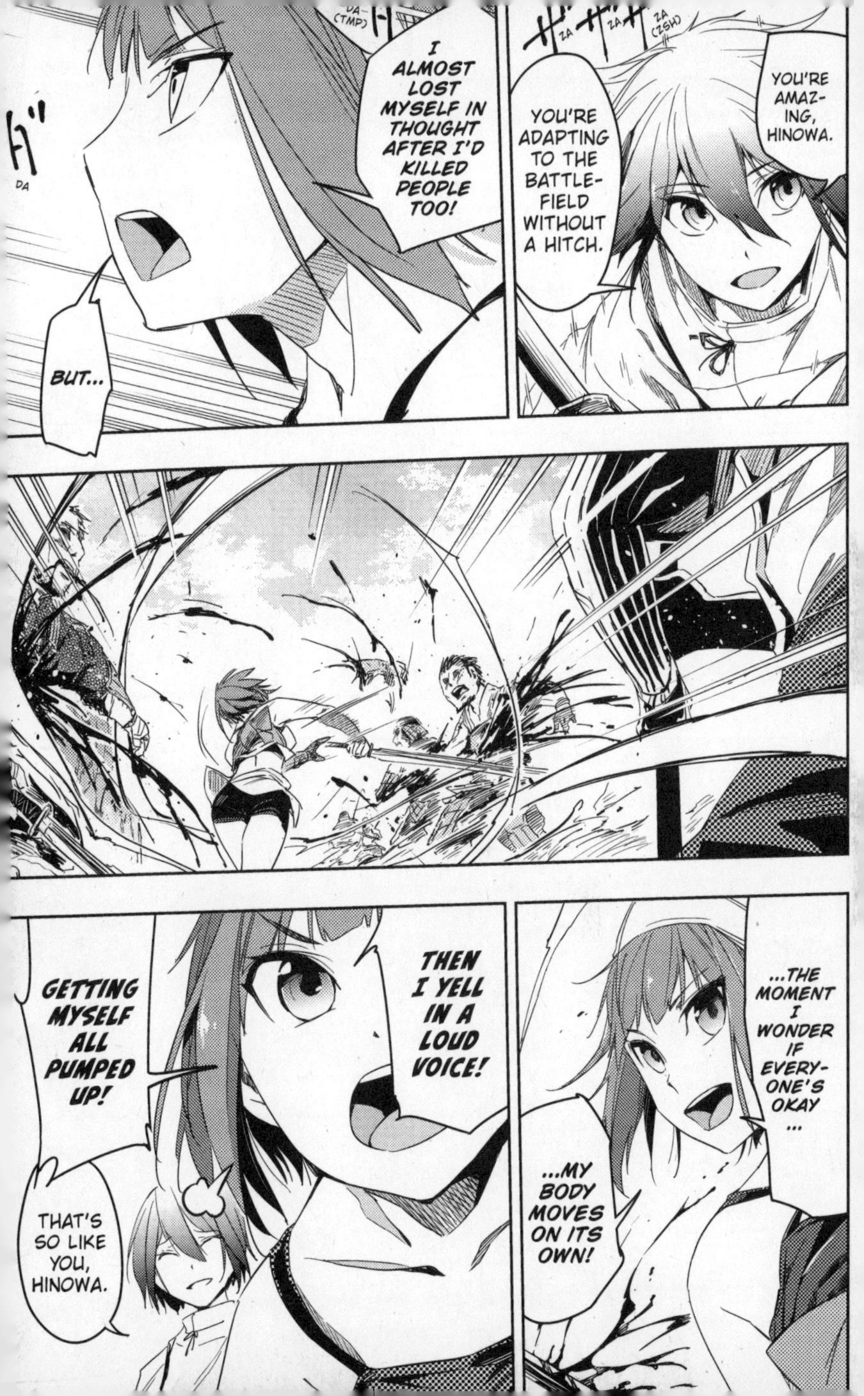
ZA ZA (ZSH)
YOU'RE AMAZ-ING, HINOWA.
YOU'RE ADAPTING TO THE BATTLE-FIELD WITHOUT A HITCH.
DA (TMP)
I ALMOST LOST MYSELF IN THOUGHT AFTER I'D KILLED PEOPLE TOO!
DA
BUT...
...THE MOMENT I WONDER IF EVERY-ONE'S OKAY...
...MY BODY MOVES ON ITS OWN!
THEN I YELL IN A LOUD VOICE!
GETTING MYSELF ALL PUMPED UP!
THAT'S SO LIKE YOU, HINOWA.

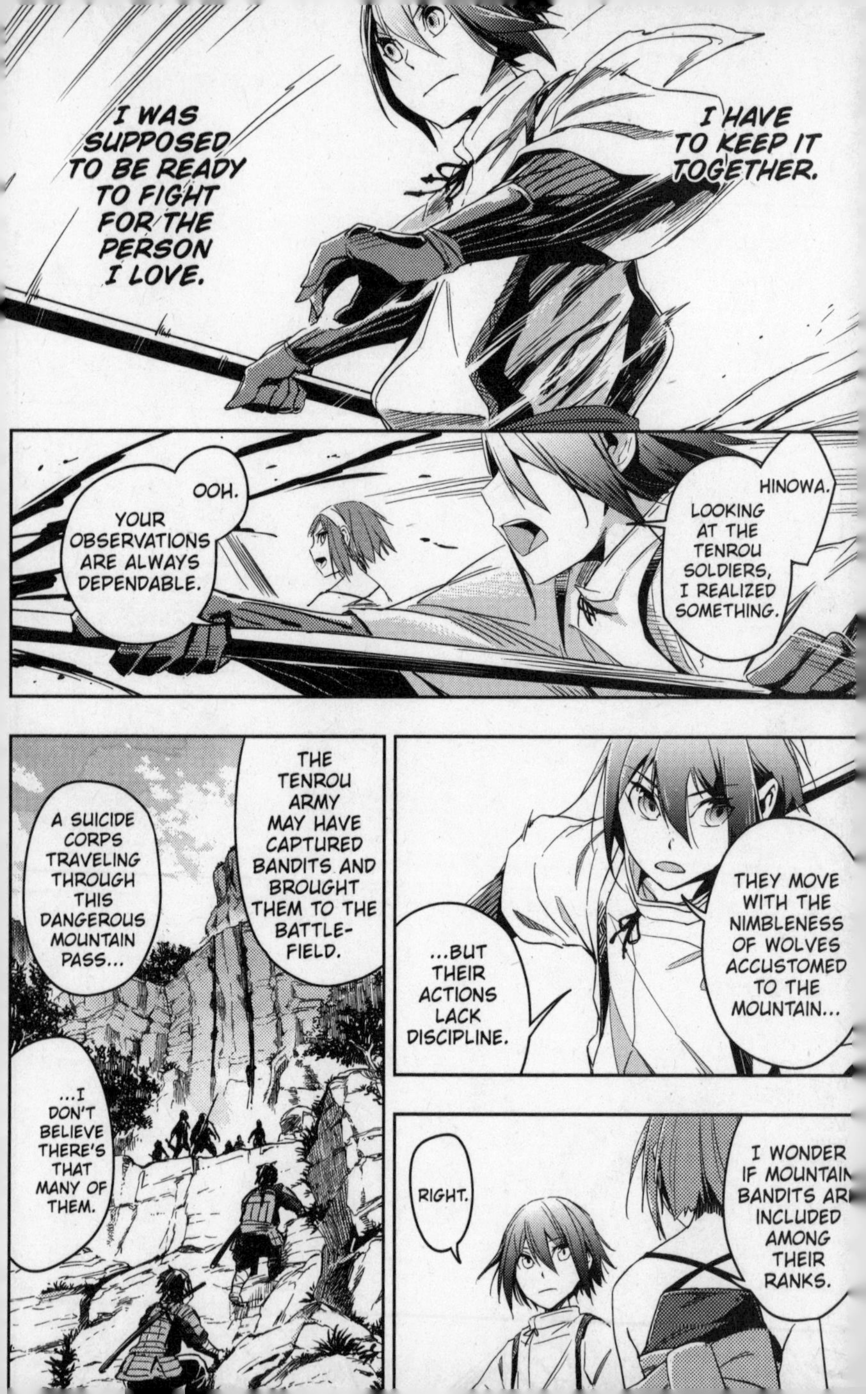
I HAVE TO KEEP IT TOGETHER.
I WAS SUPPOSED TO BE READY TO FIGHT FOR THE PERSON I LOVE.
HINOWA.
LOOKING AT THE TENROU SOLDIERS, I REALIZED SOMETHING.
OOH.
YOUR OBSERVATIONS ARE ALWAYS DEPENDABLE.
THEY MOVE WITH THE NIMBLENESS OF WOLVES ACCUSTOMED TO THE MOUNTAIN...
...BUT THEIR ACTIONS LACK DISCIPLINE.
I WONDER IF MOUNTAI BANDITS AR INCLUDED AMONG THEIR RANKS.
RIGHT.
THE TENROU ARMY MAY HAVE CAPTURED BANDITS AND BROUGHT THEM TO THE BATTLE-FIELD.
A SUICIDE CORPS TRAVELING THROUGH THIS DANGEROUS MOUNTAIN PASS...
...I DON'T BELIEVE THERE'S THAT MANY OF THEM.

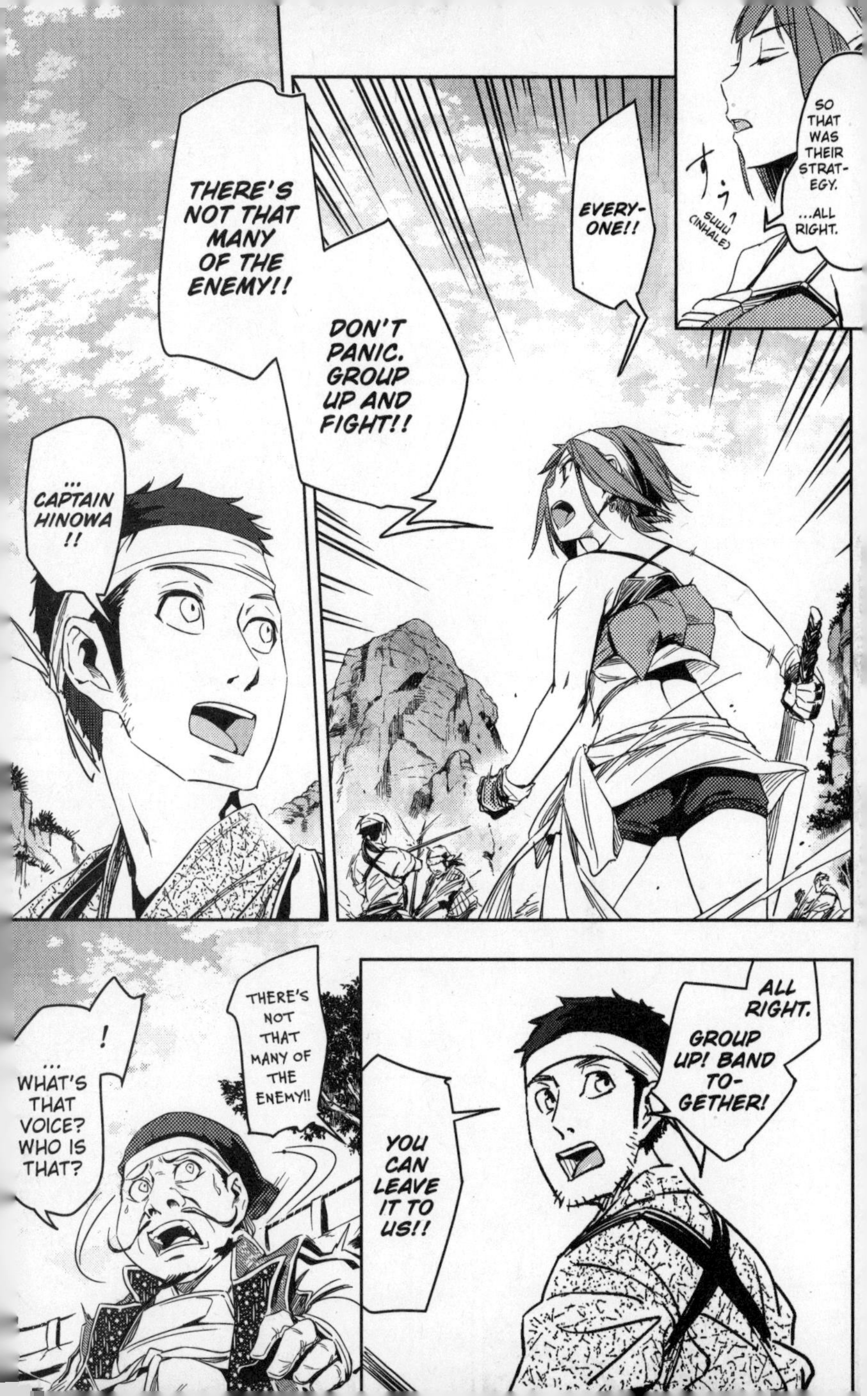
SO THAT WAS THEIR STRAT-EGY.
...ALL RIGHT.
すぅ
SUUU (INHALE)
EVERY-ONE!!
THERE'S NOT THAT MANY OF THE ENEMY!!
DON'T PANIC. GROUP UP AND FIGHT!!
...CAPTAIN HINOWA!!
ALL RIGHT.
GROUP UP! BAND TO-GETHER!
YOU CAN LEAVE IT TO US!!
THERE'S NOT THAT MANY OF THE ENEMY!!
!
...WHAT'S THAT VOICE? WHO IS THAT?

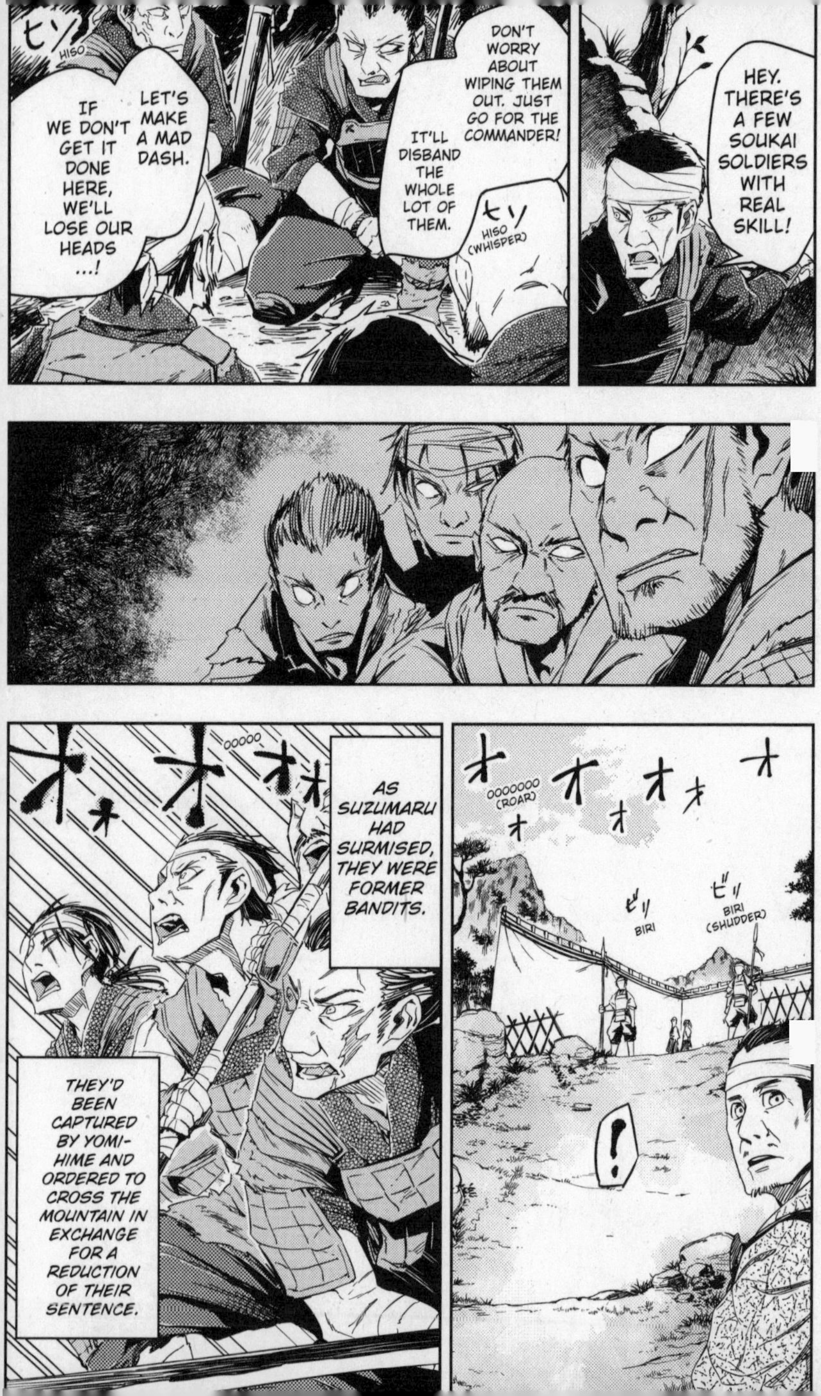
HEY. THERE'S A FEW SOUKAI SOLDIERS WITH REAL SKILL!
DON'T WORRY ABOUT WIPING THEM OUT. JUST GO FOR THE COMMANDER!
IT'LL DISBAND THE WHOLE LOT OF THEM.
ヒソ
HISO (WHISPER)
ヒソ
HISO
LET'S MAKE A MAD DASH.
IF WE DON'T GET IT DONE HERE, WE'LL LOSE OUR HEADS ...!
オオオオオオオ
OOOOOOO (ROAR)
ビリ
BIRI
ビリ
BIRI (SHUDDER)
!
AS SUZUMARU HAD SURMISED, THEY WERE FORMER BANDITS.
オオオオ
OOOOO
THEY'D BEEN CAPTURED BY YOMI-HIME AND ORDERED TO CROSS THE MOUNTAIN IN EXCHANGE FOR A REDUCTION OF THEIR SENTENCE.

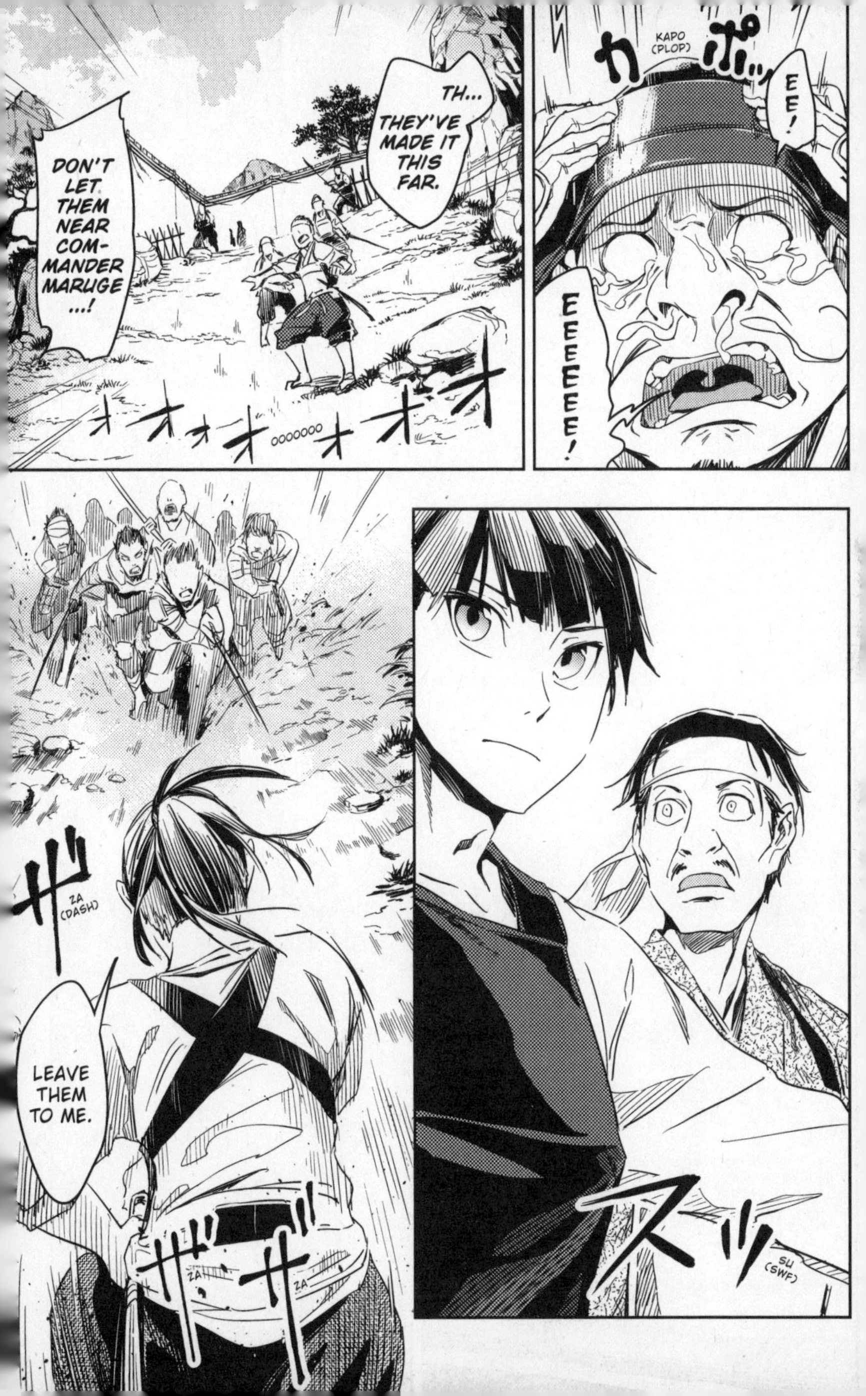

KAPO (PLOP)
EE!
EEEEEEE!
TH... THEY'VE MADE IT THIS FAR.
DON'T LET THEM NEAR COM-MANDER MARUGE ...!
OOOOOOO
SU (SWF)
ZA (DASH)
LEAVE THEM TO ME.
ZA
ZA

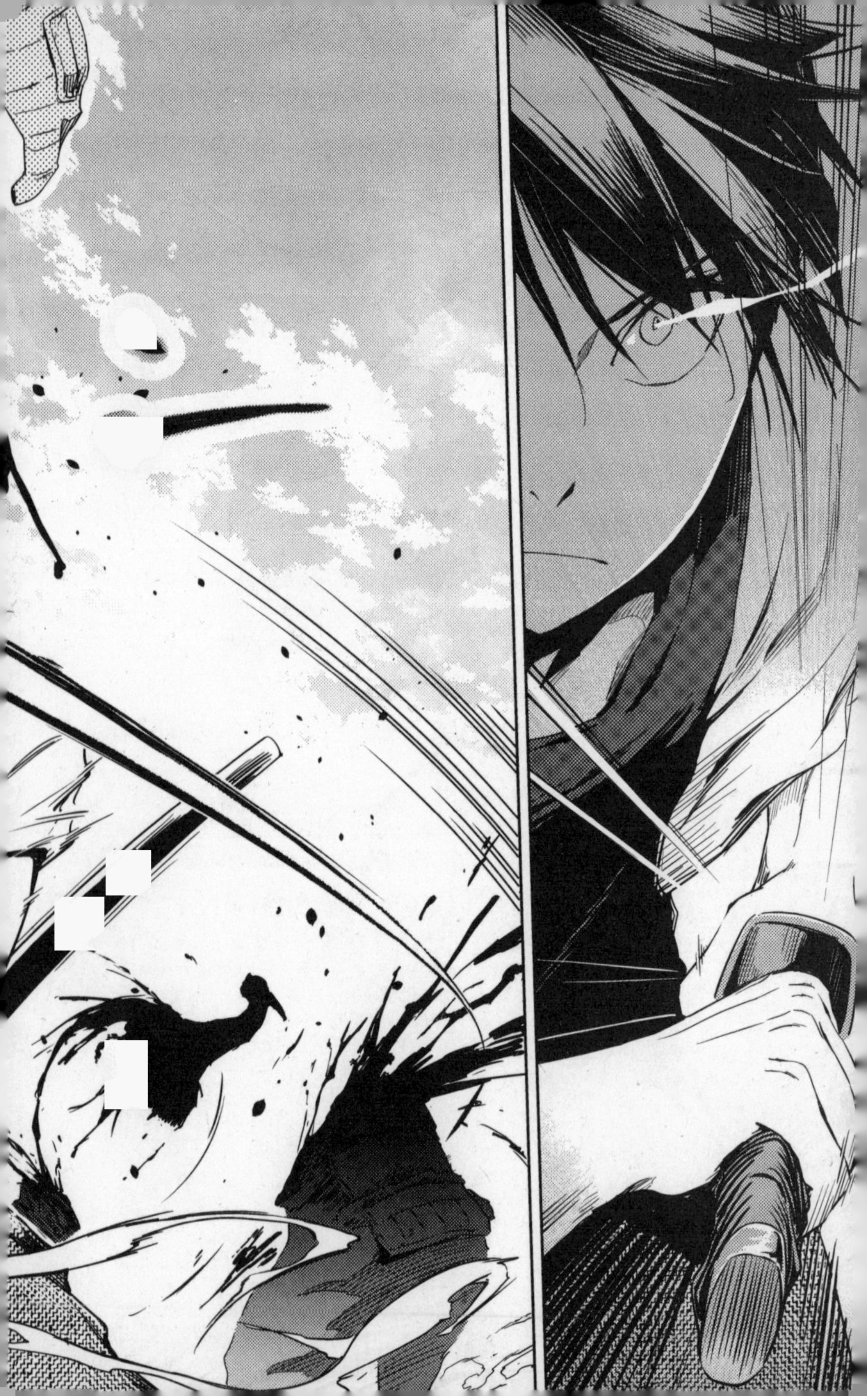

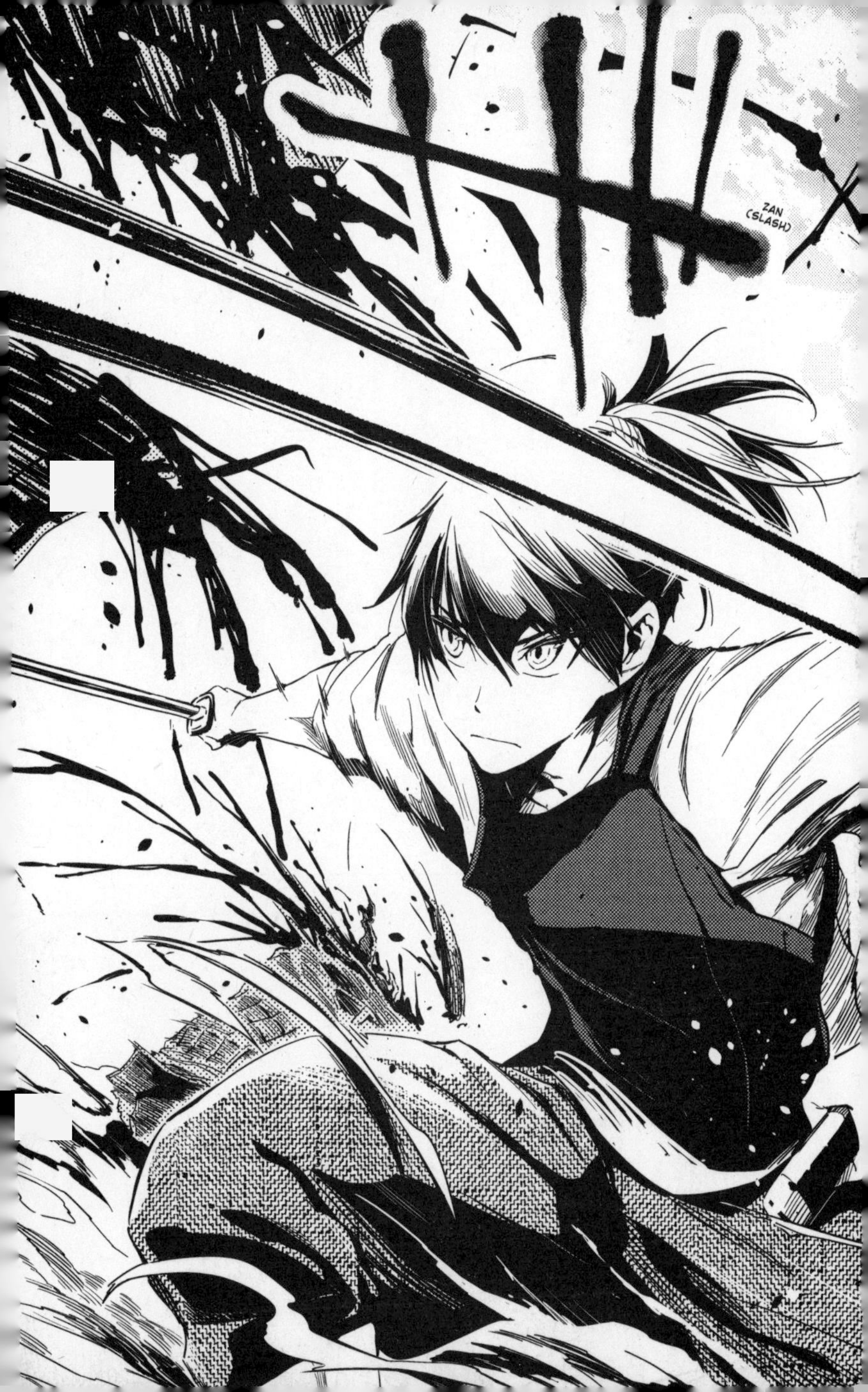
ZAN
(SLASH)

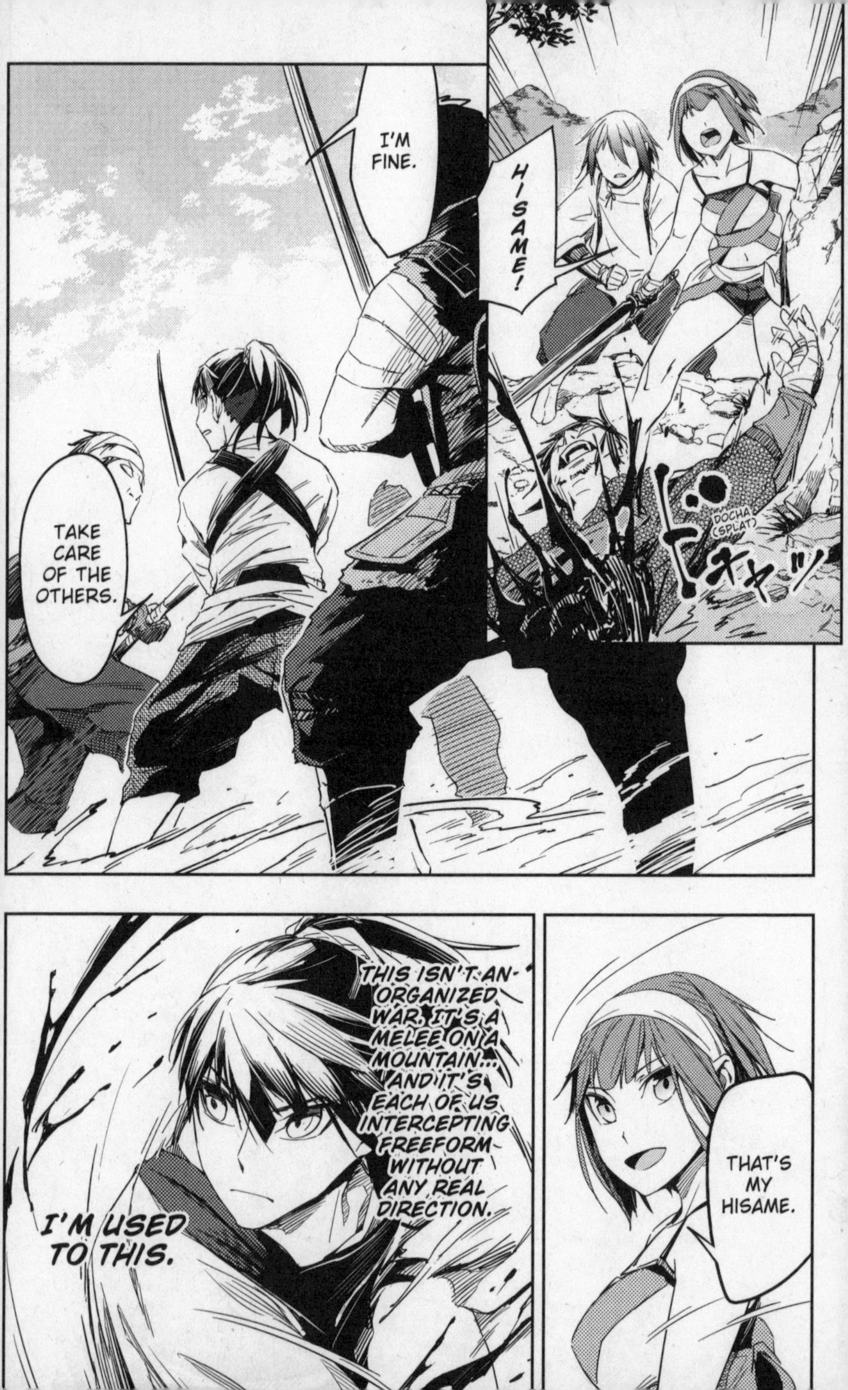
HISAME!
DOCHA (SPLAT)
I'M FINE.
TAKE CARE OF THE OTHERS.
THAT'S MY HISAME.
THIS ISN'T AN ORGANIZED WAR. IT'S A MELEE ON A MOUNTAIN... AND IT'S EACH OF US INTERCEPTING FREEFORM WITHOUT ANY REAL DIRECTION.
I'M USED TO THIS.

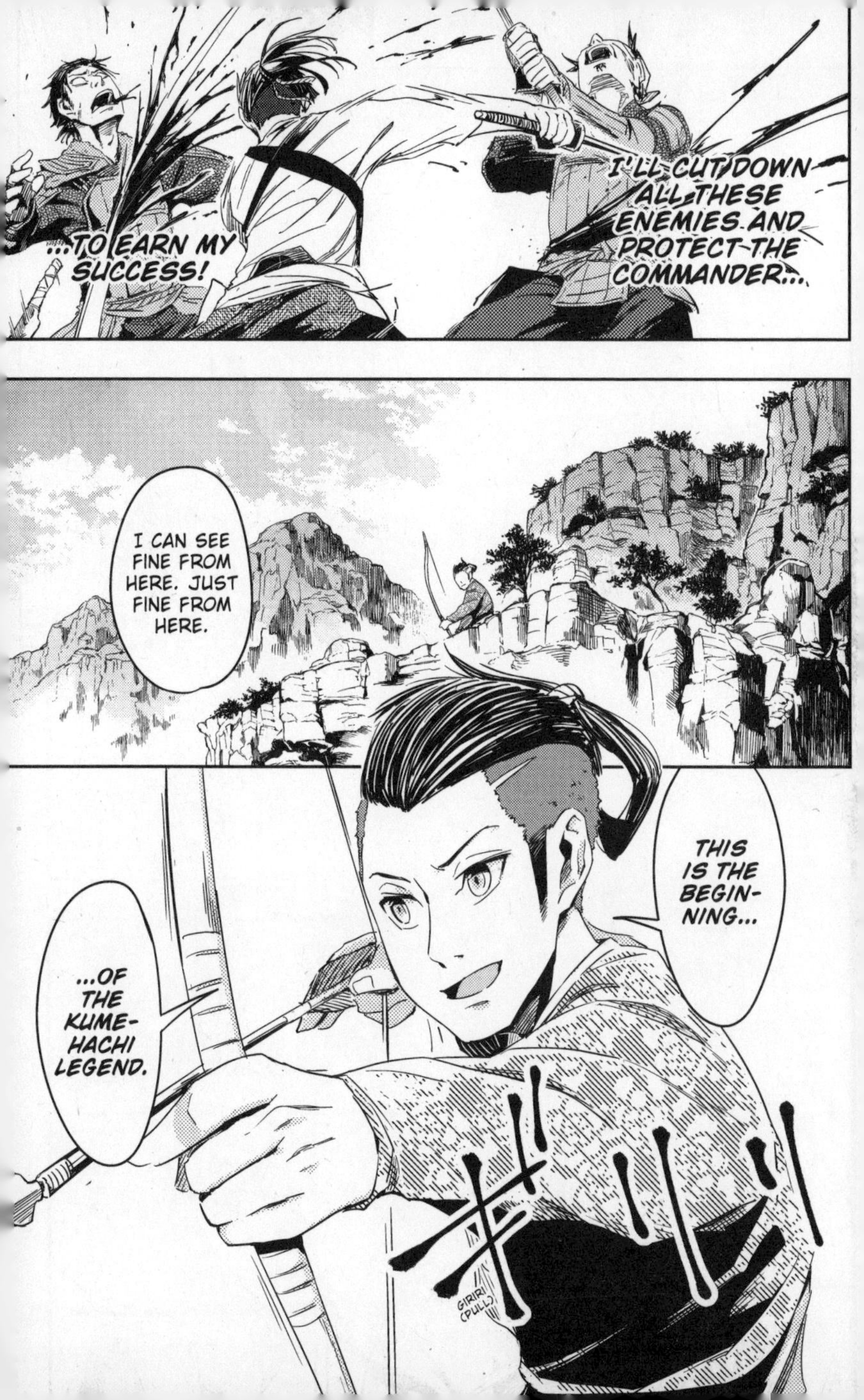
I'LL CUT DOWN ALL THESE ENEMIES AND PROTECT THE COMMANDER...
...TO EARN MY SUCCESS!
I CAN SEE FINE FROM HERE. JUST FINE FROM HERE.
THIS IS THE BEGIN-NING...
...OF THE KUME-HACHI LEGEND.
GIRIRI (PULL)

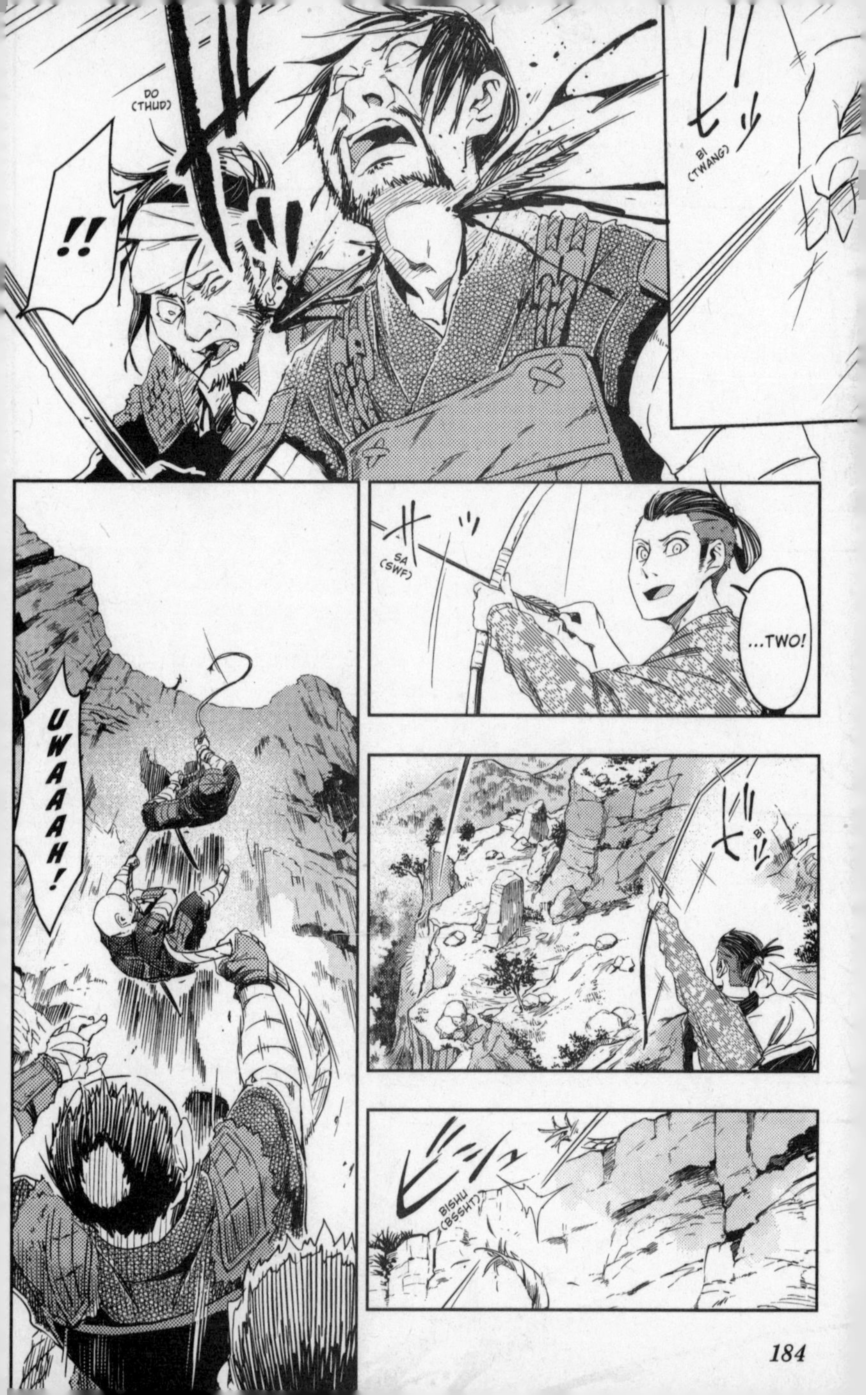
BI (TWANG)
DO (THUD)
!!
SA (SWF)
...TWO!
BI
BISHU (BSSHT)
UWAAAAH!

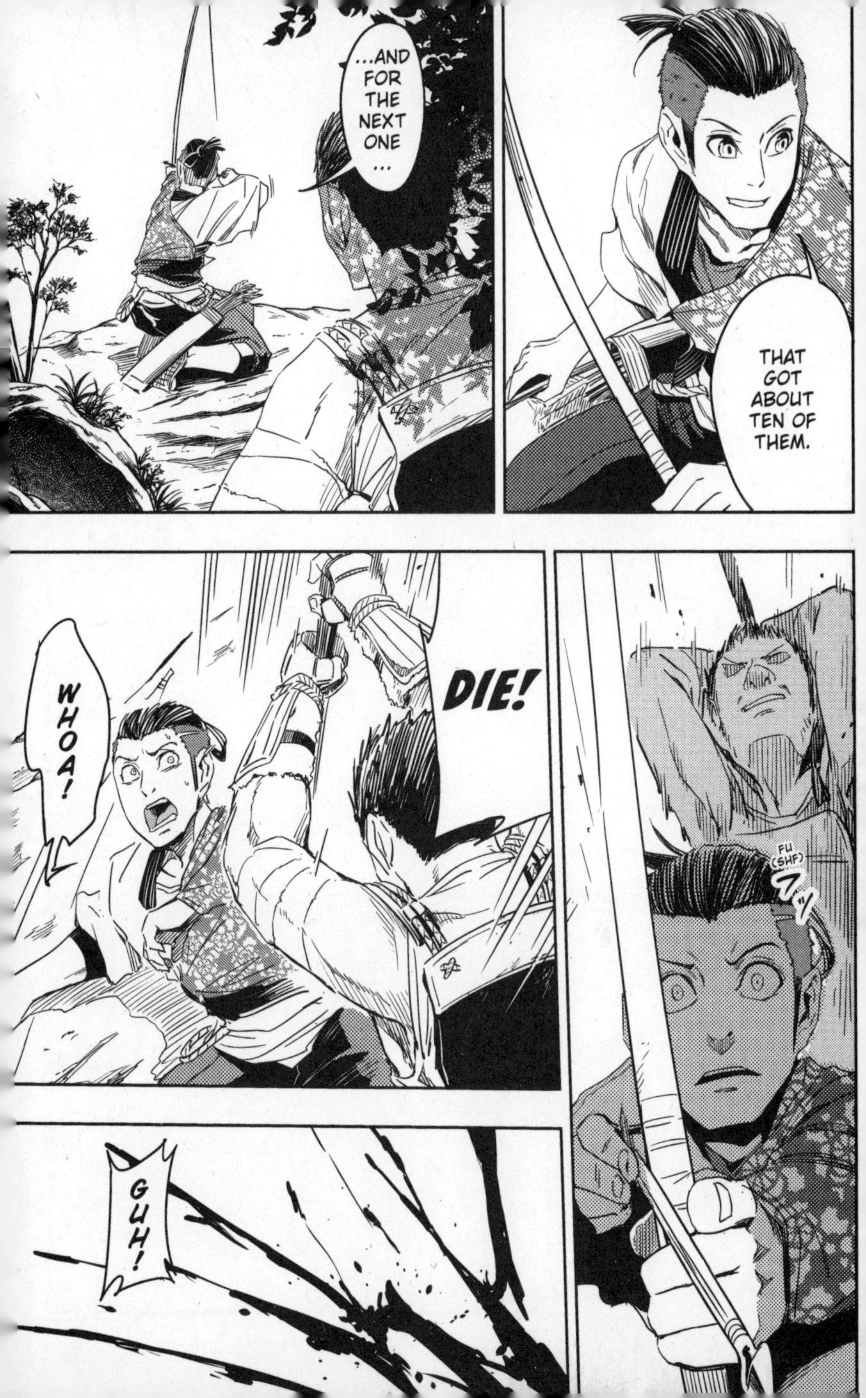
THAT GOT ABOUT TEN OF THEM.
...AND FOR THE NEXT ONE...
FU (SHF)
DIE!
WHOA!
GUH!

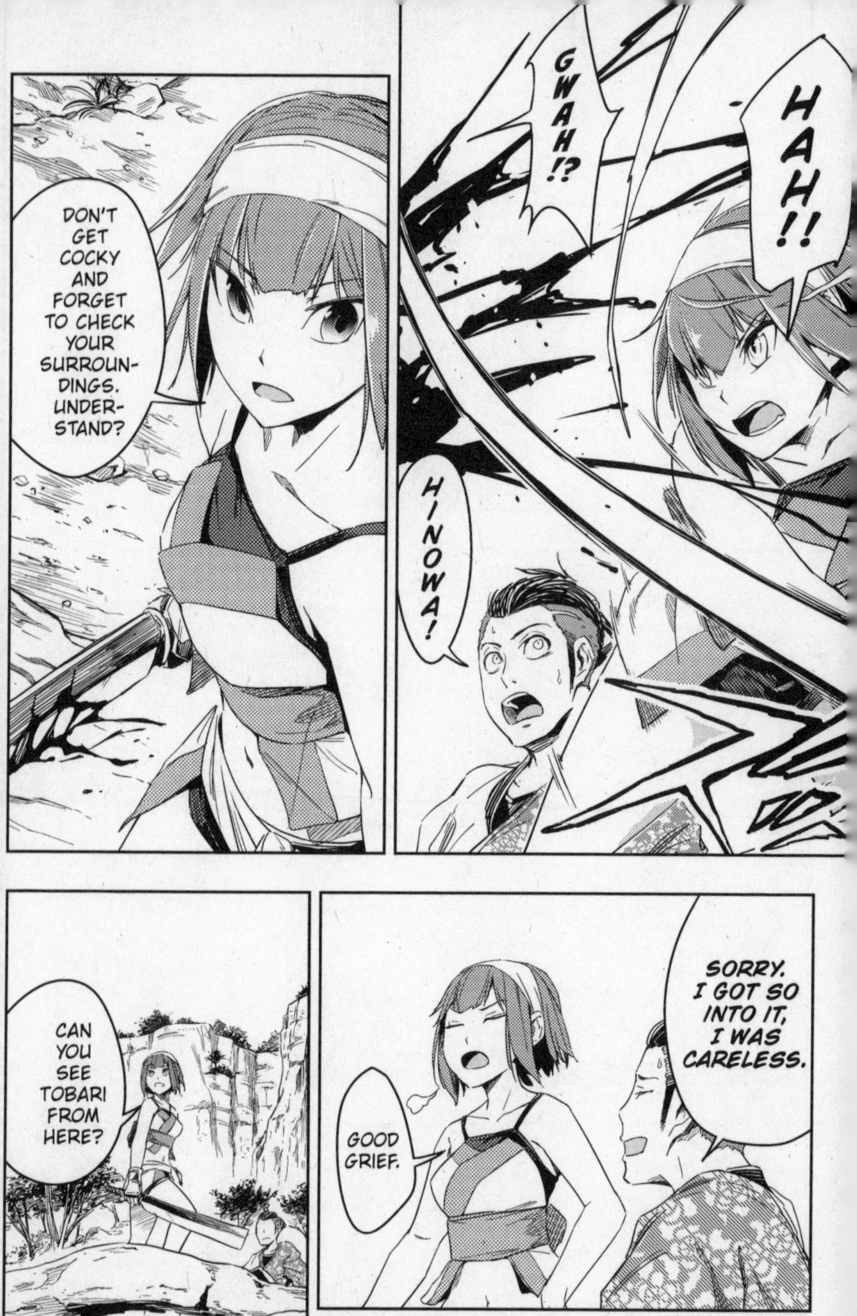
HAH!!
GWAH!?
HINOWA!
DON'T GET COCKY AND FORGET TO CHECK YOUR SURROUNDINGS. UNDERSTAND?
SORRY. I GOT SO INTO IT, I WAS CARELESS.
GOOD GRIEF.
CAN YOU SEE TOBARI FROM HERE?

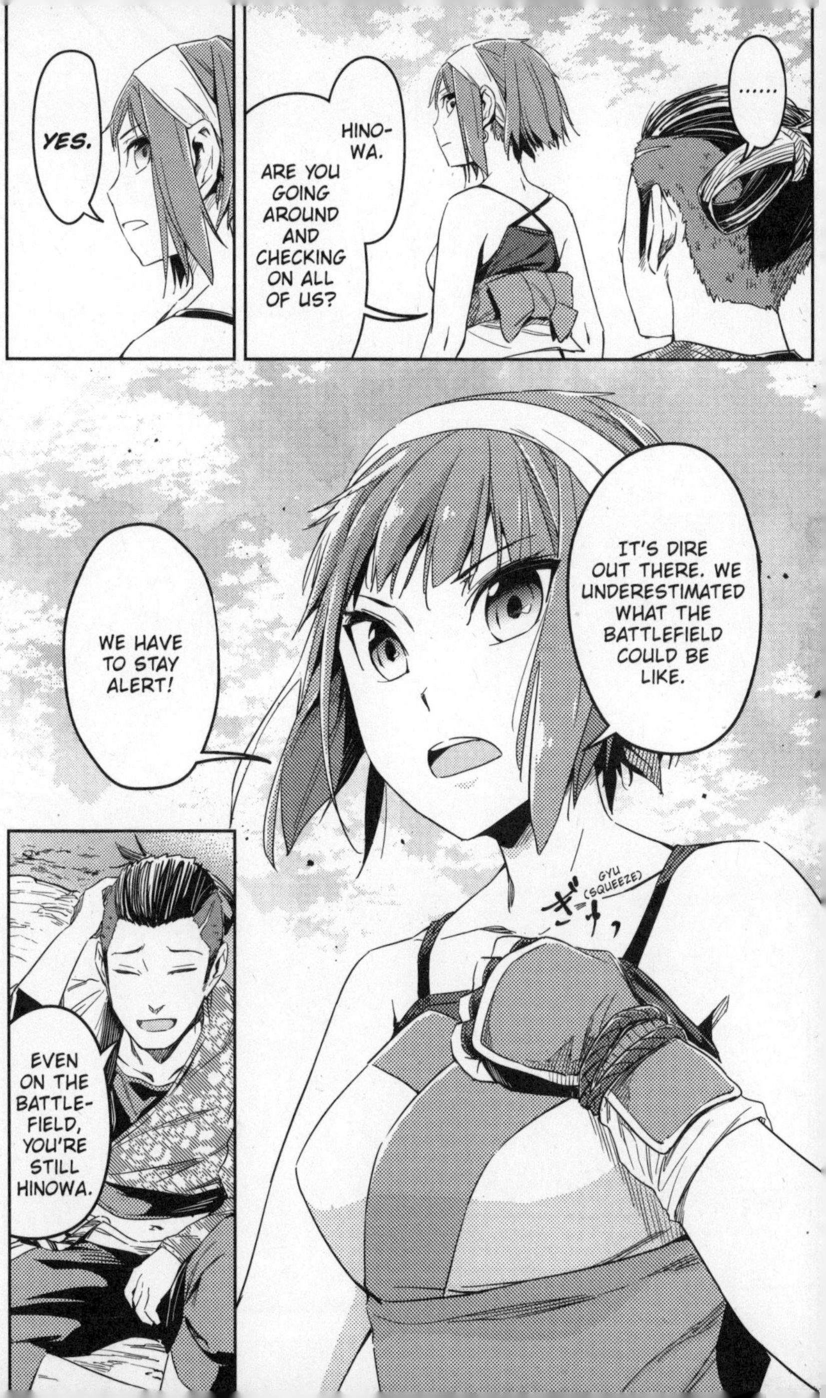
......
HINOWA. ARE YOU GOING AROUND AND CHECKING ON ALL OF US?
YES.
IT'S DIRE OUT THERE. WE UNDERESTIMATED WHAT THE BATTLEFIELD COULD BE LIKE.
WE HAVE TO STAY ALERT!
GYU (SQUEEZE)
EVEN ON THE BATTLEFIELD, YOU'RE STILL HINOWA.

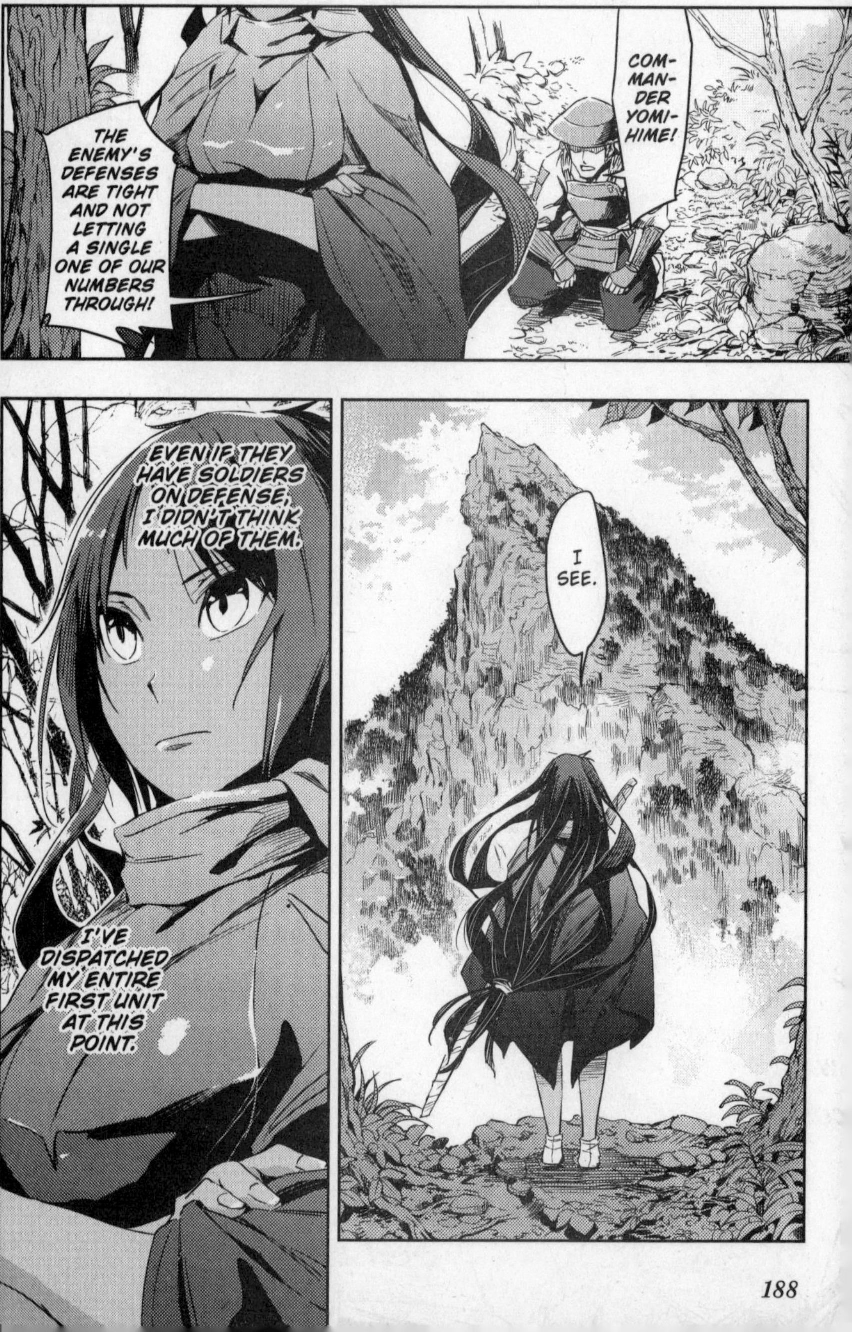
COM-MAN-DER YOMI-HIME!
THE ENEMY'S DEFENSES ARE TIGHT AND NOT LETTING A SINGLE ONE OF OUR NUMBERS THROUGH!
I SEE.
EVEN IF THEY HAVE SOLDIERS ON DEFENSE, I DIDN'T THINK MUCH OF THEM.
I'VE DISPATCHED MY ENTIRE FIRST UNIT AT THIS POINT.

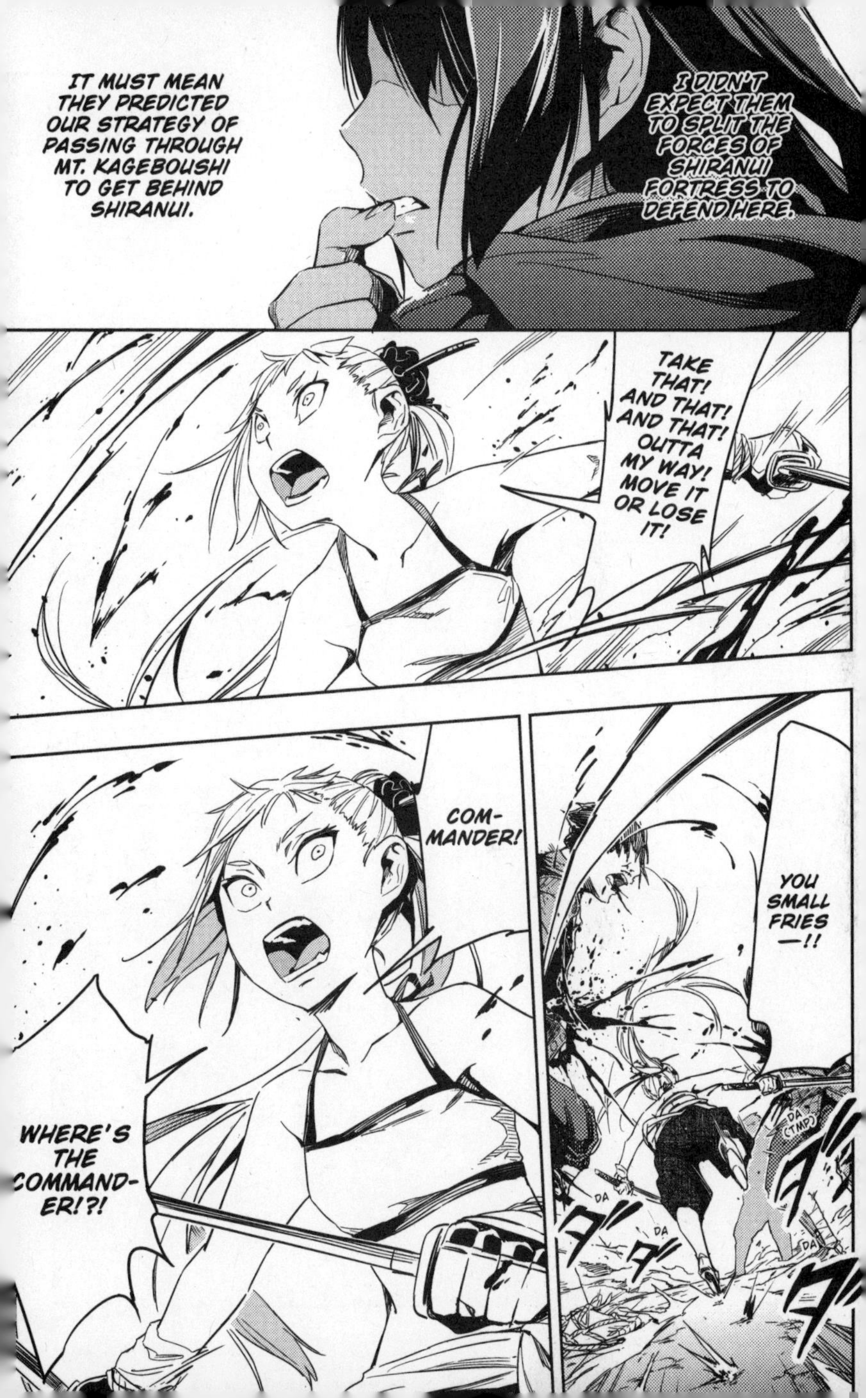
I DIDN'T EXPECT THEM TO SPLIT THE FORCES OF SHIRANUI FORTRESS TO DEFEND HERE.
IT MUST MEAN THEY PREDICTED OUR STRATEGY OF PASSING THROUGH MT. KAGEBOUSHI TO GET BEHIND SHIRANUI.
TAKE THAT! AND THAT! AND THAT! OUTTA MY WAY! MOVE IT OR LOSE IT!
YOU SMALL FRIES—!!
DA (TMP)
DA
DA
DA
COM-MANDER!
WHERE'S THE COMMAND-ER!?!

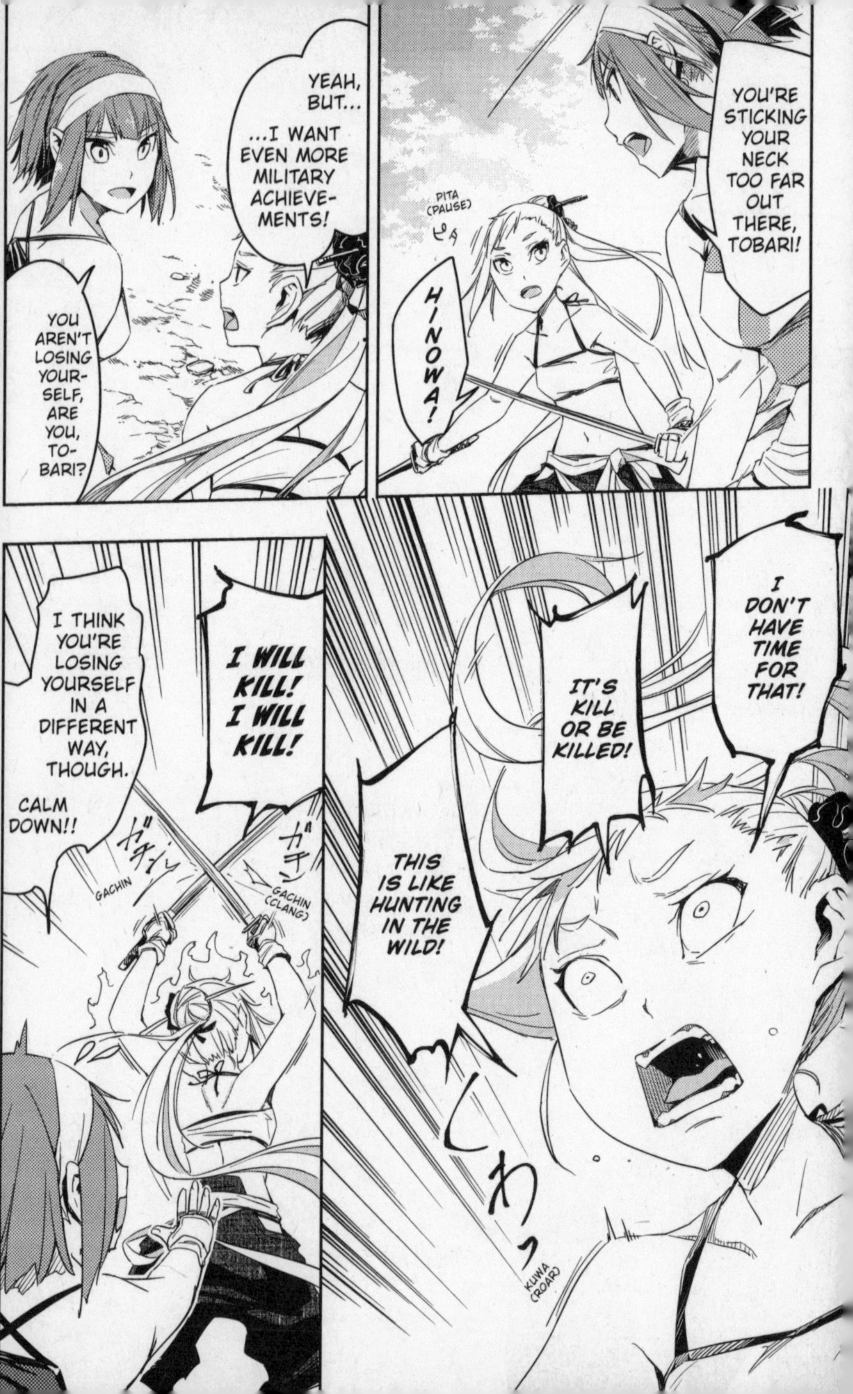
YOU'RE STICKING YOUR NECK TOO FAR OUT THERE, TOBARI!
PITA (PAUSE)
HINOWA!
YEAH, BUT...
...I WANT EVEN MORE MILITARY ACHIEVEMENTS!
YOU AREN'T LOSING YOURSELF, ARE YOU, TOBARI?
I DON'T HAVE TIME FOR THAT!
IT'S KILL OR BE KILLED!
THIS IS LIKE HUNTING IN THE WILD!
KUWA (ROAR)
I WILL KILL! I WILL KILL!
I THINK YOU'RE LOSING YOURSELF IN A DIFFERENT WAY, THOUGH.
CALM DOWN!!
GACHIN (CLANG)
GACHIN

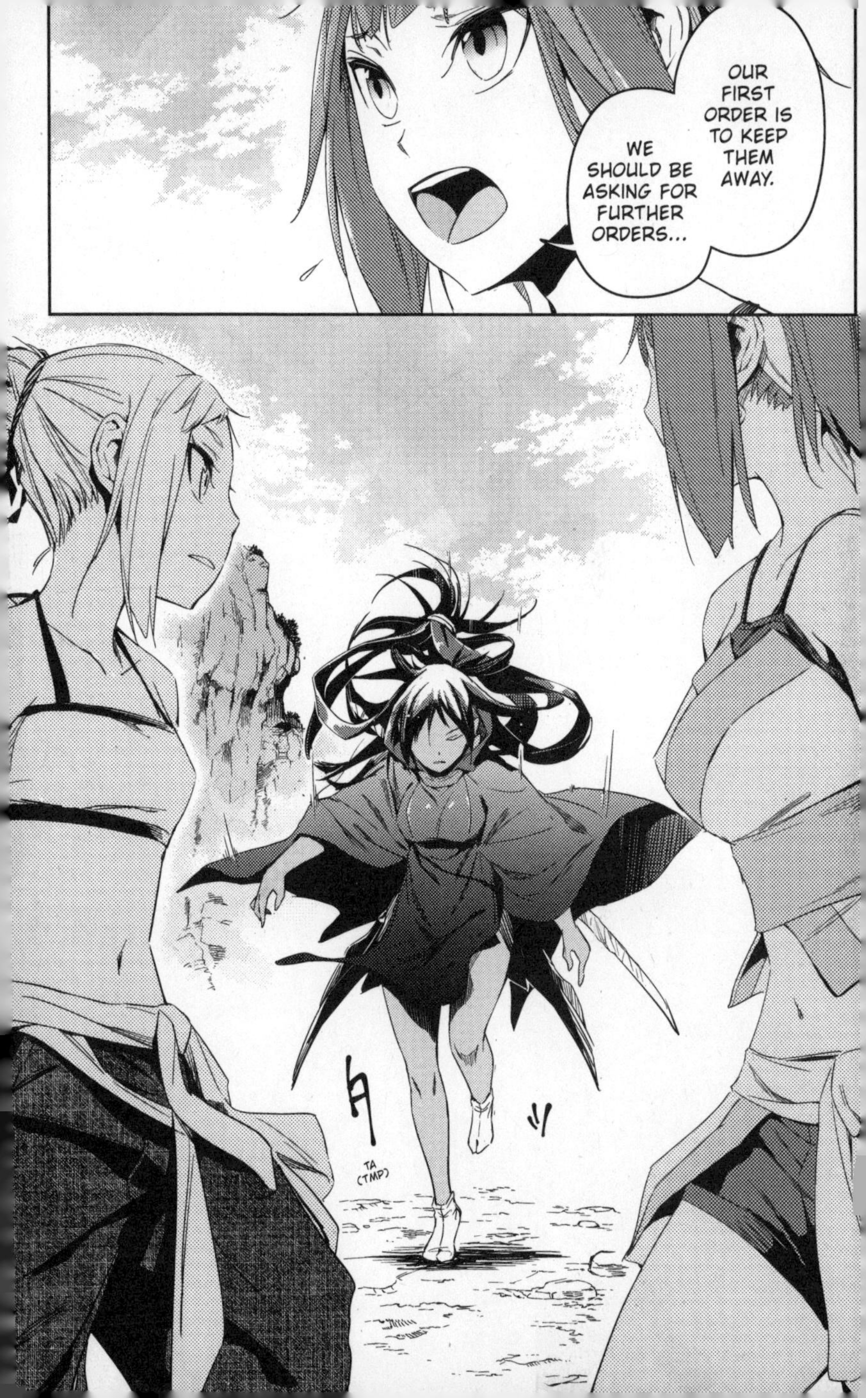
OUR FIRST ORDER IS TO KEEP THEM AWAY.
WE SHOULD BE ASKING FOR FURTHER ORDERS...
TA (TMP)

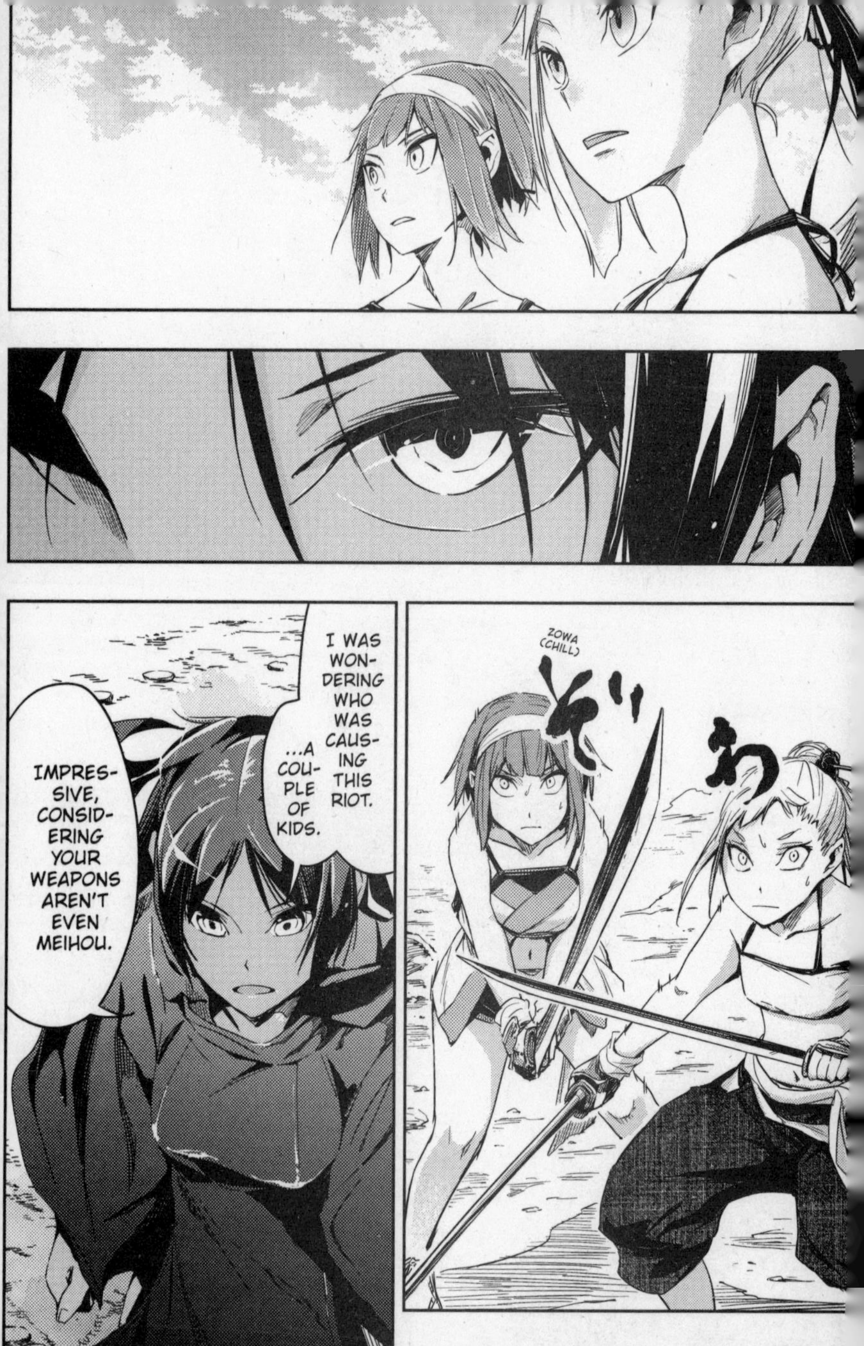
ZOWA (CHILL)
I WAS WONDERING WHO WAS CAUSING THIS RIOT.
...A COUPLE OF KIDS.
IMPRESSIVE, CONSIDERING YOUR WEAPONS AREN'T EVEN MEIHOU.

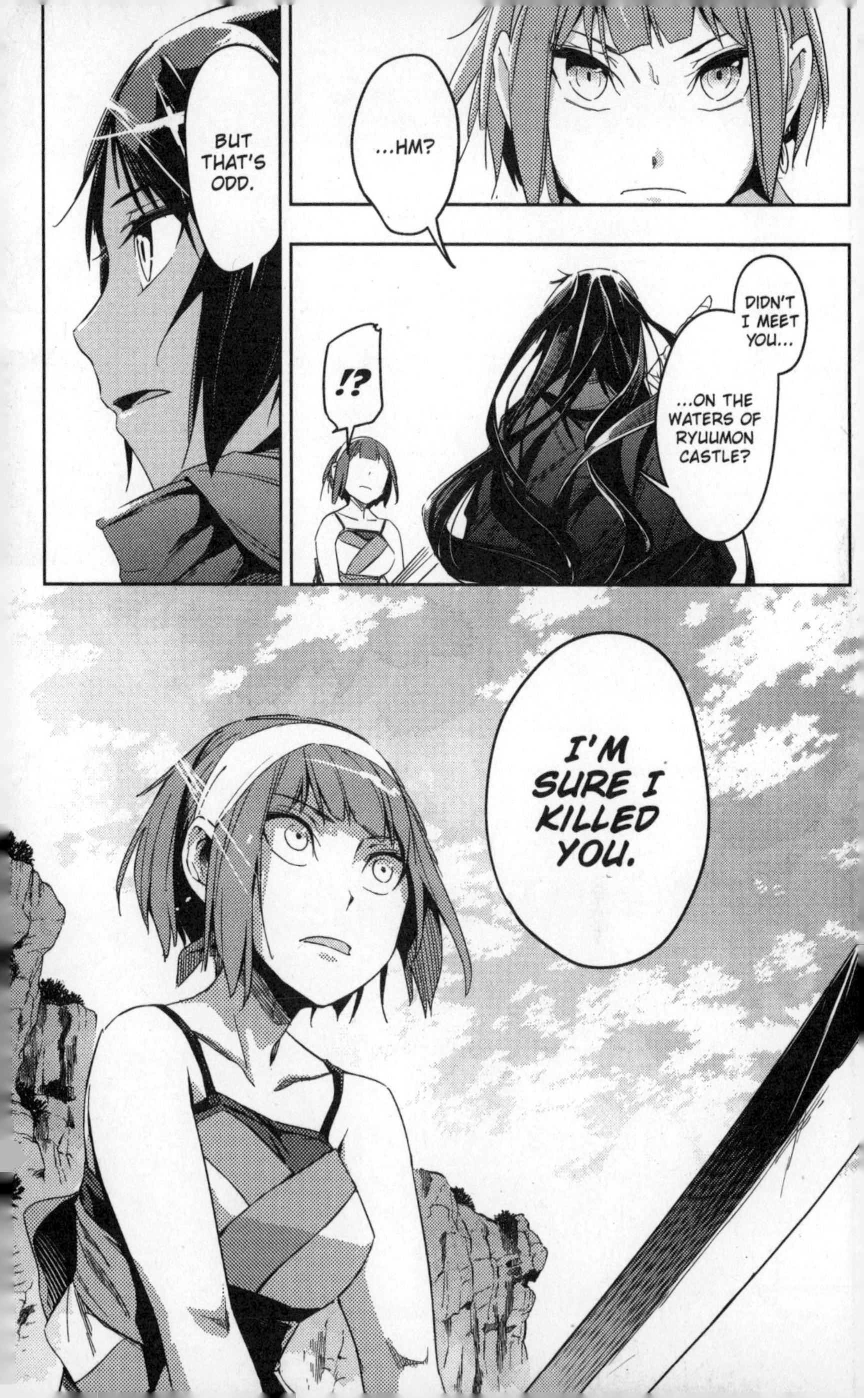
...HM?
DIDN'T I MEET YOU...
...ON THE WATERS OF RYUUMON CASTLE?
!?
BUT THAT'S ODD.
I'M SURE I KILLED YOU.

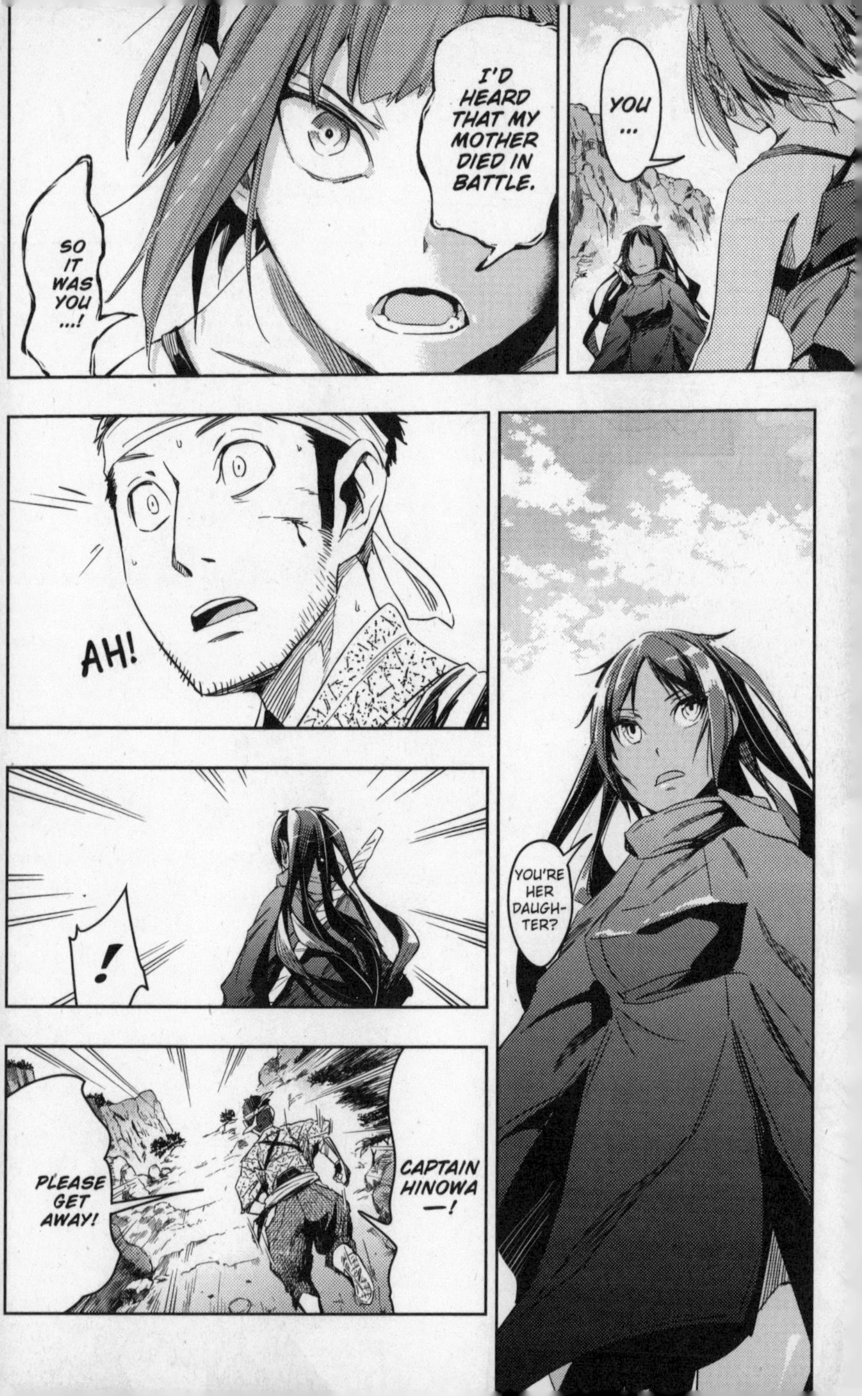
YOU ...
I'D HEARD THAT MY MOTHER DIED IN BATTLE.
SO IT WAS YOU ...!
YOU'RE HER DAUGHTER?
AH!
!
CAPTAIN HINOWA—!
PLEASE GET AWAY!

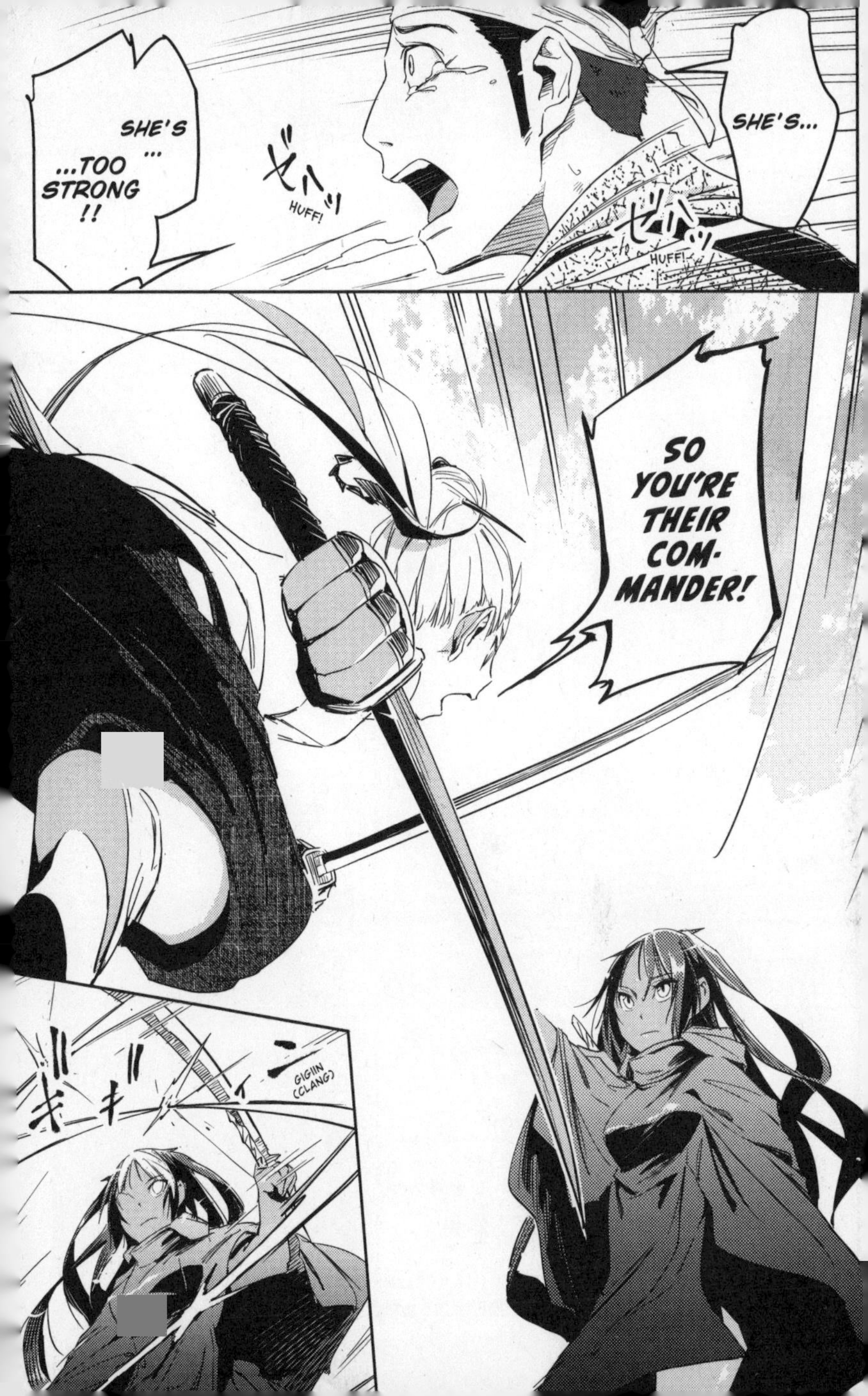

SHE'S...
ゼハッ
HUFF!
ゼハッ
HUFF!
SHE'S ... ...TOO STRONG!!
SO YOU'RE THEIR COM-MANDER!
GIGIIN (CLANG)

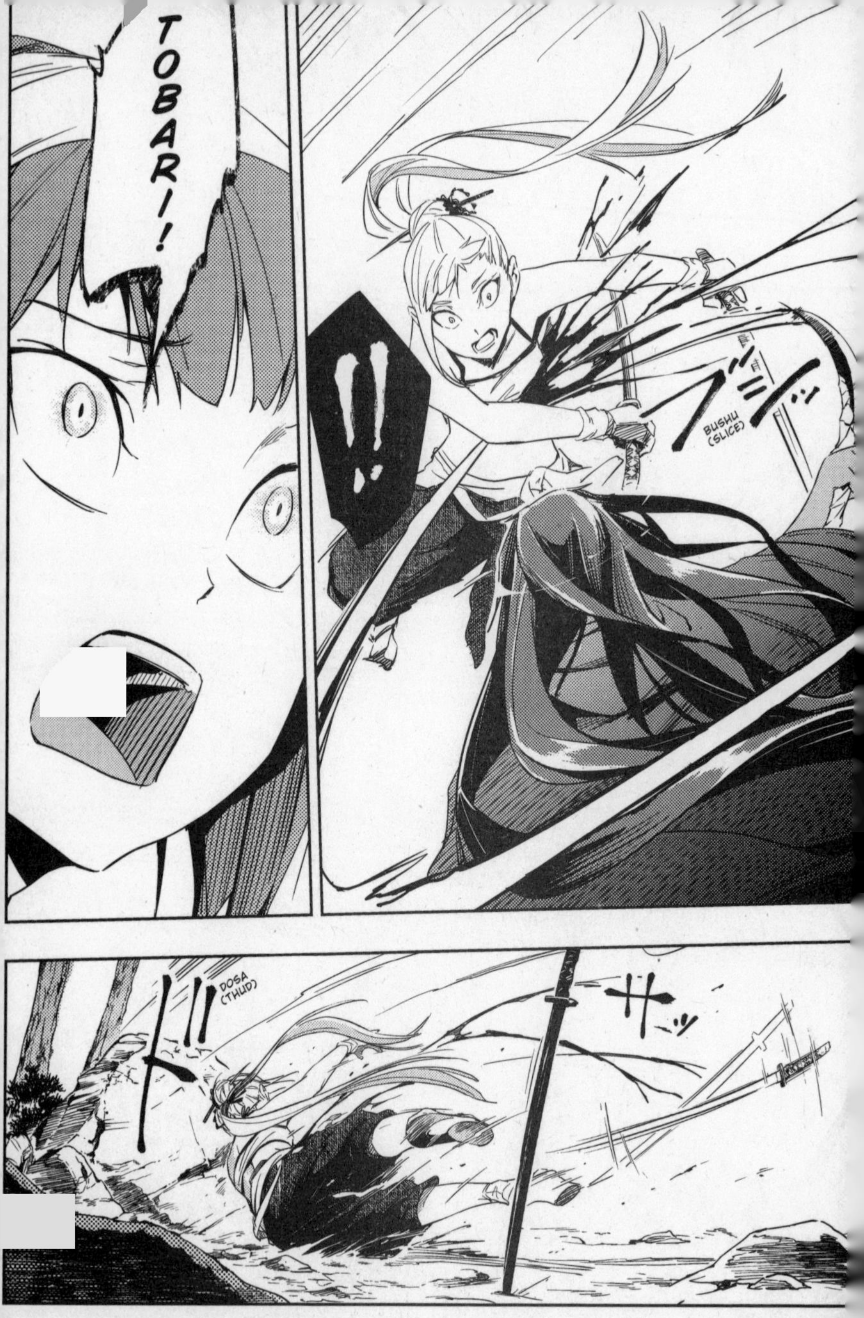
!!
BUSHU (SLICE)
TOBARI!
DOSA (THUD)

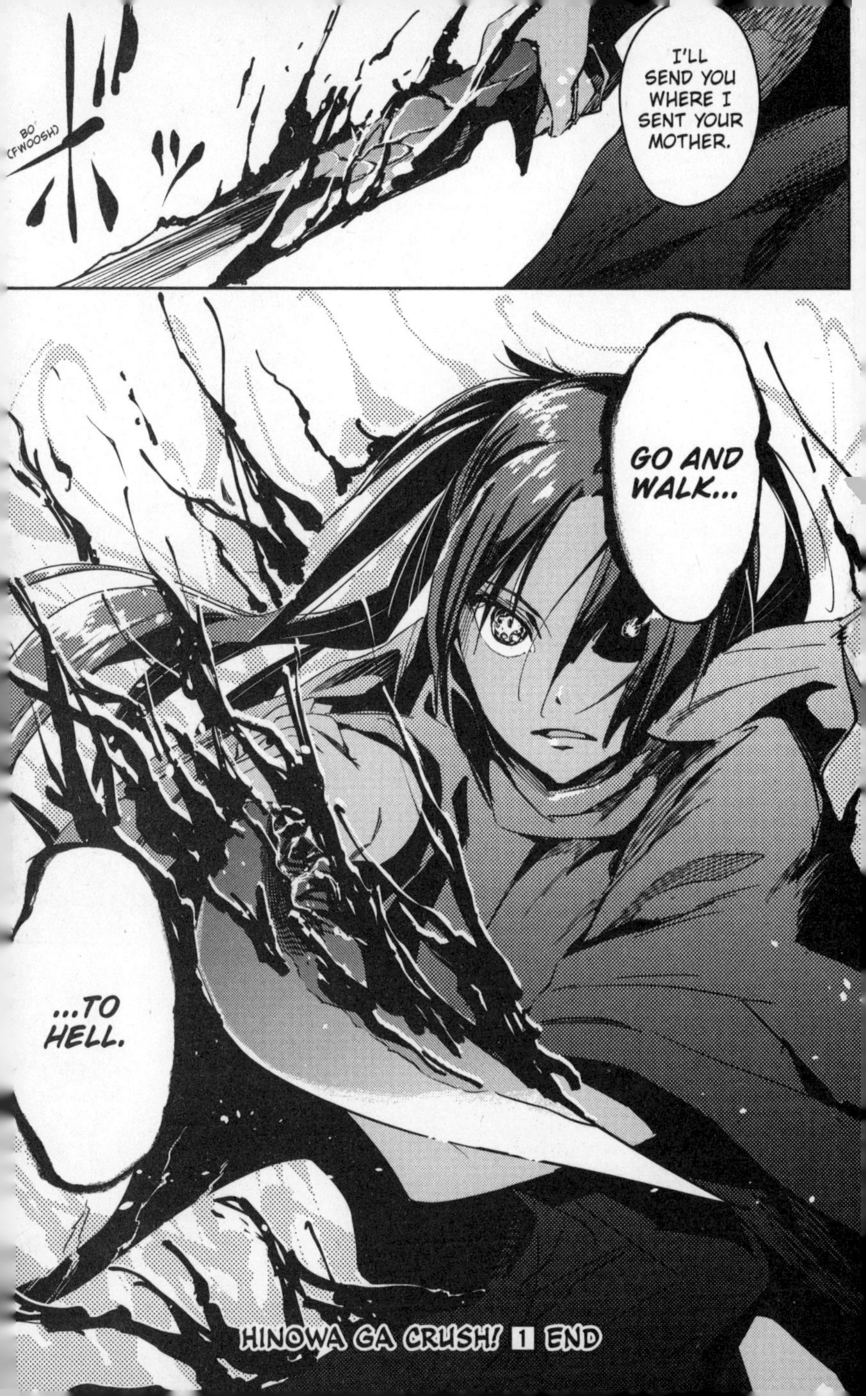
I'LL SEND YOU WHERE I SENT YOUR MOTHER.
BO (FWOOSH)
GO AND WALK...
...TO HELL.
HINOWA GA CRUSH! 1 END

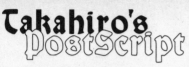

# Takahiro's PostScript

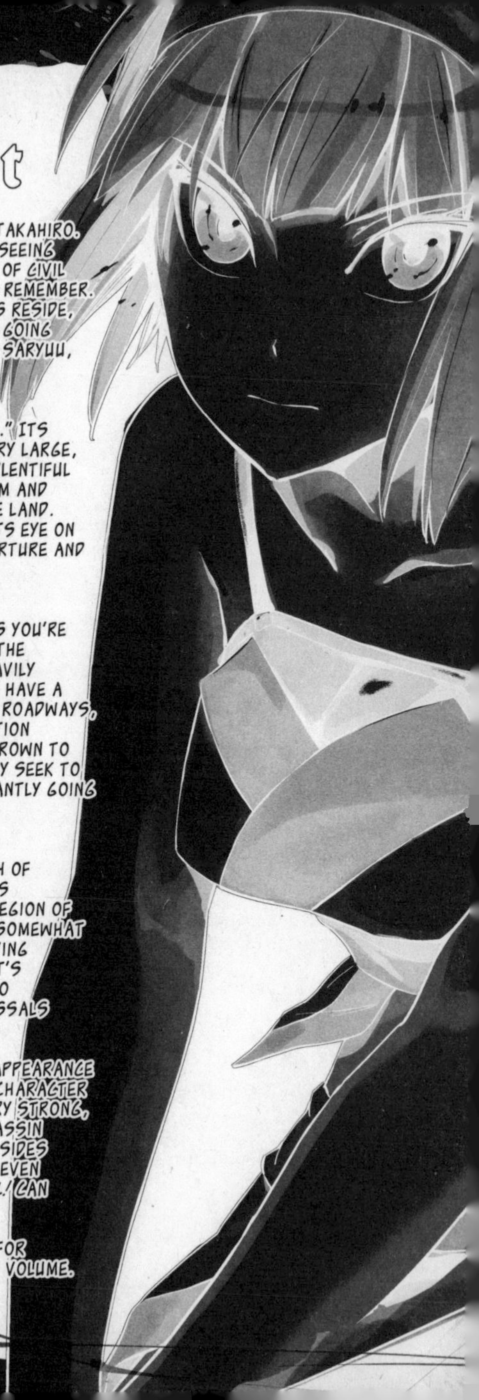

HELLO, EVERYONE. THIS IS THE AUTHOR, TAKAHIRO. AND THIS IS THE CELEBRATED VOLUME 1. SEEING AS HOW THIS STORY DEALS WITH AN AGE OF CIVIL WAR, THERE ARE SEVERAL COUNTRIES TO REMEMBER. FIRST OFF IS SOUKAI, WHERE OUR HEROES RESIDE, AND THEN THE TENROU NATION, WHICH IS GOING AFTER SOUKAI. AND WE MUSTN'T FORGET SARYUU, WHICH IS AN ALLY OF SOUKAI.

★***SOUKAI NATION***
THEIR MOTTO IS "AS MIGHTY AS THE SEA." ITS CREST IS A CRAB. THE COUNTRY ISN'T VERY LARGE, BUT WITH ITS SOUTH SEA TRADING, ITS PLENTIFUL MARINE PRODUCTS, AS WELL AS ITS WARM AND STABLE CLIMATE, IT'S A VERY FORTUNATE LAND. WHICH IS WHY THE TENROU NATION HAS ITS EYE ON IT. IT'S WHERE HINOWA MAKES HER DEPARTURE AND WHERE AKAME WASHES UP ON SHORE.

★***TENROU NATION***
THEIR MOTTO IS "KEEP GOING AS LONG AS YOU'RE ALIVE." ITS CREST IS A WOLF. THEY ARE THE CENTRALLY LOCATED WINNERS OF THE HEAVILY CONTESTED WAKOKU. AS A RESULT, THEY HAVE A MONOPOLY ON FERTILE PLAINS, MAINTAIN ROADWAYS, AND BACKDROPPED BY AFFLUENT PRODUCTION CAPACITY AND ECONOMIC POWER, HAVE GROWN TO BE THE GREATEST FORCE IN WAKOKU. THEY SEEK TO UNIFY ALL THE COUNTRIES AND ARE VIGILANTLY GOING AFTER ALL THE SMALLER NATIONS.

★***SARYUU NATION***
THEIR MOTTO IS "DON'T INCUR THE WRATH OF OTHERS." THEIR CREST IS A DRAGON. THIS COUNTRY IS LOCATED IN THE SOUTHERN REGION OF WAKOKU. IT HAS MANY DESERTS AND IS SOMEWHAT GEOGRAPHICALLY POOR, BUT IT IS SURVIVING THROUGH TRADE WITH THE SOUTH SEA. IT'S AN ALLY WITH SOUKAI, AND ITS KING IS SO DEVOTED TO THE FINE ARTS THAT HIS VASSALS ARE SUFFERING FOR IT.

A CHARACTER NAMED AKAME MAKES AN APPEARANCE HERE. AND, YES, SHE IS THE VERY SAME CHARACTER AS THE ONE IN *AKAME GA KILL!* SHE'S VERY STRONG, BUT PLEASE KEEP IN MIND SHE'S AN ASSASSIN WHO'S BEEN BURDENED WITH A CURSE. BESIDES THAT, I'M WRITING THIS STORY SO THAT EVEN THOSE WHO HAVEN'T READ *AKAME GA KILL!* CAN ENJOY IT.

AND THAT'S ALL. THANK YOU VERY MUCH FOR READING TO THE VERY END. SEE YOU NEXT VOLUME.

ATÉ BREVE OBRIGADO.

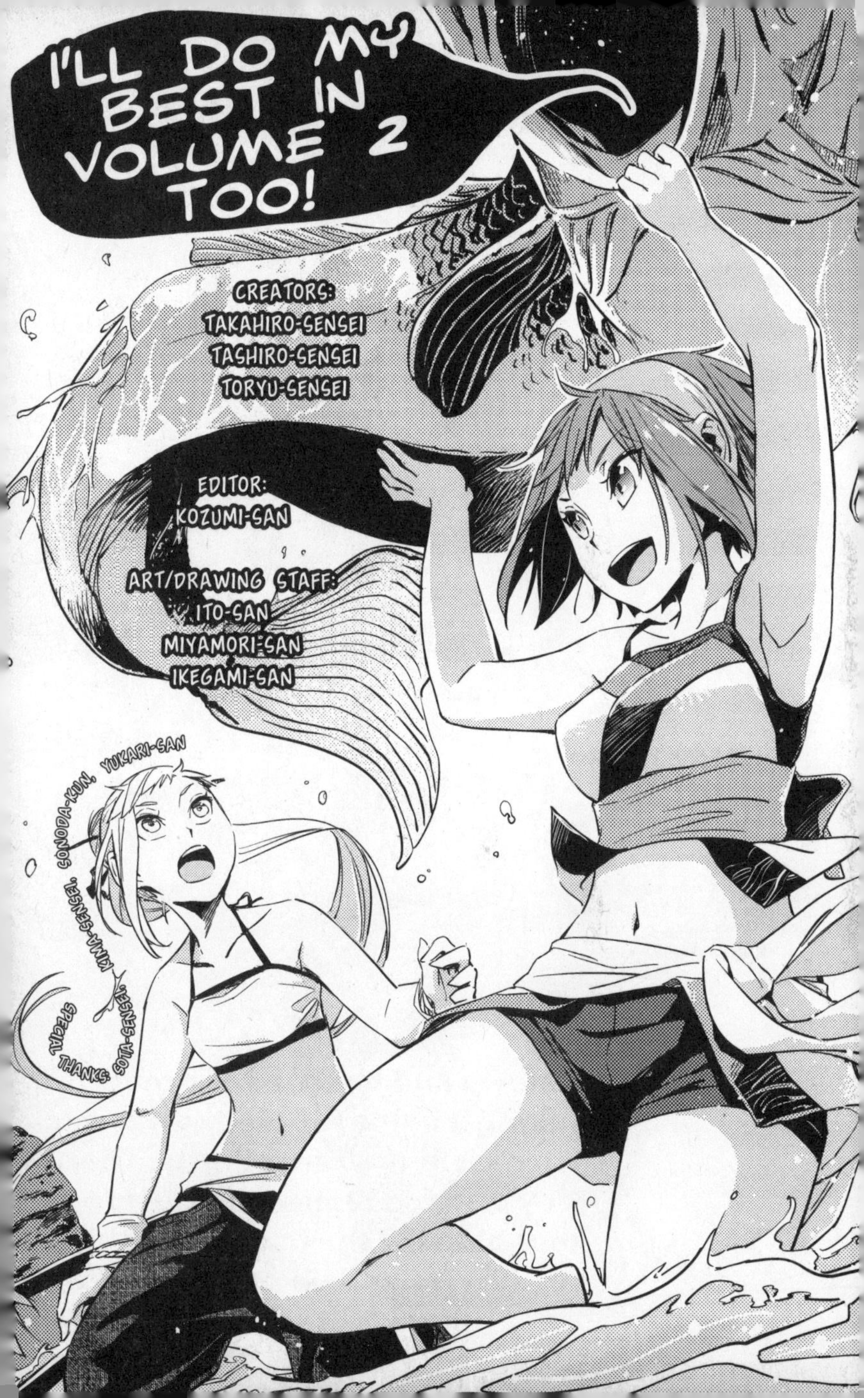
I'LL DO MY BEST IN VOLUME 2 TOO!
CREATORS:
TAKAHIRO-SENSEI
TASHIRO-SENSEI
TORYU-SENSEI
EDITOR:
KOZUMI-SAN
ART/DRAWING STAFF:
ITO-SAN
MIYAMORI-SAN
IKEGAMI-SAN
SPECIAL THANKS: SOTA-SENSEI, KIMA-SENSEI, SONODA-KUN, YUKARI-SAN

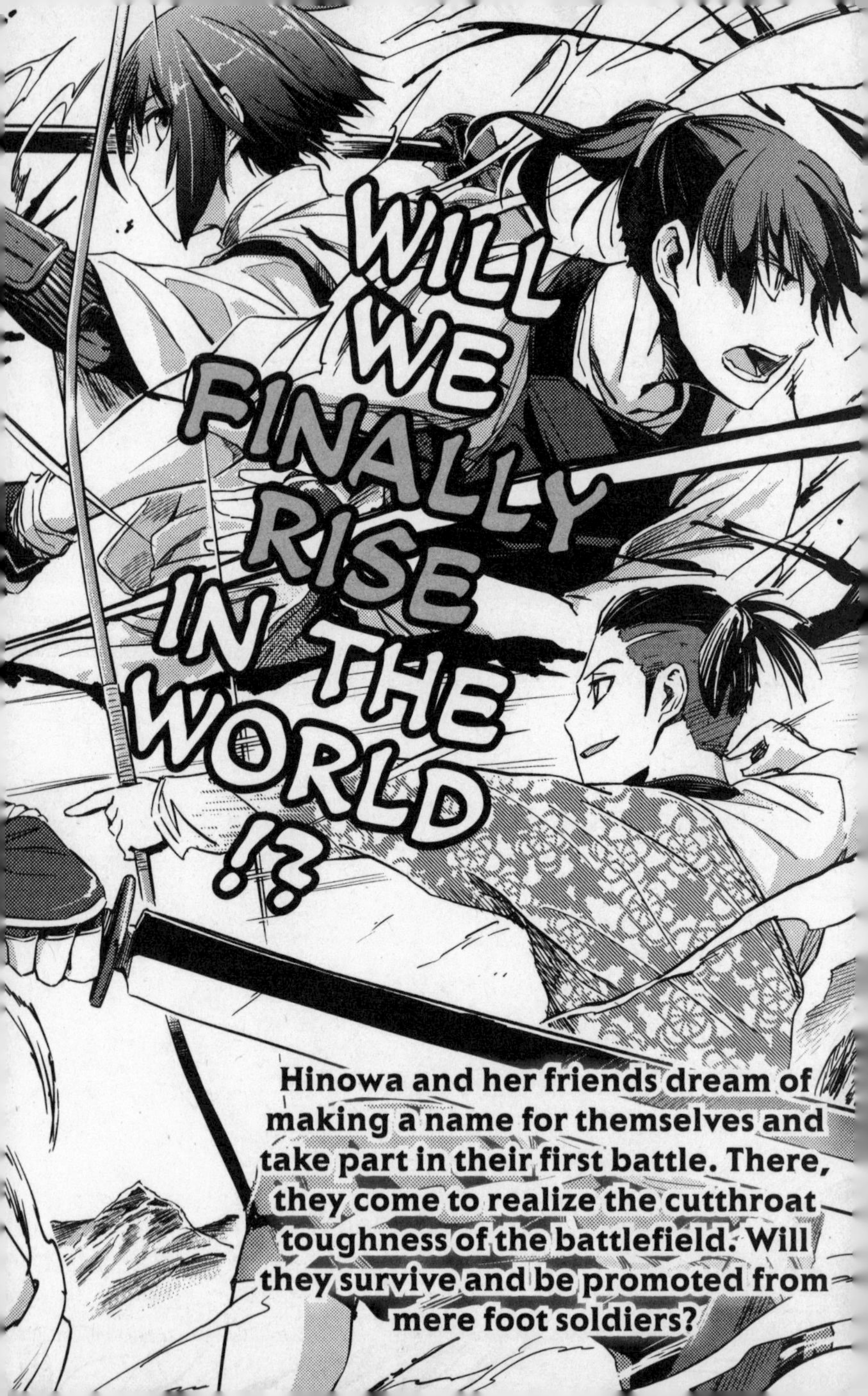
WILL WE FINALLY RISE IN THE WORLD!?
Hinowa and her friends dream of making a name for themselves and take part in their first battle. There, they come to realize the cutthroat toughness of the battlefield. Will they survive and be promoted from mere foot soldiers?

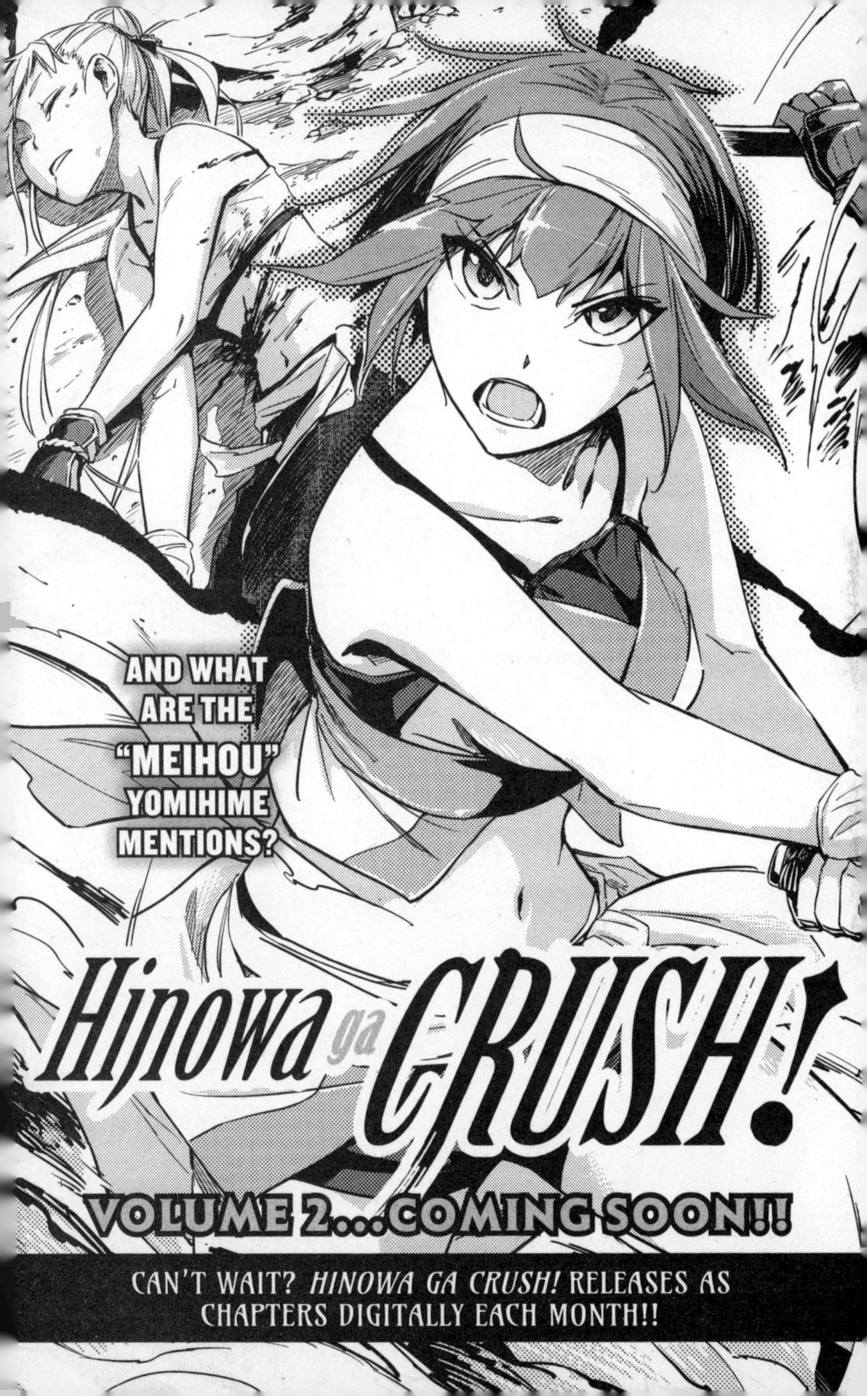
AND WHAT ARE THE "MEIHOU" YOMIHIME MENTIONS?
Hinowa ga CRUSH!
VOLUME 2...COMING SOON!!
CAN'T WAIT? HINOWA GA CRUSH! RELEASES AS CHAPTERS DIGITALLY EACH MONTH!!

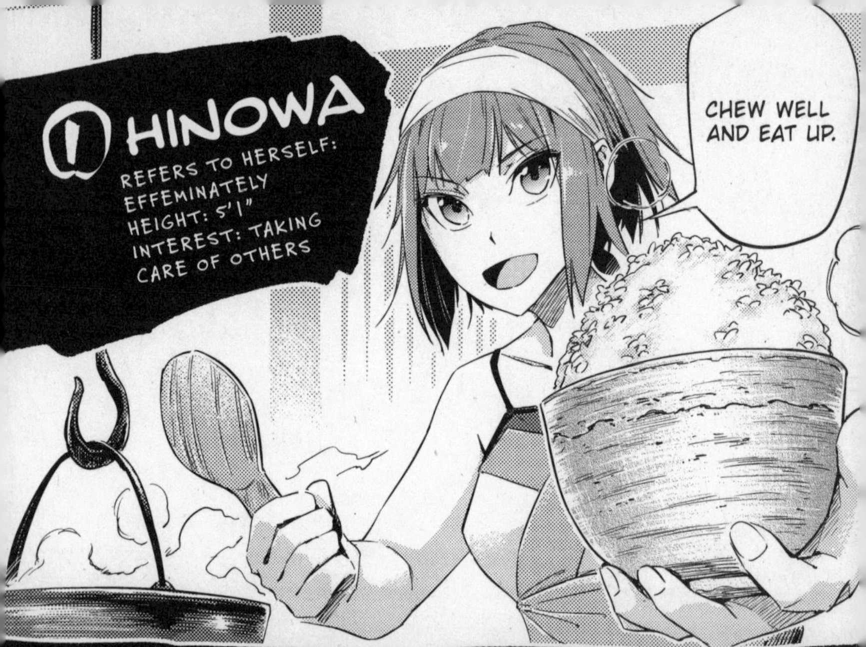
CHEW WELL AND EAT UP.
① HINOWA
REFERS TO HERSELF: EFFEMINATELY
HEIGHT: 5'1"
INTEREST: TAKING CARE OF OTHERS

HINOWA GA CRUSH!

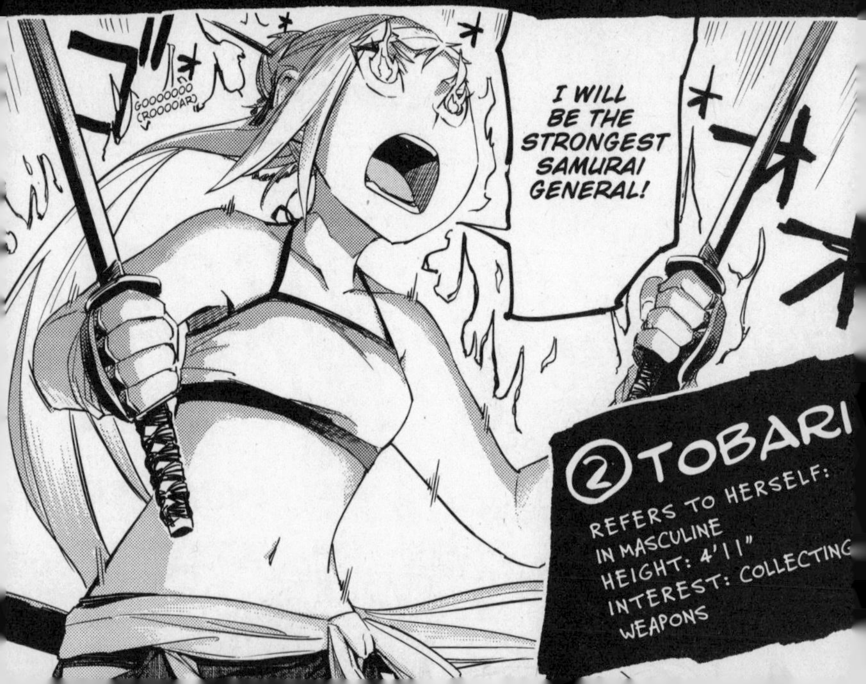
I WILL BE THE STRONGEST SAMURAI GENERAL!
GOOOOOOO (ROOOOAR)
② TOBARI
REFERS TO HERSELF: IN MASCULINE
HEIGHT: 4'11"
INTEREST: COLLECTING WEAPONS

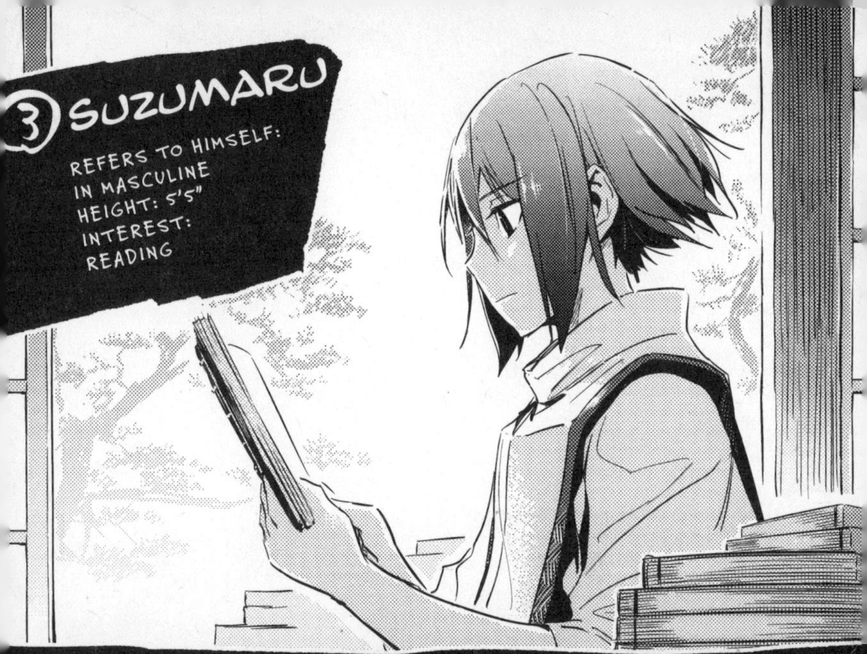
③ SUZUMARU
REFERS TO HIMSELF: IN MASCULINE
HEIGHT: 5'5"
INTEREST: READING

CHARACTER DIRECTORY

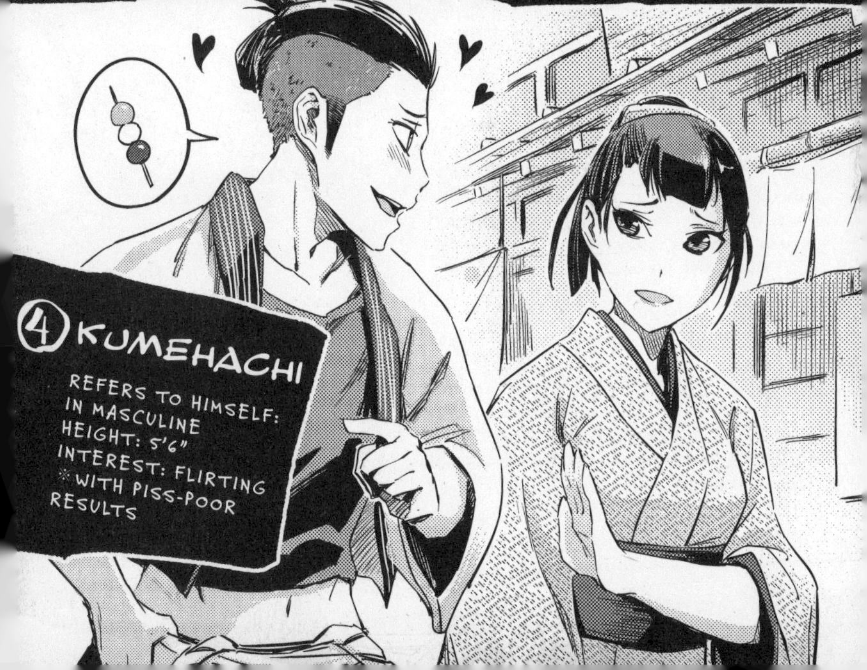
④ KUMEHACHI
REFERS TO HIMSELF: IN MASCULINE
HEIGHT: 5'6"
INTEREST: FLIRTING
※WITH PISS-POOR RESULTS

# Translation Notes

Page 13
*Isonade* is a mythical sharklike demon sea monster with a barbed tail fin.

Page 14
What Hinowa has prepared is called *namerou*, a style of preparing fish (mincing and pounding it and then serving it as a cake) that is very much like tartare.

Page 16
*Tenrou* is a name meaning "heaven wolf" and is the Japanese name for the star Sirius (of the Canis Major constellation), also known as the "dog star." This is why the shipmen derogatorily refer to Tenrou nationals as "dogs."

*Ryuumon* is spelled with characters that mean "dragon gate"—an appropriate name for the gate that leads to the rest of the Tenrou Nation's conquest.

The name of Hinowa's country, *Soukai*, means "blue sea" and reflects her countrymen, who are sea-based fishermen and ship experts.

The third nation, *Saryuu*, has a name that means "sand dragon," leaving the impression that all three realms—sky, sea, and land— have been covered by these three nations.

Page 163
The name of the *Kuroshio* nation to the south can be read as "black tide," but it also refers to the Kuroshio current, which is a north-flowing ocean current on the west side of the North Pacific. It transports warmer waters from the southern islands of Japan north toward Hokkaido.

*Hinowa ga CRUSH!*

# HE DOES NOT LET ANYONE ROLL THE DICE.

A young Priestess joins her first adventuring party, but blind to the dangers, they almost immediately find themselves in trouble. It's Goblin Slayer who comes to their rescue—a man who has dedicated his life to the extermination of all goblins by any means necessary. A dangerous, dirty, and thankless job, but he does it better than anyone. And when rumors of his feats begin to circulate, there's no telling who might come calling next...

Check out the simul-pub manga chapters every month!

Yen Press  YEN ON
www.yenpress.com

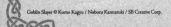

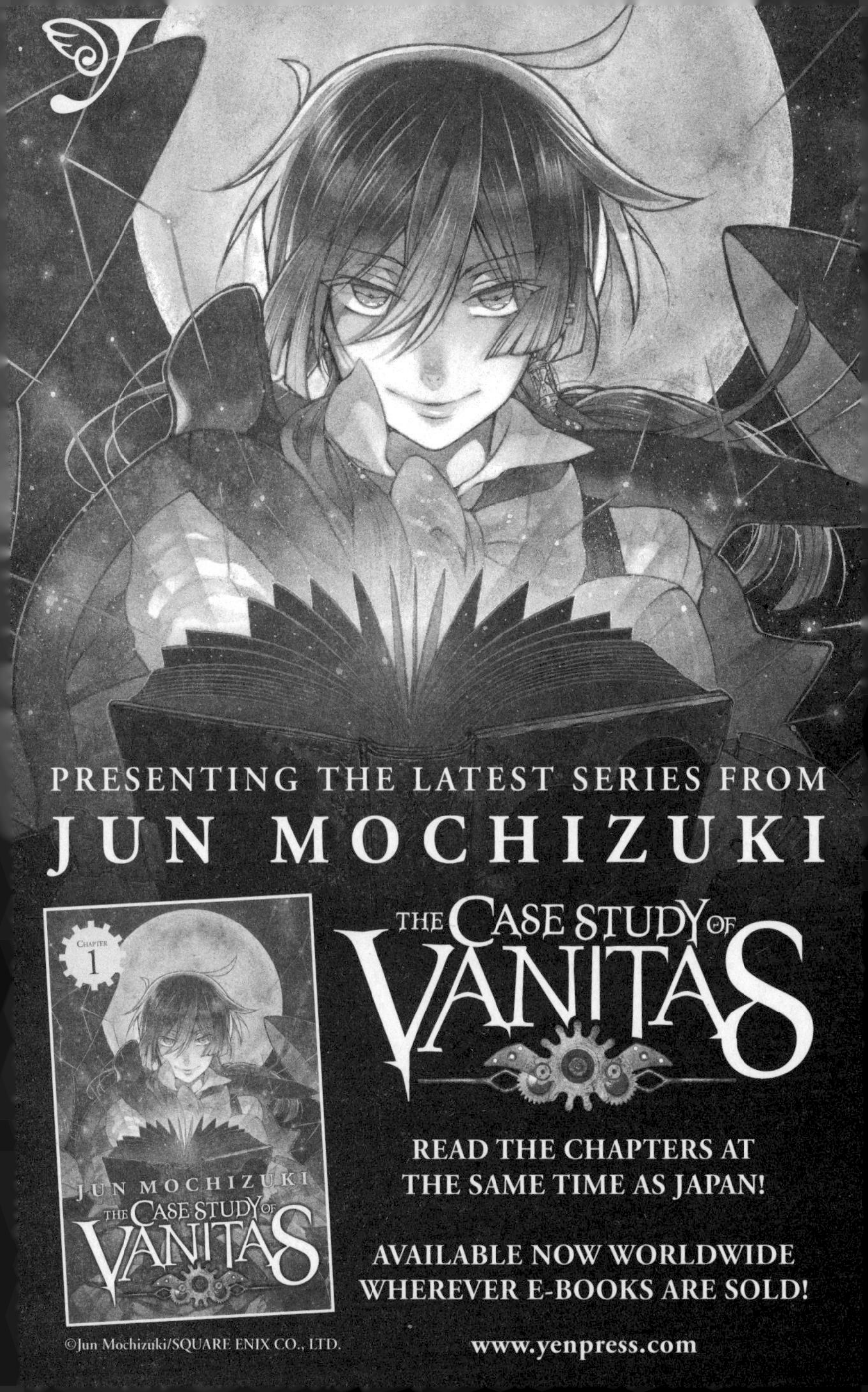
PRESENTING THE LATEST SERIES FROM
JUN MOCHIZUKI
CHAPTER 1
JUN MOCHIZUKI
THE CASE STUDY OF VANITAS
THE CASE STUDY OF VANITAS
READ THE CHAPTERS AT THE SAME TIME AS JAPAN!
AVAILABLE NOW WORLDWIDE WHEREVER E-BOOKS ARE SOLD!
©Jun Mochizuki/SQUARE ENIX CO., LTD.
www.yenpress.com

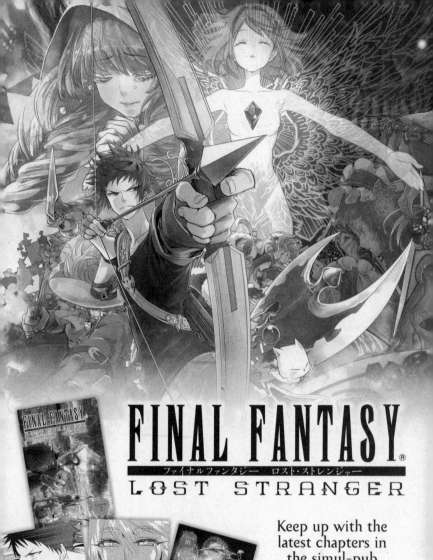

FINAL FANTASY®
ファイナルファンタジー　ロスト・ストレンジャー
LOST STRANGER
CHAPTER 7
CHAPTER 8
FINAL FANTASY
LOST STRANGER
Story: Hazuki Minase
Art: Itsuki Kameya
CHAPTER 9
CHAPTER 10
Keep up with the latest chapters in the simul-pub version! Available now worldwide wherever e-books are sold!
For more information, visit www.yenpress.com
Yen Press
©Hazuki Minase, Itsuki Kameya/SQUARE ENIX
©2017 SQUARE ENIX CO., LTD. All Rights Reserved.

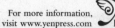

# *Hinowa ga CRUSH!*

**Story: TAKAHIRO**  **Art: strelka**

Translation: Christine Dashiell

Lettering: Rochelle Gancio & Rachel J. Pierce

This book is a work of fiction. Names, characters, places, and incidents are the product of the author's imagination or are used fictitiously. Any resemblance to actual events, locales, or persons, living or dead, is coincidental.

HINOWA GA YUKU! Volume 1 © 2017 Takahiro, strelka / SQUARE ENIX CO., LTD. First published in Japan in 2017 by SQUARE ENIX CO., LTD. English translation rights arranged with SQUARE ENIX CO., LTD. and Yen Press, LLC through Tuttle-Mori Agency, Inc., Tokyo.

English translation © 2018 by SQUARE ENIX CO., LTD.

Yen Press
1290 Avenue of the Americas
New York, NY 10104

Visit us at yenpress.com
facebook.com/yenpress
twitter.com/yenpress
yenpress.tumblr.com
instagram.com/yenpress

First Yen Press Edition: September 2018
The chapters in this volume were originally published as ebooks by Yen Press.

Yen Press is an imprint of Yen Press, LLC.
The Yen Press name and logo are trademarks of Yen Press, LLC.

The publisher is not responsible for websites (or their content) that are not owned by t

Library of (

ISBNs: 978
        978

10 9 8 7 6

WOR

Printed in the United States of America